Mothers of Invention

Mothers of Invention

Women, Italian Fascism, and Culture

Robin Pickering-Iazzi, editor

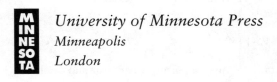

University of Minnesota Press
Minneapolis
London

Published by the University of Minnesota Press
111 Third Avenue South, Suite 290, Minneapolis, MN 55401-2520
Printed in the United States of America on acid-free paper

Library of Congress Cataloging-in-Publication Data

Mothers of invention : women, Italian fascism, and culture / Robin
   Pickering-Iazzi, editor.
      p.   cm.
   Includes bibliographical references and index.
   ISBN 0-8166-2650-2 (alk. paper). — ISBN 0-8166-2651-0 (pbk. :
alk. paper)
      1. Women in popular culture—Italy.   2. Women in politics—Italy.
   3. Women in literature.   4. Fascism—Italy.   I. Pickering-Iazzi,
   Robin Wynette.
   HQ1638.M76   1995
   305.4'0945—dc20   95-14300

The University of Minnesota is an equal-opportunity educator and employer.

Contents

Acknowledgments

I am indebted to the contributors, who generously invested their intellectual labor and creative talents in this volume of essays. I also wish to extend heartfelt gratitude to Janaki Bakhle and Robert Mosimann for the professional expertise and synergetic guidance they consistently offered while orchestrating each phase of the book's production. Paradigms of organization and efficiency, Laura Westlund and Mary Byers oversaw the final stages of manuscript preparation. The collection benefited from the copyediting provided by Judy Selhorst, whose work shows a strong regard for both the authors and the readers.

Introduction: Inventions of Women's Making, in History and Critical Thought

Robin Pickering-Iazzi

For a long time I have held the conviction that if woman wants to assert her spirituality, which the Church fathers and more recently Weininger... have denied her, she must not imitate man, but must bring out the specific attributes of her own being instead. Since these attributes have been hidden from her, she must discover them, or, more precisely, create them. In the spiritual sphere, woman must create herself.

SIBILLA ALERAMO, "Capelli corti" (Short hair), 1925/1930

Invention as a Critical Category

In his article "Scrittori e sirene" (Writers and sirens), the critic G. Titta Rosa gives us a provocative look at women and their locations in the cultural panorama of Italy in 1931, four years into the intensifying demographic campaign. This pronatalist project formed the fulcrum supporting the sexual politics the Fascist regime executed to incorporate women, with persuasion or discipline, into a separate, domesticated sphere of culture. Writing on the occasion of the prestigious Viareggio Literary Prize ceremony, Rosa treats his readers to a tantalizing cityscape lapped by the sea, while drawing attention to the female presence that outshines a supporting cast of illustrious scholars, young poets, and writers. His mise-en-scène focuses on women in public spaces where the cultural changes of modernity are enacted: as they descend majestic hotel staircases, lips shining with red lipstick, self-styled, he tells us, along the lines of their favorite movie stars; as they promenade through the streets, sporting pants; as they lie on the beach, assuredly basking in the sun and male gazes alike. More important, for Rosa, an imposing body of women has also breached the perimeters of high culture, as indicated by the metaphors and spacial imagery this critic adopts to chronicle a battle of books fought between men, and women. Playing with the theme of competition inspired by the historical event, Rosa ostensibly applauds women, announcing:

> And yet again, women are the ones who have shown the greatest enthusiasm for battle, and an Amazonian strength worthy of celebration; I'm speaking about the women candidates, our beloved and proud women writers who are now following hot on the men's heels in the literary race, not even a neck or a hair's distance behind them. Strengthened by smaller competitions, their hair streaming back in the wind... and their eyes ablaze with the love of glory, they goad their fellow male writers on, not even letting them catch their breath.

Aside from the particularly clever way Rosa draws upon classical myth and Fascist rhetoric (I am thinking of the references to Amazons, battle, glory), his perception of women as a contending, if not threatening, force in Italian culture during Fascism is by no means anomalous. Reflecting the general concern about the increasing ambiguity of gender roles, the writings by male intellectuals of the 1920s and 1930s demonstrate a preoccupation with the ongoing changes in female pratices of everyday life and culture.[1] Indeed, in the interwar period, communities of Italian women fashioned female models of their own devising, expanding the sites and ways of their engagement with cultural life.

Lest this representation give the impression of an unchecked feminization of Italian culture, we must bear in mind that the nature and function women's enterprises should assume in the authoritarian Fascist state gained monumental importance among the regime's ideologues and policy makers. While promoting the model of the woman-mother (*donna-madre*), a traditional figure that Fascist discourses reinvented by casting the bearing of children and selfless devotion to family and home as the highest political service women could perform for the state, conservative commentators inveighed against the crisis-woman (*donna-crisi*). Invoked by such other signifiers as "intellectualoide," the "masculinized woman," "*garçonne*," and "*maschietta*," this figure represented the deviant "degeneration of the female type" associated with emancipated behaviors, ideas, and desires. In addition to such discursive mechanisms, the regime constructed new apparatuses in the forms of policies, programs, and institutions designed to cultivate and manage a patriarchal agenda for female culture, a point to which I will return momentarily. Although Fascist sexual politics clearly applied pressures and boundaries on women's accomplishments and aspirations, it also created possibilities, deriving from the internal contradictions of Fascism and the politics it developed for incorporating women in national life. The dictatorship, as Victoria De Grazia amply demonstrates in *How Fascism Ruled Women* (1992), "exploited the desire to be modern as much as it curbed it.... As 'reproducers of the race,' women were to embody traditional values, being stoic, silent, and fervid; as patriotic citizens, they were to be modern, that is combative, public and on call" (p. 147).

This partial remapping of the male imaginary, where fears and desires are projected onto competing female images of the 1920s and 1930s, highlights some of the contradictions and ambiguities the title of this volume is intended to put into question. "Mothers" — in the biological sense of childbearing and in the symbolic sense of bestowing maternal care upon fathers, husbands, and offspring — thus invokes the idealized gender role re-created and diffused in dominant discourses forming the economy of margins and centers in the multiple spheres of cultural production where Fascism endeavored to exert its power. In fact, as stated in "Educazione morale, civile e fisica delle piccole e grandi Italiane" (Moral, civil and physical education of Italian girls and women), which outlines the goals the National Fascist Party set forth for female youth groups in 1929, young girls were to prepare "to serve the Fatherland as the greatest Mother, the Mother of all good Italians" (*I fasci femminili* 1929; in Meldini 1975, 157). At the same time, "Mothers" posits the concept of women as the subjects of invention, generating cultural production by means of their ingenuity, designs, and mental "conceptions." By maintaining the tension between these different notions of women as both the subjects and objects of invention, and the plurality of female models they engendered, the overarching paradigm structuring this volume seeks to avoid producing an "alternate" history of women's culture during the era of Fascism. The latter approach would reproduce the theoretical paradigm of male and female cultural production as separate, and by nature different, spheres that Fascist exponents desired yet failed to impose as a structural edifice in Italian life and society. Moreover, this framework enables us to examine the shifting positionalities—inscribed in ideas, practices, and traditional artifacts—women assumed in the hegemonic field of relations and the ideologies, discourses, and institutions (Fascist and otherwise) that constituted it. Retracing the spaces female subjects inhabited, refashioned, or disrupted, as well as those from which they were virtually shut out and alienated, also promotes an understanding of the broader dynamics of Italian culture throughout the vicissitudes of Fascism in its complexity.

As a category of interpretation, "invention" affords a range of applications for critical studies on the forms of cultural composition in "high," popular, and mass culture, as well as in everyday living in the regime. Conceived here as a process of generating ideas afresh by use of ingenuity, design, or recombination, the term *invention* offers useful distinctions from *imagination,* that I wish to maintain, recognizing, however, that inventive acts engage the faculty of imagining. Whereas the concept of invention has perhaps been undertheorized, the "imagination" has occupied a key position in Western thought from classical times to the present, its meanings now historically overdetermined. As Richard Kearney demonstrates in *The Wake of Imagination* (1988), a thorough analysis of paradigmatic shifts in concepts of imagination, the nature of this creative faculty and its relation to reality and art carries a series of problems deriving largely from the conceptual reliance upon the humanist paradigm of "imagination" as "originary" creation by an autonomous, unified subject—notions that Jacques Derrida and Jacques Lacan have effectively dismantled.[2] In contrast, the semantic valences of "invention" shift the emphasis to a mode of production more or less grounded in existing conditions, ideas, and principles.[3] The concept of "invention" can thus give a clearer sense of the gendered subject's situatedness in the historical, socioeconomic, linguistic, and certainly political formations of cultural life.

Therefore, as an interpretive category, invention furnishes an alternative to both the humanistic concept of creative imagination as "originary" essence and the "imaginary" as a semiotic regime that outlaws even the vaguest possibility of agency. And if, as critical theory contends, no space exists outside the cultural construction of knowledge and imagination, the notion of invention, I want to propose, accounts for that "insidedness" that, however, provides the terms for turns of thought and expression altering conventional associations. In fact, from its conception, *inventio,* formulated by Dante as both "the act and effects of inventing," valorizes making creative use of ideas, signs, and symbols from life and culture surround in order to bring into being different perspectives and the meanings they performatively make available. In this sense, the notion of invention — neither uniform nor definitive (comforting as definitions may be in these postmodern times) — that orients this project applies as much to the critical praxis and effects of the studies contributed to this collection as to the cultural production of women during Fascism. Through the questions they raise, their selection of textual objects, and the methods they devise to analyze them, the contributors to this volume make different artifacts and interpretations visible, thereby inventing areas of inquiry.

In a similar manner, because invention responds to and plays upon material problems and conditions, as well as desires, this category enables us to theorize the locations of women's politics of invention, not as a unified, linear movement, but as a modality of power located at multiple, micropolitical sites where authority bears upon social subjects. For example, by working through Foucault's theorization of the equivocal dynamics between discourses of power and opposition, we may see the (inter)relations between the enterprise undertaken by the regime to invent a national Fascist culture and subjectivity and women's products of counterinvention. As Foucault (1980) writes, resistances

> are all the more real and effective because they are formed right at the point where relations of power are exercised; resistance to power does not have to come from elsewhere to be real, nor is it inexorably frustrated through being the compatriot of power. It exists all the more by being in the same place as power; hence, like power, resistance is multiple and can be integrated in global strategies. (p. 142)

While keeping in mind how the intersecting determinants of gender, sexuality, class, and so forth situate women as both subjects and objects, we should not minimize how pleasure and desire figure in the xiv / Robin Pickering-Iazzi

inventive process as women redeploy signs and symbols, perhaps making the unthinkable possible. Adrienne Rich (1993) eloquently expresses this relation as she tells us, "We must use what we have to invent what we desire" (p. 215). Each of the studies here shows how this idea operates in the lives and arts of women's making, but we see the relational importance of positionality and desire particularly in the self-styled practices and creative labor of Anna Kuliscioff, a foreign-born feminist leader in the Socialist Party, and Antonietta Raphaël, a woman, Jew, and foreigner whose painting and sculpture earned her critical distinction.

Fascism and the Sexual Politics of Invention in Life and Culture

To provide a frame for reading the individual studies in this volume, which present in-depth analyses on specific issues concerning women as agents and objects of invention and how they figured in Italian society and culture in the authoritarian regime, I wish to give a brief overview of the relations of gender and power shaping the material conditions of invention. There is no doubt that the dictatorship instituted mechanisms to mediate the dispositions toward self, the body, marriage, and motherhood among targeted female communities, endeavoring, in effect, to plot the "New Italy"'s cultural terrain, redrawing the borders between male and female enterprises. Indeed, the question of how to define the proper cultural role for women, and thus establish normative behaviors, preoccupied some of the regime's most influential thinkers as they also sought to conceive a national culture, of which Mussolini was apparently the sole architect and architecture.[4] In his essay "Donne a casa" (Women at home), published in 1929, Gherardo Casini proposed a clearly repressive tack that registered the challenges female intellectuals and artists posed to male authority. He told the readers of *Critica fascista* (Fascist critique), "It will be to our credit if we can extend the restraints we've applied to women in politics to other fields, most of all, to art and literature" (in Meldini 1975, 168).

However, the majority of Fascist policy makers argued not for simple repression, but for the creation of a separate sphere for women's cultural production. Not surprisingly, the Fascist construction of female cultural identity attempted to restore woman to the traditional female role, but with a difference. The new Italian woman as exemplary wife and mother became the cultural model for the "moral" way of life in Mussolini's Italy. The text "La donna nella coscienza moderna" (Woman in modern consciousness), written by Giovanni Gentile and published in *La donna e il fanciullo* (Woman and child) in 1934, best represents this stance in Fascist discursive practice. An idealist philosopher, Gentile held the strategic position of minister of public instruction (1922–24), wrote the 1925 "Manifesto of Fascist Intellectuals," and directed the *Italian Encyclopedia* project, one of the regime's most enterprising undertakings. After claiming the death of female emancipation as a contemporary ideal, Gentile (1934) insists upon the recognition of female limits and sexual difference as the only way for women to achieve self-realization. He proposes that his concept of sexual limits is "a way of thinking and feeling as a function of the moral conception of life which, in turn, develops with the development of culture" (p. 8), a complex proposition that receives the more extensive analysis it deserves in Lucia Re's essay in this volume. Dismissing the "woman-man," the suffragist, and the "third sex" as deviant, outmoded models, Gentile deploys the woman-mother, a fundamental image and construct in the Fascist ideology of woman, to assert the importance of the family as the site where woman may best express her natural genius.

Another central component characterizing the sexual politics of Fascist culture is the renewed development of biologistic theories of female sexual difference, which hark back to essentialist concepts advanced in scientific discourses of the 1800s. This trend is exemplified in the writings of Nicola Pende, an extremist yet important figure, who was the director of special pathology at the University of Rome. In his 1941 article "Femminilità e la cultura femminile" (Femininity and female culture), published in the Fascist journal *Gerarchia* (Hierarchy), Pende defines the nature of female culture by theorizing a causal relationship between biological and cultural difference. Under the guise of magnanimity, Pende (1941/1975) introduces his thesis:

> We are not among the people who believe in woman's intellectual inferiority. But it is indisputable that the female brain is qualitatively different from the male brain. Woman is capable of doing everything that male intelligence can, but only up to a certain average level which, however, is more than sufficient for the tasks for which woman was created. The best and most objective psy-

xvi / *Robin Pickering-Iazzi*

chologists admit that woman is rarely able to rise to celebrity in those fields of thought which require the power of abstract think- ing and a sense of proportion or original invention. These fields include creative and abstract arts, like musical composition and architecture, the sciences, philosophy, history, and law. (p. 276)

The unsuitability of the female brain for "masculine" enterprises does not, Pende explains, lessen woman's importance in the Fascist state. It merely indicates difference and the different qualities of fe- male intelligence, which are predictably adapted to domestic tasks. Fashioning woman as the complementary other, Pende also claims that such female traits as practical intuition and patience are precisely the qualities the "man of genius" frequently lacks. Hence Pende ar- gues, "Woman's culture must be adapted to these sexual characteris- tics, and can in no way be equal to male culture" (p. 277).

Although writings by Fascist commentators argue against women's claims to cultural authority, employing biologistic, moral, and politi- cal arguments, the campaign to domesticate female cultural production remained primarily discursive. The Fascist state exercised its power in culture not by applying systematic forms of oppression over the citizenry, but by exerting its dominance through a changing variety of propaganda messages, programs, and organizations that addressed different sectors of the populace.[5] The ways the regime constructed these sites for the ideological production of gender identity and social relations during the formation of the Fascist hierarchical structure con- stitute the specific field of inquiry examined in Mariolina Graziosi's chapter in this volume. Therefore, the following examples will suf- fice here. The *fasci femminili* (fascist women's groups) and ONMI (National Agency for Maternity and Childhood), founded in 1925, best illustrate attempts to put into social practice the ideal of service to the Fascist state as an obligation of female citizenship, which was promoted in public discourse of the time. These organizations were instituted as a structure through which women could provide care and assistance to families, in the form of education—in the areas of health, hygiene, and moral issues—and of material aid, for example, by distributing food, clothing, and layettes among the lower classes. As indicated in the 1922 guidelines for women's groups, the Fascist regime cast female beneficent works as a social, not political, agenda. It would be a mistake, however, to assume, without distinctions, that women working within Fascist-sanctioned groups necessarily put them to the precise uses for which they were intended. In fact, De Grazia (1992, 263–64) argues that communities of middle-class women employed such programs to forge female bonds and modern networks, and, moreover, as in the case of Latin feminists, conceived of social service as political practice. This historian, and De Giorgio (1992) as well, also offers a more complex interpretation of meetings and mass gatherings of female youth staged under Fascist auspices, which have conventionally been read as signs of ideological seduction and conformity. Focusing on the use value adolescent girls attached to public space in the piazzas, both De Grazia and De Giorgio suggest that female youth utilized collective occasions to break loose of traditional family and Catholic authority, and to fashion new forms of courtship and male-female relations occasioned by modernity.

The scheme of hegemonic relations during the *ventennio* epitomizes what Edward Said (1979) calls a "diffused power system," which creates as well as inhibits sites and occasions for inventive acts. Joan Cocks (1989) eloquently underscores this point as she explains the relations between elite writers and the broader system of discursive power, stating that the authors of discourse are

> educated by its other thinkers and writers, provided a starting place by its presumptions, stimulated by its images, pressed down the avenues of reflection it has carved out, enticed to solve the perplexities it has created — their imagination determined as much by the doors swinging open one after another before them as by the doors shut and locked along the way. (p. 43)

When applied to the spheres of cultural production operating in the Fascist regime, the conceptualization of the creative dynamics structuring centers, margins, and intersections offers a point of departure for charting where women trespass, push back borders, or make inroads, altering the landscape of Italian culture. We must keep in mind, however, that the cultural elite of the interwar period represented a plurality of ideological and artistic orientations. It included not only such Fascist exponents as Gentile, Giuseppe Bottai (a journalist, founder of *Critica fascista* in 1923, and leader in the Fascist government), and the vociferous F. T. Marinetti, who founded the futurist movement. The elite also comprised figures whose relations to Fascism ranged from hostile to indifferent, and more often than not were ambivalent.

Among this latter group were, for example, Benedetto Croce, a philosopher and perhaps the most esteemed literary critic between the wars, who wrote the "Manifesto of Anti-fascist Intellectuals" (1925); the internationally acclaimed film director Roberto Rossellini; and Elio Vittorini, whose disillusionment with Fascism as a revolutionary populist movement gave rise to the novel *Conversation in Sicily* (1938–39), a cry of alienation and desperate hope amid material and ethical poverty under the regime. These diverse intellectual trends notwithstanding, dominant discourses of the 1920s and 1930s exhibit the general tendency to assert male authority within the cultural regime of the masculine and feminine. In point of fact, few women managed to gain access to the top echelons of the official hierarchy, maintained by patronage systems awarding prizes and financial assistance, and such Fascist institutions as the Academy of Italy. Among the most notable exceptions are Margherita Sarfatti, who wielded substantial power as a journalist, the founder of *Gerarchia* (1922), and the biographer of Mussolini (*Dux* 1926), to whom she was adviser and confidant,[6] and Ada Negri, a critically renowned writer and poet who was awarded the Mussolini Prize in 1930 and membership to the Academy of Italy in 1940.

This does not mean that Fascist sexual politics managed to contain or to repress women's production in cultural life. Rather, it demonstrates the need for more adequate paradigms and terminology that can move beyond common binaries — inclusion/exclusion, highbrow art/mass culture, aesthetics/politics — in order to examine different registers of cultural activity undertaken inside, outside, and in between the spaces that constitute the imbricating spheres of art and daily living. For example, the painter and sculptor Antonietta Raphaël, one among the increasing numbers of women artists who painted and exhibited their work during Fascism, created a formative role for herself in the *Scuola romana* (Roman school) and garnered critical attention from the time of the first public exhibit of her art in 1929. Similarly, women authors attracted the sustained attention of prominent critics, their literary works anthologized and examined in histories of their time. These include such award-winning writers as Benedetta, a major avant-garde novelist in the futurist movement; Grazia Deledda, who received the Nobel Prize for literature in 1926; Sibilla Aleramo, author of the internationally acclaimed feminist work *A Woman* (1906) and such collections of poetry as *Poesie* (Poems, 1929) and

Sì alla terra (Yes to the earth, 1935), and Alba de Céspedes, whose 1938 novel *There's No Turning Back* became a best-seller during Fascism despite the regime's pointed criticism of the work's lack of "Fascist ethics." The frequent contributions to the press by Teresa Labriola, the foremost theoretician of Latin feminism, and by Irene Brin, a journalist and cultural critic of notoriety, earned these writers influential positions in the public eye.

Although conventional studies highlight the regime's management of mass media and publishing, women intellectuals and artists constructed invaluable public venues for their cultural interventions. They published fiction, poetry, and essays in books, professional journals, nationally distributed newspapers, and the women's press, attaining phenomenal success among established communities of readers and the emergent mass audience.[7] Their achievements and undertakings were reported in women's publications such as the *Almanacco della donna italiana* (Italian woman's almanac) and recorded in such works as Mario Gastaldi's book on Italian women writers, *Donne, luce d'Italia* (Women, the light of Italy), published in 1930, Maria Bandini Buti's *Poetesse e scrittrici* (Women poets and writers), and the Fascist scholar Francesco Orestano's volume on exceptional women in Italian culture and history, compiled under the auspices of the national biography project of the Academy of Italy and published in 1941–42.[8] Never entirely incorporated in the center of high Italian culture, nor repressed on the furthest edges, the shifting locations of women's artistic production may induce revolutionary conditions for invention. As Gilles Deleuze and Félix Guattari (1986) tell us, "If the writer is in the margins or completely outside his or her fragile community, this situation allows the writer all the more possibility to express another possible community, to forge the means for another consciousness and another sensibility" (p. 17).

Clearly, as Alice Jardine (1984), among others, points out, we must exercise caution when applying the paradigm Deleuze and Guattari propose for deterritorializations and reterritorializations to women's art. This is especially so here, as we explore women's production of culture in a regime that addressed and legislated for different communities according to sex, marital status, class, and generation—precisely the determinants these theorists tend to gloss over. However, the notion of positionality participates in a growing body of work theorizing how a "politics of location" creates special possibilities for creative innovation. The case of Sibilla Aleramo bears out this claim. As Fiora Bassanese argues in her essay in this volume, Aleramo valuated her marginal position "as a sign of exceptionality rather than exclusion" and "separated from the norm in order to construct an exemplary self-image for her public, but also for herself." Although we cannot generalize from the example Aleramo provides, it suggests ways to speculate about how social subjects avail themselves of positionality in inventive acts designed to alter or subvert dominant social behaviors and mores, as well as symbols and associations.

As the contributors to this book show, re-viewing traditional artifacts women produced during the dictatorship—paintings, sculpture, imaginative literature, prose commentaries, and letters—enables analyses of the ways female authors of discourse negotiated dominant codes, adopting, altering, or transgressing the ideologies that prevailed. Of equal importance, particularly in examining an authoritarian regime that sought to manage cultural life, are what Michel de Certeau (1988) calls "unsigned" forms of production. His theoretical paradigm enables us to examine everyday practices—of reading, using spaces, film viewing, or self-fashioning—in order to achieve an understanding of the different ways the *bricoleur* may implement, manipulate, or thwart the signs and ideas put at her or his disposal by dominant groups. Agents of this art of invention, de Certeau speculates, "make innumerable and infinitesimal transformations of and within the dominant cultural economy in order to adapt it to their own interests and their own rules" (pp. xiii-xiv). The forms these inventions take vary, some relying on the possibilities occasioned by a situation as it unfolds, and others constructed upon collective expectations and customs. For example, impromptu plays on words, jokes, and changing the lyrics to songs constitute cultural production that, Luisa Passerini (1989) explains, disrupt the symbolic order and the power relations authorizing it. Similarly, in some cases women strategically apply their inventiveness to mediate relations between the daily life of family and state mechanisms designed to create Fascist subjectivity, fabricating, for instance, "private" circumstances to avoid participating in the regime's organizations.

Italian scholarship on the positions social subjects adopted toward Fascism brings to light operations adroitly executed in the micropolitical sphere that challenged the regime's authority at the social and symbolic levels.[9] Pushing this line of inquiry into unexplored terrain, the essays here by Maurizia Boscagli and Jacqueline Reich examine for the first time a range of modern female subjectivities constituted, respectively, in the journalistic writings of Irene Brin and in school-girl comedies produced by the Italian cinema during Fascism. These sites of cultural composition exemplify de Certeau's notion of inventive arts of modernity at the level of text, where images of female rebellion or the artificiality of women's fashion are manipulated in such a manner that they both critique Fascist codes and assume productive value for constant refashioning of identities, and at the locus of reading and viewing practices, where consumers make use of ideas, language, and signs.

As Passerini cautions, we should not overlook the symbolic significance of such interventions in collective life and the meanings attached to them. Take, for example, the brouhaha created in male cultural writings over women who cut their hair short. Although conservative commentators read women's decision to wear short hairstyles as a scandalous rebellion against tradition motivated simply by the desire to be fashionable, Sibilla Aleramo insists that the meanings of such forms of female self-invention are much more complex. In her 1925 essay "Short Hair," from which the epigraph to this introduction is drawn, Aleramo examines her own experience, maintaining that when a woman has her long hair cropped, she gains control in civilized society; her physiognomy articulates an ethical and spiritual transformation into an autonomous subject.[10] Whether transitory or long lasting in nature, arts of invention represent a formational component of subjectivity. In her study of maternal symbols produced during World War II, Anna Bravo (1991) calls for a more expansive concept of the "subject" that would account for socioeconomic determinants as well as "the role of individual inventiveness," a recurrent topic in women's oral narratives about their lives during Fascism and the Resistance (pp. 97, 103).

Reorientations: Critical Approaches to Women, Fascism, and Culture

The critical studies chosen for this collection build upon recent scholarship on Italian women and Fascism, as the authors invent paradigms that push our thinking into relatively unexplored areas of inquiry and create a different perspective on the most current scholarly debates about Fascism and culture. To be sure, the academic and popular fascination with Fascism has not waned since Susan Sontag wrote her oft-cited article "Fascinating Fascism" in 1974. The *Bibliografia orientativa del fascismo* (Introductory bibliography of Fascism), compiled by Renzo De Felice, the most authoritative scholar in the field, and published in 1991, includes more than 10,000 entries for works pertinent to nonspecialists alone. Postwar historiographic and cultural writings on Italian Fascism, and especially those on the conditions of women in the dictatorship, exhibit major paradigmatic shifts. Whereas the terms *consent* and *resistance* structured privileged categories of interpretation in the 1970s, critical studies of the 1980s all but bracketed this construction as ineffectual for examining the full range of changing attitudes and practices in a dictatorship that outlawed forms of opposition.[11] Instead, newly developed models attend to such multiple determinants as gender, class, geographic location, and generation in order to evaluate different positions adopted toward Fascist ideology and politics inscribed in sites and practices of social agency. This general approach opens onto new readings of gendered social subjects and their complicated relations to the formative discourses and institutions of Fascism, as illustrated in *Fascism in Popular Memory,* by Passerini (1987); *La nuova italiana* (The new Italian woman), by Elisabetta Mondello (1987); *La corporazione delle donne* (The corporation of women), edited by Marina Addis Saba (1988a); and *How Fascism Ruled Women,* by De Grazia (1992). Similarly, recent years have seen revisionist readings of Italian cinema, such as *Streetwalking on a Ruined Map,* by Giuliana Bruno (1993), which resituates in film history the pioneering work of Elvira Notari (1875–1946), the first Italian woman filmmaker, who worked from a marginal position within the hegemony of Italian national cinema yet produced phenomenally successful films on women and the popular culture of Naples, until her films were suppressed by changes in the industry instituted prior to and during Fascism. The breadth of archival research and approaches these works make available invites us to investigate the production of women as subjects—invented and inventing—in Italian culture.

The essays collected here also implicitly or explicitly engage with and recast growing scholarly debates about the (inter)relations among Fascism, modernism, and culture. This general problematic has inspired several volumes published in quick succession. These include a special issue of the *South Central Review* (1989) titled "Fascist Aesthetics" and an issue of the *Stanford Italian Review* (1990) titled "Fascism and Culture"; the collection *Fascism, Aesthetics, and Culture,* edited by Richard J. Golsan (1992); and *Fascist Modernism,* by Andrew Hewitt (1993).[12] The new, fundamental questions posed by this body of work concern, for example, the ways Fascism has potentially tainted postwar critical theory, as in the case of Paul de Man and deconstruction, yet also provided the impetus for productive self-critique; how avant-garde movements of the interwar years may be implicated in Fascist modernity, as exemplified by F. T. Marinetti; and the reductive postwar notion of mass culture as a Fascistic tool for engineering conformity among passive consumers. Although these discussions address issues of broad concern to us all, because of the general reliance upon canonized male writers and texts, they run the overall risk of re-presenting cultural production of the interwar years as a masculinist project.

With the purpose of appraising the cultural identities women invented during the patriarchal regime and how they relate to prevailing notions of the female and femininity, this collection addresses a lacuna in American academic discussions on Italian Fascism. The first book in English to provide a historiographic examination of the ways women belonging to different socioeconomic, generational, and geographic groups may have experienced life in the dictatorship, De Grazia's *How Fascism Ruled Women,* was published in 1992. A book-length study on the literature women authors produced during Fascism has yet to be written; the names of women artists of the period are virtually absent in American scholarship, despite their critical achievements. Hardly exhaustive, the present essays do not claim to fill in this gap.[13] Representing a broad range of topics and approaches, these chapters relocate women in the spaces they forged, thereby mapping the field of cultural relations from a different vantage point. The contributors focus primarily on arts of invention elaborated specifically during the years of Mussolini's dictatorial rule, analyzing the ideas, metaphors, concerns, and aspirations of the time that solicited and engaged women. They thus construct more articulated models of modern female subjectivity.

In the opening essay, Rosalia Colombo Ascari foregrounds issues related to the forms of invention women elaborated during the years of Fascism. She examines Anna Kuliscioff's formative role as a pioneering feminist in the Italian Socialist Party, as represented in her published works and correspondence with Filippo Turati, a leader in the Socialist Party. This study brings to light the configurations of self, political life, and praxis this intellectual styled in relation to the mobile, frequently volatile, realities of the Italian political scene from the late 1800s to the years following World War I, as Mussolini rose to power and consolidated the regime. Kuliscioff's analysis of the "woman question," which took shape as she advanced the causes of woman's suffrage and the women's labor movement within a party torn by divisiveness, gives readers an invaluable perspective on fundamental issues regarding feminism, Marxism, and the Fascist "solution."

In the second essay, Mariolina Graziosi focuses on the cultural and social program implemented by the regime to construct new models of male and female identity during the formation of the Fascist hierarchical structure, and the attendant process of normalization and moralization. In her rereading of propaganda and women's writings produced in the 1920s and 1930s, she interrogates the ideological use made of gender identity and the contradictory positions of victim and social agent made available to women by Fascism itself, which derived from the crucial role Fascist thinkers assigned to women as the moralizers/normalizers of both themselves and society.

The following three essays, which, respectively, assess the contending veins of Italian futurist discourse and chart the shifting positionalities women fashioned in avant-garde and Fascist hierarchies, clearly show the importance of examining forms of female authorship produced in movements with apparently misogynist ideologies. Clara Orban analyzes a broad range of representations of woman in the visual arts, manifestos, and fiction by, for instance, F. T. Marinetti, Umberto Boccioni, and Giacomo Balla, arguing that male futurists rendered woman transparent—lacking the virility so crucial to their aesthetic. She then locates such women futurists as Valentine de Saint Point, Futurluce, and Mina della Pergola within the field of futurist discourse, probing the space they made for themselves and the images and ideas they adopted, adapted, and contested as they created new methods of signification, primarily in the poetry of the 1920s and 1930s. Lucia Re analyzes the complex hegemony of technologies of gender constituted by Fascist discourse and by the counterdiscourse produced in experimental novels by avant-garde women writers. With a scrupulous reading of Giovanni Gentile's 1934 "La donna nella coscienza moderna" (Woman in modern consciousness) and Ferdinando Loffredo's 1938 *Politica della famiglia* (The politics of family), she first demonstrates the need to give serious consideration to Fascist theories of woman, which provide philosophical and ideological grounding for the regime's hegemonic discourse and legitimate discriminatory sexual politics. She then focuses on the alternate ways gender difference is constructed in *Le forze umane* (Human strengths, 1924) and *Il viaggio di Garará* (Garará's journey, 1931), both by Benedetta, and *Nascita e morte della massaia* (Birth and death of a housewife, 1939), by Paola Masino, which valorize female creativity and desire in the process of self-invention and thus, she proposes, may be read as a form of resistance at the level of subjectivity and self-representation. The next essay also scrutinizes the discursive regime during Fascism. However, Barbara Spackman speculates on the ideological ramifications arising when the Fascist rhetoric of virility—designed to enforce the boundaries between the masculine and the feminine—is employed not by its intended addressees, but by women. Working through Foucault's theoretical notion of "tactical polyvalence," she tests the proposition that the discourse of control may itself generate the beginnings of a "reverse discourse" with the pre-Fascist "Manifesto of the Futurist Woman," written by Valentine de Saint Point in 1912, and then with writings by the "Fascistically feminist" Teresa Labriola, which present the concepts she formulated on women and their roles in Fascist culture and society between 1918 and 1939. This analysis of how Labriola employs the Fascist rhetoric of virility, playing upon the contradictions within and between dominant codes to devise her own meanings, challenges assumptions about the "Fascist woman" and about the broader discursive field as well.

The next three critics deal with issues related to the notions and images of identity women intellectuals and artists created for themselves in journalistic prose, poetry, and the visual arts, and reconsider the performative value of their artifacts within the regime. The first of these essays gives us a new perspective on mass culture during the dictatorship, conventionally viewed as a malleable tool serving Fascistic ends. Maurizia Boscagli looks specifically at the writings Irene Brin, a journalist of sharp wit and an insider among cosmopolitan sets, contributed to the magazine *Omnibus* in the 1920s and

1930s, which were later collected in the important volume *Usi e costumi* (Manners and customs, 1981). She argues that Brin's cultural critique of modernity — a fragmentary recording of mores, attitudes, problems, and styles shaping the partial, perhaps trivial, aspects of everyday life — performs, stylistically and thematically, an ideological denoument of central myths Fascist discourse constructed about history, the Italian "race," nature, and woman. Within this frame, she focuses her analysis specifically on the ways Brin's discourse of fashion threatens the authentic and the natural by privileging artificiality; Brin posits the mixing of semiotic codes as a strategy to produce subjectivity within "a culture in uniform," inciting her readers to become producers of their own individual style.

Fiora A. Bassanese concentrates on Sibilla Aleramo's endeavor to make herself into a "living poetic myth," situating the strategies and contents she designs to create her mythic self against those employed by Mussolini to present himself as the quintessential icon of Fascism, virility, and masculinity. Using examples from Aleramo's poetry and diaries, she demonstrates the ways in which the poet, perceiving marginality as a sign of her exceptionality, inscribes will, genius, body and spirit, and eroticism under the sign of female sexual difference. The components distinguishing the mythic identity Aleramo styles in her life and poetry, Bassanese argues, constitute an original model of the new woman poet that gained popularity among female readers in the 1930s precisely because of its nonconformity. Likewise, Emily Braun interrogates questions of female identity as artistic matrix, as they intersect in the life and art of Antonietta Raphaël, whose painting, sculpture, and influence in the school of via Cavour has commanded critical attention in Italy since she first exhibited her work in 1929. The first part of this essay explains how Raphaël has been neglected by American art historians (feminists and others alike) because of biases privileging the French-American modernist mainstream and assumptions about cultural management of Italian women and art in the Fascist state. After foregrounding her interpretive arguments with a biographical profile, Braun reflects upon Raphaël's position as artist, woman, Jew, and foreigner within the regime. The analysis of her painting and sculpture demonstrates how she deployed concepts to invent a formal language that could aptly convey experiences of the female body, sexuality, procreation, and creation, positing new terms for female subjectivity with, for instance, her representations of the female gaze, mother-daughter relations, and maternity.

The two essays that follow explore the subversive refiguring of female subject positions articulated in fiction and film through different representations of collectivity, individuality, conformity, and rebellion. Carole C. Gallucci analyzes Alba De Céspedes's international best-seller *There's No Turning Back* (1938), a novel about a community of young women residing in a Roman boardinghouse run by nuns, and the different kinds of knowledge about self and society they gain. Insisting upon the interrelatedness between history and story, Gallucci proposes that De Céspedes has created a gendered female space as a site of ideological production. By reading De Céspedes's representations of women's social life against the ideals and myths promoted by Fascist exponents, Gallucci elucidates the strategic tools, images, and meanings De Céspedes has elaborated to devise female roles for social transformation while challenging, for instance, the models of the "new woman" and the "crisis woman," and the (un)holy alliance between church and state as part of an overall critique of the sociopolitical conditions in the regime.

In the final essay, Jacqueline Reich makes a strong argument for examining "minor" films that gained enormous popularity among audiences during Fascism, but have been eclipsed by the critical focus on classic neorealistic films. She proposes that filmic texts produced during Fascism offer up visual constructions of the ideal Fascist woman for public consumption and, at the same time, create openings for narrative and ideological transgression, a thesis she supports by analyzing the subversive potential of the schoolgirl comedy genre as it developed in box-office hit films produced in Italy between 1934 and 1943. Her examination, situated within the context of Fascist educational policy and practice, focuses specifically on issues associated with female sexuality and woman as spectacle, rebellion against authority, and the tension between collectivity and individuality, as illustrated in the films *Ore 9, lezione di chimica* (Nine o'clock, time for chemistry class), directed by Mario Mattoli (1941); *Teresa Venerdì* (Theresa Friday), directed by Vittorio De Sica (1941); and *Il birichino di papà* (Daddy's little devil), directed by Raffaello Matarazzo (1943).

With their assessments of signed and unsigned artifacts produced by women, the contributors to this volume make the presence of women xxviii / *Robin Pickering-Iazzi*

as inventors of meaning explicit in the dynamics of Italian culture during Fascism. They thus make a significant contribution to our understanding of women's contradictory positions, engendered by the different possibilities modernity and Fascism made available in the interwar period. Yet they also have far-ranging implications for assessing trends in Italian culture and society today. This partial reconstruction of women's interventions in cultural life sheds new light on postwar representations of Italian experiences of Fascism and the Resistance movement, a notable theme in postwar literature, cinema, and painting, as illustrated by Lina Wertmuller's film *Love and Anarchy,* Giuliana Morandini's novel *Bloodstains,* and Elsa Morante's prizewinning work *History: A Novel,* from which RAI, the Italian Broadcasting Corporation, drew its popular film version.[14] Moreover, the present studies dislodge common assumptions about women of Italy, and Fascism, as they challenge the hegemonic image of the self-sacrificing Italian mother embedded in the contemporary imaginary. They posit a different terminology that creates an epistemological category for the analysis of female subjects engaged in the active process of producing ideas, images, and artifacts of their own devising. By attending to the complex power relations women negotiated in life and art during the Fascist regime, the scholars whose works are presented here resist the tendency to demonize Fascism as a hypnotic force holding the Italian populace in an iron grip for twenty years.[15] This reappraisal—not rehabilitation—of how sophisticated mechanisms were designed during Fascism to solicit, address, and coerce different audiences may enable us to adopt a more critical perspective on how hegemonic power is constituted in "liberal" and "conservative" movements. This is a matter of much concern now, as the scandals of *Tangentopoli* (commonly translated as Kickback City) and *Mani pulite*— the "clean hands" operation designed to clean house at Montecitorio and Palazzo Madama—shift the sediments of traditional political life in Italy, perhaps enabling new powers and alliances to emerge there, and in the economy of transcultural politics.[16]

Notes

I want to thank Marina Perez De Mendiola and Panivong Norindr for their questions and critical insights, which have helped to shape this essay. Unless otherwise noted, all translations are my own.

1. The male fascination with and fear of women's nontraditional undertakings in

Italian culture of the interwar years are clearly articulated in, for example, *Le lettere italiane del nostro secolo* by Camillo Pellizzi (1929), *Contemporanei* by Giuseppe Ravegnani (1930), and the broad spectrum of writings by Fascist exponents collected in *Sposa e madre esemplare* (1975), edited by Piero Meldini.

2. I thank Ian Winter for this reference. For further work on imagination and invention as critical categories, see Joan Cocks (1989), Gerald L. Bruns (1982), and Luisa Passerini (1989).

3. This emphasis is illustrated by the definition of *invention* supplied in the unabridged *Webster's New International Dictionary,* 2d edition, which states: "The power to conceive and present new combinations of facts or ideas, to devise new methods or instruments."

4. In "Selections from the Great Debate on Fascism and Culture" (1990), Jeffrey Schnapp and Barbara Spackman provide English translations of major selections written by artists and intellectuals who engaged in the often heated discussion about the nature of and relations between Fascism and culture.

5. Victoria De Grazia (1992) brings together a comprehensive range of documentation and analysis of the institutions, organizations, and policies developed by Fascist policy makers to shape women's cultural pursuits. See also Michela De Giorgio (1992), Elisabetta Mondello (1987), and Marina Addis Saba (1988).

6. Philip V. Cannistraro and Brian Sullivan examine Margherita Sarfatti's life and works in the 1993 biography *Il Duce's Other Woman.* Nancy Harrowitz's current research, presented in her paper "Margherita Sarfatti and the Politics of Race and Gender" at the 1994 conference of the American Association for Italian Studies, explores the provocative issue of Sarfatti's Fascist feminism.

7. For English translations of short fiction written by critically acclaimed and popular women authors during Fascism, along with a revisionist reading of how their literary discourses figured in the sociocultural sphere, see Robin Pickering-Iazzi (1993).

8. See especially chapters 5–8 in Victoria De Grazia's *How Fascism Ruled Women* (1992), which discuss women's new ways of engaging with high, popular, and mass culture, as well as how male critics interpreted female cultural practices.

9. Among these important studies are Luisa Passerini's *Fascism in Popular Memory* (1987); Ilva Vaccari's *La donna nel ventennio fascista (1919–1943)* (1978); and Dianella Gagliani et al.'s "Culture popolari negli anni del fascismo" (1984).

10. The symbolic importance of a woman's wearing her hair short was also conveyed among women of the Turin working class, who perceived their cropped locks as a sign of the social progress they had made in relation to their mothers' generation. See Luisa Passerini (1987).

11. In "La donna 'muliebre,'" Marina Addis Saba (1988b) furnishes a useful examination of the major paradigms and categories of interpretation that have been applied in historiographic analyses of Italian Fascism.

12. See also Alice Yaeger Kaplan's *Reproductions of Banality* (1986), a forerunner in this field of critical inquiry.

13. Among new and unexamined areas of research are, for instance, the continuities between the construction of gender during the Fascist regime and the postwar republic, which Ellen Nerenberg investigates in "Habeas Corpus: The Gendered Subject in Prison: Reflections on Fascism and Literature in Italy, 1930–1960" (1994), and the subject of lesbian sexuality during Fascism, which has not received the critical attention it merits.

14. In addition to recent studies in Italian oral history, I wish to refer to a letter titled "La Resistenza che avete dimenticato" (The Resistance you forgot), which was

published in the June 1993 issue of the feminist magazine *Noi donne* and tells us much about the ongoing significance of this subject in the minds and memories of women who participated in the Resistance. Chiding the magazine for hardly mentioning the Resistance in its special issue (February 1993) dedicated to major historical events and figures between 1944 and 1953, the author recalls 1944 as the climactic year that saw "women engaged on all fronts, and saw women partisans and anti-Fascists killed, shot, tortured, and incarcerated." Disturbed that this chapter in the history of women and Italy is fading from memory, she reminds us that the freedoms and rights of Italian women today are rooted in the ground broken by socially and politically transformative female roles shaped in the Resistance.

15. For critiques of this tendency, see Barbara Spackman (1990), Heesok Chang (1990), and Jeffrey Schnapp (1990).

16. Less than a year after I wrote this essay, the speculative note of the conclusion requires recontextualization. Indeed, with the 1994 elections, the Italian political terrain underwent a substantial rift. Silvio Berlusconi, the head of the conservative Forza Italia movement, now holds the position of prime minister of Italy, with a coalition government including Gianfranco Fini, leader of the neo-Fascist Italian Social Movement (now called the National Alliance), and the right-wing Umberto Bossi, head of the separatist Northern League. This newborn alliance promises to provide different terms of speculation in the rapidly changing field of Italian political culture and critical thought.

Works Cited

Addis Saba, Marina, ed. 1988a. *La corporazione delle donne: Ricerche e studi sui modelli femminili nel ventennio fascista*. Florence: Vallecchi.

Addis Saba, Marina. 1988b. "La donna 'muliebre.' " In *La corporazione delle donne: Ricerche e studi sui modelli femminili nel ventennio fascista*. Edited by Marina Addis Saba. Florence: Vallecchi.

Aleramo, Sibilla. 1930. "Capelli corti." In *Gioie d'occasione*. Milan: Mondadori. Originally written in 1925.

Bravo, Anna. 1991. "Simboli del materno." In *Donne e uomini nelle guerre mondiali*. Edited by Anna Bravo. Rome-Bari: Laterza.

Bruno, Giuliana. 1993. *Streetwalking on a Ruined Map: Cultural Theory and the City Films of Elvira Notari*. Princeton, N.J.: Princeton University Press.

Bruns, Gerald L. 1982. *Inventions: Writing, Textuality, and Understanding Literary History*. New Haven, Conn.: Yale University Press.

Cannistraro, Philip V., and Brian R. Sullivan. 1993. *Il Duce's Other Woman*. New York: William Morrow.

Chang, Heesok. 1990. "Fascism and Critical Theory." *Stanford Italian Review* 8, nos. 1–2: 13–33.

Cocks, Joan. 1989. *The Oppositional Imagination: Feminism, Critique and Political Theory*. London: Routledge.

de Certeau, Michel. 1988. *The Practice of Everyday Life*. Translated by Steven Rendall. Berkeley: University of California Press.

De Felice, Renzo, comp. 1991. *Bibliografia orientativa del fascismo*. Rome: Bonacci.

De Giorgio, Michela. 1992. *Le italiane dall'unità a oggi: Modelli culturali e comportamenti sociali*. Rome-Bari: Laterza.

De Grazia, Victoria. 1992. *How Fascism Ruled Women: Italy, 1922–1945*. Berkeley: University of California Press.

Deleuze, Gilles, and Félix Guattari. 1986. *Kafka: Toward a Minor Literature.* Translated by Dana Polan. Minneapolis: University of Minnesota Press.

"Fascism and Culture." 1990. *Stanford Italian Review* 8, nos. 1–2.

"Fascist Aesthetics." 1989. *South Central Review* 6 (Summer).

Foucault, Michel. 1980. *Power/Knowledge: Selected Interviews and Other Writings 1972–1977.* Edited by Colin Gordon, translated by Colin Gordon et al. New York: Pantheon.

Gagliani, Dianella, et al. (1984). "Culture popolari negli anni del fascismo." *Italia contemporanea* 157: 63–90.

Gentile, Giovanni. 1934. *La donna e il fanciullo.* Firenze: Sansoni.

Golsan, Richard J., ed. 1992. *Fascism, Aesthetics, and Culture.* Hanover: University Press of New England.

Hewitt, Andrew. 1993. *Fascist Modernism: Aesthetics, Politics, and the Avant-Garde.* Stanford: Stanford University Press.

I fasci femminili. 1929. Milan: Libreria d'Italia.

Jardine, Alice. 1984. "Deleuze and His Br(others)." *Sub-Stance* 13, nos. 3–4: 46–60.

Kaplan, Alice Yaeger. 1986. *Reproductions of Banality: Fascism, Literature, and French Intellectual Life.* Minneapolis: University of Minnesota Press.

Kearney, Richard. 1988. *The Wake of Imagination: Ideas and Creativity in Western Culture.* London: Hutchinson.

Meldini, Piero, ed. 1975. *Sposa e madre esemplare: Ideologia e politica della donna e della famiglia durante il fascismo.* Florence: Guaraldi.

Mondello, Elisabetta. 1987. *La nuova italiana: La donna nella stampa e nella cultura del ventennio.* Rome: Riuniti.

Morandini, Giuliana. 1987. *Bloodstains.* Minneapolis: New Rivers.

Morante, Elsa. 1984. *History: A Novel.* Translated by William Weaver. New York: Vintage.

Nerenberg, Ellen. 1994. "Habeas Corpus: The Gendered Subject in Prison: Reflections on Fascism and Literature in Italy, 1930–1950." Unpublished manuscript.

Passerini, Luisa. 1987. *Fascism in Popular Memory: The Cultural Experience of the Turin Working Class.* Translated by Robert Lumley and Jude Bloomfield. Cambridge: Cambridge University Press.

———. 1989. "Immaginare l'immaginario: Rassegna di termini e di libri." *Linea d'ombra* 42: 19–23.

Pellizzi, Camillo. 1929. *Le lettere italiane del nostro secolo.* Milan: Libreria d'Italia.

Pende, Nicola. 1975. "Femminilità e la cultura femminile." In *Sposa e madre esemplare: Ideologia e politica della donna e della famiglia durante il fascismo.* Edited by Piero Meldini. Florence: Guaraldi. Originally published 1941.

Pickering-Iazzi, Robin, ed. 1993. *Unspeakable Women: Selected Short Stories Written by Italian Women during Fascism.* New York: Feminist Press.

Ravegnani, Giuseppe. 1930. *Contemporanei: Dal tramonto dell'ottocento all'alba del novecento.* Turin: Fratelli Bocca.

"La Resistenza che avete dimenticato" (letter to the editor). 1993. *Noi donne,* June, 89.

Rich, Adrienne. 1993. *What Is Found There: Notebooks on Poetry and Politics.* New York: W. W. Norton.

Rosa, G. Titta. 1931. "Scrittori e sirene." *La stampa,* August 18, 8.

Said, Edward. 1979. *Orientalism.* New York: Vintage.

Schnapp, Jeffrey. 1990. "Forwarding Address." *Stanford Italian Review* 8, nos. 1–2: 53–80.

Schnapp, Jeffrey, and Barbara Spackman. 1990. "Selections from the Great Debate on Fascism and Culture." *Stanford Italian Review* 8, nos. 1–2: 235–72.

Sontag, Susan. 1980. "Fascinating Fascism." In *Under the Sign of Saturn*. New York: Farrar, Straus & Giroux. Originally published 1974.

Spackman, Barbara. 1990. "The Fascist Rhetoric of Virility." *Stanford Italian Review* 8, nos. 1–2: 81–101.

Vaccari, Ilva. 1978. *La donna nel ventennio fascista (1919–1943)*. Milan: Vangelista.

Vittorini, Elio. 1973. *Conversation in Sicily: A Vittorini Omnibus*. New York: New Directions.

1 / Feminism and Socialism in Anna Kuliscioff's Writings

Rosalia Colombo Ascari
In memory of my father and brother

A Place in History

In the history of Italian socialism and feminism, Anna Kuliscioff stands out for her exceptional intellectual and moral stature. The publication in 1977 of the six volumes of her correspondence with Turati (1898 to 1925) allows us to better evaluate her contributions to the social and political evolution of Italian society (Schiavi 1977). She interpreted Marx and Engels with intelligence, and laid the foundations in Italy for scientific socialism (as it was first called by Marx and Engels, who claimed scientific status for their theories). She was also constantly engaged in improving the conditions of women and children in a country that, at the time, was the most backward in Europe. Virtually unknown in American scholarship, the few references made to Kuliscioff have tended to present her as an ambitious politician rather than as a dedicated feminist.

In the present essay, I intend to demonstrate that this dichotomy never existed in Kuliscioff while offering, for the first time, ample selections from her correspondence in English translation. Because so little information on Kuliscioff's life and intellectual background is available in English, I begin with a brief outline of her early ideological development and political activity. I then examine her feminist writings

1

as they engage with the problems of Italian society, using the correspondence between Turati and Kuliscioff as a constant point of reference and analysis to underline her commitment to the Socialist Party and to the feminist cause. Her independent way of thinking, acting, and developing strategies according to the mobile reality of the Italian political scene from the late 1800s to the 1920s, when Mussolini consolidated his regime, will be illustrated through her letters. They evidence, I propose, her ability to use the strength of the party for the women's cause, the impact she had on Turati's political choices, her integrity and her ability to draw a line between her political views and her personal life, and her constant, genuine devotion to the emancipation of women.

An Adventurous Life

Anna Kuliscioff was born Anna Markovna Rozenstejn at Simpheropolis, in the Crimea.[1] Her exact date of birth is not known, but, according to the most acceptable documentation, she was likely born in 1854.[2] She grew up in a rather wealthy environment, as her father, Moisey, had made a small fortune in the grain trade. After brilliantly completing her secondary education, Anna left Russia in 1871 to enroll as a student in the Department of Technical Science at the University of Zurich, and the following year she entered the Polytechnic. Switzerland had opened its universities to women, and it welcomed many young Russians in search of intellectual emancipation and many political refugees, including Pyotr Lavroff, Pyotr Nikitich Tkatscioff, Nahum Sokoloff, and other leaders of the populist movement, whose aim was to enlighten the masses until they could govern themselves (see Turati 1926, 343).[3] In Zurich, Anna began her revolutionary apprenticeship by going to Armand Ross's library, known for its history and sociology collection and enriched regularly by French and German publications on the working class. She also joined the Sanzebunist Circle. The aims of this group, which was imbued with French utopianism, are not clear. In fact, whereas Zebunev later mentioned a Bakunian influence, Vera Figner "attached a distinctly lavrist color to the group" (Casalini 1987, 20–21). These two theories appear as antithetical, because the former is insurrectional in character and the latter is pacifist. But as both propose the people's participation to achieve education, they both move from a common antistate platform, based on faith in the political maturity of the masses attainable through their natural socialist instinct.

Bakunin's influence appears to have been more relevant and lasting in Kuliscioff's political training, even though it was the propagandist idea that drove her and Pëtr Makarevic—whom she had recently married in Zurich and whom she never mentioned in her writings—to join the Odessa group when she went back to her homeland in 1873. The group spread Lavrov's teachings by disseminating universal principles of freedom, justice, and humanity among the urban proletariat. One year later she was in Kiev, one of the few members of the Odessa party to have escaped arrest. She was now part of the revolutionary organization Juznye Buntari (Haupt 1978, 240). Her changeover from pacifism to action reflects in part a weakening of the propagandist theory, caused also by the failure and dispersal of the groups to which she had belonged. Juznye Buntari commissioned her in 1876 to go to Switzerland to buy a printing press and bring it to Russia. The intention was to publish an announcement, purporting to be from the czar, in which peasants would be incited to occupy the land, which was declared to be their legitimate property. Thanks to Kuliscioff, it was printed. After the breakup of the Kiev group and a brief stay in Char'-kov, where she sang in the parks for a living, she went back to Kiev as a guest of Elena Kosac.

On April 14, 1877, with passport no. 124, issued by the city governor in the name of Alexandra Kosac, Kuliscioff left Russia for good, once again managing to avoid, by a margin of hours, falling into the hands of the police. She settled in Switzerland, probably in Lugano. Not much is known about her first months in exile. In August of that same year she got in touch with Andrea Costa, a revolutionary anarchist and a follower of Bakunin, later to become the first Socialist member in the Italian Parliament. Albonetti (1976), in his introduction to *Love Letters to Andrea Costa,* points out the historical significance of such an encounter, there locating the origin of Costa's famous shift in positions, often attributed to Kuliscioff's influence. Indeed, already in a letter of September 18, 1877, Costa wrote about the need to start afresh with a great campaign. Kuliscioff's political position, weathered by so many years of clandestine opposition ending in failure, must have motivated her populist orientation (Haupt 1978, 247). Her support for, and contributions to, Costa's ideology, even in the following years, can be understood only within this context. It was the time of their passionate love affair, which lasted until 1885, with short periods spent together and long ones spent waiting apart in prison.[4] According to Casalini (1987), the clearest expression of Kuliscioff's political creed is found in the declaration she made in December 1879 in a Florence court of law:

> Revolutions cannot be made by internationalists at their conve-nience, because it is not within the power of individuals either to make them or to provoke them; it is the people who make revolutions, and therefore it is not expedient to rise up in armed bands, but rather to wait for those revolutions and bands to take shape in order to direct them to socialist principles. Socialists ... must take part in popular movements, as well as in all other ex-pressions of the life of the people in order to direct them, but they cannot create the movements themselves. Revolution must come from the people, and it cannot be made in spite of them. (p. 41)

Obviously, Kuliscioff's extremist stance could not easily be recon-ciled with Costa's legalistic view. Their common ground had been their consideration of socialist ideology at a European level, and it was difficult for Kuliscioff to accept Costa's new line, which resulted in the founding in 1881 of the Revolutionary Party of Romagna and of the daily socialist newspaper *Avanti!*

On December 8, 1881, their daughter Andreina was born at Imola. Two months later, Kuliscioff left Italy with her and went back to Switzerland. The center of her life was now her little Ninì, who also awakened her desire to study medicine. She started her studies in Berne amid great financial and emotional hardships. Costa became increas-ingly distant and did not seem to care for their relationship, which was still very important to Kuliscioff. In Bern she rejoined the elite of European socialism and met such important figures as Karl Kautsky, August Bebel, and Georgy Plechanov. Plechanov inspired her article of April 20, 1884, which concluded her contributions to *Avanti!* In this article she introduced the program of Plechanov's group Libera-tion of Labor, the first Russian Marxist revolutionary organization, founded in 1883. She presented it as the party of the future, whose aim was to spread scientific socialism through translations of the most important works by Lassalle, Marx, and Engels. Direct contacts with the group were interrupted in 1884, when health reasons caused Kulis-cioff to move to Naples to finish her medical studies. The experience was essential because it exposed her to scientific socialism and offered her an opportunity to acquire a thorough knowledge of Marx. This intellectual foundation gave her a prestigious position in the Italian socialist movement.

For two years Kuliscioff was absent from the political scene, focusing all her energy on physical survival and on earning her degree in medicine. Medical training satisfied her aspiration to help the people, and it fulfilled her socially, by developing the early interests she had as a young girl. She faced considerable problems in the Neapolitan academic world, both as a woman and as a foreigner. Ill with tuberculosis, she fought with indomitable moral strength against physical debilitation, financial problems, and grief over the conclusion of her affair with Costa, even though she had clearly brought it to an end (see Grimaldi 1986, 28). After a period of research in Pavia at the Laboratory of General Pathology and Histology, directed by Camillo Golgi, she completed her dissertation on the etiology of puerperal fever and finally graduated in Naples in November 1886, the first woman to become a doctor in that university (Belloni 1978, 345).[5] In the meantime, on the initiative of Anna Maria Mozzoni, one of the most outspoken Italian advocates of women's liberation, Kuliscioff began to correspond with Filippo Turati, a prominent young lawyer from Milan. Within a few months, they developed a lasting relationship (Valeri 1974, 21). Turati and Kuliscioff shared "an insoluble basic contradiction between the impossibility of giving up a traditional upper-middle-class lifestyle and an equally strong aspiration to accomplish the egalitarian ideal of socialism" (Casalini 1987, 81).[6] For some years Kuliscioff remained in the political background, even though she was concerned with spreading the ideas of Marx and Engels and the ideology of German social democracy. Meanwhile, she dedicatedly practiced her profession as a *dottora* in the clinic of Via San Pietro all'Orto (Borsa 1926, 13).[7]

At the Roots of Italian Feminism and Socialism

Kuliscioff returned to the political stage in 1889, when she and Turati founded the Milan Socialist League.[8] This organization fulfilled important functions during the three years leading up to the founding of the party of Italian workers. It constituted "the head sector of the socialist movement. The final goal was socialization of producer

goods, to be attained by overtaking public power through the workers' organized struggle" (Valeri 1974, 26). The following year, on April
27, at the Philological Club in Milan, Kuliscioff gave the famous lecture "The Monopoly of Man," largely inspired by August Bebel. The
text of this lecture provides a vivid historical analysis of woman's
condition, presented as the steady monopoly of man in its various
manifestations, in its social activities and functions. Throughout the
centuries, contempt and abuse have been perpetrated by the very advocates of Christianity, Kuliscioff (1977a) argues, so that "the history of the development of the eternal feminine since primitive times
offers itself to our eyes as a long martyrology" (p.126). The way out,
she asserts, is financial independence. The desire to become independent is more and more common in woman, who demands "to cooperate in social activities, and claims to represent a social value herself"
(p. 126). The heart of the feminist question is "the great fundamental truth of modern ethics"; in other words, "Work alone, whatever
its nature, shared and compensated equitably, is the true source of
improvement for the human species" (p. 127).

To Kuliscioff, the woman factory worker is a synonym of redemp-
tion, because even though modern industrialism will make woman as
poor as man, it will rescue her from that dependence upon, and submission to, man that Kuliscioff defines as moral parasitism. Her writings diffuse an awareness of women's socioeconomic problems, which
were just beginning to take hold in hostile ground. For instance, in
1893, *Critica sociale* — a biweekly founded by Turati — published a
laudatory review of Cesare Lombroso and Guglielmo Ferrero's book
The Female Offender. The book maintained the intellectual inferiority of women, stressing the biological affinity between normal and
delinquent women. There prevailed then two different degrees of positivism; from a rationalistic kind of positivism with Marxist over-tones
to the most narrow-minded social Darwinism (Casalini 1981, 12).
Kuliscioff entered the fray with a revolutionary spirit, and, as Eugenio Garin (1962) puts it, "topple[d] positivistic determinism" (p. 37).
She argued for the need to recognize women's rights, which were
already a part of the new social order,[9] and secured for herself a
prominent position in the feminist arena until the beginning of World
War I.

Her activity as a feminist shows three stages, which Franca Bortolotti (1978) has classified in the following manner:

The first, from 1890 to 1903, is characterized by the distinction between socialism and radical feminism, and by the law on working mothers. The second, between 1907 and 1913, is the most open, and we might call it the period of Anna Kuliscioff's feminism, a socialist feminism, but clear and precise nonetheless. The third, after the war, extends from 1919 to 1924. In this period the earnestness of the theories is substantially invalidated by an insufficient perception of the political incidence of the feminist question, at a particularly dramatic juncture. (p. 104)

The term *socialist feminism* seems ambiguous to Claire La Vigna (1978), who tries to prove that for Kuliscioff the party would come first, whenever there might be conflicting interests. However, I consider Kuliscioff a representative feminist, because Italian feminism almost to this day has never been divorced from political activism.

Born into the middle class, but emancipated since early youth, Kuliscioff believed that for middle-class women oppression came from men, and for working women oppression came from capitalism. For the middle-class woman the aim is to acquire professions that used to be monopolized by men. For the working woman, "who has already acquired, or rather accepted for a long time, the right to be exploited, the aim is to narrow down her areas of employment, to prevent women from being employed in unhealthy industries, in mines and metallurgical jobs" (Kuliscioff 1977b, 168).

Among the first, Kuliscioff (1977b) points out that when unions for feminist interests presume to be above all parties, they reveal "the golden age of their very early childhood, by assuming that the question of women is something similar to love for animals, capable of uniting in one cult all men and women with one heart" (p. 164). When La Vigna (1978) writes that "socialism and feminism remained basically two parallel rather than intersecting movements" (p. 146), she confirms what Kuliscioff wrote in 1897: "Even though socialism and feminism can be parallel social currents, they will never make one cause" (Kuliscioff 1977b, 170).

During the thirty-five years in which *Critica sociale* was published, all of the articles Kuliscioff contributed and signed were directly concerned with the feminist question.[10] It was for this cause, deeply rooted in her, that she participated in and spoke at party conventions, projecting her past as a nihilist onto the present. She was inspired with such fervor as to sometimes rank together the woman worker and the professional in an interclass vision: "For as long as middle-class feminist suffragists demand suffrage for all women, we can march separately to strike together" (Kuliscioff 1977f, 200). Kuliscioff questioned the limited participation of women in the proletarian movement, and pointed out that it was the party's fault, because it seemed "to have lost its original power of expansion and to have estranged itself from the life of the proletarian mass" (p. 198). Here again she emphasized the unbridgeable gap between the social classes. For lower- or upper-middle-class women, political rights are a means of defense from men, whereas for proletarian women, those same rights are a means of economic emancipation. The social function of women is not limited to work, but also implies motherhood, which is "the highest and most delicate of all social services" (p. 201).

The 1910 controversy with Turati and with the rest of the party (except Gaetano Salvemini; see Schiavi 1977, III:1, 141) over tax, education, and military budget reform was an important moment for Kuliscioff, and a clarifying one for her thinking. Her efforts were focused in support of women's rights, and at the same time she was trying to save the Socialist Party, which, "thanks to the parliamentary environment, could extensively degenerate into just another middle-class party" (in Schiavi 1977, III:1, 115). Debate on party goals began years before, when Turati clarified the gradualistic nature of his position concerning the extension of suffrage. Kuliscioff (1977c) reaffirmed that because women had long been involved in the Industrial Revolution, they were entitled to demand "as producers and taxpayers, civil and political rights appropriate to their status" (p. 173).

Insisting on universal suffrage, Kuliscioff considered a vote made available only to women with university degrees and who had been counted in a census to be a jump backward for the proletarian cause. Precisely because woman is oppressed "by the huge burden of domestic chores," she must be called to the conquest of political rights that "may awaken her awareness in her social class, as a mother and a citizen" (Kuliscioff 1977d, 179). She concluded with a truth that is obvious to us today, but that was then unpalatable to the socialists against whom she was writing in 1910: "The vote is the defense of work, and work has no sex" (p. 179). On April 16, 1910, she directly attacked her lifetime companion, Turati, as the faithful representative of the most prominent comrades. She polemically asked him what he had done to be less of a cheater than religions, less priestly than priests, resorting to a sentimental allusion in order to refute the accusation that women have a religious "penchant," seen as a feminine weakness and therefore as a sociopolitical impairment. Kuliscioff (1977e) wrote that such a penchant

> conceals, after all, the unconscious aspiration to at least an imaginary flight from the slavery of beasts of burden, toward the idealization of motherhood, symbolized in the sweet ritual of Mary, toward a desired communion of souls, which religious marriage seems to promise for an instant under the auspices of mystery, but which hard living exposes as falsehood. (p. 182)

In the gradual change proposed by the socialists and in the granting of the vote to middle-class women, Kuliscioff saw the disappearance of the ideal and moral strength of the party itself. By associating the cause of universal suffrage with the party, which in her opinion suffered from premature old age, she hoped to attract an ardent young generation to her double cause:

> Propaganda for universal suffrage, warm with conviction, fervent with faith in the future, directed to peasants,... to women, doubly martyrs of their poverty and of male selfishness, a propaganda that, in order to triumph, must point out the endless injustices afflicting those who are most spurned, most forgotten, most exploited, such propaganda is the only one that can infuse new youth into our party. (1977e, 185)

The fact that she considered universal suffrage a way to revitalize socialism was not a clever political move, but an expression of her conviction in both causes helping each other to build a democratic society.

In addition to her elaboration of feminist ideology, Kuliscioff's political practice includes several noteworthy initiatives that provided women with means for voicing their concerns. In 1912, Kuliscioff decided to create a women's organization within the party. On July 7 of the same year it was finally formed, as a forerunner to the Women's National Socialist Committee. The committee met in conjunction with the Reggio Emilia Convention. In the meantime, Kuliscioff took on the editorship of the journal she had founded, *La difesa delle lavoratrici* (The defense of women workers). It consisted of only two pages, clearly inspired by the *Gleichheit* model. Besides addressing problems specific to women, the journal reserved ample space for general political issues. This journal was not the first of its kind, but earlier socialist publications had failed because they lacked the party's support and financial contributions. *La difesa* became the official periodical of the National Organization of Socialist Women and was published successfully until 1925. Given the broad spectrum of its readers, the publication made room for short stories that rendered socialist ideology into a simplified and romantic realism. There was also a section concerning labor disputes and the problems experienced by women workers in various fields, but the recurring themes were universal suffrage and antimilitarism.[11]

Before yielding the editorship of the journal to Angelica Balabanoff at the end of the first year, Kuliscioff spoke up in April 1912 to defend women's suffrage vehemently. She attacked Pietro Bertolini, who warned future parliaments about the danger of extending political rights to women, which might lead to "a change or switch between the two sexes of the family or social mission specific to each one of them" (Kuliscioff 1977g, 211).[12] Her response deserves special attention for the way it highlights the sexual politics of her time. Step by step, she condemned the illogical report, which accepted male illiteracy but deplored it in women: universal suffrage would grant the ballot to 6.5 million Italian women, "two-thirds of whom are thought to be illiterate," argued Bertolini. In addition, the report acknowledged the right to vote for those who had interests to defend, but it did not include women, who, Kuliscioff (1977g) stressed, have "all those needs and interests that are related to the terrible and ever-growing price increases for the necessities of life" (p. 210). In her view, the right to vote is essential for the proletariat because it constitutes a weapon to defend jobs, and it is even more valid for the most exploited of workers, women.

Just how important women's suffrage was to Kuliscioff can be seen in her letters and in her decision to go to Rome at the time of the Parliament's debate on the matter. Writing to Turati, Kuliscioff stated, "I hope to arrive in time to hear your speech and Giolitti's. Please, don't betray me. If you do not present a motion to grant all women the administrative vote, and if you do not ask for a roll-call vote on the subject, I assure you I would be deeply saddened" (in Schiavi 1977, III:2, 735). *La difesa delle lavoratrici* of June 2, 1912, had an ironic commentary on the subsequent defeat of the proposal:

The "great" reform passed.... At this point an Italian, in order to be one day a citizen, has but one precaution to take: be born a male. The idea put forth by the spokesman that all the issues concerning administrative vote would be dealt with more appropriately within the framework of a special project... was the hook on which even our friends were willing to hang their good intentions. In the meantime, women were left in limbo. (Kuliscioff 1977g, 218)

But Kuliscioff's staunch faith in her political beliefs was not shaken. In fact, with an interclass approach not frequently found in her writings, she appealed to middle-class women and wondered if the next elections might change the balance and the vision of the present assembly:

The male proletariat holds a weapon that, however faulty, is much more valid and powerful than in the past.... those who are still excluded, women workers, will cooperate for tomorrow's achievements, which will truly be for everyone.... As for middle-class suffragists... we leave them the illusion... of a professed and flaunted feminist aloofness from politics.... And yet, if only women of other social classes, of all social classes, would stop fiddling with the comfortable chimera of a cowardly aloofness, formulating platonic agendas, or sending committees to Parliament and to the prime minister in the illusion of winning over politicians of all parties, which is synonymous with no party, since solitary and scattered votes do not count and do not spread. If only they would stop bumbling in a vacuum, and would instead participate tenaciously and selflessly in the political life of their parties; if only they would bring their intellectual and moral contribution to them, by attracting new proselytes, and by giving evidence of the use and strength they can put in the service of specific ideals and of concrete interests—oh, at that point, but only at that point, they also would hasten the demise of the current male dominance, in the family, in society, in the state. (pp. 219–20)

In Kuliscioff's forceful conclusion, she once again brings together socialism and feminism with one goal in mind, universal suffrage.[13]

A new era opens up for proletarians with a conscience. Let's not leave the leaders to fight alone for us. Women workers, don't be traitors of both your sex and your class. Do not betray your husbands, your comrades, your fathers, your children, the children

of your blood and of your love because of laziness, irresponsibil-
ity, cowardice, or because of wrong and fatal concerns for public
opinion. Do not betray yourselves and mankind. (pp. 228–29)

This statement makes it amply clear that Kuliscioff believed that
only politics could promote the feminist cause.

In 1912, however, the party's internal conflicts erupted during the
war in Libya.[14] On December 1 and 2, 1911, at a joint meeting of
the party leadership and of the Socialist parliamentary group, a motion was approved stating the need to oppose the government. Seven
months later, on February 23, when the Parliament met, a split had
already taken place, despite the fact that the Socialist deputies voted
almost unanimously against a decree to annex Libya. Kuliscioff commented, "Imperialism has drowned all parties, all programs, all groups,
in Tripoli's waters" and she vented her grief in seeing "the collapse
of what little we believed we were building throughout 25 years of
work and struggles" (in Schiavi 1977, III:2, 673).[15] However, she insisted that the separation between factions must be maintained until
the next convention, otherwise it would really be a public debacle
for the party (in Schiavi 1977, III:2, 697).[16] At this time, her correspondence with Turati details problems and possibilities of action,
but it also reveals that neither of the two could find acceptable solutions (see Vigezzi 1973, 220). Kuliscioff supported Turati's position,
and, above all, she counted on him: "You need to convince yourself
that the reconstitution of the party depends largely upon you" (in
Schiavi 1977, III:2, 716). Despite Turati's and Kuliscioff's growing political isolation, their faith in the party remained constant, and on
March 2, 1912, she wrote: "I believe that instead of being on the eve of
death, we are on the eve of Resurrection" (in Schiavi 1977, III:2, 716).

In July, when the XIII National Congress of the Italian Socialist
Party took place in Reggio Emilia, a revolutionary group gained the
majority with a motion presented by Benito Mussolini, then a young
member of the Socialist Party, requesting that some members be expelled from the party.[17] Mussolini's motion passed and he triumphed.
As an immediate consequence of Turati's defeat, the direction of
Avanti! passed from Claudio Treves to Giovanni Bacci. What had been
feared had happened: "Last night," Kuliscioff wrote on June 23, 1912,
"I had a long conversation with Treves, and explained to him how
we have not lost all hope for victory. I also thought it was necessary

to prepare a defense of *Avanti!*, which will certainly be attacked by those who wish to take it over" (in Schiavi 1977, III:2, 753). There was no victory, because reunification never took place. The editorship of *Avanti!* was given to Mussolini on the first of December.[18] If initially Kuliscioff had a favorable opinion of him, by February 1913 her writings show concern about the new party policies.[19] Commenting upon an article by Mussolini, she defined his ideology as "definitely anarchical." And she paraphrased him: "In Italy we have not had either the commune or long-lasting exceptional laws, therefore a formidable clash is needed between the people and the middle class." She concluded: "How crazy! And to think that all this craziness is now the party's policy. It all seems like a bad dream to me" (in Schiavi 1977, III:2, 841).

Prior to 1913, the problems with the revolutionary group were regarded as internal conflicts. Both Kuliscioff and Turati felt that the worst danger came from the right. The peace treaty of October 18, 1912, which concluded the Italian war with Turkey and assigned Libya to Italy, confirmed a definitive break with the right.

Kuliscioff noted that there was no longer an internal policy, but only a foreign one, and even that was rather flimsy, particularly as she perceived the threat of world conflict:

The whole of Europe is hanging from a hair; the explosion of a world war may depend on Austria's whims, Italy has committed herself to the Austrian carriage, there is talk that the proletariat of individual countries should be prepared to react to a possible conflagration, and Parliament is silent, as if all this were the Shah of Persia's business. (in Schiavi 1977, III:2, 810)

The urgent state of international affairs and the climate of tension and solitude in which Kuliscioff lived, created by the dismemberment of the party, made her neither generous nor patient with her women collaborators, in whom she detected petty and selfish interests. Along with such intellectuals as Linda Malnati, Maria Giudice, and Margherita Sarfatti, she worked on the editorial board of *La difesa delle lavoratrici*.[20] However, as Kuliscioff's correspondence shows, the interests of the editorial group contrasted with her own views, reflecting an international vision of the party and of feminism. Her political position and beliefs remained constant, even as she became increasingly aware of how the right weakened the Socialist Party and, likewise, of how the government exploited the situation (Vigezzi 1973, 250). Therefore, in an attempt to find a solution, Kuliscioff sought more leeway as she estranged herself from direct participation. On November 28, 1912, she wrote:

> I am very sorry, but I will not be gulled by our famous Socialist colleagues. You must know that yesterday at a group meeting they voiced their strong disappointment because I wasn't calling them in as an editorial board to decide which articles should be printed and which problems each issue should deal with. Imagine Giudice and Malnati, who formed the so-called editorial board with me, here every day to discuss those articles. In brief, I am absolutely happy not to have them as either friends or enemies. (in Schiavi 1977, III:2, 755–56)

However, her interest never dwindled. In fact, she was always very mindful of moral or social issues that could also affect the feminist cause, and ready to lend her support. For instance, her unflagging enthusiasm was clear in 1912, when she told Turati: "I am entirely caught up by the excitement of organizing the much-talked-about women's convention." Yet her efforts also drew criticism, as we see in the comments she made in the same letter about an article published in *L'unità.* Though praising *La difesa,* the article, written by Abigaille Zanetta, questioned her influence, as Kuliscioff pointed out: "They managed to perceive me as a corruptive influence. I will answer in a few lines, especially because it would bother me if those 'half-truths' might have made the same impression on many of our readers too. Concerning free love and anticlericalism, one should be very prudent" (in Schiavi 1977, III:2, 749–50).

The constant importance Kuliscioff attributed to universal suffrage and to improving the condition of women is particularly evident in her clash with Turati in a letter of May 1913. Following the visit of Bice Sacchi and two other suffragists who asked Turati for help to present their arguments before a committee, Turati wrote, "I received them for your sake, and for your sake I will also arrange their meeting with the committee"(in Schiavi 1977, III:2, 1046). Anna responded in a bitter tone that demonstrates her strong concern over the issue:

> Don't assume, my dear, that you are doing me a huge favor wasting your time with feminists. You socialists have been won over

to the cause for reasons and principles quite different from the feminists'. If anything, all these neo-Masons . . . should turn to the representatives of the middle class. Besides, there is no reason at all that you should lend yourselves to validate a movement that is almost nonexistent. Or if it exists, it's only there to be satisfied with even a partial vote for women, even though they would deny it. In short, I am very embarrassed that you too, who are my closest relative, still have not understood what kind of behavior to adopt with feminists. True, all men are always flattered to be enticed by femininity, even when the enticement comes from a suffragist. And I am not fooling myself in any way that you are willing to see how ridiculous you are. (in Schiavi 1977, III:2, 1051–52)

This attack does not take into account Turati's affectionate irony, and is written with a very biting tone. Kuliscioff stressed the main points of her feminism, which could not be confused or associated with middle-class feminism. Her beliefs were rooted in a deep ethical vision of life that determined her political and personal choices. She could not tolerate jokes, even benevolent ones, about her ethics.[21] Kuliscioff was Turati's most faithful ally, but also his most lucid and severest critic.

Twilight

From 1913 on, Kuliscioff was confined by a serious case of arthritis to her apartment in Piazza del Duomo, which she shared with Turati for more than twenty years. Their home had been a very important meeting place for intellectuals and young politicians who were eager to be exposed to European Marxism. Even though they now received fewer and fewer visitors, Kuliscioff kept up with the political and social events of the country through the newspapers and the reports of her closest friends. Nevertheless, she increasingly missed the experience of current reality. Perhaps because of this, her correspondence from that time shows a very scrupulous and constant attention to parliamentary prerogatives.

For both Kuliscioff and Turati the most important concern on the eve of and during World War I was to keep democratic freedom alive in its parliamentary form. But they both failed to sense the deep social dissatisfaction among certain sectors of the proletariat, to whom Mussolini would soon make his appeal (see Schiavi 1977, III:2, 883–

84).[22] On neutrality, they had opposing attitudes. Turati did not support the war, and when he manifested his trust in Antonio Salandra's cabinet because Salandra was not a warmonger, Kuliscioff's far-seeing response came quickly: "Bless the dreamers, my dear! And you are among them. . . . For my part I am convinced that the war has already been decided. . . . there isn't the slightest doubt that intervention, for the government, is already out of the question" (in Schiavi 1977, III:2, 1191). Scholars on Kuliscioff have maintained that she had unclear or ambivalent attitudes toward the war, steeped more in feeling than in rationality. For instance, Casalini (1987) concludes, "It is not possible to categorize her thought bluntly with the labels of 'neutralism' or 'democratic interventionism' " (p. 251). However, in a letter of March 4, 1915, Kuliscioff outlined her ideas with clarity: "Surely I don't want the war either, but this does not prevent me from deeply sensing the prevailing reality, and even Italy will not be able to get out of the general conflagration. . . . In short, either Italy will march in a few days, or she will remain isolated and damaged in the future" (in Schiavi 1977, IV:1, 33). The following day she underscored her position: "Indecision is not possible anymore: either we live by taking action or we will vegetate in the future, if we remain neutral" (in Schiavi 1977, IV:1, 38). Contemporary historians tend to justify her interventionism, first, because patriotism and internationalism are not viewed as irreconcilable for a certain generation of socialists. Second, she believed the great war would empower Italian capitalism and destroy Hapsburg domination, through the alliance of Italy with countries that were more advanced politically and economically, such as France and England (Casalini 1987, 252–53).

This position differs substantially from Turati's. In fact, even after Italy entered the war, he remained unequivocally neutral. He continued to insist on the disastrous consequences of war, whereas Kuliscioff seemed to consider it as a means of accelerating the country's process of democratization. Turati wrote to her in a letter of March 12, 1915:

> This is your obsession: believing that the war can save or defend us. War is like disease: it can kill, it can debilitate, nothing else. It will make us neither richer, nor wiser, nor more productive, nor freer, nor more honest, nor happier than we are. Why should we apply criteria to foreign policy that are so different from those we have adopted for internal policy, concerning revolution and upheavals? (in Schiavi 1977, IV:1, 62)

The respective positions Kuliscioff and Turati adopted on the war represented deeper differences within the party. For instance, the anti-Leninism of the reformists, who called Lenin the first czar of communism, accentuated the fracture that had already occurred in the party. In fact, their neutralism had been opposed by the democratic interventionists led by Gaetano Salvemini and Leonida Bissolati, and by Mussolini's revolutionary interventionists. For both groups, the war was a means of taking back the initiative in foreign and internal affairs, and a way to distance the party from the middle class, seen in general as opposed to armed intervention.

During the last ten years of her life, Kuliscioff gave all her intellectual strength to save the unity of the Socialist Party from its internal crises and from the growing Fascist movement. With the escalation of violence, democratic ideals faded away as the feminist cause lost its power. In September 1919, when Parliament approved the law for the nonpolitical vote for women, Kuliscioff duly noted the indifference that surrounded the issue: "The vote for women has been born, but I see no one is welcoming the newborn. Indeed, after the fact, everybody grumbles and finds it hard to swallow" (in Schiavi 1977, V, 186). In Kuliscioff's correspondence there are no comments on the Fascist project of 1923 granting the vote to women with patriotic merits. At that point she was more concerned with the broader Italian political scene. She never ceased urging Turati to act. Kuliscioff saw that the same problem affected the two factions of the party, Reformists and Maximalists:

> You want daring reforms, and you don't dare to take over the government, whereas this would be your chance. Maximalists want communism through proletarian dictatorship, but they do not have the courage to exploit the rebellious movements in various parts of the country in order to establish their dictatorship. Both factions... blame each other for not doing anything, accusing each other, as an alibi for their own impotence.... It is not enough to create programs, one must also aim at implementing them. (in Schiavi 1977, V, 364)

In 1920, Turati considered being part of the government an absurd idea, because it would have meant taking on "the direct and terrible responsibilities to become liquidators of a bankruptcy we by no means caused" (in Schiavi 1977, V, 370). Hesitation, internal strife, aloofness from real and local problems (Granata 1978), an incapacity to voice "the class struggle of the low middle class, which had become like a wedge between the middle class and the proletariat" (Salvatorelli 1923/ 1977, 12), are precisely elements that such contemporary historians as Ivano Granata and Luigi Salvatorelli use to explain the rise of the Fascist regime. De Felice (1976) characterizes the actual promoters of Fascism in the rural and urban middle class emerging at the end of World War I as "trying to acquire participation, and to acquire political power, having become a social force" (p. 30).[23] A reading of the correspondence between Kuliscioff and Turati from 1920 to 1925 shows a frequently dramatic attention to details, to violent episodes, a recurrence of exclamations, and disorientation about the madness of the times, but we don't find an in-depth analysis, only attempts. Kuliscioff could not see the nationalistic spirit of the low middle class yet, and she remained convinced that the upper middle class acted within Giolitti's sphere. Faithful to Engels's theory about the relationship between democracy and socialism, she thought that a possible dictatorship could not last long, because of the inevitable reaction of the industrial middle class, "which, in order to develop, has the same needs as the proletariat" (in Schiavi 1977, V, 899).

In the meantime, after the XIX Congress of the Socialist Party, held in Rome in October 1922, reformists were expelled from the party. The split marked the end of a lifelong commitment. In commenting upon Turati's farewell speech, Kuliscioff wrote on October 4: "*Consummatum est!* . . . at the bottom of my soul there is a great sadness: it seems to me as if we too are finished with the debacle of that party which was born and grew along with us!" (in Schiavi 1977, V, 895). As a consequence, the Partito Socialista Unitario (Unitarian Socialist Party) was formed. After the march on Rome on October 28, 1922, and the formation of the Mussolini cabinet, Kuliscioff still hoped "that some good might come out of the bad" (in Schiavi 1977, V, 900). As De Felice points out, Mussolini's great fortune was precisely that many Italians thought Mussolini represented "a lesser evil, a price to pay to get out of a dead end, and to reorganize energies, no one having yet realized what Fascism was, and not just what difficulties they would have to get rid of it, but also what difficulties Mussolini himself would have to control it and channel it according to his goals" (quoted in Colarizi 1973, 11). When Turati appeared to consider the possibility of an alliance among the leftist parties to form a united proletarian front against the dictatorship, Kuliscioff did not support the idea. One would lose, she wrote, "not only a battle, but also that amount of respect and consideration in public opinion toward the most valued and serious personalities on our side" (in Schiavi 1977, V, 906).

As Turati was willing "to gang up with the devil, if only Fascism could be defeated," she called him a pessimist; she poured oil on troubled waters, advising him to let time take its course, and not to push in order to get a possible artificial victory in administrative elections. In her opinion, Mussolini must "go full circle" and one should not "strengthen Fascism with leftist blocs of any kind" (in Schiavi 1977, V, 909). But in summer 1923, even though "Mussolini's parable is not yet concluded," she suggested "a bloc of all oppositions against the government and its majority group, because only a union of all will be able to represent an element of resistance against all the acts of violence organized by both volunteer and militarized praetorians" (in Schiavi 1977, VI, 77).

The last years of the correspondence indicate a constant vacillation between fleeting hope and deep sadness. Turati, disappointed by the policies of opposition parties, set his hopes on foreign intervention (Schiavi 1977, VI, 191), whereas Kuliscioff was convinced that foreign democratic governments did not want to intervene in Italy's internal miseries, and therefore, she concluded, "hoping that France or England would isolate our government is almost a reckless idea" (in Schiavi 1977, VI, 251).[24] The speech delivered on May 30, 1924, by Giacomo Matteotti, secretary of the newly formed Unitarian Socialist Party, denouncing the illegality of the elections of April 1924 gave both Kuliscioff and Turati new energy. But Matteotti's assassination just ten days later, which would lead to the opposition's abstention from all parliamentary activities (known as the Aventino secession; Turati and Kuliscioff 1945, 5–6), also became a cause for new illusions: "The stone that has been laying on our chests for years is crumbling into dust. Our work … is about to be rewarded. We will not die angry" (in Schiavi 1977, VI, 323).

In contrast with the optimism of Turati, who was uplifted by the favor of public opinion, Kuliscioff recommended the possibility of a military regime,[25] and later she put all her faith in the National Democratic Union, founded by Giovanni Amendola in November 1924. For her, that party represented the beginning of a political pluralism that could win over Fascism and form the basis of a new government.

This government would be directly responsible for Italy's economic and social development. Her hopes were thwarted by the Fascist aggression against Amendola in July 1925.[26] A few months later, in November, Turati's Unitarian Socialist Party was dissolved, because one of its members, Tito Zaniboni, had organized an attempt to kill Mussolini.

Even in the ruin of the democratic ideals for which Kuliscioff had fought all her life, she did not yield to despair. She strongly opposed Turati's idea of letting the main socialist periodical *La critica* "commit suicide" after its seizure by the totalitarian authorities.[27] On December 29, 1925, she died in her house in Milan, which for many years had remained the center of Italian reformism, and where, with the help of Turati, she had fought to give a new ethic to Italian society.

The Legacy

Kuliscioff's advocacy of women's suffrage came to fruition in 1945, after twenty years of Fascist dictatorial rule, World War II, and the Resistance movement against the Fascists and Nazi occupation. Women obtained the right to vote in a bill cosigned by Alcide De Gasperi and Palmiro Togliatti, leaders of the Christian Democratic Party and of the Communist Party, respectively. However, "the woman question," as Marxist thought posed it, was hardly resolved; women's relation to the Communist Party remained fraught with contradictions. It is true that the Communist Party sponsored the first official edition of *Noi donne,* the publication of UDI (the Italian Women's Union), published in Naples in 1944. By 1949, UDI with more than a million members, spearheaded a strong campaign for women's rights. In *L'unità,* the Communist daily, Togliatti closely followed the growth of the women's union and, foreseeing its impact, encouraged the plurality of the association, which could also represent Catholic women fighting for the same rights. Furthermore, the Communist Party supported the Merlin law in 1958, which abolished legalized prostitution and thus had a direct effect on income for the state.

On the other hand, the party never embraced the feminist cause in the manner the majority of women wanted, and in fact perpetuated male dominance, a practice later reproached by Communist women. Indeed, in the 1970s some Italian feminist groups adopted a radical separatist position against institutional politics. Other women followed the path Kuliscioff pioneered, advancing feminist politics within the

Communist Party. In part as a result of their efforts, in 1975 Italy passed new legislation on family rights, finally abrogating the Fascist laws that had stipulated that only women could be considered adulterous. The new law guaranteed equal rights for men and women in the family, and repealed *patria potestas*. Then, 1978 saw the landmark passage of the law legalizing abortion. Despite these notable achievements in women's rights, debates over women's contradictory positions in the Communist Party, newly renamed the Democratic Party of the Left, have intensified, as illustrated by the publication *Reti,* the Communist women's journal. In a recent article, Rossana Rossanda, a central figure in the party, responded to "the woman question" in a way that uncannily echoed the political praxis Kuliscioff elaborated, as she insisted that women in the party be both feminist and communist, stating, "Women are not a constituency to be added on [to party membership] but a different constituency, whose centuries-old history of difference, positively exploded in the past few years, entails a reconstitutive *self-consciousness* and thus a rethinking of the *entire* horizon and method of the party" (quoted in De Lauretis 1990, 14). Although we cannot minimize the more than seventy years of material and political differences shaping these perspectives, Kuliscioff stands as an important precursor to the new direction contemporary Communist women propose.

Notes

1. According to Maria Casalini (1987), "Kuliscioff's biographies (as she was going to have herself called in the years of emigration) have used in different cases the names of Anna Markovna, Anna Michajlovna, Anna Moiseevna" (p. 15). Unless otherwise noted, all translations in this chapter are my own.

2. Claudio Treves (1926), in an issue of *Critica sociale* dedicated to the memory of Anna Kuliscioff, notes, "Anna Michailewna Kuliscioff was born 69 years ago, on January 9, 1857, in a well-to-do family, at Moskaja (Kerson) in Little Russia" (p. 5). Pietro Albonetti, in his introduction to *Lettere d'amore a Andrea Costa* (1976, 17) points out the problem of documenting Kuliscioff's date of birth.

3. The appendix to the 1926 Turati volume contains information drawn from an article and from the book *Jews in the Russian Revolutionary Movement,* by Leo Deutsch, who had known Anna as a young woman.

4. For a chronology of Costa's and Kuliscioff's lives, see Martelli (1980, 111–23).

5. See also Lipinska (1900, 467). Antonio Pala (1973, 79) names Turin as the city where she graduated. Actually, Kuliscioff appears to have been an assistant at the obstetrical clinic in Turin's university (Mondolfo and Pagliari 1926, 7).

6. Casalini (1987) stresses the leading role Anna had in Turati's Marxist training and in his mental well-being. She also points out that some critics tend to minimize the importance of her political influence on Turati.

7. She was called *dottora* by the common people. Many of her patients also came from the middle class. Her charm touched everyone.

8. This league replaced a previous one that had been founded in 1881 by A. M. Mozzoni, and had adhered to Partito Operaio Italiano in 1888. See Bortolotti (1963, 191).

9. See figures concerning the predominance of women workers in Kuliscioff's "Monopolio dell'uomo" (1977a, 133); see also Kuliscioff (1977f).

10. The first issue of *Critica sociale* was published January 15, 1891 (see Valeri 1974, 28). Throughout its existence, many of the periodical's articles were signed "T.K.," "Noi," or "Critica sociale." It is clear that the contents of the articles were the result of collaboration, as can be seen from a letter of May 4, 1910: "The signature 'Critica sociale' was always considered, at least by those few who know us, as our joint signature, now it's not a joint one anymore, and so it is appropriate that it be signed by you alone" (in Schiavi 1977, III:1, 124–25).

11. At the end of the first year, the direction of the periodical passed from Kuliscioff to Angelica Balabanoff. In a letter of February 27, 1912, Kuliscioff wrote to Turati that she had been "massacred" by women, and wondered, "When will I ever make up my mind to slacken the bridle?" (in Schiavi 1977, III:2, 687). Speaking of Balabanoff, on November 28, 1912, she wrote: "Bal[abanoff] made her debut in *Avanti!* The article is long, but... always the same things expressed in a very childish way. It is her way of thinking; all her historical-philosophical-Marxist culture is of little or no use to her" (in Schiavi 1977, III:2, 755).

12. Bertolini had been elected spokesman of the parliamentary committee charged with what Kuliscioff called "the great reform" of Giolitti.

13. Concerning the fusion of the two causes, it is interesting to read the appeal published in *La difesa delle lavoratrici* at the time of the founding of Unione Nazionale delle Donne Socialiste: "The issue is not... to start a kind of 'socialist feminism,' which would be in total contrast with the theoretical principles of socialism, and with the very nature of the class movement. The aim is not to create a socialism for women, and to separate the crowd of women from that of men, like in country churches. The aim... is the exact opposite. The idea is to prepare, to facilitate, to secure a more and more tangible and active blending of the consciences and the forces of the whole army of workers" (quoted in Della Peruta 1961, 129). The issues of *La difesa delle lavoratrici* originally published from 1912 through 1917 were reprinted in March 1992 by the European Institute of Social Studies (Polotti 1992).

14. On September 29, 1911, Italy declared war on Turkey without consulting Parliament, in application of Article 5 of the 1848 statute that gave the crown the prerogative to declare war.

15. In this letter of February 23, one can sense the awareness of dissent within the party: "That vote of forced discipline is really deplorable. If only a dozen deputies had remained seated while the Bissolatis and the Ferris were all excited applauding Spingardi and Cattolica [minister of the navy], the event would have been no less historical than that historical session itself."

16. In a letter dated February 3, 1892, Kuliscioff noted: "I think it would be a serious mistake to go back to unity. I was hoping you would opt for separation, and the Congress would decide and then judge."

17. "He had a motion approved by which deputies Bissolati, Bonomi, and Cabrini were declared expelled from the party because they had visited the king, and Podrecca was expelled as a warmonger" (Valeri 1974, 98). The visit had been paid on March

14, 1912, after the attempt on the king's and queen's lives by the anarchist bricklayer Antonio D'Alba. As a result of the expulsion, on July 10 the Partito Socialista Riformista Italiano was formed.

18. Valeri (1974) notes that "on November 1, 1912, the newspaper was entrusted to Mussolini" (p. 98), but in the correspondence the reference is to December 1, and this date is accepted by most historians dealing with this period.

19. She wrote letters on December 2, 14, and 16, 1912, that were favorable (in Schiavi 1977, III:2, 771, 811, 823), but in a letter dated December 20, she wrote that Mussolini would like to have her opinion for *Avanti!* but she felt "very embarrassed expressing my opinion, because the newspaper is done very poorly" (III:2, 838).

20. *La difesa delle lavoratrici* began publication on January 7, 1912. Other members of the editorial board included Carlotta Clerici and Gisella Brebbia.

21. According to La Vigna (1978), Kuliscioff modified her feminist view in 1912, the year of the party's most serious crisis.

22. The letter of February 15, 1913, is especially enlightening.

23. On the "new petty bourgeoisie" see Forgacs (1986).

24. Casalini quotes this letter of May 28, 1924, as a declaration of hope in McDonald's government.

25. She made such a recommendation in letters of June 20 and 22 and November 14, 1924 (see Schiavi 1977, VI, 326, 334, 447).

26. She wrote on November 18, 1924: "Did you carefully read the manifesto to the country by the newly formed Unione Nazionale? I think it is a document of very great political, and even historical, value, if this adjective had not been too misused and downgraded by the Fascist press. The old democracy has died, old-style radicalism has died, and modern democracy arises, essentially inspired to the proletarian movement, which understands and comprehends the inevitable slow shifting of social life toward the main protagonists of modern living, the working classes, both manual workers and intellectuals" (in Schiavi 1977, VI, 459).

27. She expressed her opposition in letters dated November 17, 19, and 20, 1925 (see Schiavi 1977, VI, 776, 785, 786).

Works Cited

Albonetti, Pietro. 1976. "Introduction." In *Lettere d'amore a Andrea Costa*. Edited by Pietro Albonetti. Milan: Feltrinelli.

Belloni, Luigi. 1978. "Anna Kuliscioff, allieva del Cantani e del Golgi, e le sue ricerche sulla etiologia della febbre puerperale." *Physis* 20, nos. 1–4.

Boggio, Maricla, and Annabella Ceriani. 1977. *Anna Kuliscioff*. Venice: Marsilio.

Borsa, Mario. 1926. "La sua bontà." *Critica sociale*, January 3.

Casalini, Maria. 1981. "Femminismo e socialismo in Anna Kuliscioff, 1890–1907." *Italia contemporanea* 33 (June).

———. 1987. *La signora del socialismo italiano*. Rome: Riuniti.

Colarizi, Simona. 1973. *I democratici all'opposizione: Giovanni Amendola e l'Unione Nazionale (1922–1926)*. Bologna: Il Mulino.

De Felice, Renzo. 1976. *Intervista sul fascismo*. Bari: Laterza.

De Lauretis, Teresa. 1990. "Introduction." In Milan Women's Bookstore Collective, *Sexual Difference: A Theory of Social-Symbolic Practice*. Translated by Patricia Cicogna and Teresa De Lauretis. Bloomington: Indiana University Press.

Della Peruta, Franco, ed. 1961. *I periodici di Milano* (vol. 2). Milan: Feltrinelli.

24 / *Rosalia Colombo Ascari*

Forgacs, David. 1986. "The Left and Fascism: Problems of Definition and Strategy."
In *Rethinking Italian Fascism: Capitalism, Populism and Culture*. Edited by David
Forgacs. London: Lawrence & Wishart.
Garin, Eugenio. 1962. "La questione femminile." *Belfagor* 17 (January 31).
Granata, Ivano. 1978. "Ascesa e crisi del socialismo nel primo dopoguerra (1919-
1922): Il 'caso' di Milano." In *Anna Kuliscioff e l'età del Riformismo: Atti del
Convegno di Milano, dic. 1976*. Milan: Mondo Operaio, edizione Avanti.
Grimaldi, A. 1986. "Foreword." In Paolo Pillitteri, *Alle sarte di Corso Magenta*.
Milan: F. Angeli.
Haupt, Georges. 1978. "Rôle de l'exil dans la diffusion de l'image de l'intelligentsia
révolutionnaire." *Cahiers du monde russe et soviétique* 19 (July-September).
Kuliscioff, Anna. 1977a. "Monopolio dell 'uomo." In *Anna Kuliscioff*. Edited by
Maricla Boggio and Annabella Ceriani. Venice: Marsilio. Orginally delivered as a
lecture at the Philological Club, Milan, April 27, 1890.
———. 1977b. "Il femminismo." In *Anna Kuliscioff*. Edited by Maricla Boggio and
Annabella Ceriani. Venice: Marsilio. Originally published in *Critica sociale*, June
16, 1897.
———. 1977c. "Il congresso delle donne italiane." In *Anna Kuliscioff*. Edited by
Maricla Boggio and Annabella Ceriani. Venice: Marsilio. Originally published in
Critica sociale, May 16, 1908.
———. 1977d. "Suffragio universale?" In *Anna Kuliscioff*. Edited by Maricla Boggio
and Annabella Ceriani. Venice: Marsilio. Originally published in *Critica sociale*,
March 16-April 1, 1910.
———. 1977e. "Suffragio universale a scartamento ridotto." In *Anna Kuliscioff*.
Edited by Maricla Boggio and Annabella Ceriani. Venice: Marsilio. Originally
published in *Critica sociale*, April 16, 1910.
———. 1977f. "Proletariato femminile e Partito Socialista." In *Anna Kuliscioff*.
Edited by Maricla Boggio and Annabella Ceriani. Venice: Marsilio. Originally
published in *Critica sociale*, September 18, 1910.
———. 1977g. "Per il suffragio femminile." In *Anna Kuliscioff*. Edited by Maricla
Boggio and Annabella Ceriani. Venice: Marsilio. Originally published in *La difesa
delle lavoratrici*, June 2, 1912.
La Vigna, Claire. 1978. "The Marxist Ambivalence Toward Women: Between
Socialism and Feminism in the Italian Socialist Party." In *Socialist Women*. Edited
by M.J. Boxer and J.H. Quataert. New York: Elsevier.
Lipinska, Melanie. 1900. *Histoire des femmes médecins*. Paris: Librairie G. Jacques.
Martelli, Mino. 1980. *Andrea Costa e Anna Kuliscioff*. Rome: Edizioni Paolino.
Mondolfo, Ugo Guido, and Fausto Pagliari. 1926. "Anna Kuliscioff: La vita e
l'azione." *Critica sociale*, January 3.
Pala, Antonio. 1973. *Anna Kuliscioff*. Milan: Librimarket.
Palotti, Giulio, ed. 1992. *La difesa delle lavoratrici* (vol. 1). Milan: European Institute
of Social Studies.
Pieroni Bortolotti, Franca. 1963. *Alle origini del movimento femminile in Italia,
1848–1892*. Turin: Einaudi.
———. 1978. "Anna Kuliscioff e la questione femminile." In *Anna Kuliscioff e l'età
del Riformismo: Atti del Convegno di Milano, dic. 1976*. Milan: Mondo Operaio,
edizione Avanti.
Salvatorelli, Luigi. 1977. *Nazionalfascismo*. Turin: Einaudi. Originally published 1923.
Schiavi, Alessandro. 1977. *Filippo Turati, Anna Kuliscioff: Carteggio* (6 vols.). Edited
by Franco Pedone. Turin: Einaudi.

Treves, Claudio. 1926. "Anna Kuliscioff." *Critica sociale,* January 3.

Turati, Filippo, ed. 1926. *Anna Kuliscioff: In memoriam.* Milan: Tipografia Lazzari.

Turati, Filippo and Anna Kuliscioff. 1945. *La tragedia di G. Matteotti.* Forlì: Editrice Socialista Romagnola.

Valeri, Nino. 1974. *Turati e la Kuliscioff.* Florence: Le Monnier.

Vigezzi, Brunello. 1973. "Giolitti, il Partito Socialista, la guerra di Libia nelle lettere di Filippo Turati e Anna Kuliscioff (1912)." In *Omaggio a Nenni.* Rome: Quaderni di Mondo Operaio.

2 / Gender Struggle and the Social Manipulation and Ideological Use of Gender Identity in the Interwar Years

Mariolina Graziosi

During the Liberal and Fascist eras, two waves of visible gender struggle appeared in Italy. The first gained momentum in the early years of industrialization, and the second surged after World War I. In both cases, the driving force of male-female strife was "economic." As Italy became industrialized, men strove to obtain and keep jobs as more women sought employment, whereas in the postwar years, men struggled against women just to secure jobs in a period of high unemployment. Certainly, such conflictual sexual relations in the socioeconomic sphere can be classified within the general formation of a gender power struggle in patriarchal culture. Here, however, I am concerned with examining the particular "ideological use" made of gender identities to suppress gender struggle in the interwar years and to discriminate against women. My analysis focuses on the ideological use of gender identity that is explicitly revealed in propaganda and journalistic writings dating from 1919 (during the "Liberal" state) through the years of the Fascist regime's ascendancy. A rereading of these discourses illustrates how the open gender struggle of the early 1920s was repressed during Fascism and replaced with a "sociocultural program" articulated in high moralistic terms to define norms of gender identity and to create a number of "truly feminine" jobs. Normalization and moralization thus became synonymous. Working through

Foucault's paradigm of master-slave morality,[1] I intend to analyze the ways gender identities were deployed in the formation of the Fascist hierarchical structure—a hierarchy disavowed by propaganda presenting Fascist Italy as an organic society where cooperation, rather than power and class struggle, dominated. In point of fact, while displaying the "ideological mask of cooperation," Fascist propaganda turned women's "inferiority" into the contradictory mission of women as both the moralizer of society and the symbol of Fascist values of abnegation and life's struggle.

Gender Struggle after the War

The years between 1919 and 1922—that is, from the end of World War I to the nomination of Mussolini as prime minister—prepared the terrain for the success of Fascism.[2] Deep social changes caused by the war emerged and gave rise to a strong wave of civic strife that took the form of class struggle and conflicts among different social groups.[3] The large intergroup conflicts derived from the ways the war had emphasized collective bonds but also destroyed ideological barriers, thus making each group feel entitled to ask for more social recognition and benefits. This feeling also arose from the emphasis the dominant Fascist ideology naturally placed on unity rather than social differences: different groups felt entitled to ask for social recognition that, before the war, had seemed to belong only to specific groups and classes. The newspaper *Il corriere della sera* (1919a) gave a clear idea of this situation in an article titled "Questions of Demobilization": "The question of demobilization is at a critical point. Letters written by soldiers, agendas composed by military comrades or professional colleagues, [and] observations made by experts crowd the newspaper columns more than ever before. Every group wants its voice to be heard. There are as many groups as there are interests and specific situations" (p. 2). Fascists in general, and Mussolini in particular, encouraged and used such group conflicts, actually enhancing them in order to make the shift from class conflict to conflicts along several other lines of cleavage. Fascists made this transition their political program, which they realized by representing themselves as the fighters opposing any form of class struggle. Yet they also played one group against another. Mussolini, for instance, emphasized the importance of social rewards for veterans. He made them his first constituency, leading them against working-class organizations and other group struggles, such as the gender struggle.

The gender struggle was one of the central group conflicts that developed after the war. Women's abilities to do a broad range of jobs during the war collapsed stereotypes from the prewar years (Camarda and Peli 1980). After the war, however, women's employment assumed a completely different character. Men wanted their jobs back, and when the economic situation made this difficult, they transformed the economic crisis into a fierce gender struggle. Articles in daily newspapers, magazines, and the women's press reported this reaction, conveyed by such slogans as "Women's employment is causing men's unemployment" and "Women go home, because home is the place where you really belong" (*La difesa delle lavoratrici* 1922a, 1923).[4] The strong gender struggle of those years, and the support socialists gave to it, emerges very clearly from the pages of the socialist magazine *La difesa delle lavoratrici* (The defense of women workers). For instance, in 1919 more than a few articles were dedicated to unemployment and the demobilization of women. The magazine criticized the strong development of gender struggle—defined as fratricidal—as well as the popular slogan "Women's employment is causing men's unemployment." It opposed this position with the view that "the capitalist mode of production" was the cause of unemployment and other social problems. Nevertheless, even in this magazine, the shared view was that female employment in industry, in the trade sector, and in public services damaged men's chances for employment (*La difesa delle lavoratrici* 1919a).[5]

Among the different groups, veterans vociferously opposed employed women. They organized demonstrations at post offices and banks, because white-collar jobs were the highest in demand, and shouted the slogan "Down with women." An article in *La difesa delle lavoratrici* (1921a) pointed out, "Both women who work and the sharks that exploit workers and enjoy themselves are grouped together, in the same invective."[6] The same magazine defended women's employment in an article titled "Disabled Soldiers and Women Clerks," reminding veterans that women had held positions in the postal service since the birth of the telegraph and telephone industry. Moreover, women worked for many years at the same monthly salary of just 15 or 30 lire, whereas men could now get that salary after just six months of employment (*La difesa delle lavoratrici* 1921b). However, the veterans gained increasing power, which they leveled against women workers with growing threats of violence. At rallies, *La difesa* (1922c) reported, the National Association of Soldiers (Associazione Nazionale Combattenti) ordered owners and managers of public companies to fire all female employees, threatening them with the possibility of violent action if they did not comply. The same article also mentioned the show of Fascist support for the veterans, which in large part accounted for their violent behavior.[7]

Articles published in the women's press illustrate how the intensified gender struggle swung public opinion against women as well as the discursive strategies women adopted to defend female socioeconomic advances. The following passage is representative in this respect, capturing the general hostility toward women and the author's attempt to reveal the irrational bias supporting this stance:

> Public opinion repeats all the commonplaces: women must go knit—The newspapers—oh—the newspapers... *Il corriere* proclaims: "When there is not a place for everybody, men come first and then women." What a beautiful discovery, what depth of thought. You have taught us in school that the nation is a family, etc. What would that family be like if your theories were applied? Men eat first. Then, if there were leftovers, women would eat. (*La difesa delle lavoratrici* 1921b)

Another article openly discusses and critiques the question of discrimination against women. The author argues that women suffer both gender and class discrimination, and concludes that men still see women as property. Men, she tells us, are afraid of educated women. Therefore, their ideal woman is uneducated (*La difesa delle lavoratrici* 1922b).

Amid the fierce competition for jobs, males deployed a variety of arguments to have women expelled from public employment. For example, men claimed that white-collar women had inferior job skills. The magazine *Il giornale della donna* reported that not one day went by without magazines of varying persuasions receiving letters from men that accused white-collar women of not knowing grammar, spelling, and typing. On these grounds, they claimed, women had to be fired (Casertelli-Cabrini 1921, 3). But the most popular and effective arguments emphasized men's role as the heads of families. Unemployment among men hurt those who depended upon them, whereas women, some insisted, worked only to satisfy their frivolous attitudes. Thus, working women were accused of committing the worst of crimes — stealing men's jobs and jeopardizing the lives of entire families. The fact that women were also parts of families, and often even the heads of families, was not considered. Women's jobs were associated only with their doll houses, as the following quotation demonstrates:

> [Women] were reproached — all of them, which is a shortcoming of the campaign — for their conspicuous consumption.... Silk stockings, candies, movies, perfumes, dresses, hats, and all sorts of infamous articles have appeared in the national press.... In any event, rightly or wrongly men keep repeating that women steal their jobs, with which they [the unemployed men] would buy bread for their families. (Casertelli-Cabrini 1921, 3)

The argument that women steal men's jobs was even applied to elementary school teaching, a field that had been considered the domain of women since its beginnings.[8] The profession, in fact, was represented as a natural extension of the maternal role, and therefore more suited to women than to men. The "feminization" of the profession naturally implied low wages and many inconveniences.[9] After the war, however, male interest in this profession grew. Men immediately regulated measures that would make teaching a male profession. Not surprisingly, they requested better salaries (*Il corriere della sera* 1919b, 1919c).[10]

According to male discourses, women would not only have to vacate jobs that used to be done by men, they would also be forced to go back home and relinquish almost all jobs to men. The commentary provided in an article with the provocative title "The Trench of Male Privilege" tells us much about how professional women viewed the socioeconomic conditions. This female commentator sums up the situation:

> Let us be explicit, every woman who replaced a man by "occupying" his job during the war must give it back. This has been happening all along, and the process is now complete. But now we are facing a different problem. It is now requested that women who hold jobs legitimately acquired on the basis of their education, practical training, or proven ability be fired from public ad-

ministration. One witnesses recurrent practices aimed at obstruct-
ing (even more than is already happening) the way to women's
advancement up the hierarchical ladder. In practice, all of this
amounts to a more or less declared war against women's participation in public administration. (Lombardo 1921, 7–8)

In the fall of 1920, the Ministry of Treasury, in agreement with the
prime minister, established that all laws in favor of women's employment would no longer be valid as of April 30, 1921 (Loschi 1921). By
so doing, the government essentially legislated women's expulsion from
key jobs and sectors. As women were expelled from important jobs,
a significant trend toward revising the emancipationist view of the
prewar years emerged at both economic and cultural levels. In the years
prior to and during the war, the feminist movement had critiqued the
notion that home is women's natural place.[11] However, a cultural process that institutionalized norms restating women's inferior position
accompanied the socioeconomic process of expelling women from
the labor market.

By adopting Foucault's analytic paradigm, we see the deep ideological nature of both praxes. In his work Foucault (1961/1965, 1975/
1977) interrogates the "normative" nature of social practices. He
proposes that normalization is a process of social control that has
the function of preventing the formation of subjectivity and, in so
doing, operates to maintain the status quo. Therefore, for Foucault,
social discourse becomes an act of violence, a concrete social praxis
of violence against the individual who is forced to be what society
requests he or she to be: "We must conceive discourse as a violence
that we do to things, or to all events, as a practice we impose upon
them; it is in this practice that the events of discourse find the principle of regularity (Foucault 1969/1972, 229). This is why the redefinition of gender identity becomes crucial in a moment of deep social
changes. Redefining gender identity functions as the vehicle through
which society legitimates its concrete process of discrimination, and, in
general, its sociopolitical needs. I propose that in Italy immediately after
World War I, and during the Fascist regime, society needed to control
unemployment, and consequently a new redistribution of economic
resources was needed. Gender struggle was the expression of this
need, and the formation of a new gender identity was the ideological

mask that covered the concrete process of violence exercised against women through the social practices of expulsion, segregation, and moralization.

Women's Segregation and the Ideology of Femininity

The Sacchi Law of July 17, 1919, which listed the employment positions that women could not occupy—mostly high-ranking positions in the military and public employment—inaugurated the process of women's segregation in the workplace. For instance, women were not allowed to be general directors of any public office (*Il giornale della donna* 1920d). Initially, the law did not cause an uproar among the women's organizations that continued to be active during the early 1920s. These feminist organizations believed the exclusions enacted by the Sacchi Law could be avoided if women obtained the right to vote. Feminists argued that if a woman could be an elected public official in a local administration, it would no longer be possible to deny her the right to be minister, alderman, and so on. Such a prohibition would lose any logical ground (Lombardo 1920). Feminist organizations also considered the Sacchi Law a real achievement for women because it gave them access to positions that were previously closed. For instance, the Sacchi Law did not deny women the right to teach in senior all–male high schools, as had a previous law passed in 1915. Unfortunately, feminists were wrong in both cases. It was a long time before women could be elected either as representatives or as public officials. Furthermore, the Board of Education continued its established hiring practices, conforming with the 1915 law that denied women the right to teach in all–male high schools long after the Sacchi Law was instituted. Only after a lawsuit in which the Board of Education lost did the Sacchi Law replace the 1915 law (Una Professionista 1920).

The Sacchi Law failed to alleviate the struggle between men and women for jobs in the early 1920s. The surviving feminist organizations negotiated the social and juridical attempts to restrict female access to the labor market by attempting to persuade women to accept leaving their jobs, and by formulating a new ideology that justified this new attitude. Their ideological scope was to transform the wish and the right of women to be full citizens, like men, into the wish to be "moral subjects." The most active group in this period was the organization Il Consiglio Nazionale delle Donne Italiane (the National

Council of Italian Women).[12] This heterogeneous association formulated the new ideology, which it diffused through magazines such as *Il giornale della donna* and through a series of sociocultural programs, both designed to educate women. The female role promoted by this organization conformed with the traditional Catholic notion of woman, which claimed femininity as the true essence of womanhood, defined in terms of patriarchal morality. This paradigm stressed gender specificity as opposed to gender equality, and made morality and femininity synonymous. To be a real woman and to be a moral human being were presented as coterminous. The process of educating women to the new female identity assumed a moralistic tone; the project's explicit aim was to "moralize women" who had lost their morality in the struggle for emancipation.

The pages of the "female" magazine *Il giornale della donna* specifically outlined this position, stating that the goal of female organizations was to "reeducate women" because the "Italian woman of our days has gone through a crisis that on the one hand has sharpened and increased her potential return to the social and economic spheres, but at the same time has diminished her, almost deprived her of her moral energy.... This is the issue: our woman has to be assisted so that she can find herself again, her value, her reason for being in these new times" (Boni 1920, 1).

To legitimate this feminine paradigm—intended to induce women to rethink their real vocation in life—many authors proposed new values. They asserted that female citizens could be feminine, real women, and therefore moral human beings, only by staying at home and performing their roles as mothers, spouses, and sisters (*Il giornale della donna* 1920c). Kristeva (1986) clarifies the role of such feminine values within a patriarchal social formation, which was the case of Italy before and after the Fascist regime. She argues that the "reabsorption of femininity within the maternal construct" has the twofold function of overcoming the fear of death and of establishing the will to power as the main goal. According to Kristeva, overcoming death and power go hand in hand. The Virgin Mary symbolizes both, the absence of death and power. She is the guardian of power, male power (p. 120). Hence, the moralization of women that was pursued within the new paradigm was the necessary guise of the reaffirmation of male authority. The moralizing project sought to legitimate a social order firmly grounded in the patriarchal values of male superiority—men's right to be first and women's duty to work for the maintainance of the hierarchical social order. This discourse, which emerged before Fascism, became the dominant discourse during the Fascist regime. In both periods, Catholic discourse provided the model for the definition of the meaning of "femininity."[13]

In order to define and institutionalize the recoded notion of the "feminine," female groups, with the financial help of the state, inaugurated a series of sociocultural programs. These consisted primarily of schools reserved for women that would train them in jobs considered truly "feminine," and therefore suited to women. The main sectors considered female were the home and welfare.

One of the first important schools designed for "social workers" was opened in 1920, with state aid, under the auspices of the National Council of Italian Women (*Il giornale della donna* 1920a, 3). In the same period, we also find the creation of professional schools for nurses, who were called health workers. These schools were presented as the ideal solution for women who were forced to work. But before this undertaking, other initiatives were taken in the same direction. In 1919 a commission for women's employment was formed within a local administration. The female organization called Associazione per la Donna (Association for Woman) participated in this commission, together with Catholic organizations. With the primary goal of retraining unemployed women, this commission organized vocational courses (*Il giornale della donna* 1920b). Because of the more radical orientation of Associazione per la Donna, the courses included, among others, a class for typists, a form of work no longer considered appropriate for women (*Il giornale della donna* 1920e).

An article in *Il giornale della donna* (1920e) placed great emphasis on the creation of different vocational schools for housekeepers, housewives, and workers in small workshops, intended to retrain women fired from "male" jobs. The new position on female roles and jobs was represented as being in perfect line with the emancipationist feminist view, as is clear in the following example:

> What were we, the pioneers of feminism, asking through our propaganda? That a woman be granted her independence through wage labor, which would save her personal dignity. But now, why should independence and dignity be more the result of a factory job than a household job, of the wage earned as a blue-collar worker than that earned as a maid? In either case the

woman lives off her own work, and in neither case is she now subject to the head of the household who, apparently, kept her. (Sierra Cammeo 1921, 1)

This author seems to forget, however, that in the course of new training women lost crucial jobs and, most of the time, the opportunity to work. For this reason their economic dependency increased, making them vulnerable to any kind of personal and social threat. In a few years this "cultural revolution," based exclusively on women's particularity, would become clearer and surer of its path.

During the Fascist regime, women's exclusion from the labor force and segregation in a few "nonexistent" vocational jobs became more prevalent. Both were legitimated with an intensive propaganda campaign whose aim was the formation of the real feminine woman: the Fascist woman. Teresa Labriola, one of the main ideologues of the Fascist moral revolution, clarifies the core of the Fascist definition of women's identity: to be the symbols of patriarchal values and, at the same time, the social agents of the patriarchal morality that emphasized subjection to male authority within the family and in society at large. "The typical and original feminine function of a woman is precisely that of forcing pure values into every generation of men. This is what I think, and this is what I have been writing for a long time" (Labriola 1920b, 2). Labriola (1920a) also says that women, more than men, "make possible the subordination of the individual to larger and higher dimensions" (p. 14). This assertion expresses the central idea of the Fascist cultural program. Women were considered to have the tendency to accept a higher authority given that they more easily tend to merge with it. For this "deeply conservative nature" they were chosen as the symbol of abnegation and total acceptance of collective goals (Labriola 1920a). It is thus clear that for moralization Fascist propaganda meant what Foucault has defined as normalization: conformity.

The Fascist Cultural Revolution: The Denial of Social and Political Rights

In contrast to the Liberal era, during the Fascist regime open gender struggle was delegitimated through a series of laws that expelled women from important jobs and through the creation of social organizations along with a corresponding system of values that had gender difference and gender hierarchy at its core. Because of these changes, the processes of expulsion and segregation of women were no longer represented as discriminatory measures, but simply as the ways the Fascist regime restored social order after the chaos of the Liberal era. The process of expulsion initiated by the Sacchi Law became widespread during the Fascist regime, with the result that women lost many important jobs and were directed toward limited vocational jobs that the regime created and presented as the "real female jobs." For instance, a 1926 bill prohibited women from holding tenured positions in post offices (*Il giornale della donna* 1926b). In the following year, women lost their right to teach history, philosophy, and Italian literature in public high schools, with the exception of those high schools reserved for the education of elementary school teachers (Benedettini-Aferazzi 1927; Cicatelli 1927). In the meantime, a bill passed in January 1927 established that female salaries had to be half of male salaries. Another bill established separate curves for the selection of women and men in the national competition for the assignment of elementary school positions. Men wanted and obtained the separation, arguing that women were better prepared for their jobs and therefore obtained the best positions (*Il giornale della donna* 1928b). Other measures taken by the state to restrict female employment in and access to education included the stipulation that women could not be principals in middle schools and the increase in female student school fees to double the amount paid by males at both high school and university levels. Similarly, the government proposed bills to limit the number of women working in public offices. For example, one bill, approved November 28, 1933, stipulated that the male rate of employment in public offices had to be higher than the female rate. Later, in 1938, another bill fixed female employment at just 10 percent of all public employment.

Women's labor relations in the industrial and rural sectors during the dictatorship exhibit complex changing trends that were affected by a variety of factors. Industry did not follow an overt program to expel women from jobs, but the world economic crisis of 1929 strongly affected Italy, and females were among the first to be fired in both the industrial and the rural sectors. For instance, Chiara Saraceno (1979–80), in her analysis of the working-class family during the Fascist regime, reports the following statistics:

In 1921–22 the index of female unemployment was lower than that of males; in 1924–1925 it was at the same level; in 1926–1932 it was higher. Beginning with 1933–1935, the index of female unemployment stayed below that of male unemployment, not because women were more employed than men, but because they were getting out of the active population. (p.209)

Although many women worked in the rural sector, the official level of female employment was very low, because women were usually counted as family helpers, not as part of the labor force (Saraceno 1979–80, 198).

The expulsion of women from both industrial and rural sectors was not the result of direct government action. The regime left capitalists free to use the labor forces they needed most. For this reason, as Saraceno points out, the expulsion of the female labor force from the industrial sector occurred in ways and times that varied from one region to another.[14] The factors that accounted for the decrease in female employment in the industrial sectors included the reduction of men's salaries, which made the male labor force competitive in relation to the female labor force; the development of heavy industries, in which male occupation always prevailed; and the corresponding crisis of the textile sector, traditionally dominated by the female labor force. These factors also exacerbated the insecurity characterizing forms of temporary employment positions, such as shop clerk, apprentice in dressmaker workshops, or maid—the occupations women generally held. It is not surprising that increased female unemployment in industry and agriculture swelled the ranks of women doing factory labor at home—the main form of female labor in this period. Saraceno tells us that unemployed women had to accept "clandestine work" because the decrease in men's salaries forced them to accept any kind of work, under any conditions. Among the most negative aspects of clandestine work was that it provided no pension or any other benefits.[15]

Although women's battle for social and political rights was still open in the years just prior to the Fascist regime, all the main themes of emancipation paled within the "modern" feminine paradigm. In general, female organizations rephrased emancipationist discourse in terms of the feminine paradigm, so that the negation of women's rights, and any other defeat for women— from the emancipationist point of view— could be perceived as a victory, as an affirmation of women's true "identity." This was particularly apparent in the struggles for divorce and for the extension of voting rights to women.[16] In the new view, divorce could be allowed only in very rare cases, and never when the parties concerned had children (Avel 1920, 15–16). Divorce had to be refused, just as jobs that did not express the female vocation in life—that is, to be mother and caregiver—had to be refused. A 1920 article concerned with defining the female paradigm clearly outlines this perspective: "The woman problem is basically a problem concerning ideals. This should not be forgotten or obscured. Social advancements, and political and practical improvements do not constitute the essence of the problem, nor its solution. Rather, they are a consequence of achieved dignity and a means to increase such dignity" (Pintor Dore 1920, 1).

The shifting positions on women's suffrage adopted by Mussolini as he sought to gain female support are of particular importance here. Although he supported extending the vote to women in 1919, he later opposed the right of women to vote.[17] In an interview with a journalist of *Petit Parisien,* he declared: "I am a supporter of universal suffrage, but not of female suffrage, especially considering that women always vote for their men" (quoted in *Il popolo d'Italia,* November 12, 1922, 1). In 1923, at the first Fascist Female Congress (Il Congresso Femminile delle Tre Venezie), his answer was not so frank as in the press interview. First, he stated that if women really wanted the right to vote, then they would obtain it. Then he moved to the devaluation of such achievement, declaring that "even in times when women did not vote, yet wished to vote, in those faraway times, ancient, close, remote times, women always had an overwhelming influence on the destiny of human societies" (quoted in *Il popolo d'Italia,* June 2, 1923, 6).

This histrionic position reached the point of an open lie when, on the occasion of the Congress of the International Alliance for the Extension of the Right of Women to Vote, Mussolini announced: "As far as the government is concerned, I feel authorized to state that, save unforeseen events, the Fascist government is committed to grant the right to vote to many groups of women, beginning with administrative elections" (quoted in *Il popolo d'Italia,* May 15, 1923, 6). On the same occasion, the duce announced his project to extend the right to vote to women in administrative elections and, sometime in the future, the right to vote in political elections. Yet he did not miss the opportunity to shift the focus from the right to vote to the traditional roles with which Fascist women had to be more properly concerned. At the end of his speech, in fact, he made a special tribute to all mothers who had lost their children in the war. In 1923, a bill in favor of the extension of the right of women to vote in administrative elections was presented in Parliament. It became law on November 22, 1925. Unfortunately, women never had the chance to exercise their right to vote; the following year, the Fascist regime abolished administrative elections as part of reform that institutionalized the new administrative position of *podestà* in place of the elected local administration (*Il giornale della donna* 1926a, 1).

The Fascist Moralizing Discourse: Women as Guardians of Fascist Patriarchal Values

The question most frequently posed in articles of the time that analyzed new laws denying women access to specific jobs was, Which profession is most suitable for women? The answer provided in different articles published in *Il giornale della donna* was that most suitable for a woman is a job that is also a mission. Only this kind of job, writers argued, could allow a woman to have a "political role." In one of its numerous and repetitive articles on the subject, the magazine called professional women to this collective mission, claiming: "These women with degrees in medicine and Italian literature ought to go visit some of their neighbors. Then they would see a mass of female workers and shopkeepers.... They ought to join the assistance organizations of the National Fascist Party and teach, through practical examples, the fundamental principles of the family" (*Il giornale della donna* 1929, 1).

For the Fascist regime, the ideal female job took women among the people to educate them—that is, to transmit the basic moral principles of Fascist doctrine. Fascist ideologues presented social work as the occupation that would allow women to assume both political and moral roles and, at the same time, to achieve the highest development of their personalities. Fascist thinkers presented women's development as the result of their being and feeling part of the state.

> In the Liberal paradigm an individual is nothing but an individual. We Fascists...must make every effort to transform this individual into a personality. This is what we all ought to strive for. And we have to convince women that they should not rest on

their natural "individuality." Once their personality is achieved, we should not deny them the opportunity to act on the basis of all their potential. Once the personality has been acquired, which is the ability to be part of the state, women can contribute usefully as well. Why then should women be excluded? . . . Beyond the struggle is the realization of pure values. (*Il giornale della donna* 1929, 1)

This quotation clarifies the main scope of the cultural revolution operated by the Fascist regime: to convince women to give up any socioeconomic and political achievements and to accept the symbolic role of main signifier of the Fascist ideology—the symbol of the life-and-death struggle, of abnegation to collective goals that the regime required of all citizens.[18] For a woman, to be a moral human being meant to accept the symbolic role and become the "moralizer" of society. This program, however, aimed exclusively at remodeling women's forms of self-perception: to convince them of their real need to be at home, to see themselves suited only for specific jobs, to endorse the patriarchal values that the Fascist state represented. The Fascist intellectual Ferdinando Loffredo (1938) clearly explains the ideological link between the two processes of expulsion and moralization:

The abolition of female work must be the result of two convergent factors: the prohibition sanctioned by the law and the prohibition sanctioned by public opinion. The woman who leaves the domestic walls to go to work; the woman who, in promiscuity with a man, goes around the streets, on trains, on buses, and lives in factories and in offices, most importantly must become an object of reprobation, more so than of legal sanction. (p. 365)

Adopting a similar position, Mussolini outlined in 1934 the dangerous effects working has on women, men, and the pronatalist campaign:

With work a woman becomes like a man; she causes man's unemployment; she develops an independence and a fashion that is contrary to the process of childbirth, and lowers the demographic curve; man is deprived of work and dignity; he is castrated in every sense because the machine deprives him either of his woman or of his virility. (p. 2)

The redefinition of the female role in the Fascist regime made women victims and at the same time protagonists of the state's key activity: social moralization that asked women to fulfill their maternal role at home or in state-sanctioned welfare associations, renouncing any form of economic, political, or intellectual autonomy. The women's Fascist organization Fasci Femminili took on the task of reeducating women to the new female identity and role. This organization's entire educational activity may be divided into three levels. At the highest level were the schools for the formation of the elite, for those who would proceed to inculcate the people with the official Fascist credo. At the intermediate level were a number of professions related to the field of social assistance, intended to enforce the idea of work as a social mission. The third level included the mass organizations and activities organized by the Fasci Femminili to educate the masses in Fascist values, thereby contributing to the formation of the collective consciousness.

The Fasci Femminili elite were women of the bourgeoisie who, after obtaining their college degrees, decided to enter one of the Fascist party's three superior schools. These three schools opened in 1929, after years of the rejection of women from intellectual and white-collar jobs. The schools included the School of Home Economics, the School for Factory Fascist Social Workers, and the School for Rural Teachers. On the basis of the kind of training they received and the type of work they were expected to do, the women who attended these schools could be defined as organic intellectuals.[19] For instance, the factory social worker had to be among people, especially among workers, and the help she gave was strictly linked to the work of propaganda for the Fascist regime. The following prescription, pronounced in a public ceremony attended by the duce himself, demonstrates the "political" nature of this kind of profession:

> Make the state closer to the masses; generate roots to spread deep into the masses; organize the masses; take better and better care of the economic and spiritual conditions in which the masses live; become interpreters of the masses' needs and aspirations. By going to the factories, by talking to the worker like watchful Fascist sisters, we will make sure that he will take ever greater advantage of those facilities that you, Duce, wanted and realized. (*Il giornale della donna* 1930, 1)

The social workers for factories received their instruction at the school of San Gregorio, which offered rigorous formal training. It consisted of three years of postuniversity education in which women with college degrees had to take courses in law, economics, medicine, hygiene, and practical social work. After the three years, these women received legal degrees and were hired by the Confederation of Industry, which sent them to factories (F.D. 1930). From the information given in the Fascist press, it seems that very few women went to the school for factory social workers. This was probably because of the admission requirements, which included a college education, militancy for the party, single marital status, and board and tuition at 350 lire a month.[20]

For rural teachers, educated in the Fascist Party School of Santo Alessio, the admission requirements were less demanding and there was a shorter training period. The school for rural teachers required only a high school diploma for teaching elementary school. Furthermore, the students did not have to pay tuition or board, because there was a special state connection between the school and the "Enti delegati dal Ministero dell'Educazione Nazionale" (the organizations appointed by the National Board of Education), which paid 2,000 lire a year to each student (*Il giornale della donna* 1933).[21] After a ten-month training period, the rural teachers went to the countryside to struggle against the process of urbanization. They performed their duty by organizing courses of interest to peasant men and women within the local section of Fasci Femminili. These included courses in child care, techniques for raising chickens and rabbits, and other kinds of information useful for people in the countryside. In the case of rural teachers we can also speak of organic intellectuals, because the goal of these professionals primarily concerned diffusing propaganda by providing "watchful, continuous, moral and technical assistance" (*Il giornale della donna* 1932, 3).

The third type of organic intellectual included women educated in the school of household education. The first International Congress of Household Education called for a school that would create women who could run perfect households (*Il giornale della donna* 1927). Like the rural teachers, the students at this school received degrees for teaching elementary school. Financial aid for the students covered the cost of fulfilling the prerequisite. One article reported that the majority of students were tenured elementary school teachers who had asked for a year of paid leave (*Il giornale della donna* 1932).[22] After a training period of one year, the graduates taught courses in home economics in elementary and high schools, or gave private lessons. The goal adopted by these schools clearly illustrates their propagandistic function of inculcating women with traditional values of family, motherhood, and country: "We will force them to love their families; we will teach good management of the house, the rational way to raise children, the value of time, of money, of individual energies" (*Il giornale della donna* 1930, 1).

Apart from these three professions, each of which had directive functions of mediation, the Fasci Femminili organized different kinds of social assistance and created other social work positions. Although we can still speak of organic intellectuals in this case, the positions did not have directive functions. Instead, the work involved operational activities of assistance, requiring no prior degree. These positions could be paid or voluntary. Among these "professions of social workers," the first job invented by the regime was the *segretaria sociale* (social secretary). This position involved mediating between workers and capitalists. Women were trained to go into factories and help workers see their jobs as part of a collective process, so that they could acquire a moral view of their jobs and of their social place, thereby relinquishing any idea of class struggle. The state preferred women to men for this job because, it was said, men were too politically oriented and too inclined to organize workers. Therefore, they would tend not to limit themselves to informal meetings for developing morals (Istituto Italiano per L'Assistenza Sociale 1923). The Istituto Italiano per L'Assistenza Sociale (Italian Institute for Social Workers) was created in Milan for the specific task of creating such professionals. This private institute was financed by industrialists, medical doctors, and other esteemed citizens, and received official approval. It offered women with college degrees a brief period of training that covered a few classes on basic tenets of Fascist credo and basic courses in hygiene, law, and economics.

Nursing represented another popular profession at this level. In 1923 a congress organized by a group of nurses asked for the institutionalization of a school for nurses that would be entitled to give proficiency certificates. In addition to the education of nurses, the congress also requested the formation of an organization for *assistenti sanitarie* (medical assistants), who would prepare courses on different medical subjects for the elementary and high schools. Medical assistant students had to be certified nurses (Istituto Italiano per L'Assistenza Sociale 1923). In 1926, the Fascist state instituted both positions and ordered the creation of boarding schools for nurses and schools of public medicine, hygiene, and social assistance. Such schools had to be in hospitals and were under the direct surveillance of the Ministry of Interior and Education. The program consisted of two years of training for the certification of nurses, after which nurses could take another year of training in order to assume directive functions within the school or enter a training program for *assistenti sanitarie visitatrici* (medical assistants) (Arpesani 1926).

Before the Fascist decree of 1923, only one school for nurses and ambulatory health assistants existed, established in 1919 by the Lega d'Igiene Sociale of Liguria (Ligurian Social Hygiene League). In 1923, the school was transformed into a boarding school for both professions (Arpesani 1926). An article in *Il giornale della donna* dedicated to women's role in social assistance makes it clear that these professions were seen as part of the moralizing process. The article's main argument is that the "social question" arises from the jealousy and envy felt by people who are less talented and thus have less wealth and power:

> We could define as political and social the science that teaches the measures flowing from the powers of the state and directed to the solution of the social question in a way that is biased in favor of those classes who, because of their nature, are less favored.... We can foresee the opening up of enormous areas of intervention in the field of public assistance that would match up perfectly with the mission of a woman as mother. As examples, I will list just a few of the most important activities in a modern society: the protection of motherhood and children, and moral and material assistance to the handicapped, is the mission of nurses and sanitary assistants visiting the sick; women with degrees of union organizer [*organizzatrice sindacale*], social worker in the factory [*assistente di fabbrica*], vocational counselor [*orientatrice professionale*], and director of cooperatives and workers' shelters [*direttrice di cooperativa e di convitti operai*] will engage in those activities related to the protection and organized defense of the working classes. (Dalmazzo 1926, 1)

In time, the army of moral workers grew to unprecedented dimensions and led to the creation of new jobs in social work. In 1928, the Fascist Party asked the Rome section of the Red Cross to offer a one-year course for *infermiere familiari Fasciste* (Fascist family nurses), the first volunteer job (*Il giornale della donna* 1928a). Another volunteer job, the *visitatrice Fascista* (Fascist visitor of the needy) was institutionalized in 1934, and the Fasci Femminili itself held courses for the women's preparation. Partly propagandistic, the job assigned the volunteer the task of telling needy families about the different kinds of assistance the Fascist state would give them. In 1935, yet another volunteer job was created, this time within nursing. The Fascist Party asked the Red Cross to train volunteer nurses by offering two-year courses. Graduates of this course could offer their services free of charge (*La donna Fascista* 1935).

Women thus became the signifier of the Fascist ideology of life and death, of rebirth and war, and the social agents of the parallel moralizing-normalizing process. Men were the warriors and the heros, whereas women formed the troop deployed to enforce the patriarchal values of war and duty as Fascist imperatives.

Notes

Unless otherwise noted, all translations in this chapter are my own.

1. Hegel (1807/1985) was the first to use the master-slave metaphor to describe the internal dynamic of the process of self-consciousness. Even though Hegel saw the process of self-consciousness as linked to the cultural dimension, his main goal was to describe the essence of the process—that is, its ontological aspect. Foucault, following Nietzsche's (1881–82/1969) idea of the link between a specific morality and the form of consciousness, has proposed the thesis of the absence of a subject in the modern society, for the dominant master-slave morality has transformed the process of moralization in the process of normalization. Foucault defines normalization as a system of social practices that do violence to the individual ontological sphere, and in so doing prevent the individual from having the possibility to be born as a subject, that is, outside of the collective repressive dimension. (See note 19, below.)

2. The Fascist movement was born in January 1919 as a movement of veterans who held a nationalist ideology. After a moment of uncertainty in which it appeared ready to present a program of reforms in favor of the working class, the movement took the road of violence. From the spring of 1919, its actions largely concentrated on the physical destruction of the working-class movement. The violent actions of the Fascist bands initially went undisturbed, as the liberal political leaders of this period thought it convenient to let the Fascist bands go ahead with their violent destruction of the working-class movement. In this manner, liberal institutions would not be directly involved in the violent repression of the working class. In this very favorable atmosphere, the Fascist movement developed and found ample room to act as an armed organization (De Luna 1978, 395).

3. World War I, and the economic and social crisis that immediately developed, caused a crisis of hegemony in Giolitti's government. The main sign of the hegemonic crisis was the outbreak of class struggles, which were so strong and so widespread that the Socialist Party and the working-class unions could not control them. Because of the intense class struggle, this period has been called *Biennio Rosso*. In such deep

turmoil, the simple activity of mediation was no longer sufficient to restore social order. In order to maintain the status quo, the solution of violent repressive action, led by the Fascist movement, was chosen (Ragionieri 1976).

4. An article in *Il giornale della donna* (The woman's newspaper) responding to the prevailing struggle of men against women denounced the situation: "At this point in time, the great revelation is taking place. That is, experience shows that women do have the attitudes, as well as the intellectual and physical abilities, necessary to carry out tasks for which only men were previously deemed suitable" (Pertici 1920, 1). *Il giornale della donna* (a weekly magazine concerned with the social education of women) was founded in 1919 by feminist movements that were close to the republican party. It became the official publication of the feminist organization Federazione pro Suffragio Femminile (Federation in Favor of the Female Vote). When the Fascist regime imposed a series of legal restrictions on the press, the magazine made the Fascist ideology its own. The name of the magazine was maintained until 1934, but the subtitle became *Per i Fasci femminili* (For the female Fascist organization). In 1935 the name of the magazine changed to *La donna Fascista* (The Fascist woman).

5. In another article in the same magazine it was reported that the National Congress of Typographers had discussed the possibility of admitting women to the trade, but had decided against it. Furthermore, male typographers asked that women employed in their sector leave the jobs they had held during the war. They argued that women damaged the sector by agreeing to work when men were on strike (*La difesa delle lavoratrici* 1919c).

6. The article, titled "Demobilization of Woman?" openly denounces the anger of veterans against women: "It is incredible. After four years of war, veterans want to solve the problem of unemployment by simply throwing out hundreds of women." The article goes on to argue that this will not solve the problem, and that the solution lies in fighting the capitalist system. Finally, it argues that women had, after all, taken men's jobs only because of the war (*La difesa delle lavoratrici* 1919b).

7. About this event, *La difesa delle lavoratrici* (1922c) reported: "Florence, in fact, has seen wonderful acts of politeness and courtesy. Young ladies have been followed and hissed on the street, others have been locked up in the offices and forced to go out only under the protection of policemen."

8. In 1859, Casati's Law established compulsory education for the first two grades of elementary school. La Scuola Normale was opened for the preparation of elementary teachers. The law allowed women to enroll at the age of 15 and men at age 16. This decision was explained with the justification that women, given their maternal instinct, could learn more easily how to teach children (Tomasi, Genovesi, et al. 1978, 172).

9. Elementary school teachers were paid by the local administrations, which generally attempted to keep salaries to a minimum. Furthermore, the teaching positions were often far away from the teachers' hometowns, so they needed to move. Being alone in a town was not safe for women, who many times faced sexual aggression and ostracism (Tranfaglia 1978).

10. An article in *Il giornale della donna* commented, "What we have been expecting all along has happened: in the hunt for jobs, gender egotism has gone so far as to upset the primary school, questioning woman's right to a job that everybody had acknowledged to be the most fitting for her nature, the job that most requires the warmth with which she has carried out such a crucial duty" (P.A.B. 1922, 1).

11. The important feminist voices in these years belonged to Anna Maria Mozzoni

and Anna Kuliscioff. Mozzoni was one of the first radical feminists belonging to Mazzini's movement. Her activity began immediately after the Italian unification, with a strong critique of the New Code. She denounced the position of subjection these laws assigned to women, which ratified the subjection they suffered during the preunification period (Mozzoni 1865/1975). Until her death, she was the main leader of the republican feminist movement.

Kuliscioff was instead the feminist leader of socialists. As Rosalia Colombo Ascari argues in her chapter in this volume, she brought the awareness of the specificity of the female struggle into the Socialist Party. She countered the different theories rationalizing women's lower wages as the result of their needing less, or being less productive, with the thesis that women were paid less for two reasons: first, they were less organized than men; second, because they were considered appendages to men, their salaries were always considered to be merely complementary. Kuliscioff (1894) concluded by declaring that "a woman is regarded as an appendage to a man, rather than a person in herself, a person with a right to work and to live off her job" (p. 33). For an overview of the development of feminism in Italy, see Pieroni Bortolotti (1963, 1974).

12. The National Council of Italian Women was formed on the occasion of the third National Congress of Italian Women, held in May 1920. With the new organization, the feminist movement attempted to overcome its fragmentation of the war period. It was in fact an organization that united different groups without asking for political homogeneity, as Pieroni Bortolotti (1974) notes: "The Council [of Italian Women] was nothing more than a group of associations, each with its own perspectives, and it is difficult to find a definition that would fit all of them" (p. 141). This political heterogeneity allowed the organization to survive during the early 1920s, without, however, producing any political success for women. The organization, in order to survive, increasingly accepted the emerging Fascist regime's antifeminist view. The first feminist organizations were formed toward the last decade of the eighteenth century, and became very strong and active at the turn of the century (Pieroni Bortolotti 1963, 1974).

13. For an overview of the Catholic view, see Gaiotti De Biase (1963).

14. Saraceno (1979–80, 208) distinguishes two periods in the curve of female industrial employment. In the period from 1921 to 1931, female employment did not diminish in the north, for women were better organized and their jobs were more stable. After 1931, when heavy industry developed, women's employment diminished more rapidly than did men's employment. In the south, instead, there was only one period in which female employment grew a little: between 1931 and 1936, when Italy went to fight in Africa. Saraceno points out that the increase in female employment concerned mostly the textile sector, which developed in the central regions while it was diminishing in the other parts of Italy.

15. It is clear that the Fascist regime allowed industrialists to return to a form of intense labor exploitation, both male and female, that usually occurs in the phase of early accumulation: low salaries, long working hours to the point of exhaustion, no working-class organization, only "cooperation"!

16. In these early days, the strongest opposition came from Anna Maria Mozzoni. In the years from the unification to Depretis's project of electoral reform, Mozzoni's political activity was carried out within the republican groups following Mozzoni's political view and program. Since her first struggle, she claimed equal rights for women in all aspects of social and political life, from the right to administer her patrimony to the guardianship of her children to the right to be employed in any public office (Mozzoni 1865/1975). Anna Kuliscioff was also in favor of the extension of rights to women.

She was the only figure within the Socialist Party who spoke in favor of women's emancipationist claim (Kuliscioff 1908, 1910a, 1910b).

17. The Fascist movement directly attacked the Liberal state on October 28, 1922, an event recorded as the "March on Rome." This event came after a process of institutionalization through which the Fascist movement gave itself legality that helped it "conquer" the government. On November 7, 1921, the Fascist National Party was formed. The second phase of institutionalization was the official declaration of the state as a Fascist state, on January 3, 1925.

The Fascist government formed a new capitalist state, characterized by a different way of achieving consent and by a new way of separating the state from the particularistic interests of the economically dominant class. The formation of this new capitalist state began when Mussolini assumed the role of prime minister and began work to dismantle the liberal state and to reinstall absolute power of the bourgeoisie over the working class. In order to achieve these two goals, Mussolini adopted two kinds of political measures: (1) the abolition of those political measures that would block the paternalistic project of the bourgeoisie, and (2) administrative reforms that would reinforce the state administration over the local administration, which, in this case, meant the transformation of the Liberal state into a charismatic dictatorship. The Liberal era and the Fascist era represent two patterns of the bourgeoisie's hegemonic process. The former is a pattern in which traditional social relationships were framed within the elitist liberal framework of suffrage, elections, and political representatives. The latter is a pattern in which traditional social relationships were framed within the authoritarian framework that refused democracy and substituted the direct control of the masses.

18. The Fascist regime made motherhood the symbolic representation of that aspect of the Fascist ideology concerned with the "natural dimension" of life, that is, the life-and-death struggle (Evola 1934). Mothers became the symbol of the Fascist value of total abnegation to collective goals, to the point of sacrficing life for them. In this way, both motherhood and collective symbols assumed a sacred character. They formed the "sacred canopy" within which the meanings were formed, with the result that the ontological and political spheres became strictly intertwined and social repression was experienced as an existential dimension.

19. "Organic intellectuals" is an expression first used by Gramsci (1949/1971), who defines it in the following way: "Intellectuals in the functional sense fall into two groups. In the first place there are the 'traditional' professional intellectuals, literary, scientific and so on, whose position in the interstices of society has a certain inter-class aura about it, but derives ultimately from past and present class relations and conceals an attachment to various historical class formations. Secondly, there are the organic intellectuals, the thinking and organising element of a particular fundamental social class. These organic intellectuals are distinguished less by their profession, which may be any job characteristic of their class, than by their function in directing the ideas and aspirations of the class to which they organically belong" (p. 3). The crucial aspect of Gramsci's new concept is the internal link he sees between the organic intellectual and the group within which he or she operates.

20. The school had a closed admission policy. It admitted only thiry-seven female students per year.

21. This school also had limits on enrollments, admitting twenty-five students between the ages of 20 and 30.

22. In this case the number of students admitted was twenty, in the age range of 20–30.

Works Cited

Primary Sources

Arpesani, M. 1926. "La donna fra i malati." *Il giornale della donna,* nos. 7–10.

Avel. 1920. "Femminismo." *Il giornale della donna,* no. 23.

Benedettini–Aferazzi, P. 1927. "La donna e il suo lavoro." *Il giornale della donna,* no. 1.

Boni, P. 1920. "Per la coscienza morale." *Il giornale della donna,* no. 12.

Casertelli–Cabrini, L. 1921. "La donna lavoratrice in Italia." *Il giornale della donna,* no. 4.

Cicatelli, B. 1927. "La revoca di un decreto mai decretato." *Il giornale della donna,* no. 3.

Il corriere della sera. 1919a. "Questioni di smobilitazione." January 10, 2.

———. 1919b. "L'agitazione dei maestri: Dichiarazioni del Ministro Berenini." June 8, 2.

———. 1919c. "Lo sciopero dei maestri." June 12, 3.

Dalmazzo, F. 1926. "La questione sociale e l'opera della donna." *Il giornale della donna,* nos. 15–16.

La difesa delle lavoratrici. 1919a. "La smobilitazione della donna e la disoccupazione." November 2, 3.

———. 1919b. "Smobilitare la donna?" November 16, 3.

———. 1919c. "La donna nel lavoro tipografico." November 16, 4.

———. 1921a. "Donne e mutilati." January 2, 1.

———. 1921b. "Mutilati e donne impiegate." April 23, 2.

———. 1922a. "La donna e la disoccupazione." June 3, 1.

———. 1922b. "A parità di doveri, parità di diritti." June 3, 2.

———. 1922c. "Una odiosa rappresaglia." September 17, 4.

———. 1923. "Signorine d'ufficio." October 15, 3.

La donna Fascista. 1935. "Infermiere volontarie." No. 17.

Evola, J. 1934. *La rivolta contro il mondo moderno.* Turin: Fratelli Bocca Editori.

F.D. 1930. "L'assistente sociale in regime fascista." *Il giornale della donna,* no. 17.

Il giornale della donna. 1920a. "La scuola professionale." No. 2.

———. 1920b. "Assistenza sociale." No. 6.

———. 1920c. "Parole chiare." No. 6.

———. 1920d. "La capacità giuridica della donna." No. 7.

———. 1920e. "Scuole professionali e smobilitazione femminile." No. 12.

———. 1926a. "Istituzioni del podestà." No. 2.

———. 1926b. "Il diritto al lavoro." Nos. 17–18.

———. 1927. "V Congresso Internazionale di Economia Domestica." No. 18.

———. 1928a. "Le infermiere familiari fasciste." No. 3.

———. 1928b. "A proposito di insegnanti." No. 16.

———. 1929. "La funzione della donna." Nos. 16–18.

———. 1930. "L'interessamento del duce per le tre scuole femminili del partito." No. 14.

———. 1932. "Le tre scuole superiori femminili del Partito Nazionale Fascista." No. 24.

———. 1933. "Le tre scuole superiori femminili del Partito Nazionale Fascista." No. 19.

Istituto Italiano per L'Assistenza Sociale. 1923. "Orientamenti nuovi dell'attività femminile." *Il giornale della donna,* no. 4.

Kuliscioff, A. 1894. *Il monopolio dell'uomo*. Milan: Uffici Della Critica Sociale.
———. 1908. "Il congresso delle donne Italiane." *Critica sociale*, no. 10.
———. 1910a. "Suffragio universale?" *Critica sociale*, nos. 6–7.
———. 1910b. "Per conchiudere sul voto alle donne." *Critica Sociale*, no. 9.
Labriola, T. 1920a. *Il dovere nazionale della donna*. Rome: Associazione Nazionale Italiana.
———. 1920b. "I valori spirituali del matrimonio." *Il giornale della donna*, nos. 32–33.
Loffredo, F. 1938. *Politica della famiglia*. Milan: Valentino Bompiani.
Lombardo, E. 1920. "Sulla capacità giuridica della donna." *Il giornale della donna*, no. 9.
———. 1921. "Le trincee del privilegio maschile." *Il giornale della donna*, no. 4.
Loschi, M. A. 1921. "Abbasso le donne. *Il giornale della donna*, no. 9.
Mozzoni, A. M. 1975. *La liberazione della donna*. Edited by F. Pieroni Bortolotti. Milan: Mazzotta. Originally published 1865.
Mussolini, B. 1934. "Macchina e donna." *Il popolo d'Italia*, August 31, 2.
Pertici, A. 1920. "Il lavoro femminile nelle industrie belliche." *Il giornale della donna*, no. 24.
Pintor Dore, A. 1920. "Femminismo." *Il giornale della donna*, no. 25.
P.A.B. 1922. "Maestri e maestre." *Il giornale della donna*, no. 21.
Una Professionista. 1920. "Una delle più belle missioni femminili." *Il giornale della donna*, no. 14.
Sierra Cammeo, N. 1921. "A proposito del lavoro delle donne." *Il giornale della donna*, nos. 13–14.

Secondary Sources

Camarda, A., and S. Peli. 1980. *L'altro esercito*. Milan: Feltrinelli.
De Luna, G. 1978. "Fascismo: Le origini." In *Storia d'Italia* (vol. 1). Edited by N. Tranfaglia. Florence: La Nuova Italia.
Foucault, M. 1965. *Madness and Civilization: A History of Insanity in the Age of Reason*. New York: Pantheon. Originally published 1961.
———. 1972. *The Archaeology of Knowledge: The Discourse on Language*. New York: Harper Torchbooks. Originally published in 1969.
———. 1977. *Discipline and Punish*. New York: Pantheon. Originally published in 1975.
Gaiotti De Biase, P. 1963. *Le origini del movimento cattolico femminile*. Brescia: Morcelliana.
Gramsci, A. 1971. *The Prison Notebooks*. New York: International. Originally published in 1949.
Hegel, F. 1985. *Fenomenologia dello spirito*. Florence: La Nuova Italia. Originally published in 1807.
Kristeva, J. 1986. "The Stabbat Mother." In *The Kristeva Reader*. New York: Columbia University Press.
Nietszche, F. 1969. *On the Genealogy of Morals*. New York: Vintage. Originally published 1881–82.
Pieroni Bortolotti, F. 1963. *Alle origini del movimento femminile in Italia, 1848–1892*. Turin: Einaudi.
———. 1974. *Socialismo e questione femminile in Italia, 1892–1922*. Milan: Mazzotta.

Ragionieri, E. 1976. "La storia politica e sociale." In *Storia d'Italia* (vol.4). Edited by E. Ragioniezi. Turin: Einaudi.

Saraceno, C. 1979–80. *La famiglia operaia sotto il fascismo*. Milan: Fondazione Gian Giacomo Feltrinelli.

Tomasi, T., G. Genovesi, et al. 1978. *L'istruzione di base in Italia (1859–1977)*. Florence: Vallecchi.

Tranfaglia, N. 1978. "Fascismo: Il regime." In *Storia d'Italia* (vol. 1). Edited by N. Tranfaglia. Florence: La Nuova Italia.

3 / Women, Futurism, and Fascism

Clara Orban

In any discussion of the artistic scene during the years of Fascist rule in Italy, the futurist movement plays an important role. Because of this strong association, futurist studies lay almost dormant for several decades after World War II before undergoing a revival of interest. Similarly, in recent years, the paradigms used to discuss Fascism have shifted to include women. In a sense, both the futurist and the Fascist movements, linked as they were, constitute areas of study examined in new ways. However, in discussions on futurism and Fascism, the role of women has been a sublimated discourse. More "important" areas of scrutiny have seemed to be futurism's political implications and avant-garde connections. Yet women during this period were obligated to discover new ways of articulating the codes of both political and artistic life, because the dominant culture conspired to push them to the fringes. Women added to the dominant culture as they invented new methods of signification. Futurism, for instance, as is well known, created an openly misogynist atmosphere, yet many women became associated with the movement as it developed through the years of World War I, the 1920s, and the 1930s.

In this essay, I plan to reexamine the misogynist pronouncements of F. T. Marinetti and his colleagues in order to contextualize my discussion of women and futurism. Then, by rereading the often forgotten work produced by women futurists against male futurist discourses, I will interrogate the ways female artists adopted futurist rhetoric and adapted their strategies to the movement, modifying it to include their presence. Subsequently, a reappraisal of the connection between futurism and Fascism brought to light through the study of futurist manifestos will help to underline their relationship. Several secondary sources in recent years elucidate the changing role of women in Fascism, and all these elements together will provide a picture of the ways in which women's voices served to complement the two movements as well as to alter them.

Masculine Agendas

On the surface, one cannot deny the extremely misogynist nature of Marinetti's pronouncements, especially in the early manifestos. The "Fondazione e manifesto del futurismo" (Foundation and manifesto of futurism), first published on the front page of *Le figaro,* February 20, 1909, contains the now famous statement: "We want to glorify war, the only hygiene of the world, militarism, patriotism, the destructive gesture of the libertarians, the beautiful ideas for which one dies, and the despisal of women" (Marinetti 1990, 11). This statement, the ninth of eleven listed that punctuate the futurist plan, coexists with other statements declaring death to passéist aesthetics, replacing it with mechanical beauty and the glorification of the machine, and those declaring the love of war. Despising women goes hand in hand with the new aesthetic of war, the purification of the masculine gesture, and the death that may result from it. Women, therefore, no longer exist merely as objects of poetic contemplation and romantic idealism, but as objects of loathing as well. A reversal of aesthetic order that Marinetti will develop in future manifestos already appears implicit here. Yet, even in this first official pronouncement, Marinetti betrays a certain ambiguity with respect to women: as a class of people he tells us they are to be rejected, yet his imagery contains soft echos of maternal longing reminiscent of the most sentimental nineteenth-century prose. Before he begins his list of futurist desires and demands, Marinetti describes the critical event leading to the production of the manifesto: he had an accident while driving his car and thereafter, ironically, the great champion of the machine abandoned motorcars, never to drive again. When his car turned over as he tried to avoid cyclists on the road, it fell into a ditch, which he describes as a "maternal ditch, nearly full of muddy water! Beautiful workshop of a ditch! I avidly tasted your fortifying slime, which reminded me of the sacred black breast of my Sudanese wet nurse" (Marinetti 1990, 9).[1] This return to the womb, precipitated by the failure of the machine he so loved, presents a partial reversal of Marinetti's despisal of women. In this scenario, the female body, when regressively linked to maternal, intrauterine memory, survives intact in Marinetti's new world order. In the first "manifesto of futurism," women play two roles, mother and outcast, neither of which represents a departure from traditional representations.

As the futurist movement developed, Marinetti continued to include statements on the role of women in his manifestos, an ever-present element of the way in which he defined and promulgated his movement. In the *Daily Mail* on November 21, 1913, Marinetti published his first manifesto on theater, "Il teatro di varietà" (Variety theater), which sings the praises of this new form of theater over the passéist, sentimental drama. One of its advantages is that it provides

> a school of instruction in sincerity for males, since it exalts their rapacious instinct and rips away all of women's veils, all the phrases, all the signs, all the romantic cries which deform and mask them. Instead, it brings out all of women's admirable animal qualities, their force, their seduction, their treachery and resistance. (Marinetti 1990, 84)

Further, Marinetti categorically dismisses "ideal love and its romantic obsession" (p. 85). These pronouncements clarify the ones he made four years earlier. Women fulfilling nonmaternal roles are no longer categorically rejected. Although he falls back on the worn stereotype of the female seductress, the perfidious female, Marinetti realizes women can have "admirable animal qualities." These stereotypes of the sighing, whimpering, weak woman are joined with images of women who exhibit animal strength and resistance. The picture of women again appears ambiguous, as it did in the first "manifesto of futurism," although now Marinetti proposes new possibilities for female roles. It is the romantic ideal they have been forced to represent as love objects that he loathes. Women as subjects are capable of "masculine" traits, the strength and virility Marinetti prizes above all others.

Years later, Marinetti would build on this idea in "Contro il lusso femminile" (Against female luxury) (March 11, 1920). This fascinating document opens by declaring that females have been forced by males to concentrate great efforts on their outward appearance, and this has had deleterious effects on both sexes (Marinetti 1990, 546). Marinetti sees a transfer of desire from the flesh, its rightful place, onto clothing and jewels, a fetishistic displacement. The sensation of the flesh remains potent, whereas the "indefinite and completely artificial sensibility, which only responds to silk, to velvet, to jewels and to furs," must be stopped (p. 547). This would seem to suggest that Marinetti blames men for objectifying women, which has not only turned females into prostitutes but softened men in the process. However, the reason for Marinetti's concern becomes clear: "We speak in the name of the race, which demands ardent men and impregnated women" (p. 548). Here we cannot miss the similarities between Marinetti's position and the pronatalist rhetoric Mussolini later employed. Voicing his preoccupation with procreation, which I shall discuss below, Marinetti reveals that his chief concern is not for women's social advancement, but for their continued desirability as organs of reproduction. Once again, in the same manifesto, Marinetti seems to liberate women and conversely to relegate them to their stereotypical role of womb-producer.

As futurism developed during the teens and twenties, and became entwined with budding Fascism, futurist political manifestos proliferated. Women's role in the new political order was spelled out, yet again, ambiguously. In the "Manifesto del Partito Futurista Italiano" (Manifesto of the Italian Futurist Party), among the details of his program Marinetti lists "abolition of authorization to marry. Easy divorce. Gradual devaluation of marriage for the gradual increase in free love and creation of children of the state" (1990, 154). He also calls for universal suffrage. Marinetti once again seems to be championing an environment in which women gain certain freedoms in personal relationships. In "Contro l'amore e il parlamentarismo" (Against love and parliamentary government), however, Marinetti's liberal ideas take a regressive turn. He proposes the vote for women, but specifies that he supports it only because of women's inferior character and intellect. If women are allowed to vote, their stupid choices will certainly bring down the Parliament, another hated form of passéist conventions (Marinetti 1990, 293). For Marinetti, women's suffrage has nothing to do with liberating female citizens, and everything to do with subverting the political order to replace it with futurist institutions.

In 1919, Marinetti wrote a tract titled "Contro il matrimonio" (Against matrimony), in which he attacks the family as an organization that saps the energy of individuals through constant contact and bickering. Even a nondysfunctional family remains nothing more than a symbol of passéist notions and emotions. He states that "a man who does not know how to give joy and strength to a woman must not impose his will or company on her. Woman does not belong to man, but to the future and to the development of the race" (Marinetti 1990, 370). Again, woman's role is to procreate, and for that she must be granted certain freedoms from constraints. Children are to be educated outside the home so that they may grow, away from the suffocating domestic atmosphere. Thus, the supposed emancipation of women prepares the way for Marinetti's notion that the ideal universe remains devoid of women, consisting only of men and machines, first introduced in the 1915 text, "Uomo moltiplicato e il regno della macchina" (Multiplied man and the reign of the machine), the title of a manifesto from the collection *Guerra, sola igiene del mondo* (War, sole hygiene of the world), which specifies that the ideal universe remains devoid of women, consisting only of men and machines. For this to happen, men must eliminate all traces of affection or eroticism (Marinetti 1990, 300). Women have become not only ambiguous in this transformation, but superfluous. It is as though the futurists view woman as neither a positive nor a negative entity. She has become transparent. In a sense, this is the worst fate, for she becomes expendable. Even the enemy has a role to play, but woman has none. Cinzia Blum (1990) notes that woman is consistently erased as a subject in the manifesto, yet this in itself exposes a latent anxiety, as "virulent misogyny, homophobia, and the erotization of violence add up to a paranoid self-definition" (p. 209). I would add that Marinetti's indecision on the role of women, at once quite liberal and regressive, reinforces the "paranoid self-definition." Although the declarative style of the manifestos presents futurist ideas as categorical realities, the texts contain a hidden uncertainty.

As we have seen, woman's only important role, as procreator, must be assumed by some other entity if she disappears. Procreation, or at least continued multiplication of the species, was central to Marinetti's vision, yet he certainly saw that, given women's mollifying potential, an alternate form of replication was useful. In some of Marinetti's texts, machines replace women; in others, men perform the sole procreating function. Very early in his career, in *Mafarka, il futurista* (Mafarka, the futurist), Marinetti had already developed these ideals of sexual self-sufficiency. The novel was first published in French in 1910, and in the same year Decio Cinti's Italian-language translation appeared. *Mafarka* exemplifies an early Marinettian text, written while he was abandoning his symbolist style and language and developing his futurist themes. Mafarka, the warrior king of the African city of Tell-el-Kibir, has wrested control from his uncle Boubassa. Magamal, Mafarka's brother, possesses decidedly feminine traits, providing a strange counterpoint to Mafarka's hypervirility, perhaps as a way of implying that absolute virility is difficult to achieve and is not automatically passed down genetically. One of the first scenes in the novel involves the conquest of the rival army and the mass rape of female prisoners, who enjoy the sexual attack (Marinetti 1910, 30–32). In this male-centered universe, women are not raped but sexually aroused. Mafarka conquers other cities and negotiates various other sexual encounters. Toward the end of the novel, while on an ocean voyage, Mafarka wakes up as a futurist. He abandons the soft life, rejects his fawning followers, and leaves Tell-el-Kibir. What concerns him most in these later sections of the novel is engendering a child himself. Mafarka tells his followers that this type of self-sufficient procreation remains the only assurance of complete domination of the will:

> Because you should know that I have engendered a son without the aid of the vulva!... You don't understand?... Then listen.... [I] concluded that it is possible to push from one's flesh, without the stinking complicity and help of the female womb, an immortal giant with infallible wings! Our will must go forth from us to seize matter and modify it to our whims. This way, we can mold everything that surrounds us and endlessly renew the face of the world.... That is the new Voluptuousness which will rid the world of Love, when I have founded the religion of the exteriorized Will and of daily Heroism. (Marinetti 1910, 214–16)

Voluptuousness has become a religion, the world of sentimentality must disappear. When man can use his will to procreate without woman, without the vulva, he will have gained the power to create the god that everyone has inside. In the meantime, women have been reduced to sexual organs. Mafarka's wish to procreate represents the ultimate relationship of creator to object created. When Mafarka does produce his son, Gazourma, this mechanical winged monster exemplifies all that can be done without women. Mafarka rebuffs Colubbi, his concubine, when she approaches Gazourma, because Mafarka insists his seed was divine (p. 272). He was able to create without her, so she must disappear. Gazourma originated only from man. Mafarka represents a transitional character in Marinetti's dialectic of sexual politics. He does not care only for autogratification without procreation; self-sufficiency in procreation equates with divine creation in Marinetti's novel. When Mafarka engenders his own son, he affirms the creative process, thereby implying that women have no role in it. David Dollenmayer (1986, 140) has identified a fundamental fear of women in *Mafarka*. They are no longer even useful for their *valeur animal* (animal value), but must be hated and feared for their sexuality, which threatens to sap the strength of the warriors. Marinetti later developed these ideas in his manifestos, as we have seen. Romolo Runcini (1981, 271), speaking of the importance of gesture in futurism, goes so far as to posit that these artists sublimated their world vision into an erotization of technology, a notion exemplified by *Mafarka*.

Mafarka does not represent the only text of this period that glorifies the status of male autosufficiency. In order to explore its importance further, we must situate Italian futurism within the larger context of the avant-garde movements flourishing during the early decades of this century. Artists working within the confines of cubism, dadaism, and surrealism, although approaching art from a vantage point different from that of futurism, constructed many of the same artistic paradigms. Avant-garde movements share several traits, as Andreas Huyssen (1986, 197) has noted, among which are the following: a desire for experimentation, a persistent exploration of language in literature and of the medium itself in painting, the rejection of all classical systems of representation, the effacement of "content," the erasure of subjectivity, and an adversarial stance toward bourgeois culture.

It is useful to explore misogynist pronouncements in other avant-garde writers to determine the place that futurists occupied within the avant-garde with respect to the discourse on the feminine. Guillaume

Apollinaire stands as a literary giant during the historical avant-garde period, and was connected to artists in almost all the movements in one way or another. His play *Les mamelles de Tirésias* (The breasts of Tirésias) stands as an important example. In the play, which was first performed at the Conservatoire Renée Maubel in Paris, June 24, 1917,[2] Thérèse refuses to produce children for the nation of Zanzibar because she is a feminist: "I am a feminist, and I do not recognize the authority of men" (Apollinaire 1972, 119). She wants to go to war, so she transforms herself into a man, renamed Tirésias. Consequently, her husband, known in the play only by his marital status as *le mari,* decides he will produce the offspring necessary for the state. In fact, he produces 40,049 children in one day (p. 141). When the gendarme of Zanzibar courts *le mari,* the latter realizes he must become fertile, stating:

> Woman in Zanzibar wants political rights
> And suddenly renounces prolific love
> You hear her cry, No more children, No more children
> To populate Zanzibar, all we need is elephants
> Monkeys, serpents, mosquitos and ostriches
> And, as sterile as the inhabitants of the hornet's nest,
> Which at least make wax and honey,
> Women are nothing but neuter before heaven
> And I want to tell you, dear Mr. Gendarme [on the megaphone]
> Zanzibar needs children [without the megaphone]
> Sound the alarm
> Cry out at every corner and on the boulevard
> That we must make more children in Zanzibar
> If women won't make any more, too bad
> Let men make them. (Apollinaire 1972, 134)

Several issues emerge here. The woman forces man's decision to self-sufficiency because she seeks liberation. She is "neutral/neuter," so men must take over, enforcing a dialectic of abdication-empowerment. The climate in Europe at the end of the nineteenth century, and especially after World War I, was ripe for this type of discourse. Both the French and Italian governments, fearful of the consequences of population decimation during the war, openly campaigned for increased birthrates. Apollinaire's play provides a parable of this situation, a playful spoof on procreative self-sufficiency. Apollinaire plays on the notions set out by Marinetti, but renders them into parody.

Several years later, Salvador Dalí, an important representative of the surrealist movement, dedicated a great part of his career to the theme of the "great masturbator," both in painting and in poetry. Dalí's pictorial works disturb the viewer because they portray surreal subjects using traditional techniques, such as three-point perspective and chiaroscuro. In 1929 he launched a canvas, *Le grand masturbatuer,* that depicts the fantasy life leading up to the act of male masturbation.[3] A huge head, yellowish and waxlike, appears pointed toward the barren landscape typical of Dalí's works. It balances on the tip of its nose, its eyes closed. Where the neck would appear Dalí has configured an ornamental shape. He has replaced the mouth with a grasshopper, itself being consumed by ants.[4] From this waxen face protrude several images, one indistinguishable mass, a gargoyle head licking its lips, and, much larger, a beautiful female bust and face (a portrait of Dalí's wife Gala) in ecstasy licking male genitals attached to two legs with bloody knees. This painting does include the image of a woman, who appears as a mere phantasm of the male imagination. Her image is still "required" for sexual satisfaction, but the image will suffice. In a strange sense, Dalí recaptures some of the sensual dynamic of the troubadouric *amor de lonh,* transforming it into a pornographic exchange. The sexual act itself can be accomplished as an act of autogratification.

A year later, in *La femme visible* (The visible woman), Dalí published a lengthy poem by the same name. This oniric text depicts various acts of coupling and sexuality during twilight. The text speaks of "great agate staircases," so presumably the sexual acts take place in palatial settings (Dalí 1980, 144). The cadre contains echoes of the Marquis de Sade's sexual fantasy in *Les 120 jours de Sodome,* in which orgies take place in a castle. The same year, Dalí made allusions to the Sadian text in his film *L'age d'or* (The age of gold) (1930), a collaborative effort with Luis Buñuel. In fact, *Le grand masturbateur* contains many passages of Sadian inspiration, including references to the ingestion of feces and urine as a sexual practice. Although certain portions of the poem suggest sexuality between men and women, as the scene evolves it concentrates on the hermaphrodite, "remarkable, irresistible person / and delicate with a chignon and with female breasts / with a huge penis and with huge testicles" (Dalí 1980, 146). This text glorifies not only the elimination of women even as objects of sexuality and procreation, but also the complete disappearance of sexual differentiation. Dalí's nightmare world consists of men who reach sexual satisfaction without women, even of women who become men.

In retrospect, there is evidence that male autogratification and its corollary, male self-sufficiency, constitute a relatively common literary theme in several countries during the early twentieth century. Perhaps this theme, which prescribes the complete exclusion of women, even from their most biologically dictated role of procreator and womb, belies a fear of women's increasing role in society. We have seen that Marinetti's texts are ambivalent, at times glorifying and at times debasing women. Furthermore, several historical reassessments of Fascism note that women's roles changed substantially after World War I, and Fascist ideologues were obligated to confront and ultimately try to suppress this reality. Literary and artistic attempts to suppress women and render them transparent, nonexistent, and to substitute a male worldview demonstrate the same sorts of pathological behavior noted by Blum (1990) and Dollenmayer (1986) in Marinetti. When women become "equals," men attempt to do away with even the uterine necessity of the female.

The thematic treatments of women Marinetti constructed in the manifestos reappear in his other artistic works. I have already discussed *Mafarka* in this context. Marinetti's *parole in libertà* (free word) composition "Dune" (Dunes) (1914) also contains segments that portray women, but again merely as objects of scorn because of their sentimental attachments to things. The *tavola parolibera* (free word table) "Sentimentale" (Sentimental) included in the longer poem describes the conquest of women as an expedition, yet the young explorers are "cheated on by wives lovers / solemnity of a cuckold / on the line of the equator" (in Caruso and Martini 1974, 37). This composition describes a soldier's discovery of his wife's unfaithfulness right before being forced to continue his march in the "dune," during which he reaches "Parma here I am kisses traditional **zing zing** of / a provincial bed" (p. 37). The women evoked in this passage are once again reduced to the social-sexual role of *moglie-amanti* (wife-lovers) and completely lose individuality, suffocated by the militaristic male context. This text highlights the way in which misogynist pronouncements are mingled with the militaristic glorification typical of futurism. This scenario echos the situation Marinetti outlines in the manifestos, in which women's role remains subjugated to men's virility.

Similarly, Umberto Boccioni's *parole in libertà* poem, "Scarpetta da società + orina" (Little society shoe + urine), published in 1914, revives Marinetti's pronouncements against female adornments and their corrupting influence. The noise of the shoes, "plicche-ploc plicche-ploc," represents "cadence swaying / prostitute" (in Caruso and Martini 1974, 52). The entire poem emphasizes the economic aspect of the woman's elaborate exterior dress, building to the conclusion, in which Boccioni decries the "fat man / married sucked Sunday excitement café chantant frees the stupid Monday." The prostitute's client has become a weak, unvirile shell because of his association with women. This poem precisely outlines Marinetti's concern for society. When women focus so much attention on their appearance because of male pleasure at seeing it, the situation must be put to a stop, not because it debases women, but because the men involved with these women risk losing their fighting spirit.

In pictorial futurist art, women once again represent a transparent subject. Clearly, given that futurists desired to eliminate sentimentality in their art, they had to eliminate women as pictorial subjects. Women traditionally had been the ideal subjects of the sentimental gaze in art and literature, and thus are not often depicted in futurist poetry or painting, which demanded that sentimentality be banished. The elimination of women as subjects was in some ways unique to futurism among the avant-garde movements of this period; even casual reference to cubist or surrealist painting proves that women continued to occupy a central place in the iconography of these groups. In surrealism, for example, the feminine subject played a central role in pictorial depictions of sexuality and "convulsive beauty," a key concept of André Breton's surrealist terminology. In futurism, however, when women are depicted, they appear gender neutral. Boccioni, certainly better known for his painting than for his poetry, almost always depicted either his mother or his sister as subject. He did this especially in his early works, during his divisionist, prefuturist period, but also in purely futurist works such as *Antigrazioso* (Antigracious) (1912).[5] Some of his earlier works include women in relatively traditional poses—in barrooms, for instance, such as in *La risata* (The laugh) (1911),[6] possibly inspired by some of Henri de Toulouse-Lautrec's pictures of the Moulin Rouge. Boccioni's work *Idolo moderno* (Modern idol) (1911) uses the *topos* of woman as idol, but modifies it for the new electric age.[7] The woman depicted appears demented because of her enlarged eyes. Her hat, with its huge brim and flowers, seems almost Renoiresque. Yet the painting's colors all reflect garish yellows, blues, and greens, as though the image were viewed under a gas lamp. In fact, the modern idol is the woman of the machine age, or the electric age. Although this last work modifies an accepted artistic stereotype, in essence, Boccioni's depictions of women on the canvas do not modify the traditional view of woman as idol, woman as object. Giacomo Balla, who depicts women on the canvas even more rarely than Boccioni, also presents women as gender neutral. One of his canvases with human subjects depicts a girl running on a balcony as though viewed through the freeze-frame mode on a movie camera (*Bambina che corre sul balcone* [Girl running on a balcony], 1912).[8] The dynamism of the object in motion proves essential, so all reference to gender appears secondary. From this brief overview of futurist poetry and painting, it seems clear that a reinforcement of traditional depictions of women is much more important than any real discussion of gender differences. What truly count for the futurists are speed, dynamism, glorification of the machine, and virility. All else disappears in the new futurist landscape.

At this point, having reconstructed the male futurist perspective on women, I can offer a closer examination of the suggestions of several critics that futurist texts belie a certain pathological behavior with respect to women. Sigmund Freud and Jacques Lacan both provide possible avenues into this discussion. Furthermore, feminist critics furnish material that is helpful in the assessment of possible justifications for women artists within such a misogynist movement. Freud's central lecture "Femininity," combines his various earlier pronouncements on female sexuality, adding new material. He posits the famous idea of "penis envy." In his conception, little girls feel wronged because they want "to have something like it [the penis] too" (Freud 1965, 125). In his essay "The Signification of the Phallus," Lacan continues to assess the importance of the male organ for sexual differentiation. He describes the phallus as the ultimate signifier, intended to designate as a whole the effects of the signified (Lacan 1977, 285). For Lacan, the penis stands for the organ, whereas the phallus represents the symbolic penis, that which stands for something else. It represents a mark of difference, the fact that the subject is not complete unto itself. It represents the break of unity caused by the symbolic father whose presence ruptures the mother-child bond and imposes the

"*non*" *du père*. The phallus allies with the logos because recognition
of difference remains a condition for logic and language. It propels
subjects into speech (Brennan 1989, 4).

Feminist critics have seized upon these attempts by male psychoanalysts to describe the female psyche and have refined them to include a "truer" vision of women. Luce Irigaray (1985) states that she
does not wish to redefine woman as subject or object, but to wrest
control from the economy of the logos. Woman must no longer allow herself to be defined as lack, deficiency, imitation, or negative image of the subject, but must create a *positive excess* on the feminine
side (p. 78). In other words, the problem, as it is posed, is not sufficient to define women. Hélène Cixous (1976) builds on this idea and
posits that the new logos, the new way of describing, is inscribed
within. It must be a language of the body, especially the female body
(p. 887). Jane Gallup (1989, 38) discusses implications of Lacan's
theory, the Lacanian "split," as problematic of Western culture, split
as it is from everything biological that leads to the domination and
exploitation of women. Women had certainly been written under the
sign of "lack" by male futurists. The subject is not complete unto itself, lacking the virility so central to the futurist aesthetic. Male futurists rendered woman transparent, at times seeming to endorse her
freedom from societal constraints, which they demanded for themselves, at others rendering her prisoner of her own body, a pure procreation machine. Feminist critics argue that women must demand
their own voices, based on logic predicated on their own bodies. As
we shall see, Italian futurist women struggled between these poles,
attempting to carve out space for themselves in futurism.[9] They tried
to reappropriate the language of their male counterparts as well as to
invent a language of their own.

Feminine Revisions

Valentine de Saint Point rebutted the claims Marinetti made in his
manifestos by creating the "Manifesto della donna futurista" (Manifesto of the futurist woman) (March 25, 1912). Both men and women
merit *disprezzo* (disdain) because of humanity's mediocrity. In fact, humanity should not even be divided into male and female (Marinetti et
al. 1914, 69). She speaks of women as warriors (Marinetti et al. 1914,

71), similar to the feminist language in Monique Wittig's *Les guérril-lères* (the English translation retains the French title) (1968/1971) and the mythic reappropriation of the past in Maxine Hong Kingston's *The Woman Warrior* (1977). Wittig composes a "feminary," a text that "presents numerous blank pages in which they [the women] write from time to time" (p. 15). The tribe of warrior women creates not only a new language, but a new, circular system of symbols to replace the phallocentric system. Wittig's vision is of a mythic future of warrior women, similar to de Saint Point's view. Kingston, instead, reaches back to an ancient Chinese myth of a woman warrior who saved the village. This warrior, and all the Chinese women who lived in the repressive male society of China, provide a justification for Kingston's view of herself, a Chinese American woman, caught between conflicting ideas of past and present. For de Saint Point, women must reacquire cruelty and violence; they must become unjust, like all the forces of nature (Marinetti et al. 1914, 73).

Echoes of feminist critics can be heard in de Saint Point's desire to annihilate the categories of men and women, the bipolar subdivision that predisposes a master/slave dialectic. Yet she recognizes that futurism is right. Its emphasis on force, on strength, and on destruction of the past fits within the female futurist's worldview. She sings women's intuition, just as Marinetti praises intuition as a linguistic force behind analogies and syntactic connections in the manifestos. Like male futurists, de Saint Point follows the heroes, becoming warrior or nurse (the more traditionally feminine role in war) (Marinetti et al. 1914, 71). She must create children, not only for herself but as warriors for the nation. In effect, de Saint Point here attempts at times to break from the female stereotypes, but ultimately succumbs to Marinetti's virile propaganda. She tries to inscribe female futurism within the male paradigm. As Barbara Spackman points out in chapter 5 of this volume, de Saint Point could be seen to argue for a mixing and matching of gender, the goal of which is a virilization of women. Similar tactics are at play in her manifesto of lust ("Manifesto futurista della Lussuria") (January 11, 1913). Lust remains essential to dynamism, therefore it must be embraced (Marinetti et al. 1914, 118). "Art and war are the great manifestations of sensuality; lust is their flower" (p. 119). Yet lust must be stripped of all the veils that cover it (p. 122). Like Marinetti, de Saint Point perceives lust as a potentially liberating force, yet it remains firmly anchored within a futurist dialectic of power and dynamism. She represents perhaps the first of a long succession of women futurists.

Another early text of *tavole parolibere* (1916) proposes Marinetti as a subject. Marietta Angelini, Marinetti's maid and later futurist poet, produced a *tavola* in which the futurist leader is portrayed as a phallic number one, with the words above him *vesuviano cervello* (Vesuvian brain) (Salaris 1982, 51). He is a man of blood, *l'uomo rosso* (the red man), whose heart is made of steel. Marinetti appears as a volcano, ready to erupt. Here, Angelini inscribes Marinetti as object entirely within the futurist masculine dialectic.

Later, some women futurists became associated with the Florentine journal *Italia futurista* (1916–18), whereas others were subsequently associated with *Roma futurista* (1918–20) in Rome. Several important figures endeavored to find their own voices. Enif Robert and Marinetti collaborated on the text "Conversazione fra il sole e il mio ventre" (Conversation between the sun and my belly) (1919). Certainly, this text still belies the rhetoric of masculine power as embodied in the sun, which brings spasms of pleasure to the woman (see Verdone 1973, 168). Yet Robert infuses the text with the kind of feminine-centered language of the body that Cixous advocates. The speaker examines her stomach and discovers that "her wound" is certainly more eloquent than her mouth (p. 169). The gulf of Santa Margherita appears as a uterine environment, whose stomach has engendered a dolphin, a "virile member" in its "humid penombra" (p. 172). Here, female iconology centers on procreation, the womb and the vulva, but on its own terms, not as an instrument of male desire for dominance. The female body takes its place in this text beside the male futurist discourse of domination. Here, the discourse on the female body does not replace male discourse but proposes itself as an added dimension to male futurist imagery.

The futurist writer Futurluce (pseudonym of Elda Norchi) provides a particularly significant example of the way the female avantgarde artist may redeploy futurist propaganda techniques while articulating a uniquely feminine mode of discourse. In her piece "Le donne e il futurismo" (Women and futurism, published in *Roma futurista,* February 9, 1919), she begins by asking polemically "Cosa volete da noi? Cosa chiedete? [What do you want from us? What are you asking?]" (Salaris 1982, 134). But Futurluce refuses to ask questions passively. She quickly reveals her desire to declare the principles, the ground rules governing how futurism will discuss women:

> And now to us: you faithfully, honestly hold out your hands to us, well, good, here we are, we extend ours to you, we shake them virilely, it will be the mutual pact for present and future action and collaboration. I do not speak for myself but I want to speak for all women who are convinced that they exist as organs of this society, not as playthings and dolls which more or less have a voice, but as women who live, who have in their veins the generous Italian blood, of women who know that they want to fight, of women who perhaps will die but who will not move backwards. Here we are, comrades, we come to you. (in Salaris 1982, 135)

The dialectic is still predicated on power, but this time women and men coexist in a relationship of equality instead of domination. Futurluce uses the futurist style, depicting a virile world of comrades marching toward a common enemy of the homeland, but here both men and women are virile. Although de Saint Point also continues the futurist rhetoric and inscribes women within it, Futurluce goes further. She proposes new images that include women alongside men, not merely subservient to them, the handshake replacing the passéist kiss as gesture of male-female union.

Mina della Pergola perhaps most dramatically demonstrates the rupture of the male mold in her poem "Il trionfo dell'F" (The triumph of the letter F) published in *Dinamo,* March 1919. The letter *f* is both graphically and phonically disseminated throughout the work. The poet begins by describing an "incubo di questa notte afosissima con tanti F [nightmare of this suffocating night with so many fs]" (in Salaris 1982, 157). The *f* triumphs in the word *fumare* (to smoke) and *profumare* (to have a perfumed smell). In this text, the poet decides to substitute *f* for all the letters of the alphabet, even to dress in "fs." She desires to "ferire la mia fissazione / Fenditura su tutto il mio corpo Femmineo / (comincia la pazzia?) / Impossibile FFfioritura nell'Io [wound my fixation / gash in my entire female body / (does madness begin here?) / Impossible flowering of 'I'] (p. 157). Ultimately the search for the "I" remains predicated on a feminine logos, both of signifier (f / fenditura / femmina) and signified (feminine). The logos — speech — has been reclaimed. Lucia Re (1989, 262) sees Della Pergola's poem as an almost Derridian play of signifier and dissemination of the *f*. Again, the feminine appears as a "wound," as it does in Robert's text, similar to the lack described by early psychoanalysts, but through language Della Pergola attempts to regain some terrain lost to male futurism. The word *futurism* itself now modulates and associates with the feminine through the common consonant.

In the later decades of futurism, especially in the 1930s and 1940s, futurist women once again seemed to appropriate the male dialogue of power and, in the process, to sacrifice some of their feminine/feminist language. A decidedly nationalistic and militaristic content can be discerned in some texts by women futurists. Laura Serra's poem "Golfo di Napoli" (Gulf of Naples) builds on the kinds of analogies between the feminine and water seen in Robert's text. The gulf is the "madre sirena" (mother siren) containing grottos in which nymphs play (in Viazzi 1978, 665). Yet, on the whole, what the poet really declaims are the fires of the old volcanic crater (Vesuvius), which produces the steel for Mediterranean power (p. 665). Serra sings the glory of "Italia madre" (mother Italy), which launches, through discipline and glory, the light of the reign and empire (p. 667). She decries those who have gone to look for bread beyond the shores of the motherland, because safety and certainty reside only within. We see here a definite shift in emphasis. This poem begins with feminist/feminine evocations, only to restore the dialogue of power. This time, the terms under which this power is inscribed appear not merely male futurist dominated but also heavily dependent on Fascist rhetoric of empire and sacrifice. Interestingly, women futurists may seem to abandon their desire to speak with their own voices and to succumb to the voice of political power.

Maria Goretti's "Canzone del petrolio" (Song of petroleum) again subverts the dialogue of the sexes for political ends. Petroleum appropriates the feminine voice and calls out, sirenlike, to man to look at her, because she is beautiful (in Viazzi 1978, 697). She appears as light that will bring power and glory. Why this curious choice of poetic subject? A possible answer lies in the historical context. The Fascist government's alliance with Nazi Germany was precipitated by an oil crisis. After the Ethiopia campaign of 1935, the Allies blockaded oil shipments to Italy as a punishment, as Italy was almost entirely dependent on foreign oil. Petroleum became the privileged signifier of power, a key element in the dialogue of empowerment. Goretti understood this and inscribed the raw material into the stereotypically female role as object of desire. Once again, we see later female futurists abandoning the search for a feminine voice as they attempt to rewrite the feminine stereotypes within the larger, newly urgent political framework.

My analysis has focused mainly on poetic texts, but Anna Nozzoli (1978) verifies a similar shift in prose works by female futurists during the 1930s, following the consolidation of the Fascist regime. Nozzoli sums up the development of women futurists:

> The road of female narrative during the "crisis" years of futurism thus seems to move in the sign of constant, unalterable, repeated antifeminist vocation, reflected in various examples of feminine typology: mother and obscure object of desire, the genius-woman attracted in the orbit of futurist phallocentrism and the passionate creature apt to exercise aggression on male eroticism. (p. 59)

Although we have seen that certain texts by male futurists provide more ambiguous views of women than Nozzoli allows, her assessment of the general climate in futurist circles as reflected in their texts appears valid. Nozzoli supports her argument through contextual references to the political climate, stating that a similar process of transformation took place on the social plane during the years of Fascism. Likewise, Lucia Re (1989, 271) argues that during the later phase of the movement, futurist women shifted positions, rehabilitating motherhood in an attempt to inscribe the movement within a traditional discourse. Elisabetta Mondello (1987, 45) notes a shift in language as well. Several binomials established by male futurists to discuss women, such as *donna-sentimentalismo* (woman-sentimentalism), give way to *donna-stirpe, donna-razza* (woman-progeny, woman-race). However, as Re amply demonstrates in her contribution to this volume, women futurists such as Benedetta Cappa Marinetti did attempt to propose radical expressions of alternative modes of constructing gender differences. In *Le forze umane* and *Il viaggio di Gararà*, Benedetta highlights the theories of female creativity and desire, distancing herself from the rhetoric common in male futurist texts. The new light shed on these forgotten female futurist texts, among others, shows that all in all, women futurists represent a much more complex tableau than originally thought.

Political Perspectives

Now that the relations between women and futurism have been documented, we still must ask in what way the shift outlined above sprang from the changing political climate in Italy. Chronologically, the futurist movement was virtually contemporaneous with the Fascist Party, although it began about a decade earlier. Futurism began in 1909 and virtually disappeared as a movement when Marinetti died in 1944, only a few months before Mussolini died. The movement went through several modulations during these decades, so far-reaching that futurism is often divided into two phases. The first—sometimes called the "heroic" phase—lasted approximately until the early years of World War I. Several important futurists, such as the architect Antonio Sant'Elia and Boccioni, were killed in the war, and the loss of these key members had a great impact on the direction of the group. Furthermore, during the second phase, futurism expanded its experimentation into para-artistic genres, such as cuisine and fashion. Even in the visual arts and poetry, new forms of expression were tried, such as "aeropittura." Futurism itself became a political party, and during the teens and twenties, Marinetti wrote several manifestos with explicit political intent. In many of these, he discusses the role of women. As stated earlier, in "Manifesto del Partito Futurista Italiano," Marinetti declares that matrimony must be abolished and divorce rendered easy. This would favor free love and children raised by the state (Marinetti 1990, 154). Again, Marinetti seems to declare acts to free women from traditional bonds when his primary aim remains procreation. In the 1920s, as he continued producing manifestos and tracts such as "Al di là del comunismo" (Beyond communism) (1920) and "Futurismo e fascismo," Marinetti increasingly embraced the ideals of Mussolini. Only when Mussolini decided to ally himself entirely with the Catholic Church in 1929 did Marinetti find it necessary to break definitively from him.

Although chronologically the two movements overlap, Fascism developed independent of futurism, as Alberto Schiavo (1981, 10) reminds us. Mussolini alone spearheaded its rise. Futurism did, however, inform and augment Fascist rhetoric. Mussolini displayed an early fascination with futurist innovation well before he founded his "revolutionary" movement. As Schiavo points out, on November 14, 1914, Mussolini wrote a letter to Paolo Buzzi (he had already met Boccioni) in which he stated that, even in the domain of art, all his sympathies lay with the innovators, in other words, the futurists (p. 17). In his history of futurism and Fascism, Schiavo argues that even politically, the futurists paved the way for Fascism because they founded their own political party. In December 1918, after launching the Futurist Party, the exponents of futurism organized the *Fasci politici futuristi,* the backbone on which Mussolini would, four months later, build the *Fasci di combattimento* (Schiavo 1981, 22). Certainly, the two movements were closely allied for a time, even proposing a common slate of candidates. Yet, as mentioned, a rupture took place when Mussolini decided he needed the support of the Catholic Church, a move that alienated Marinetti's profoundly anticlerical nature. Futurism and Fascism represent a moment in which the goals of an artistic movement and those of a political party coincided: to replace the old with something else, by force if necessary. Yet not all artists in Italy during this period reacted in this way. Lino Pertile (1986, 162) notes that the futurists and Gabriele D'Annunzio, as well as Giuseppe Ungaretti, were all allied or sympathetic to the Fascist movement, but that often this connection did not translate into literature, above all in the poetry of Ungaretti. Some writers consciously endeavored to dissociate their art from the political, so that it did not necessarily become a part of their art. Thus, the futurists and the Fascists to some extent represent a unique alliance.

In what way did futurism develop along with Fascism? Julie Dashwood (1972, 100) notes that Marinetti supported the movement as long as it remained a movement rather than a political entity. She maintains that futurism was attracted to the propaganda of Fascism, but once it became codified and needed outside support to survive, Marinetti rejected it. Even before Mussolini attempted to gain the support of the church, thereby antagonizing Marinetti, these two protagonists occupied incompatible positions on the Libya campaign of 1911, as Judy Davies (1988) notes. The futurists had declared their support, whereas Mussolini, in his socialist days, had condemned it. Like Schiavo, Davies also notes that Mussolini allowed Marinetti to establish the tone for his *fasci,* which were to become a sort of political and ideological avant-garde (p. 95). In fact, as Barbara Spackman (1990) amply illustrates, the roots of allegiance run much deeper. She outlines the ways Mussolini's movement was predicated on notions of virility conceptualized by futurists. The duce was to be seen only in virile poses; he shaved his head to hide gray hairs; and so on. This position certainly inscribes itself directly within the futurist rhetoric of virility outlined above. In fact, Andrew Hewitt (1992, 43) goes even further and notes that Italian futurism is radically and fundamentally Fascist, because the entire futurist program links politics and aesthetics in a sort of Fascist modernism. Futurism and Fascism appear intimately linked in their bombastic, militaristic style, their use of propaganda, and their linking of politics and aesthetics, as well as their overall worldviews.

As a final note, we could elaborate the way in which futurist women positioned themselves in the context of the regime. In effect, the female futurists from the later period, of the late 1920s and the 1930s and 1940s, are artists whose work merits further study. A thorough examination of these texts would certainly yield interesting results with regard to the connections between the regime and the female futurists. We can state, given the analysis conducted thus far, that a consideration of female futurist discourses elaborated during the interwar period changes our perception of Italian modernism and Italian women writers in general. It also poses new questions that have been forestalled by an almost exclusive focus on male exponents of futurism and avant-garde movements in general. To elaborate a relationship between female futurists and the larger question of the artistic milieux of the first decades of the century, we could incorporate critical parameters already established to discuss the distinctions between "high art" and "mass culture," respectively associated with the "masculine" and the "feminine." Huyssen (1986) takes as his model Emma Bovary, whose love of romance novels is scorned by Flaubert, an exponent of "high art." During the last half of the nineteenth century and into the modernist movements of the twentieth century, masculinity was increasingly linked with action and business, femininity with the arts (Huyssen 1986, 189). A division thus arose between mass culture (the feminine "art") and high culture (the masculine "art"). Huyssen states that, although recent studies on the avant-garde attempt to redefine these movements as feminine or feminized, it is impossible to deny their misogynist nature (p. 193). In fact, he attributes the powerful masculinization of texts by writers such as Marinetti to the contemporaneous feminization of mass culture (p. 198). Yet, we must remember the extent to which "mass culture," especially advertising, penetrated the avant-garde. Cubist collages often contained ads within their frames, artists from all the movements used ads on their canvases and produced advertisements for products. Futurism was art of a public nature, meant to be consumed rapidly, as are advertisements. A few decades later, Magritte worked extensively in advertising, especially during the early years of his career. Mass culture began to integrate with high art with the arrival of the avant-garde. Thus, Huyssen concludes that "the road from the avant-garde's experiments to contemporary women's art seems to have been shorter, less tortuous, and ultimately more productive than the less frequently traveled road from high modernism" (p. 204). When mass culture met high art, the distinctions between exclusively female and male art worlds collapsed. Women futurist artists had begun, more so than their male colleagues, to join the two divided spheres. Their works used and transformed the language of the avant-garde, the logos of male dominance, into a world that could accept the feminine voice. Consequently, I propose, the gap between the masculine and the feminine in art narrowed.

Women's roles in misogynist societies have come under intense scrutiny of late, an almost lost body of information to discover. The futurists, promulgators of virility, forwarded contradictory postures toward women. Yet women writers and artists adopted and adapted themselves to this movement that would attempt to subjugate them. Some adopted the male rhetoric; others adapted it to the female voice. Women found ways to stake small claims to their speech, as well as their bodies, even during the height of political repression. Within the male world of Italy between the world wars, where the social, political, and artistic climate conspired against them, women writers and artists carved out a space of their own.

Notes

All translations in the text are my own, unless the text cited in the bibliography appears in translation.

1. Marinetti spent most of his early years in Alexandria because his father, a banker, was stationed there. He often recalls the exotic encounters of his early Egyptian experience, as he does here, as formative ones.

2. Perhaps the most noted aspects of this play remain the prologue and subtitle, both which employ the newly coined word *surrealist*. The artists of that movement continually harkened back to Apollinaire as one of their spiritual leaders. He states in the prologue that most of the play was written in 1903, but performed only many years later.

3. For illustration, see Dalí (1980, 143, plate 71).

4. Dalí describes the importance of the grasshopper in his work *La vie secrète de Salvador Dalí*. As a child, he caught a small fish in his hands. When he went to look at it, he noted its resemblance to a grasshopper, and in later years the association of the two creatures still made him scream in horror (Dalí 1980, 142). He does not elucidate the fear, but we are to understand that it is sexual in nature. Also, ants appear as a sign of sexual passion not only in Dalí's poetry and paintings, but also in key scenes in his films. In *Un chien andalou* (1929), one of the men who attempts to rape the female character in the film notices ants crawling on the palm of his hand during moments of intense arousal. It seems logical to conclude that the image of the combined insects in *Le grand masturbateur* stands for sexuality.

5. For an illustration, see Coen (1988, 150, plate 66).

6. For an illustration, see Coen (1988, 107, plate 53).

7. For an illustration, see Coen (1988, 113, plate 55A).

8. For an illustration, see Braun (1989, plate 7).

9. Jean-Claude Marcadé and Valentine Marcadé (1983) note that the situation for Russian futurist women was much more liberal than in most of Europe, perhaps because women's juridical status had improved under the empire as of 1860. That is why I specify here that the discussion centers only on Italian futurists.

Works Cited

Apollinaire, Guillaume. 1972. *L'enchanteur pourrissant suivi de Les mamelles de Tirésias et de Couleurs du temps*. Edited by Michel Décaudin. Paris: Gallimard.

Blum, Cinzia. 1990. "Rhetorical Strategies and Gender in Marinetti's Futurist Manifesto." *Italica* (Summer): 196–211.

Braun, Emily, ed. 1989. *Italian Art in the Twentieth Century: Painting and Sculpture 1900–1988*. London: Royal Academy of the Arts.

Brennan, Teresa. 1989. "Introduction." In *Between Feminism and Psychoanalysis*. Edited by Teresa Brennan. London: Routledge.

Caruso, Luciano, and Stelio M. Martini, eds. 1974. *Tavole parolibere futuriste 1912–1944* (vols. 1–2). Naples: Liguori.

Cixous, Hélène. 1976. "The Laugh of the Medusa." Translated by Keith Cohen and Paula Cohen. *Signs: Journal of Women in Culture and Society* (Summer): 875–93.

Coen, Ester. *Umberto Boccioni*. New York: The Metropolitan Museum of Art, 1988.

Dalí, Salvador. 1980. *Salvador Dalí, rétrospective 1920–1980*. Paris: Centre Georges Pompidou.

Dashwood, Julie R. 1972. "Futurism and Fascism." *Italian Studies* 27: 91–103.

Davies, Judy. 1988. "The Futures Market: Marinetti and the Fascists in Milan." In *Visions and Blueprints: Avantgarde Culture and Radical Politics in Early Twentieth-Century Europe*. Edited by Edward Timms and Peter Collier. Manchester: Manchester University Press.

Dollenmayer, David. 1986. "Alfred Döblin, Futurism, and Women: A Relationship Reexamined." *Germanic Review* (Fall): 138–45.

Freud, Sigmund. 1965. "Femininity." In *New Introductory Lectures on Psychoanalysis*. Edited and translated by James Strachey. New York: W. W. Norton.

Gallup, Jane. 1989. "Moving Backwards or Forwards." In *Between Feminism and Psychoanalysis*. Edited by Teresa Brennan. London: Routledge.

Hewitt, Andrew. 1992. "Fascist Modernism, Futurism and 'Post-modernity.'" In *Fascism, Aesthetics and Culture*. Edited by Richard J. Golsan. Hanover: University Press of New England.

Huyssen, Andreas. 1986. "Mass Culture as Woman: Modernism's Other." In *Studies in Entertainment: Critical Approaches to Mass Culture.* Edited by Tania Modleski. Bloomington: Indiana University Press.

Irigaray, Luce. 1985. "The Power of Discourse and the Subordination of the Feminine." In *This Sex Which Is Not One.* Translated by Catherine Porter. Ithaca, N.Y.: Cornell University Press.

Kingston, Maxine Hong. 1977. *The Woman Warrior: Memoirs of a Girlhood among Ghosts.* New York: Alfred A. Knopf.

Lacan, Jacques. 1977. *Ecrits: A Selection.* Translated by Alan Sheridan. New York: W. W. Norton.

Marcadé, Jean-Claude, and Valentine Marcadé, eds. 1983. *L'avant-garde au féminin: Moucou-Saint-Petersbourg-Paris 1907–1930.* Paris: Artcurial.

Marinetti, F. T. 1910. *Mafarka le futuriste.* Paris: Sansot.

———. 1990. *Teoria e invenzione futurista,* 2d ed. Edited by Luciano De Maria. Milan: Mondadori.

Marinetti, F. T., et al. 1914. *I manifesti del futurismo: Prima serie.* Florence: Lacerba.

Mondello, Elisabetta. 1987. *La nuova italiana: La donna nella stampa e nella cultura del ventennio.* Rome: Riuniti.

Nozzoli, Anna. 1978. *Tabù e coscienza: La condizione femminile nella letteratura italiana del Novecento.* Florence: La Nuova Italia.

Pertile, Lino. 1986. "Fascism and Literature." In *Rethinking Italian Fascism: Capitalism, Populism and Culture.* Edited by David Forgacs. London: Lawrence & Wishart.

Re, Lucia. 1989. "Futurism and Feminism." *Annali d'italianistica* 7: 253–72.

Runcini, Romolo. 1981. "La parola e il gesto tra futurismo e fascismo." *Problemi: Periodico quadrimestrale di cultura* (September/December): 262–74.

Salaris, Claudia. 1982. *Le futuriste: Donne e letteratura d'avanguardia in Italia (1909/1944).* Milan: Edizioni delle donne.

Schiavo, Alberto. 1981. "Futurismo con e senza fascismo." In *Futurismo and Fascismo.* Edited Alberto Schiavo. Rome: Giovanni Volpe.

Spackman, Barbara. 1990. "The Fascist Rhetoric of Virility." *Stanford Italian Review* 8: 81–101.

Verdone, Mario, ed. 1973. *Prosa e critica futurista.* Milan: Feltrinelli.

Viazzi, Glauco, ed. 1978. *I poeti del futurismo 1909–1944.* Milan: Longanesi.

Wittig, Monique. 1971. *Les guérrillères.* Translated by David Le Vay. Boston: Beacon. Originally published 1968.

4 / Fascist Theories of "Woman" and the Construction of Gender

Lucia Re

Fascist Theorizations of Gender

During the 1920s and 1930s, a number of theories were developed in Fascist Italy regarding the essence, function, and place of woman. These theories constituted veritable "technologies of gender": discursive practices that contributed to the cultural construction of sexual difference in Fascist Italy. Teresa De Lauretis (1987, 18), who has adapted to the study of gender Foucault's notion of the "technology" of sex (those mechanisms, tactics, and devices — other than simply prohibition and the law — through which power has access to and controls sexuality), has remarked that gender in any given period is a cultural construction rather than a simple derivative of biological or physiological difference. It is, furthermore, a construction that is constantly *in process*, shaped and reshaped through discourses — such as the cinema or philosophical theories produced in the academy — that have a more or less direct, institutional power to influence the field of social meaning and therefore to generate, promote, or reinforce specific notions and representations of gender. The cultural construction of gender is never one-way, of course. Although in any given period certain technologies of gender become so entrenched as to acquire the dominance of a hegemonic model, there are also *counter*technologies at work on the margins or between the lines of the dominant discourse. These countertechnologies, although less easily visible and detectable, influence the construction of gender—and its representation—either by deconstructing or destabilizing hegemonic models and discursive practices or by positing new and more or less radically different alternatives.

I will consider two theoretical texts that are—in different ways—representative of the hegemonic discourse of Fascism on woman: Giovanni Gentile's 1934 "La donna nella coscienza moderna" (Woman in modern consciousness) and Ferdinando Loffredo's 1938 *Politica della famiglia* (Politics of the family).[1] I will then turn briefly to three literary texts by women that, in my view, constitute forms of counterdiscourse, actively "resisting" the Fascist construction of woman.[2] These are the experimental novels *Le forze umane* (The human strengths) (1924) and *Il viaggio di Gararà* (Gararà's journey) (1931), both by the futurist novelist and artist who called herself Benedetta, and the 1939 novel *Nascita e morte della massaia* (Birth and death of the housewife) by Paola Masino, which is also an experimental text.[3] Before turning to the texts, I would like to summarize briefly the terms of the current scholarship and critical debate on women and Fascism, in order to make my own position more clear.

One of the most familiar images of the traditional "Fascist woman" appears in Ettore Scola's highly praised 1977 film *Una giornata particolare* (A special day), which is set against the background of Hitler's triumphal visit to Rome in 1938. Antonietta, the female protagonist—played by Sophia Loren—is the quintessential Fascist *massaia,* or housewife. She is self-sacrificing and totally devoted to her brutish husband, a state brothels keeper, and to her numerous children. Although she works like a slave in her own house and has to struggle with the family budget to feed her children, she looks forward to having another child to please the duce and help fulfill the demographic aspirations of the fatherland. The duce appears as a powerful erotic and heroic ideal to her; she fainted once, overwhelmed by seeing him on horseback in the Villa Borghese, and keeps a scrapbook of clippings and pictures of him cut out from the popular, gossipy tabloids that are her only reading material. Her brief encounter with a homosexual man—an anti-Fascist radio announcer (played by

Marcello Mastroianni) who lives in the same building and is about to be sent into political confinement—exposes all the painful limitations of her understanding of sexuality, gender roles, and sexual politics, portraying her as a prisoner of the Fascist regimentation of women's bodies and minds. As powerful as this film is, however, especially owing to the outstanding performances of the two lead actors, it falls, at least as far as the depiction of the woman is concerned, squarely within the stereotype of female "consensus" for the regime's policy of keeping women in the home, reinforcing patriarchal authority, and confining female destiny to childbearing. Although there is considerable truth to Scola's image of the Fascist woman, the film rests too easily within the terms of its own stereotype. Moreover, it indirectly ends up reinforcing the common notion that uneducated lower- and lower-middle-class women (and men) were more easily the victims of Fascist propaganda regarding gender roles than were upper-class or better-educated women and men, who are presumed to have held more enlightened positions.

Since Maria Antonietta Macciocchi's pioneering 1976 work on the Fascist woman (*La donna "nera"*), however, it has become increasingly clear that the Fascist construction of woman goes well beyond the simple and easily deconstructible formula of the *sposa e madre esemplare* (exemplary wife and mother) of Fascist propaganda. During the Fascist era, there were several competing, even contradictory, discourses on woman and sexual difference, rather than a single monolithic ideology.[4] These discourses changed considerably in the years between the early 1920s and the mid-1930s. Early Fascism not only advocated women's right to vote (a right that women in Italy actually gained only after the end of World War II), but, before 1925, was far from advancing the notion of woman as subaltern or reducible to the maternal role. Mussolini's speech of May 26, 1927, launching his new demographic campaign, marked the turning point in the regime's attitude toward women, inaugurating its policy of antifeminist repression, which symbolically may be said to have culminated in Mussolini's 1932 statement regarding the position of women in the Fascist state: "La donna deve obbedire. . . . La mia opinione della sua parte nello Stato è in opposizione ad ogni femminismo. Naturalmente essa non deve essere schiava, ma se io le concedessi il diritto elettorale mi si deriderebbe. Nel nostro Stato essa non deve contare [Woman must obey. . . . My idea of her role in the state is in opposition to all feminism. Naturally she shouldn't be a slave, but if I conceded her the vote, I'd be laughed at. In our state, she must not count]" (in Ludwig 1932; cited in Meldini 1975, 34–35).[5] Yet, as Elisabetta Mondello has shown in her thoughtful 1987 study on woman in Fascist discourse and in the popular press, the integrally antifeminist and authoritarian character of the regime's official vision of woman coexisted with much more complex and contradictory models of female behavior and gender roles in the so-called *stampa femminile* — especially in magazines such as *L'almanacco della donna italiana* and *Lidel*. Although not explicitly oppositional, these publications appealed to and contributed to the creation of a female readership that was much more emancipated and culturally open than the traditional iconography of the regime appeared to allow.[6]

The institutional misogyny of the regime, especially after its militarization in 1935, has been well documented by Victoria De Grazia in her monumental book, *How Fascism Ruled Women* (1992).[7] Like Mondello, De Grazia outlines a highly diversified range of female responses to the regime's policies toward women that goes well beyond the traditional notion of female consensus; she argues that only Gramsci's notion of "contradictory consciousness" can explain the complexity of the belief systems and the strategies pursued by women to come to terms with the dominant order (p. 14). Although she illustrates with punctilious precision the policies of the regime and its bias against women, De Grazia — and a large portion of the current scholarship on Italian Fascism, culture, and women — gives only scant attention to Fascist *theories* of woman, stating simply that the regime took it as axiomatic that women and men were different by nature, and politicized this difference to the advantage of males (p. 7).[8] This disregard for theory is a result of two common misconceptions, one regarding theory itself and the other regarding the ability of Fascism to produce a theory worthy of this name. According to the former, theory is a superstructural, abstract discourse, devoid of any real historical meaning or impact. At most it is a justification ex post facto of specific economic or social practices. Theory in and of itself therefore deserves little attention on the historian's part. According to the latter misconception, still common among Italian historians of Fascism, there can be by definition no authentic theory produced by Fascism because Fascism had no real culture (or literature). All it could produce was ideology, or propaganda. Elisabetta Mondello (1987) and Piero Meldini (1975) substantially subscribe to both prejudices when they argue that Fascist antifeminism at a theoretical level was only a secondhand rehash of stereotypes taken from nineteenth-century and turn-of-the-century misogynist thought, in particular the work of Lombroso and Mantegazza, as well as Nietzsche ("Woman is an enigma whose solution is called maternity"), Schopenhauer, Moebius, and Otto Weininger ("Women have neither existence nor essence, they are *not*; they are nothingness").[9]

An extension of the second prejudice—which denies the depth or resonance, or even the existence, of a Fascist "culture"—leads both Mondello and De Grazia to either ignore or dismiss the cultural production of futurist women writers, and of women writers in general. Mondello in particular acknowledges that women intellectuals were the privileged target of Fascist misogyny—portrayed as hysterical, perverted, sterile, masculinized, or homosexual—yet she suggests that no substantial form of cultural resistance developed among futurist women because, being too close to Fascism in the first place, they ended up internalizing completely its maternalist ideology (p. 51). De Grazia also takes an either/or stand toward women intellectuals under the Fascist regime, which is at odds with her claim to have adopted the Gramscian notion of "contradictory consciousness" as her theoretical framework. For De Grazia there was only *accommodation* to Fascism among women intellectuals (or self-annihilation).[10] The claim often made by cultural critics that significant forms of resistance *can* develop—even though unconnected to any explicit broader political design of subversion—in micropolitical practices and discourses on the margins or between the lines of the dominant order would seem unfounded in De Grazia's view.[11] In particular, no real form of feminist cultural resistance can be said to have actually developed in Italy during Fascism, she claims, because the effects of such supposed resistance on the larger system cannot be empirically proven (pp. 274–75).

It will have become clear at this point that, in my view, if we want to gain a less limited understanding of all the levels and complexities of the cultural construction of gender in the Fascist era, we need to consider the ways in which the hegemonic discourse of the regime finds philosophical as well as political and ideological grounding in its *theories* of gender. We also need to look at how the terms for a *different* construction of gender exist as well, at the margins of the regime's hegemonic discourse, in the micropolitical practices of literary writing by women, for example. My hypothesis is that whereas the former discourse not only legitimates the politics of the regime but also contributes to the foundation of the logic of its discrimination against women (and therefore needs to be taken seriously), the political effects of the latter constitute a kind of resistance to Fascist theories of gender at the "local" level—in other words, at the level of subjectivity and self-representation.

What better place to start a discussion of Fascist theories of woman than the work of the philosopher Giovanni Gentile? Gentile was a convinced supporter of Fascism and its most authoritative ideologue. As minister of public instruction between 1922 and 1924, he initiated major educational reform that was to have a strong impact on discrimination against women in Italian society during and after the Fascist era. Gentile was a member of the Fascist Grand Council from 1923 to 1929; he was the founder and president of the Italian Institute of Fascist Culture, the general editor of the monumental Giovanni Treccani *Italian Encyclopedia,* the director of the prestigious *Giornale critico della filosofia italiana,* and the major arbiter of Fascist cultural policies in the 1920s. In 1925 he drafted the famous "Manifesto of Fascist Intellectuals." The well-known 1932 article on Fascism in the encyclopedia that appeared under Mussolini's name was clearly derived from Gentile's work. Gentile was, in short, the official thinker of the regime, and he remained loyal to Mussolini to the very end.

Far from being a mere conglomerate of secondhand misogynist stereotypes from the turn of the century, Gentile's essay is to a large extent a careful, thoroughly constructed, and in many ways sophisticated argument about sexual difference, rather than about the inferiority of woman. Its principal rhetorical strategy is, as we shall see, the unmasking or deconstruction of paradox as prejudice, so that rather than the expression of a deviant logic, the paradox itself turns out to be the expression of a deeper, more authentically modern, and therefore superior cultural reason. Gentile's essay contains no direct mention of Fascism or the Fascist state, yet its theory of woman is entirely predicated on them. It starts out by stating that feminism is at present, fortunately, dead, and that it has therefore now become possible to speak of woman without taking either a feminist or antifeminist stand. Feminism is dead, in Gentile's view, because the notion of equal rights on which it was based has become obsolete. The philosophical foundation of the equal rights movement—the idea that individuals,

whether men or women, are endowed with certain fundamental, natural, rights that it is the task of elected representatives to guarantee
and protect—has been shown to be a fallacy, according to Gentile.
He therefore ironically begins his argument by showing how indeed—in the Fascist state—women are *not* inferior to men, for men
and women are equal: equal in having no rights at all. Gentile states
as a matter of fact, as if it were a historically verified, empirical
given, that men and women have been shown to have no rights, but
only duties: "doveri da adempiere, cioè non beni da godere, ma ide-
ali da realizzare con lo sforzo, con la lotta e col sacrificio, che trae il
singolo dal suo primitivo egoismo per fargli trovare la sua vera vita
fuori di sè [duties to fulfill, not goods to enjoy, but rather ideals to be
realized through one's efforts, through struggle and sacrifice, which
take the individual from his primitive egoism to make him find his
true life outside of himself]" (pp. 81–82). "Outside of oneself," or, in
other words, in the state. As will become increasingly clear, Gentile's
principal model in his assessment of woman is neither the misogyny
of Otto Weininger nor that of Walter Moebius, Nietzsche, or Schopenhauer. Rather, the relevant philosophical subtext is Hegel, who places
woman squarely within the economy of the family and, therefore, of
the state. For Gentile, the state *is* the Fascist state: there are no others.
The Fascist state represents a definitive break with the legacy of the Enlightenment and the French Revolution, and indeed, it has superseded
all forms of democratic state, becoming the sole truly *modern* form
of government. Let's not forget that the title of his essay is "Woman
in *Modern* Consciousness," in which *Fascist* and *modern* are meant
to be synonyms. We shall also see shortly that *consciousness* is synonymous with *male consciousness* for Gentile.

The death of feminism and of the equal rights movement is, Gentile claims, a fundamental achievement of modernity because it has
restored the sharply defined *difference* between man and woman,
which had become blurred in the years of the development of the
women's movement, when the "false and ridiculous ideal" of a *donna-
uomo* (woman-man) and even of a "third sex" had developed (pp. 82–
83). The maintenance of difference—sexual and gender difference
first and foremost—as a strong, sharply defined, either/or binary
logic is fundamental to the Fascist philosopher. The blurring of this
difference threatens to weaken, if not abolish, modern, or in other
words Fascist, consciousness, and the Fascist state. Indeed, we are only

now beginning to understand more clearly through feminist and gender studies just *how* central the ideology of gender difference as a binary logic is to the construction of racial and class difference as well, at all levels of social and political discourse. The weakening or blurring of gender difference was a threat to the entire Fascist hierarchy of values. The demographic campaign launched by Mussolini in 1927, for example, which was intended to refeminize women by taking them away from the workplace and other masculinizing positions and restoring them to their proper role of childbearers for the race, was stimulated in part by the paranoid perception that people of other, "inferior" races were reproducing themselves much too quickly and were threatening to overwhelm the white and Latin races.[12] In Gentile's discussion of woman, therefore, much more is at stake than the need to keep women in their place; the entire Fascist ideological edifice may be said to hinge on the point of gender difference.

Yet, unlike what one might expect based on superficial assessments of the Fascist vision of woman, Gentile's position is far from being a variant of a predictably vulgar biological essentialism. On the contrary, Gentile elaborates his own theory of woman's, and of gender, difference, as a historical and *cultural formation,* rather than a biological given. For Gentile, woman possesses entirely the humanity of man; she *is* man, in other words, "but in a different form: a difference which is the limit of her sex" (p. 83). Difference as limit, then. But what exactly is the nature of this limit? Is it purely a physiological limit? asks Gentile. The answer is no. The limit that constitutes the otherness, the difference, of woman, is, for Gentile, a cultural construction: "Questo limite, che non è ... un limite naturale, ma un concetto, un modo di pensare e quindi di sentire, si viene determinando in funzione della concezione morale della vita; la quale a sua volta, si sviluppa con lo svolgimento della cultura [This limit, which is not ... a natural limit, but a concept, a way of thinking and therefore of feeling, is determined as a consequence of a moral conception of life, which in turn takes form with the development of culture]" (p. 84). Yet this limit, which separates woman from man, although it is not to be understood as an intrinsic limitation or inferiority of woman, is a form of otherness with respect to *man*; it is what, by making woman *the other* of man, makes her desirable.

I do not need to emphasize how male centered, in spite of all his universalizing pretensions, Gentile's perspective (and his conception of gender and desire) is. Desire seems to be exclusively male; there is no such thing as female desire, or consciousness, or subjectivity, apparently. In acknowledging this, however, we must also observe that more modern and presumably more enlightened theories of desire, consciousness, and subjectivity, such as Lacan's, are really not that far removed from Gentile's position. The female body in itself does not exist, argues Gentile in a paradox worthy of Lacan: the female body as different and other exists only insofar as it becomes the object of male desire. "La verità è che questo corpo materiale (anatomico e fisiologico) nella donna che si ama, che si cerca come donna, che si vede come tale, non esiste.... [Esso] è sempre vita spirituale perchè si attua mediante il sentimento e l'intelligenza. La differenza che fa cercare all'uomo il suo altro nella donna è bensì anche fisiologica, ma elevata a differenza spirituale [The truth is that this material body (anatomical and physiological) of the woman one loves, the woman one looks for as woman, who is seen as a woman, does not exist.... This body is always spiritual because it becomes real through man's feeling and intelligence. The difference that makes man seek his other in woman is, to be sure, physiological to an extent, but elevated to spiritual difference]" (p.84).

Although Gentile provides us with a cultural, rather than biological or essentialist, definition of gender difference, his definition of culture is implicitly univocal and totalitarian. There is only one authentically modern culture (just as there is only one truly modern state), and that is, implicitly, Fascist culture. This culture is—it must be remembered—perceived as the culture of a specific race, the Latin race, in its difference and opposition to all other races. It is in this and only this culture, in this and only this state, that ethics and politics coincide, and individuals—both as men and women and as members of a social class—find themselves fulfilled and realize their freedom. The woman and the slave (Gentile discusses them in the same paragraph) are redeemed not when they are actually freed from their subjection (which is only apparent), but when both they and their master understand that this subjection is really the expression of their inner freedom and dignity. By the same token, woman actually *loses* her individuality at the very moment when she seems to acquire it, for a woman is an individual only when and if she belongs to a man: her individuality corresponds to her position as a man's woman (her being his mother, wife, or the mother of his children): "La donna . . . è del marito, ed è quello che è in quanto è di lui [Woman belongs to her husband, and is what she is because she is his]" (p. 92). Every healthy and well-ordered society, Gentile argues, following once again in Hegel's footsteps, has at its core the family and religion, and it is the woman who acts as the principal agent and guarantor of the ethics and sanctity of the family. In the more virile ages of antiquity, woman belonged in the home, Gentile claims, and in the home, spiritually if not materially, remains the woman to whom modern man pays homage.

Gentile's essay culminates in the exaltation of woman as mother. Although the unmasking of paradox as prejudice is still the dominant strategy, there is a curious break in the essay's tone and language at this point, as Gentile tries to move from a discussion of love between man and woman to a discussion of maternal love. The philosophical, almost technical discourse of the opening pages turns into a fragmented rhetoric that abandons rational or pseudorational argumentation in favor of a melange of clichéd literary citations from Dante, Petrarch, Leopardi, and the Gospels, as well as mystical images and even popular sayings, such as "Di mamma ce n'è una sola [You only have one mother]." This rhetorical and stylistic breakdown is symptomatic perhaps of a cultural schizophrenia that still afflicts Italian men in their veneration for their mothers and their difficulty in mediating between images of woman as mother and images of woman as erotic object. Motherhood is the holiness that makes of woman the self-sacrificing link between man and God, Gentile states. Motherhood is, furthermore, something innate, original, and essential to woman, to the point that every virgin is also by definition already a mother. Those who do not respect this quality of "virginal motherhood" in woman, of which the Virgin Mary is the noblest emblem, destroy the woman in woman, and extinguish love in the world, Gentile concludes. (Earlier on, he inveighs against those who "materialize woman, and thus extinguish the ideal light that suffuses her head with a halo, and defends her from the bestial perversions of sexual life"; p. 87.) Thus the essentialism that was surprisingly lacking in Gentile's original definition of sexual difference in the opening pages of the essay makes its return with a vengeance. It is as if the need to legitimate the maternalist ideology of the regime forced the author, at a loss for terms of a coherent or even apparently coherent rational argument, to lapse back into a language of suggestiveness and emotionalism—the very rhetoric the regime commonly used to obfuscate the real issues behind its coercive policies.

The second Fascist theory of gender that I wish to analyze briefly is found in *Politica della famiglia,* by the young, ambitious, right-wing Fascist sociologist Ferdinando Loffredo (1938). Loffredo's discussion, which is part of an extended study of the "demographic problem," represents a more brutal, pragmatic approach to the question of woman. For Loffredo—unlike Gentile—there is no question that sexual and gender difference actually translates into a definite *inferiority* of woman, rather than, as Gentile delicately puts it, a complementarity. Yet there is an essential continuity between the two thinkers as well, and the latter actually helps to clarify the ideological implications of the former's more abstract and apparently disinterested discourse. Furthermore, Loffredo's radical approach to the question of woman and his critique from the right of current Fascist policies regarding the education and social roles of women reveal the Fascist technologies of gender to have been less monolithic and univocal, and much more complex and contradictory, than is often assumed. Also, once again, the notion that Fascist misogyny is purely a convenient reworking of nineteenth-century and turn-of-the-century stereotypes about the inferiority of woman turns out to be mistaken. Although these stereotypes are indeed present in Loffredo, and may in fact be said to constitute the deeper ideological structure of his argument, their rhetorical efficacy—that which turns them into the components of a Fascist technology of gender—is predicated on their being reworked into the language of scientific theory.

Loffredo's text, with several footnotes on almost every page, presents itself as a sociological treatise based on a careful examination of demographic statistics and the most recent international literature in English, French, and German on the family and the condition of woman in contemporary societies. Its principal argument is that the emancipation of women—their being allowed to be educated and to work outside the home—has had devastating consequences for all modern societies. These consequences include not only a dangerous decline in birthrates, but also the physical and spiritual alienation of women, their estrangement from the home and family life. Loffredo strikes at the very heart of the contradictions in the Fascist regime's policy toward women. Fascist Italy, he argues, is to a considerable degree free of the devastating consequences of female emancipation that plague countries such as France and the Soviet Union. For example, no Italian minister is compelled to address women as members of political parties, no feminist association is in a position to challenge the hierarchical structure of the family, and no equal rights law is ever likely to be proposed, Loffredo states (p. 349). Nevertheless, he continues, even the limited degree of female emancipation that the regime has allowed has had a negative impact and poses a threat to its survival. Only the blind, feverish rhythm of modern civilization, with its ever-faster economic development, can explain the success of the otherwise contradictory and degenerate notion that two beings such as man and woman, different by nature and destined to have entirely different functions, should receive the same kind of education and cultural formation:

> La donna, costituita in modo da maturare nel suo corpo il figlio, per i tre quarti di un anno, costituita in modo da poter nutrire il figlio, con una secrezione del suo organismo, per oltre un anno, dotata di qualità che la rendono adatta ad allevare ed educare il figlio almeno fino alla adolescenza, ciononostante riceve, nella nostra civiltà, la stessa istruzione che riceverebbe se le sue funzioni fossero eguali a quelle dell'uomo.

> [Woman, made to ripen a child within her body for three-quarters of the year, made to nourish this child, with a secretion of her organism, for longer than a year, endowed with qualities that make her able to raise and educate the child at least through adolescence, nevertheless receives, in our civilization, the same education as if her functions were equal to man's.] (p. 351)

It is hard to imagine a more concisely brutal definition of woman's biological destiny. Yet Loffredo's statement is interesting also because it testifies to a dissent from the right regarding Fascism's allegiance to capitalism, and the way it has allowed the traditional family structure to be altered by the need to bring women into the workforce. Loffredo declares the invention of the typewriter one of the most pernicious events leading to the dissolution of the family structure. He even opposes women's sports, on the grounds that they take woman outside the home and lead to an overestimation of the attractiveness of the body. Moreover, sports endanger the female reproductive apparatus and waste physical energies that should be devoted to childbearing (p. 359).

Loffredo concludes his argument by making a series of proposals for changes that must be enacted if the regime is to protect the interests of the state and forestall its own degeneration. First and foremost is the "restaurazione della sudditanza culturale-intellettuale [restoration of the intellectual and cultural subjection]" of woman to man: "La donna deve tornare sotto la sudditanza assoluta dell'uomo: padre o marito; sudditanza, e quindi inferiorità: spirituale, culturale ed economica [Woman must return to a state of absolute subjection to man: father or husband; subjection and therefore inferiority: spiritual, cultural and economic]" (p. 369). Professional and secondary school instruction for women must be forbidden. Special educational programs for women must be initiated that are geared toward making them excellent housewives and homemakers. Home economics must be the fundamental subject of instruction, and it must emphasize the priority and nobility of manual labor in the home (p. 361). The right of women to work outside of the home must be reversed juridically by the Fascist state into a right of women *not* to work and, at the same time, public opinion must be influenced to condemn "la donna che— senza la più assoluta e comprovata necessità—lascia le pareti domestiche per recarsi al lavoro, la donna che, in promiscuità con l'uomo, gira per le strade, sui trams, sugli autobus, vive nelle officine e negli uffici [the woman who—without the utmost and proven necessity— leaves the domestic walls to go to work, the woman who lives in promiscuous contact with man, goes around in the streets, on trams, on buses, lives in factories and offices]." Loffredo evokes, in short, as his ideal, the image of a woman segregated in the home, buried alive, an image that will return, in a parodic key, in Masino's (1982) wonderful novel on the *massaia*.

There was arguably a strong sexual bias in Fascist schools, and schools with exclusively or almost exclusively female constituencies did exist—such as the short-lived *liceo femminile* and the vocational schools for secretaries and clerical workers. However, as Victoria De Grazia (1992) has shown, the regime never actually segregated or excluded women.[13] Women were not barred from any branch or level of the educational system, a system that produced, for example, the Nobel Prize winner Rita Levi Montalcini and women such as Natalia

Ginzburg and Elsa Morante. The main axis of discrimination after the Gentile reform was across social class rather than gender difference (although this of course meant that lower-class women were doubly discriminated against, and had the highest illiteracy rates); only the elite were promoted, so as not to overload the market for intellectual labor. In 1939, the year after the publication of Loffredo's *Politica della famiglia,* a new school charter drafted by Giuseppe Bottai — the minister of education and author of a lukewarm preface to Loffredo's book — proposed a series of reforms to correct the Gentile laws and to create special schools for women that would "prepare them spiritually for running households and teaching in nursery schools." None of this ever actually happened. Indeed, Bottai affirmed in the charter that such institutes could be implemented only as "the corporative order defined the new direction of female labor" (De Grazia 1992, 156). Pending such a time — which, with the events of mobilization for war, Bottai implied, was clearly not at hand — things continued as they were and women remained, at least theoretically, able to attend any school they wanted.

If Gentile and Loffredo represent, respectively, the more moderate and the more radical facets of the Fascist theory of gender, and show us, the former from within institutionally sanctioned discourse, the latter from outside, how theory functions as a technology of gender, the evidence of these theories' resonance within the body of social discourse lies not only in the actual policies of the regime toward women, but also in the ways in which the antifeminist challenge posed by these theories elicited responses, and generated countertechnologies, in the micropolitical discursive practices of, for example, women writers.

Avant-Garde Women Artists and Countertechnologies of Gender

It is not coincidental that we find the most radical expression of alternative modes of constructing gender difference in the practice of avant-garde, experimental women writers and artists, rather than in the work of more traditional authors who followed prescribed formal and generic conventions.[14] Ironically obscured by the fame (or infamy) of her husband, Filippo Tommaso Marinetti, whose own views on Fascism as well as feminism are still the subject of a lively critical debate, Benedetta's novels and graphic illustrations have received little attention, or they have been assumed to subscribe entirely to the anti-feminist and maternalist ideology of the regime.[15] Yet even a summary reading of two of her experimental works, *Le forze umane* and *Il viaggio di Gararà*, reveals quite a different picture. Although they are very different, the central theme of both works is female creativity and desire—a theme that in itself, if we think back on Gentile's and especially Loffredo's texts, is practically heretical. *Le forze umane* starts out as an autobiographical narrative about the author's childhood, the trauma of her father's mental illness and death following the war, and her first confrontation with poverty, ignorance, and social injustice when—while still pursuing her degree in education—she teaches underprivileged children. The narration of facts and events is reduced to a minimum, however, almost a bare outline, written in short, paratactic sentences, often of only one or two words, with fragments of dialogue. The task of communicating the meaning of the events narrated and of the feelings evoked by them in the narrator is entrusted to a series of abstract graphic tables that are interspersed throughout the text and bear equally abstract titles. "Sforzo differenziatore" (Differentiating effort), "Diversità raggiunte" (Diversities achieved), "Ironia" (Irony), "L'io ottimista fra le rotaie del pessimismo" (The optimistic I between the tracks of pessimism), and "Armonia di forze dissimili" (Harmony of dissimilar forces) are some of them. The tables represent a kind of abstract visual writing, an attempt to express meaning directly through the graphic mark on the page, and they constitute an original and personal variant of futurist experimentation with visual poetry.

What is most striking about this combination of visual and written text, however, is that in telling the story of the formation of her self as a complete and unified entity ("Sogno di creare il mio spirito in armonia perfetta, uno in sè e completo [I dream of creating my spirit in perfect harmony, one in itself, and complete]"), Benedetta is implicitly rejecting Gentile's thesis that the female self is but the completion of the male, and that woman exists only as the other of man. Indeed, Benedetta implies that her self-formation can take place only in conjunction with the loss—no matter how painful—of the dominant father figure in her life. Furthermore, as the title indicates, Benedetta takes her experience of self-formation as a paradigm of the development of human consciousness, male *and* female, thus undermining both Gentile's and Loffredo's notion of the primacy of male consciousness. When desire and love come to interfere with the sense of her inner unity and self-fulfillment, the narrator tells of her struggle to overcome the resistance of the self to accept another, staging a kind of dialogic passion play between the allegorical figures of "Unity" and "Love." Finally, contrary to the Fascist vision of female subordination, Benedetta envisions the relationship of man and woman as a conscious relationship between equals, the contact and eventual fusion of two equally powerful "nuclei," body as well as mind. It is from this fusion that a child will be born, Benedetta adds, devoting only one short paragraph to this privileged topic of the Fascist theory of woman, and thus decentering and demystifying it. The text ends with a self-reflexive celebration of her own writing and art as the true expression of her creativity, and of what she calls the "identità di volontà e di materia nello spirito divenuto realtà [identity of will and matter in the spirit become reality]" (p. 144).

In *Le forze umane,* and even more so in *Gararà,* Benedetta carries out a double process of denaturalization. She denaturalizes woman in that she removes her from the sphere of the biological and the maternal, which are her only natural place according to the Fascist technologies of gender, and recasts her in a more complex role as cultural agent and creator; she denaturalizes writing by pushing it toward the realm of graphic abstraction, which requires the reader's creative interpretation rather than a simple decoding and, at the same time, makes the reader aware of the arbitrary and conventional nature of graphic and linguistic signs. This work of estrangement and denaturalization becomes even more radical in *Gararà,* a very difficult text to read and understand because it is almost entirely nonanthropocentric, lacking human characters as they are normally conceived in traditional narrative. In fact, Benedetta calls this work a "cosmic drama," for it fuses narrative with theatrical spectacle, music, and drawing in a great allegorical representation about the shortcomings of Enlightenment reason and rationality in its attempts to control and quantify matter and to master desire. Devoid of human characters until just before the conclusion, the text stages nonhuman agents such as Matter (Mata), Reason (the dwarfish Gararà, with legs made out of a compass), Quantity, Colors (*Gli Allegri,* or Little Joyful Ones), Desire, Light, and Fire. Just before the end, after the demise and dissolution of Gararà, the *Allegri* tell the story of how a young girl, *la fanciulla,* discovers creativity and succeeds in reinventing herself and the world. It is as if in order to emerge from the prisonhouse of the Fascist technologies of gender and to envision the coming into being of an entirely different kind of woman, the entire edifice of Enlightenment rationality, with its pretenses of universality and its nightmarish involution in the totalitarian state, had to — as in Horkheimer and Adorno's critique of the "dialectics of enlightenment" — be reevaluated as dangerously spurious and illusory.

Although Paola Masino's mock-heroic novel *Nascita e morte della massaia,* written in 1938–39, is not as radical in formal terms as either of Benedetta's texts, it is nevertheless experimental in its use of alienation devices such as doubling, a Brechtian kind of theatricality, interpolated narratives, and paradoxical situations bordering on the surreal and the fantastic. The novel starts with a premise worthy of Calvino's *Barone rampante* (The baron in the trees): the protagonist, a young girl from a wealthy upper-middle-class family, refuses to live with her siblings and chooses to spend her life shut off in a trunk, reading, writing, and eating moldy bread crusts. She does so because she intuits what awaits her if she comes out and becomes a woman. She is expected to become a homemaker, a mother, and above all a *massaia,* a domestic worker and careful administrator of the home, and to that form of enslavement she prefers remaining in her trunk, where she is free to read, write, and dream. Unlike Calvino's protagonist, however, who spends (almost) his entire life up in the trees, she does not stick to her pronouncement and finally emerges — enticed by her mother — to take part in the ball (the greatest comic scene in the novel) celebrating her debut into society. The debut marks the beginning of her adventures as a rebel in a world bent on normalizing her and making her a *sposa e madre esemplare* (an exemplary wife and mother). "Stai tranquilla. Sarò normale [Don't worry. I will be normal]" (p. 43), she announces to her mother during the party. The entire novel is precisely about this quest for normalization (as in a kind of mock-heroic female version of Moravia's *The Conformist*) and its impossibility.

The Massaia (we never learn her real name; she is just "la Massaia") marries a rich uncle and moves with him to the provinces, where he has a mansion full of servants whom it is her duty to instruct and rule over with the utmost watchfulness and discipline, so that there will be no waste and the entire household will function like clockwork. Despite the fact that she has all these servants, and partly because of it, she is a slave in her own house, bound to a merciless system of coercion and control that leaves her no time for anything else. Masino clearly chose an upper-class *massaia* as her protagonist precisely with the aim of dramatizing the issue of subjection and subordination—issues that are central to both Gentile's and Loffredo's visions of woman's role in the family and the state. The key role of Masino's Massaia is that of ruling over the servants while being ruled over by her husband as a kind of servant herself.

During her life as a *massaia,* the protagonist often wishes she were back inside her trunk: "Quando uscii da là...ero quella di oggi, per sempre; imbalsamata, dentro [When I came out of there...I became what I am today; embalmed forever, inside]," she reflects toward the end of the narrative. Her encounter with the home is a progressive enslavement. The regime of the home, even its very physical being, its furniture and layout, turn out to be a reflection of the hierarchy and bureaucracy of the Fascist state:

La donna vedeva benissimo i mobili intorno a sé. Erano mobili senza vita, ostinatamente mobili: non ne volevano sapere di essere stati alberi vivi, non ricordavano il grembo del cielo e della terra. Ora si sentivano saliti di un grado, a fare i servi degli uomini. Avevano ognuno una funzione e ci tenevano. La poltrona tiene a distanza lo sgabello, il letto matrimoniale la branda, la brocca ha ai suoi ordini una centuria di bicchieri, la pentola grande urta la piccina, le candele stanno sull'attenti davanti alla lampada a diffusore. La gerarchia è un fatto cosmico, si comincia dai cherubini e si finisce agli uscieri, ma crederci è gratuito: la sposa non ci credeva, o per meglio dire, fin qui, la aveva ignorata. Soltanto, durante i primi giorni della sua nuova vita si era accorta dell'importanza della burocrazia, sociale e domestica.

[The woman saw the furniture around her perfectly well. It was lifeless furniture, stubbornly furniture: it did not want to know anything about once having been living trees, it did not remember the cradle of the sky and the earth. Now these pieces of furniture felt promoted, having become the servants of men. Each had its function and was proud of it. The chair keeps the stool at a distance, the double bed keeps away from the camp-bed, the pitcher has a hundred glasses under it, the large pot beats the small one, the candles stand at attention in front of the lamp. Hierarchy is a cosmic fact, from angels to ushers, but to believe in it is gratuitous: the new bride did not believe in it, or, rather, up to now, she had known nothing about it. Only during the first few days of her new life had she realized the importance of bureaucracy, social and domestic.] (p. 65)

As her metamorphosis into a *massaia* progresses, the protagonist is overtaken by a cleaning frenzy, and her vision becomes wholly saturated with the concerns of home economics: "A poco a poco non vide intorno a sé che cose da governare: traverso gli uomini le pareti che li proteggono, nella voce delle donne le masserizie cui soprintendono [Little by little she saw only things around her that needed straightening up: through men she saw the walls that protect them, and in women's voices the things and goods that they must oversee]" (p. 70). But the metamorphosis is never wholly achieved, and an inner conflict develops in the Massaia between insubordination and the pressure to conform. She holds heretical views on politics, power, and modern capitalism, and she derides the Fascist rhetoric of motherhood, yet the voice of ideological insubordination is constantly checked and held back by a form of self-censorship. In a sequence that is a triumph of comic estrangement, the imperatives of home economics and the housewife's duties seem to come to her from the most unlikely sources, including an opera by Igor Stravinsky, Goethe's *Faust*, and Beethoven's diaries. Central to this sequence and to the entire novel is the notion that the need one feels as a subject to take on a specific gender and social position is far from a "natural" process. Rather, it the product of a complex discursive dialectic that is essentially linguistic: "Vedi come le cose degli uomini sono coerenti," the Massaia reflects at one point. "Scegli una parte e te ne nasce subito il linguaggio: adopera un linguaggio e susciti in te l'individuo cui tal linguaggio appartiene [See how coherent human things are. You choose a role and immediately its language emerges in you: you use a language and you gather up within you the kind of individual to whom that language belongs]"(p. 215).

The conflict between the impulse to conform and the urge to rebel generates an actual splitting of the Massaia, who at various stages during the novel actually meets with her double, who is apparently the obedient half of her personality. Even her obedient double, however, eventually refuses the role of housewife. Increasingly, as she perfects her housewife skills, the Massaia feels alternately the wish for her home, and even the entire nation and race, to disappear and the desire to die herself. In one of her attempts at escape, during which, as in a parody of the medieval errant knights, she travels without a precise goal, she looks at the men who travel with her in the same train or airplane with a feeling of horror: "Li guatava e li vedeva in funzione di mariti, di padri, di fratelli, dunque di aguzzini delle donne: coloro che riducono le fanciulle in massaie, che portano camicie i cui bottoni oltre la stoffa agganciano e chiudono per sempre i cervelli delle mogli [She glanced at them and saw them as husbands, fathers, brothers, or, in other words, torturers of women: those who turn young girls into housewives, those who wear shirts whose buttons, besides the cloth, hook onto and close forever the brains of their wives]" (p. 248). Finally the Massaia, after having achieved perfection and even fame as one of the most accomplished housewives and charity ladies in the country, goes insane. Only then, and for a brief time before her death, does she experience freedom once again, roaming through the city and seeing it as a fantastic projection of her imagination.

The Fascist censors read Masino's book in proofs, and judged it to be cynical and defeatist, although they did not prohibit its publication. They only asked that all references to authorities, public figures, national institutions, the church, and the Bible be removed, as well as all irreverent uses of words such as *patria* (fatherland), and *nazione* (nation). All specific allusions to Italy that made the locale of the novel recognizable also had to be cut out. Thus purified, the book was about to come out in 1939 when a fire caused by an aerial bombardment in Milan destroyed the warehouse where all the copies were stored. The book was to appear only in 1945, reconstructed in part by the author from memory on the basis of the surviving proofs.

Certainly works such as Benedetta's and Masino's fully deserve to be read for their literary qualities and originality, and deserve to enter the canon of modern Italian literature next to other great works of the 1920s and 1930s such as Alberto Moravia's *Gli indifferenti* (Time of indifference) and Carlo Emilio Gadda's earlier fiction. Moreover, reading the experimental writing women produced as expressions of a "countertechnology" of gender, with and against Fascist theories of gender such as Gentile's and Loffredo's, can help us not only to see these texts and their contexts in their fuller ideological and political implications, but also to gain a deeper understanding of how literature itself can be a form of political praxis.

Notes

Unless otherwise noted, all translations in this chapter are my own.

1. I have chosen these texts in particular because they typify the spectrum of Fascist theorizations of woman. Although it belongs in part to the same category, the monumental *Rivolta contro il mondo moderno* (1935), by the "mystical" and controversial (to Fascist "orthodoxy" during the *ventennio*, and still today in light of his unexpected revival among young neo-Fascists) theorist Julius Evola, is highly idiosyncratic in its attempt to introduce Oriental philosophies (Hinduism, Taoism) into Italian culture, and deserves a fuller investigation of its own.

2. I mean *resistance* as Foucault does, not necessarily as an organized, collective political struggle, but rather as a form of opposition that, like power itself, can arise and become manifest in a multiplicity of diverse discursive fields. The relation between the discourses of power and of resistance is, to be sure, complex and ambivalent; the very nature of discourse allows no resistance without complicity. Yet, as Foucault (1978) writes in *The History of Sexuality*, "We must make allowance for the complex and unstable process whereby discourse can be both an instrument and an effect of power, but also a hindrance; a stumbling block, a point of resistance and a starting point for an opening strategy" (pp. 100–101). For a feminist critical discussion (and critique) of Foucault's notion of resistance, see McNay (1992) and the essays in Diamond and Quinby (1988). In particular, Jana Sawicki (1988) argues that "if relations of power are dispersed and fragmented throughout the social field, so must resistance to power be.... Freedom lies in our capacity to discover the historical links between certain modes of self-understanding and modes of domination, and to resist the ways in which we have already been classified and identified by dominant discourses. This means discovering new ways of understanding ourselves and each other, refusing to accept the dominant culture's characterization of our practices and desires, and redefining them from within resistant cultures" (pp. 185–86). For an interesting use of a similar notion of resistance in the practices of women's everyday life and oral culture under Fascism, see Passerini (1984).

3. Masino's novel was recently republished by La Tartaruga in its esteemed Novecento series.

4. On the "duplicity," "ambiguity," and contradictory nature of the Fascist vision of gender difference, women's roles, and sexuality, see Zunino (1985, 294–99). Zunino points out in particular that the mythology of female virtue and the puritan ideology of the regime propagated by the press were intended for and addressed to the "masses," whereas different, even opposite, codes of behavior were implicitly reserved for the elites.

5. On the importance of Mussolini's so-called Discorso dell'Ascensione of 1927, announcing the demographic campaign that would shape the entire course of Fascism's policy toward women, see Santarelli (1976).

6. According to Zunino (1985, 290–93), the initial ideology of activism in the first decade of the regime, and its promise of universal transformation, encouraged the development of a dissonant, tentative new "feminism" within Fascism itself (he cites in particular the newspaper editorials by Maria Villavecchia and Teresa Labriola) that ran counter to the more traditionalist official views and was soon to be vehemently rebuked in the press. On Fascist feminism, see also De Grand (1976, 955–56) and Follacchio (1988).

7. See also Alexander De Grand's "Women under Italian Fascism" (1976), Piero Meldini's *Sposa e madre esemplare* (1975) (which includes an anthology of Fascist

articles and pronouncements on woman, unfortunately excerpted without much regard to context), and the extremely useful and diverse 1988 collection of historical and cultural analyses of various facets of women's lives and responses to Fascism in *La corporazione delle donne* (The women's corporations), edited and with an introductory essay by Marina Addis Saba. Specifically on the question of consensus, see Mario Marazzitti and Roberto Sani (1986). In her "Unseduced Mothers" (1990–91), Robin Pickering-Iazzi proposes an interesting reading of models of female behavior that opposed or countered the Fascist "woman-mother" in the practices of everyday life and in short fiction by women published on the cultural "third page" of the Italian daily press. For an overview of the scholarship on women and Fascism until 1985, see Bartolini (1985).

8. De Grazia gives only a brief reading of Gentile's essay on woman, interpreting it as being entirely and avowedly antifemale (p. 152). A similar disregard for the specificity and significance of Fascist theories of woman can be found, for example, in De Grand (1976), Caldwell (1986), and, most recently, in Cannistraro and Sullivan's (1993) biography of Margherita Sarfatti. Zunino (1985) acknowledges the contradictory complexity of the regime's discourse on woman and sexuality, but offers no sustained analysis, providing rather a quick overview of some of the prevalent traditionalist and antifeminist views in the press of the period.

9. See Mondello (1987, 26–27). According to Caldwell (1986), on the other hand, Fascist attitudes toward women were only an extension of the traditional Catholic views of womanhood and woman's maternal role.

10. "It seems no coincidence that the years 1924, 1927, and 1928 registered the highest number of female suicides in modern Italy," De Grazia (1992, 240) points out.

11. On this point, see De Grazia's debate with Luisa Passerini in "Alle origini della cultura di massa: Cultura popolare e fascismo in Italia" (1983, especially pp. 19–22). Summarizing some of the findings in her research on oral popular culture, and especially the comic spirit, in Turin under Fascism, Passerini outlines a notion of cultural "resistance" that is neither a form of organized struggle nor explicit political action, but consists rather of momentary, spontaneous acts of communication (for example, jokes or graffiti) that "break" with the orthodoxy of the regime and demystify it. This type of discursive resistance, she points out, often goes hand in hand with forms of pragmatic acceptance of the regime, and is marked by deep ambivalence. Nevertheless, it cannot be ignored or dismissed, for, according to Passerini, even though it may not be *directly* productive of political action, it has on the one hand an autonomous value, and on the other hand it can function as a base for other forms of resistance that have a clearer impact on the political sphere.

12. See, for example, Loffredo (1938), who claims that "l'esperienza ha dimostrato che l'apporto dato dalla donna emancipata allo sviluppo della civiltà è negativo; la emancipazione della donna, mentre non ha prodotto vantaggi apprezzabili nel campo delle scienze e delle arti, costituisce il più certo pericolo di distruzione per tutto quanto la civiltà bianca ha finora prodotto [experience has shown that the contribution given by emancipated woman to the development of civilization is a negative one; the emancipation of woman has failed to produce any appreciable advantages in the sciences and the arts, and it constitutes the most certain danger of destruction for all that white civilization has produced thus far]" (p. 369).

13. Women were, however, barred at various points from teaching in certain fields, such as Latin, Greek, and history, and from occupying certain posts, such as *preside* of technical institutes (see De Grazia 1992, 153).

14. For a view of how more "traditional" women writers also challenged both the canon and traditional notions of gender difference, see Robin Pickering-Iazzi's afterword to *Unspeakable Women* (1993).

15. See, for example, Mondello (1987, 33–51) and Nozzoli (1978, 61). For a different view, see my "Futurism and Feminism" (1989). Marinetti is often still invoked as the sole or principal signifier of futurism, of the politics of the avant-garde in Italy, and of futurism's dealings with Fascism. See, for example, Schnapp (1990), Hewitt (1993), and Golsan (1992).

Works Cited

Addis Saba, Marina, ed. 1988. *La corporazione delle donne: Ricerche e studi sui modelli femminili nel ventennio fascista*. Florence: Vallecchi.

Bartolini, Stefania. 1985. "Le donne sotto il fascismo." *Memoria* 10: 124–32.

Benedetta [Cappa Marinetti, Benedetta]. 1924. *Le forze umane: Romanzo astratto con sintesi grafiche*. Foligno: Campitelli.

———. 1931. *Il viaggio di Gararà: Romanzo cosmico per teatro*. Milan: Monreale.

Caldwell, Lesley. 1986. "Reproducers of the Nation: Women and the Family in Fascist Policy." In *Rethinking Italian Fascism: Capitalism, Populism and Culture*. Edited by David Forgacs. London: Lawrence & Wishart.

Cannistraro, Philip V., and Brian R. Sullivan. 1993. *Il Duce's Other Woman*. New York: William Morrow.

De Grand, Alexander. 1976. "Women under Italian Fascism." *Historical Journal* 19: 947–68.

De Grazia, Victoria. 1992. *How Fascism Ruled Women: Italy, 1922–1945*. Berkeley: University of California Press.

De Grazia, Victoria, and Luisa Passerini. 1983. "Alle origini della cultura di massa: Cultura popolare e fascismo in Italia" (dialogue edited by Amalia Signorelli). *La Ricerca Folklorica* 7: 19–25.

De Lauretis, Teresa. 1987. *Technologies of Gender: Essays on Theory, Film, and Fiction*. Bloomington: Indiana University Press.

Diamond, Irene, and Lee Quinby, eds. 1988. *Feminism and Foucault: Reflections on Resistance*. Boston: Northeastern University Press.

Evola, Julius. 1935. *Rivolta contro il mondo moderno*. Milan: Hoepli.

Follacchio, Sara. 1988. "Conversando di femminismo: 'La donna italiana.'" In *La corporazione delle donne: Ricerche e studi sui modelli femminili nel ventennio fascista*. Edited by Marina Addis Saba. Florence: Vallecchi.

Foucault, Michel. 1978. *The History of Sexuality* (vol. 1) *An Introduction*. Translated by Robert Hurley. New York: Pantheon.

Gentile, Giovanni. 1969. "La donna nella coscienza moderna." In *Preliminari allo studio del fanciullo*. Florence: Sansoni. Originally published 1934.

Golsan, Richard J., ed. 1992. *Fascism, Aesthetics, and Culture*. Hanover: University Press of New England.

Hewitt, Andrew. 1993. *Fascist Modernism: Aesthetics, Politics, and the Avant-Garde*. Stanford: Stanford University Press.

Loffredo, Ferdinando. 1938. *Politica della famiglia*. Milan: Bompiani.

Ludwig, Emil. 1932. *Colloqui con Mussolini*. Verona: Mondadori.

Macciocchi, Maria Antonietta. 1976. *La donna "nera": "Consenso" femminile e fascismo*. Milan: Feltrinelli.

Marazzitti, Mario, and Roberto Sani. 1986. "La cooperazione femminile nel periodo fascista: Ideologia e esperienza." In *L'audacia insolente: La cooperazione femminile 1886–1986.* Venice: Marsilio.

Masino, Paola. 1982. *Nascita e morte della massaia.* Milan: La Tartaruga. Originally published 1939.

McNay, Lois. 1992. *Foucault Feminism.* Boston: Northeastern University Press.

Meldini, Piero, ed. 1975. *Sposa e madre esemplare: Ideologia e politica della donna e della famiglia durante il fascismo.* Florence: Guaraldi.

Mondello, Elisabetta. 1987. *La nuova italiana: La donna nella stampa e nella cultura del ventennio.* Rome: Riuniti.

Nozzoli, Anna. 1978. *Tabù e coscienza: La condizione femminile nella letteratura italiana del novecento.* Florence: La Nuova Italia.

Passerini, Luisa. 1984. *Torino operaia e fascismo.* Bari: Laterza.

Pickering-Iazzi, Robin. 1990–91. "Unseduced Mothers: The Resisting Female Subject in Italian Culture of the Twenties and Thirties." Working Paper No. 1, fall–winter, University of Wisconsin-Milwaukee Center For Twentieth Century Studies.

———, ed. 1993. *Unspeakable Women: Selected Short Stories Written by Italian Women during Fascism.* New York: Feminist Press.

Re, Lucia. 1989. "Futurism and Feminism." *Annali d'italianistica* 7: 253–72.

Santarelli, Enzo. 1976. "Il fascismo e le ideologie antifemministe." *Problemi del socialismo* 4: 75–106.

Sawicki, Jana. 1988. "Identity Politics and Sexual Freedom: Foucault and Feminism." In *Feminism and Foucault: Reflections on Resistance.* Edited by Irene Diamond and Lee Quinby. Boston: Northeastern University Press.

Schnapp, Jeffrey. 1990. "Forwarding Address." *Stanford Italian Review* 8: 53–80.

Zunino, Pier Giorgio. 1985. *L'ideologia del fascismo.* Bologna: Il Mulino.

5 / Fascist Women and the Rhetoric of Virility

Barbara Spackman

Perhaps no discursive regime so energetically enforced compulsory heterosexuality as did the Fascist regime. Prolific mothers and virile men people its imaginary, and its rhetoric of virility collapses gender and sex, biologizing both. As do all such naturalizations of gender and sex, the Fascist rhetoric of virility requires that virility be the property of the male and femininity the property of the female. Any redistribution of properties, any mixing and matching of terms — a feminine man, a masculine woman — is counted as an unnatural monstrosity, perversion, or aberration. Fascism as discursive regime is, in this sense, merely a particularly feverish example of a more general formation. One might even suggest that its eroticization, which inspired Susan Sontag's influential essay "Fascinating Fascism" (1980), is less an eroticization of a political regime than it is an eroticization of the very compulsoriness of heterosexuality, which the political regime makes so palpable.[1] Sadomasochism decked out in SS uniforms would in that case be not so much "a response to an oppressive freedom of choice in sex," as Sontag (1980, 104) argues, as the mastery through parody of an oppressive regime of necessity, a substitution of choice for necessity that recalls the compulsion to repeat of the sufferers of war trauma in Freud's *Beyond the Pleasure Principle* (1955/1986).[2] The trauma for these sufferers would be the imposition and enforcement of heterosexuality; that its repeaters should be, as Sontag claims, gay men, would therefore mark them not as somehow politically suspect (which Sontag's essay homophobically does) but rather as survivors of a war refought in every social formation governed by the "heterosexual matrix." Fascism comes to be a figure for that war and the trauma it produces; sadomasochism functions as the parody that theatrically denaturalizes the necessity of the heterosexual regime itself.[3]

Fascism offers a particularly virulent example of a more general discursive formation, then, but what is of interest here is its particularity — the precise forms it takes on during the "black twenty years." In the Fascist topography of gender and sex, stepping out into the public sphere "masculinizes" and "sterilizes" women, whereas the loss of a position in the public sphere necessarily "devirilizes" men. Production and reproduction are strictly, and asymmetrically, linked for men and women: only men involved in economic production are figured as capable of sexual reproduction, whereas involvement in economic production is presumed to destroy the woman's ability to reproduce. Thus the adjectives *masculine* and *virile* as applied to women were terms of abuse meant to deride the intellectual, "feminist," and hence supposedly sterile woman not properly devoted to her reproductive mission, and the "feminine" as applied to men named first the soldier returning from the barracks to find himself jobless, and later the taxed "celibate" who produced no offspring.[4] The representation of the devirilized man dipped into homophobic fantasy to produce the "pederast" of Marinetti's manifestos and the limp-wristed "*gagà*" of Asverio Gravelli's *Vademecum dello stile fascista* (Vademecum of Fascist style) (n.d.).[5] The representation of the "virile woman" for the most part skirted the historical association of the virilization of women and lesbianism (the nonreproductive woman is, in Gravelli's caricatures, still a mother, but mother to a dog) and concentrated on more overtly political connotations, for women's entry into the public, economic sphere threatened the very reproduction of the means of production. This threat was recoded as a threat to women's own reproductive equipment, and its political force retained in the repeated association of the "masculine woman" and feminism. This is not, of course, an innovation on the part of the Fascist regime or even of the Fascist movement, but has roots in the reaction of late-nineteenth-century medicolegal anthropology and sociology to women's suffrage and emancipation movements.

Scipio Sighele, sociologist and popularizer of Weiningerian notions about women, neatly summarizes the ideologeme of the sterile feminist in his *Eva moderna* (Modern Eve) (1910):

> Those who aspire to emancipate themselves, those who through intelligence, activity, or will have acquired a more or less legitimate reputation, have something masculine in their physical persons as in their moral physiognomy. One would say that in them a male soul lives and moves. One would say that they feel as men, and that it is precisely this male consciousness that forces them to ask for spiritual liberation.
>
> Today, the reemergence of feminism is due in great part to the increase in the number of masculine women, the *hoministes,* as Remy de Gourmont calls them with an expressive neologism. (pp. 51–52)[6]

In a move characteristic of turn-of-the-century antiegalitarian politics, Sighele translates a demand for political equality into a diagnosis of physical similarity: the woman who requests equality is, in body and in soul, a man, so unthinkable a notion is emancipation of women for Sighele. Once women have entered, and been forced to exit, the workforce during and after World War I, the threat of substitution of men by women becomes more concrete and more immediate, and the discursive prohibition on entry into the public sphere becomes more urgent, more explicit. Women should not "take on masculine attitudes and invade the male sphere of action," reads a 1921 statute of the Gruppo Femminile Fascista Romano (Roman Fascist Women's Group), and the propaganda of the regime will spread the Mussolinian word that work masculinizes women and robs their husbands of their virility.[7]

This is familiar territory, surveyed by Piero Meldini's (1975) selection of rank-and-file writings on the subject of the Fascist woman, and mapped by the works of a growing number of historians, including Victoria De Grazia (1992), Marina Addis Saba (1988a), and Elisabetta Mondello (1987), to name only a few.[8] What I would like to do in this essay is to build upon the work of these historians, and, as a literary critic, probe the ideological ramifications of the adoption of the Fascist rhetoric of virility by women themselves. Does the rhetoric of virility swerve from its intended course when adopted by unintended users? The underpinnings of this question can be traced to Foucault's theorization of the "tactical polyvalence" of discourses in *The History of Sexuality* (1980, esp. 100–102). Against the notion that the world of discourse can be divided into dominant and dominated discourse, Foucault argues for a conception of discourse as "a series of discontinuous segments whose tactical function is neither uniform nor stable." This instability means that the beginnings of an opposing strategy are not located "outside" a discourse of control, repression, or prohibition, but rather are produced by that same discourse. Foucault offers as an example the nineteenth-century psychiatrization of homosexuality, which at once extended social control of the "perversion" that it established and made possible the emergence of a "reverse discourse" that used the same vocabulary and categories to argue for the legitimacy and "naturality" of homosexuality. Is it possible that the rhetoric of virility, when wielded by women, produces a similar "reverse discourse"? Or does women's adoption of the rhetoric simply recirculate the same strategy, leaving intact the logic of its exclusions and prohibitions?

I hope to begin to answer these questions by examining the works of two of what Sighele would have called *les hoministes*: the pre-Fascist futurist Valentine de Saint Point and the properly and devotedly Fascist Teresa Labriola, both women who flaunted the prohibition against virilization.

Valentine de Saint Point's 1912 *Manifeste de la femme futuriste* (Manifesto of the futurist woman) is explicitly a response to the "scorn for women" trumpeted in Marinetti's founding manifesto. In women's defense, de Saint Point seems to argue for a mixing and matching of gender and sex that makes possible a virilization of women. Though pre-Fascist, the following passage nicely illustrates the way in which Fascist ideology will bind together ideologically incompatible elements, both progressive and reactionary, left and right, in order to appear, as Zeev Sternhell (1986) puts it, neither left nor right:

> *It is absurd to divide humanity into women and men.* It is composed only of *femininity* and *masculinity*. Every superman, every hero no matter how epic, every genius no matter how powerful, is only the prodigious expression of a race and an epoch insofar as he is composed at once of feminine and masculine elements, of femininity and masculinity: that is to say insofar as he is a complete being. (de Saint Point 1912/1973, 329)

The binding mechanism operates here to yoke recognizably Weiningerian concepts—masculinity and femininity as characteristics loosened from their supposed biological moorings—to an argument for androgyny foreign to the xenophobic Weininger, for whom the combination of masculinity and woman was abhorrent. Whereas on the one hand such a discourse begins to glimpse, however obscurely, what we would now call the social construction of gender, on the other it also produces an argument for a very problematic kind of bellicose androgyny.[9] Indeed, by turning Marinetti's argument against him, de Saint Point succeeds in turning it back against women as well; whereas Marinetti argued that men had become too feminine and women too masculine, de Saint Point finds women not virile enough: "What women as well as men lack most is virility" (p. 330). Is such a call for a virile woman merely the recirculation of the logic according to which the only good woman is a good man, or can we, as Foucault's example suggests, find in its polyvalence the beginnings of a reverse discourse?

The logic is certainly a familiar one, and points to precedents in the literature of defense or praise of women. As Juliana Schiesari (1989) has argued in her work on the humanist discourse of *virtù,* one of the highest "compliments" that phallocentric discourse can pay to women is to efface their difference and laud their approximation of a masculine ideal. Such is the case in the Renaissance notion of the virago, in the praise of learned women such as Christine de Pisan as "virilis femina," and "beyond their sex," and in the underlying classical notion of self-sacrificing women such as Lucretia as "virilis."[10] Beyond their sex, but still firmly implanted within phallocentric discourse, for the suggestion is that the only subject is a virile one, and that equality can be attained only at the price of the erasure of sexual difference. The self-sacrificing woman sacrifices her difference from man. (This is, parenthetically, the reasoning at the bottom of the refusal of equal rights on the part of contemporary Italian philosophers of sexual difference: as Paola Bono and Sandra Kemp [1991] put it, "The polis is open only to women who agree to neuter themselves. Outside the polis sexual difference is recognized, but only in the form of a sexual role which implies inferiority. Becoming equal thus means becoming like a man" [p. 15].)[11] De Saint Point's sister futurist, Enif Robert (1917/1982) provides a vivid example of this topography of virility:

There are women whom a most felicitous correspondence, a perfect adhesion of soul and senses, renders luscious when they give
themselves in a room "shadowy and perfumed" but who, at the
right time, know how to be lively, courageous, strong, VIRILE,
INTELLIGENT, beside their man. (p. 108)

Deeply ensnared within the discourse it aims to refute, this declaration describes a movement that takes women out of the bedroom
and into the public sphere, a public sphere that can only be imagined
as "at the side of their man." Going out means going virile.

But de Saint Point (1912/1973) goes even further when she produces a list of viragoes, amazons, and other women who went "beyond
their sex":

Women: they are the Furies, the Amazons, the Semiramis', the
Joans of Arc, the Jeanne Hachettes, the Judiths and the Charlotte Cordays, the Cleopatras and the Messalinas, the women
warriors who fight more ferociously than the males, the women
lovers who incite, the women destroyers who, demolishing the
weakest, help in natural selection through pride or the "despair
by which the heart gives its all."

May the next wars give rise to heroines like that magnificent
Caterina Sforza who, besieged in her castle, seeing from the bat-
tlements the enemy threaten the life of her son to force her to
surrender, heroically exposing her sex, cried out: "Kill him, I still
have the mold to make others!" (p. 330)

The invocation of the virago Caterina Sforza involves de Saint Point's
manifesto in a dense intertextual web that includes not only Machiavelli's *Discourses,* but also, and more contemporaneously, Gramsci's
reading of the topos in Machiavelli and D'Annunzio's speeches at Fi-
ume.[12] I have not the space here to plumb those depths, so will concentrate on the function of the Caterina Sforza episode within the context of de Saint Point's employment of the rhetoric of virility. If de
Saint Point meant to provide an example of the self-sacrificing mother
who would give her sons to the state, such as the heroic mother invoked at the end of her manifesto, she picked the wrong lady. Caterina sacrifices not herself for the sake of her sons, but her sons for
the sake of her own political power. The threat to kill Caterina's children is, after all, an attempt to castrate her politically, and her gesture
can be read as a refusal to be castrated. The exposure of her "sex" is

thus at once an exhibition of virility—she makes the private public, exposes what should remain private, and refuses to be drawn back into the private sphere by the tug of the umbilical cord—and an affirmation of femininity, of her sexual difference from men. She points to "her sex," her genitals, but also her sexual difference from men, in the very moment in which, in true virago fashion, she goes "beyond her sex." The "impropriety" of her gesture figures the threat she poses to property relations, understood both as the relations of reproduction and as the "proper" relations of gender and sex.[13] This version of the topos also underlines her status as antimother, for Caterina both violates the rigidly gendered, and ultimately Aristotelian, opposition between virile courage and maternal love (an opposition that Mussolini will elaborate in the famous equation "la guerra sta all'uomo come la maternità alla donna" [war is to man as maternity is to woman]) and claims ownership of the mold or form, precisely what the male is, for Aristotle, presumed to supply in reproduction.[14]

These are the beginnings of a "reverse discourse," both in the sense that they reverse the Aristotelian underpinnings of the essentialization of gender and sex and in the sense that they use the rhetoric of virility in defense rather than scorn of women. But just as a mere reversal remains governed by the oppositions it overturns, so is the "antimother" of de Saint Point's text governed by the antifeminist, antiegalitarian, pronatalist ending of the manifesto, in which de Saint Point calls for mothers to provide heroes for humanity. Rita Guerricchio (1976), in fact, argues that despite its apparently polemical form, de Saint Point's manifesto in reality corroborates the image and ideology of woman promoted by Marinetti. As a strategy for dealing with the coexistence of progressive and reactionary elements in Fascist ideology, the model of appearance versus reality employed by Guerricchio is well worn, perhaps even worn out; versions can be found in notions of a "*paese reale*" or of collective nicodemism, and in explanations of the way in which Fascism is supposed to have appeared to be on the left when in fact it was on the right.[15] An alternative to this (ultimately apologetic) use of the appearance/reality paradigm has been proposed by Ernesto Laclau (1977) and Alice Kaplan (1986), who have argued that Fascist discourse works precisely by binding together the progressive and the reactionary. This latter approach allows us to discover the glimmerings of opposing strategies even within

Fascism as discursive regime, and is, I find, particularly useful in understanding the contradictory position of women within Fascism both as discursive and as juridico-political regime. With its contradictory strategies, de Saint Point's manifesto already participates in the Fascist matrix.

Indeed, Fascism issues a contradictory interpellation to those it constitutes as women: as Marina Addis Saba (1988b, 5) has observed, it at once excludes women, depriving them of rights they never had and fixing them in the role of wife and mother, and calls them loudly to participate in political life.[16] It thus at once rigidly enforces the boundary between private and public spheres and calls for its transgressive crossing. One response to this divided interpellation produces what Emma Scaramuzza (1983), and Marina Addis Saba (1988b) after her, have called "la donna muliebre," the active, intellectual, and Fascistically feminist woman. Borrowed from the Alleanza Muliebre Culturale Italiana (Italian Ladies' Cultural Alliance), a women's organization active from 1930 to 1939, the term itself is a coinage that responds to and refashions the rhetoric of virility. Available in Italian as an erudite alternative to *femminile,* the Latinate *muliebre* was perceived as belonging to the appropriate Romanizing register: "Muliebre," writes Scaramuzza, transfers onto the feminine the "high moral tone attributed to 'virile'" (p. 114n). One such *donna muliebre,* Teresa Labriola, was not deaf to the contradictory interpellation; indeed, in 1929 she described the position of Italian women as "with one foot in the past and one in the present, with one ear cocked to the 'Internationale' and another to 'Giovinezza'" (Labriola 1929, 656).[17] Labriola's position as Fascist feminist and ex-suffragist turned antiemancipationist theorist awkwardly straddles the worlds of past and present, and, though the stereophonic mixing of left and right often produces noise one would rather not hear, it also produces unexpected chords and discords. I will concentrate here on a small sampling of her extremely prolific activity — in particular, on the 1918 *Problemi sociali della donna* (The social problems of woman) and on her frequent contributions to the periodical *La donna italiana* (The Italian woman) in the years 1924 to 1939.

In a 1923 referendum in *L'almanacco della donna italiana* (The almanac of the Italian woman), Labriola was named one of the "ten most famous women alive," and the word chosen to pinpoint her "essence" was *maschilità* (see Mondello 1987, 180–81). As the virile woman, however, Labriola is neither a Lucretia who sacrifices her difference to a patriarchal code of honor nor an Ines Donati, the woman squadrista whose dying words, "I wanted to be too virile and forgot that, in the end, I was but a weak woman," were all too easily enthroned by the regime.[18] Both of those representations work to maintain the propriety of gender and sex. Labriola, on the other hand, exploits a disjunction already operative in the rhetoric of virility itself to produce a notion of the woman who could be virile yet not masculine. That disjunction is created by the elevation to the status of "universality" of the term *virility,* and its consequently occluded relation to masculinity. By exploiting this disjunction, Labriola inadvertently denaturalizes the relation between sex and gender, and ends up denaturalizing maternity itself.

I describe this exploitation as inadvertent, as the result of a logic not entirely under Labriola's control, for the paths taken by her reasoning are, to use the two adjectives most used to describe Fascist ideology, confused and contradictory. In Labriola's case, the confusion results from a collision of two competing ideological imperatives, one the "feminist" strain left over from a barely audible "*internazionale,*" and the other the nationalist strain, which is dominant.[19] Labriola's "Latin feminism" brings with it a defense of women's qualities (rather than of their rights) and a rejection of the overvaluation of male qualities in what she refers to as "masculine society."[20] Hers is (at least in part) an antiegalitarianism that argues against equality on the grounds not that equality collapses a hierarchy that should be maintained, but rather that equality masks a hierarchy that remains undisturbed. In the 1918 *Problemi sociali della donna,* she argues, for example, not that women should be barred from the workplace or university, but that the workplace itself is modeled on masculine qualities and needs, and that the new postwar, Fascist workplace should be reformed to accommodate women and feminine qualities. Insofar as the aim of her arguments is the reconciliation of maternity and work, she opposes the rhetoric of virility that excludes women from the workforce on the grounds that production and reproduction are antithetical.

Labriola's nationalism, on the other hand, comes to her bound up with a rhetoric of virility, for, as George Mosse (1985) has convincingly shown, the ideal of manliness accompanies the development of nationalism itself. Labriola's goal is to nationalize women, educate them as Fascists, and bring them into the workplace without sacrificing their "feminine qualities." But how to bring about such a nationalization without betraying the "Latin feminist" imperative and accepting a masculinization of women that Labriola repeatedly condemns? Labriola's solution is to split off "virility" from masculinity by exploiting the ambiguity of "virility" as a universalist moral category available to "all humanity." Making the words of an anonymous (and anomalous, in such a fiercely nationalistic text) Frenchman her own, Labriola (1918) writes that "women should retain their feminine qualities but at the same time acquire virile qualities" in order to achieve her goal of forming "a national spirit in the Italian woman" (pp. 60–61). Those virile qualities consist in the awareness of a sense of belonging to a race and to a nation. Rather than exposing its gender neutrality to be an ideological mystification, Labriola makes the mystification work to her advantage, severing masculinity from virility and installing femininity in its place.[21] Yet because "virility" can never be cleansed entirely of its relation to "masculinity," the attribution of virility to women implies the detachability of gender from sex.

Lest this sound more radical an operation than it is, it should be said that the qualities Labriola works with are not redefined, but merely recombined; she can produce a Fascist woman "with a maternal heart, and yet with a virile mind" (1933a, 67), but cannot imagine womanhood apart from motherhood; indeed, she rejects egalitarianism also because it does not take into account "the infant that gallops behind the woman" (1930b, 547). But as the (merest) beginnings of a strategy that adopts the categories and terms of the discourse it opposes, Labriola's strategy at once accepts the logic of identity that posits the male term as unmarked and refuses the erasure and denigration of feminine difference that the logic requires.

This paradox would be more manageable if it described a chronology, a position adopted and then superseded by another. But at least in the materials at hand, the paradox persists from 1918 until the late 1930s. As both practitioner and refuter of the rhetoric of virility, Labriola is at war with herself. Thus in the 1924 essay "Il femminismo italiano nella rinascita dello spirito" (Italian feminism in the rebirth of the Spirit) she posits a (Fascist) realm of values beyond sexual difference:

The very communion within which we live, whether religious or national, implies the existence of values that are not masculine but spiritual. They have roots and origin in that natural existence which is sexual. But they continually rise above and continually negate that which is, in its brutal naturality, instinctive in the differentiation of the sexes. (p. 13)

In a 1930 article, she exposes the underlying masculinity of the erasure of difference, which she labels "egalitarian":

It seems that every virtue is in man and every lack in woman, so much so that every individual attitude of man, as a being of the male sex, is considered an index of complete humanity and raised up as the culmination of the emancipation of woman.... No, my adversarial women friends, no! I fight against the error of identifying male and humanity. (1930b, 544)

And in a 1934 response to the essentialization of the relation between gender and sex in Julius Evola's *Rivolta contro il mondo moderno* (Revolt against the modern world) (1934/1969), Labriola reaffirms the existence of "rational, asexual qualities, of asexual truths that woman possesses not as woman but as participant in an undifferentiated human nature" (p. 258).[22] The paradox has her trapped in a cage whose bars are binary oppositions, as she scrambles to refute the "antifemminism of so many Fascists," and yet to remain the "Fascist of the first hour" that she paints herself to be (Labriola 1927a, 562).

Thus, on the one hand, her "feminism" is characterized by an antimimetic impulse with respect to male standards of values, assumed to be universal. Labriola bases her criticism of Anglo-American emancipationist feminism on a rejection of *mimetismo*, "the external and servile imitation of masculine activities" (1927b, 645). This position allows her to be remarkably astute when it comes to the ways in which femininity is constituted as a defect according to a male symbolic order, and women are bound to failure in masculine cultural institutions. Thus in a 1932 article titled "La donna nella cultura e nelle professioni" (Woman in culture and in the professions), Labriola writes:

The masculine type is prevalent in civil society and, face it, is what has given the principal form to human history. The lady friends of kings and ambassadors of love don't count! Women

stayed locked away in gated gardens! That's the way it was!...
given the male type considered the "specimen" of the human race,
women were left with a very limited choice: either perish or imitate. (p. 537)

To argue for women's equality on the basis of successes obtained in
imitating such a model is, Labriola argues, the mistake made by egalitarian feminism.[23] Women are set up for failure, and only rarely suc-
ceed in becoming honorary men. More often than not, they resort to
a strategy that resembles Joan Rivière's (1929/1986) notion of "womanliness as masquerade," an exaggeration of femininity designed to
mask a competitive threat:

> Since the masculine type is the norm of conception and conduct
> in higher institutions of learning and culture, it is obvious that
> the means for arriving at the goal was and still is to intensify to
> the maximum, in a true exasperation, nakedly intellectualistic
> qualities, thereby mortifying the spirit in its luxurious wealth,
> and to simulate the characteristics of aggressivity; or, in a re-
> verse move, to make oneself into a slave of the male professor,
> exasperating the custom of slavishness (as most women students
> have done) by exaggerating beyond believability the characteris-
> tics of femininity. (Labriola 1932, 537)

Coupled with a defense of women's intellectual abilities, and directed
against "the campaign that many Italian men have launched against
Italian women and young students," Labriola's argument champions
the cause of the "rights of female intellect" to a place within the university and cultural institutions, and "not outside but inside the vast
panorama of the spiritual ascent of our people" (1932, 538).[24] That
such a cause runs counter to the regime's policies and propaganda
does not deter Labriola from finding the solution to the problem
in Fascism, "insofar as it means to reconstruct the table of values"
(1931, 71).

Among these values, Labriola would like to place an ideal of femininity, neither mimetic nor servile, that gradually takes shape as the
sacerdotal, spiritual mother (see, e.g., Labriola 1935a, 10–12). One
is tempted to argue that insofar as the ideal allows her to mute the
threat of substitution of men by women, and to retain her claim for
women's place, as women, in the public sphere, its function is primarily strategic, an adoption of womanliness as masquerade on Labriola's

part. Indeed, her own notion of femininity at once enables and pro-
hibits such a strategic use, for it at once posits femininity as "artificial" and as "natural." That is to say that whereas Labriola condemns the exaggeration of "the characteristics of femmininity in
intellectual fields" because "women [thereby] perform an antibiologi-
cal function... because the characteristics of femininity must be
sharpened only in order to arrive at the natural destination of the female sex, which is maternity" (1932, 537), her ideal of femininity requires the very disjunction that allows the strategic swerving and
"sharpening" of femininity. Here the paradox that governs Labriola's work produces its most interesting knots, for in order to maintain the paradox and remain faithful to the nationalist rhetoric of
virility, Labriola ends up constituting an ideal of womanliness whose
logic mimes that of the ideal of manliness.[25] The fortitude and for-
bearance shown by the virile subject in relation to his own sensuality
is matched in Labriola's ideal by the jettisoning of female sexuality.
As Labriola puts it, "Giardino si è il nostro, ma Armida ha da fare
bagaglio [Ours is a garden, but Armida's got to go]" (1927b, 648). So
drastic is the abjection of sexuality that maternity (understood as
Italian and Fascist) comes to be an exclusively spiritual, nonbiologi-
cal operation. In other words, in order to give to femininity the moral
form that would correspond to degendered virility, Labriola must de-
naturalize maternity itself.

The denaturalization of the Fascist mother is possible, however, only
on condition that other women be figured as the nature and sexuality that she has overcome. Here the rhetoric of virility replicates its
genealogical precedent, the humanist discourse of (virile) *virtù*, for,
as Schiesari (1989) argues, the concept of *virtù* may "work at times
in an emancipatory fashion... but it may also function to 'castrate'
women, to deny their feminine sexuality in such a way that the discourse of virtue keeps the 'exceptional' woman separate from other
women" (p. 80). Indeed, banished from the garden of Italy, Armida
has a destination all picked out: the land of Bolshevik biologization,
populated by "amoral" proletarian women. Women must be educated
to be mothers and nationalists, Labriola argues in the 1918 *Problemi
sociali della donna,* because the winds of socialism have passed over
the masses of peasants and proletarian women and wiped from their
heads all sense of moral judgment in sexual matters (p. 49). Left alone,
such women "abandon themselves to crazy utopianisms" and non-

reproductive sex—they'd rather be commies than mommies. Hence the need for a "training for motherhood for women" that includes "the desire and aptitude to work for national ends" (p. 106). Whereas Labriola changes many of her positions, sometimes simply reversing them (most dramatically from suffragist to antisuffragist, but also from a position that sees a covert subordination in protectionist measures to one that recommends them on the basis of women's "physical inferiority"), she retains and bolsters this notion of a Bolshevik state of nature until 1938 (she stopped writing in 1939, and died in 1941).[26] In a 1930 article titled "Problemi morali del femminismo" (Moral problems of feminism), Labriola argues against the recognition of "natural maternity," invoked as a legal category: mothers have rights and duties insofar as they occupy a juridical position, claims Labriola, not insofar as they may have physically given birth; faithful to Roman law, that juridical position is dependent upon marriage.[27] In fact, Labriola's Fascist mother appears to be a revival of the social fiction that was Roman motherhood, in which maternity was limited to motherhood within marriage and the materfamilias was such not because she had children but because she was the wife of a paterfamilias.[28] Mothers are legally constructed as mothers, but do not exist in nature; "natural maternity" refers instead to the unwed *genitrix* who, for Labriola, exists in Bolshevik nature.[29] Labriola gives it specific geographical coordinates in the 1938 article "Il pericolo latente" (The latent danger): "The biological conception, I mean the merely biological conception of maternity, is located geographically in Russia" (p. 2).

Labriola thus ends up turning women over to the state, reimprisoning them in the patriarchal family, and condemning them to compulsory heterosexuality if they are to have "rights and duties" in the Fascist state. Yet in spite of this congruence between Labriola and the ideology of the regime, the notion of motherhood as legal and social fiction has a certain demystificatory force in relation to the Fascist naturalization of motherhood. Thus in 1938, she once again argues against the rhetoric according to which entry into the public sphere masculinizes women. Renewed in the 1930s in reaction to the involvement of women in sports, the charge was rebiologized by practitioners of sports gynecology who were eager to show the physical effects of "masculinization"; it is in this context that Labriola takes another shot at the opponents of the "new woman:"

You, reader, perhaps believe that there is a latent danger of the masculinization of women. Much has been said about this famous masculinization; it is still bandied about and will continue to be so for God knows how long. The opposition to the new woman, or better, to a hypothetical, almost fantasmatic woman comes from prejudicial questions that are . . . prejudices. (1938, 2).[30]

The latent danger turns out to be a different one: "a materialistic conception of a maternity stripped of spiritual attributes" that Labriola attributes to "an excess of Bolshevik materialism . . . in us men and women at the present moment." Fascist discourse here turns against itself, the pot calling the kettle red, as it were. This is indeed a "reverse discourse," for by recirculating the terms of the rhetoric of virility Labriola comes to reject (by repudiating as "Bolshevik") the grounds of her own Fascist idealism, which, like all idealisms, necessarily posits women as matter and strips them of "spiritual attributes."

As in de Saint Point's manifesto, however, the dominant Fascist tone in Labriola's work drowns out the dissonant note, and the discourse proceeds undisturbed by its own implications. If we can hear it now, it is because the context has changed, and feminists have begun not only to reverse but also to rewrite the terms that constitute the rhetoric and politics of virility. That rewriting makes it possible, and necessary, for us to hear the dissonant notes within Fascist discourse both as the product of the contradictory ways in which women accommodated themselves to the gendering of power and as a reminder of the tangled ruses of the rhetoric of virility itself.

Notes

Unless otherwise noted, all translations are my own.

1. On "compulsory heterosexuality," see Adrienne Rich (1980).

2. See also Kaja Silverman's (1980) discussion of *Beyond the Pleasure Principle* in relation to Liliana Cavani's *Night Porter.*

3. See Judith Butler's (1990) theorization of parody as denaturalizing strategy.

4. The tax on "celibates," or nonreproductive men, was instituted in 1926 and exacted 25 percent of the offending man's wages.

5. On Marinetti and "pederasty," see Barbara Spackman (1990, forthcoming-b).

6. The notion of a masculine soul in a female body, of course, recalls the medicolegal notion of male homosexuality as "a woman's soul trapped in a man's body."

7. See, for example, Benito Mussolini (1934/1961): "The demographic question intersects with the question of unemployment in the working woman. When work is not a direct impediment to reproduction, it is a distraction, foments an independence and resultant physical and moral habits contrary to childbirth. Man, disoriented and

above all 'unemployed' in all senses, ends up renouncing the family. Today, the machine and woman are the two major causes of unemployment. In particular, woman often saves a family in trouble or even herself, but her work is, in the general framework, a source of political and moral bitterness. The salvation of a few individuals is paid for with the blood of a multitude. There is no victory without some deaths. The exit of women from the workforce would undoubtedly have an economic repercussion on many families, but a legion of men would raise their heads, now hung in shame, and a hundredfold new families would suddenly enter into the life of the nation. We must convince ourselves that the same work that causes the loss of reproductive attributes in woman brings to man a robust physical and moral virility. A virility that the machine should help along" (pp. 310–311).

8. See also Macciocchi (1976), De Grand (1976), Bartolini (1976), Fraddosio (1986), and Santarelli (1976a).

9. Lucia Re (1989) makes this argument in her reading *in bono* of Valentine de Saint Point's position. It is, to be sure, the *lectio difficilior,* for de Saint Point's manifesto also proclaims itself antifeminist and ends with a call to mothers to produce heroes. For readings *in malo,* see Anna Nozzoli (1978) and Rita Guerricchio (1976).

10. See Schiesari's brilliant essay, "In Praise of Virtuous Women? For a Genealogy of Gender Morals in Renaissance Italy" (1989). I take the expression "beyond their sex" from the collection of that title edited by Patricia H. Labalme (1984).

11. See also Carla Lonzi (1991) and the Milan Women's Bookstore Collective (1990). On the equality versus difference debate within feminism, see Joan W. Scott (1990). For a proposal of "equivalent" rather than "equal" rights, see Drucilla Cornell (1992).

12. I discuss this intertexual web in *Fascist Virilities: Rhetoric, Ideology, and Social Fantasy* (Spackman forthcoming-a).

13. See the dossier of discussions that ends with an invocation of Caterina Sforza in Neil Hertz (1985a, 1985b) and Catherine Gallagher (1985). See also John Freccero (1993).

14. Maternal love, for Aristotle, is the unique source of courage in women, as it is in bears. Summarizing Aristotle, Suzanne Saïd (1983) writes: "Au courage virile s'oppose l'amour maternel, chez les hommes comme chez les animaux" (p. 98).

15. For a critique of such notions, see Pier Giorgio Zunino (1985).

16. This divided call is itself riven by yet other divisions, among them the contradiction between the representation of woman as rural mother, product of Fascism's demographic delirium, and the construction of woman as urban consumer, product of the "Americanization" that accompanies capitalism. See Victoria De Grazia (1991, 1992) and Mondello (1987, 111).

17. On Teresa Labriola, see Luigi dal Pane (1942), Enzo Santarelli (1976b), Ivana Rinaldi (1987), Marina Addis Saba (1988b), Sara Follacchio (1988), Victoria De Grazia (1992), and Elisabetta Mondello (1987).

18. Quoted in Denise Detragiache (1983, 227). On Donati, see Ivana Rinaldi (1987).

19. The leftist strain is so faint that some hear it not at all. Certain that the egalitarian, emancipationist route is inseparable from feminism, Franca Pieroni Bortolotti (1963, 1974, 1978) in particular is unwilling to grant any authenticity to Labriola's "feminism." Already in the pre-Fascist era, writes Pieroni Bortolotti (1974), "Labriola called for the advancement of European women in order to counterbalance the rise of 'negroes' " (p. 12). The term *emancipation* linked the abolitionist and feminist causes, something that Pieroni Bortolotti claims Labriola knew quite well. Labriola's severing of those causes, and attack on emancipationist feminism (of the left) in an attempt to distinguish from it a "pure feminism" (of the right) are, Pieroni Bortolotti (1978)

argues, evidence of "indifference to truth, ideological ignominy, and a talent for imbroglio" (p. 244). Pieroni Bortolotti blames on Labriola the subsequent resistance of the Italian proletariat to feminism: "From that moment, within Italian democracy and its corresponding worker's movement, the term 'feminism' will be unconsciously associated with antidemocratic and antisocialist positions, and as such it will be unconsciously rejected" (p. 244).

20. On Latin feminism, see De Grazia (1992).

21. This splitting causes confusion even within a single work, where virility and masculinity at one moment appear to be synonyms and at another virility is degendered. Thus in *I problemi sociali della donna* Labriola (1918) writes: "In a society that has so clearly shown itself to be animated by virile spirit, guided by virile will and capable of expansion solely through the traditional means of male society, that is war, the development of feminine activities necessarily follows the line of development of masculine organization. Feminine activity is locked within dams" (p. 32). When, however, Labriola turns to the development of women's activities in the new nation, "virility" returns as a positive rather than negative term, the connotation of which is clearly that of ungendered dedication to the nation.

22. Evola's (1934/1969) elaborate theories can be boiled down to two statements. The first is that, "in special regard to the sexes, whoever is born a man must complete himself as a man, and whoever is born a woman must complete herself as a woman in everything and for everything, overcoming any mixture or promiscuity" (p. 202). Second, "mixed beings," as Evola puts it, smack of "the abnormal inclinations of the 'third sex,'" beings who "in their souls are neither man nor woman, or rather the woman is a man and the man, a woman" (p. 209).

23. See Labriola (1931). Her point is not that women should be expelled from professions; rather, "the profession is the condition for the harmonious development of feminine qualities, it is above all beneficial from an intellectual, ethical, and economic point of view. And besides, it corresponds to the concrete way of life of modern society" (pp. 72–73).

24. Alexander De Grand (1976) attributes to Labriola the position that "the desire to send young women to the universities was mere middle class snobbishness" (p. 958), and cites in support her 1933 article "Per la riforma della cultura" (Labriola 1933b). Although it is true that she associates the bourgeoisie with a "paper chase" mentality interested only in degrees and diplomas for pragmatic reasons, she does not address the question of the university in that article, which is devoted to the problems of childhood and adolescence, nor does she draw the conclusion that De Grand attributes to her. In a follow-up essay, "Sempre in tema di cultura," Labriola writes that culture is of no use to woman understood as "a completely physiological being" (a conception she rejects); that woman understood as "a spiritual, sacerdotal being" also has no need of culture, because she comes "originally" to that vocation; but that culture is indispensable for woman as "educator of the nation, for the nation, understood as a living reality that transcends the species," which is to say, as nationalized mother (see 1933c, 466–67).

25. On the ideal of (homosocial) manliness and its abjection of certain sexualities and sensualities (particularly male homosexuality), see George Mosse (1985).

26. In a 1930 essay, Labriola writes that "under the pretext of protection, there has been and in part still is today in world history a sort of enslavement of women" (1930b, 545), but in a 1935 article, she argues that "woman must be protected above all" because of her "natural physical inferiority" (1935a, 11–12).

27. See Labriola (1930a, 334). On Roman law, see Yan Thomas (1992).

28. Though Labriola never quite arrives at this conclusion explicitly, she tiptoes around it, introducing the materfamilias in a 1935 article titled "Suffragismo francese e sodalismo italiano" and reluctantly admitting that physical maternity has a role to play in a 1936 article, "Madri e istitutrici": "Okay, physical maternity is the basis, or better, it is the condition for the exercise of complete maternity. But it is not enough. We must affirm the value of spiritual maternity. If we don't affirm it, we are in Bolshevism" (p. 246).

29. Labriola was reacting to the recognition of "natural maternity" by the National Agency for Maternity and Infancy, which provided services for unwed mothers and illegitimate children. Its roots, according to De Grazia (1992, 60–68), were indeed in "prewar social reformism rather than fascist pronatalism." On Fascist maternity policies, see also Annarita Buttafuoco (1991) and Chiara Saraceno (1991).

30. On women and sports during the Fascist regime, see Rosella Isidori Frasca (1983, 1988).

Works Cited

Addis Saba, Marina, ed. 1988a. *La corporazione delle donne: Ricerche e studi sui modelli femminili nel ventennio fascista.* Florence: Vallecchi.

———. 1988b. "La donna 'muliebre.'" In *La corporazione delle donne: Ricerche e studi sui modelli femminili nel ventennio fascista.* Edited by Marina Addis Saba. Florence: Vallecchi.

Bartolini, Stefania. 1982. "La donna sotto il fascismo." *Memoria* 10: 124–32.

Butler, Judith. 1990. *Gender Trouble: Feminism and the Subversion of Identity.* New York: Routledge.

Bono, Paola, and Sandra Kemp. 1991. "Introduction: Coming from the South." In *Italian Feminist Thought.* Edited by Paola Bono and Sandra Kemp. Cambridge, Mass.: Basil Blackwell.

Buttafuoco, Annarita. 1991. "Motherhood as a Political Strategy: The Role of the Italian Women's Movement in the Creation of the *Cassa Nazionale di Maternità.*" In *Maternity and Gender Policies: Women and the Rise of the European Welfare States, 1880s–1950s.* Edited by Gisela Bock and Pat Thane. New York: Routledge.

Cornell, Drucilla. 1992. "Gender, Sex, and Equivalent Rights." In *Feminists Theorize the Political.* Edited by Judith Butler and Joan W. Scott. New York: Routledge.

dal Pane, Luigi. 1942. "Antonio e Teresa Labriola." *Rivista internazionale di filosofia del diritto* 22, series 2: 49–79.

De Grand, Alexander. 1976. "Women under Italian Fascism." *Historical Journal* 19: 947–68.

De Grazia, Victoria. 1991. "La nazionalizzazione delle donne: Modelli di regime e cultura commerciale nell'Italia fascista." *Memoria* 33, no. 3: 95–111.

———. 1992. *How Fascism Ruled Women: Italy, 1922–1945.* Berkeley: University of California Press.

de Saint Point, Valentine. 1973. "Manifeste de la femme futuriste: Réponse a F.T. Marinetti." In *Futurisme: Manifestes, proclamations, documents.* Edited by Giovanni Lista. Lausanne: Éditions L'Age d'Homme. Originally published 1912.

Detragiache, Denise. 1983. "Il fascismo femminile da San Sepolcro all'affare Matteotti (1919–1925)." *Storia contemporanea* 14 (April).

Evola, Julius. 1969. *Rivolta contro il mondo moderno.* Rome: Edizioni Mediterranee. Originally published 1934.

Follacchio, Sara. 1988. "Conversando di femminismo: 'La donna italiana.'" In *La corporazione delle donne: Ricerche e studi sui modelli femminili nel ventennio fascista*. Edited by Marina Addis Saba. Florence: Vallecchi.

Foucault, Michel. 1980. *The History of Sexuality* (vol. 1) *An Introduction*. Translated by Robert Hurley. New York: Vintage.

Fraddosio, Maria. 1986. "Le donne e il fascismo: Ricerche e problemi di interpretazione." *Storia contemporanea* 1: 95–135.

Freccero, John. 1993. "Medusa and the Madonna of Forlì: Political Sexuality in Machiavelli." In *Machiavelli and the Discourse of Literature*. Edited by Albert R. Ascoli and Victoria Kahn. Ithaca, N.Y.: Cornell University Press.

Freud, Sigmund. 1986. *Beyond the Pleasure Principle*. In *The Standard Edition of the Complete Psychological Works of Sigmund Freud*. Edited and translated by James Strachey. London: Hogarth. Originally published 1955.

Gallagher, Catherine. 1985. "Response from Catherine Gallagher." In *The End of the Line: Essays on Psychoanalysis and the Sublime*. Edited by Neil Hertz. New York: Columbia University Press.

Gravelli, Asverio. n.d. *Vademecum dello stile fascista, dai fogli di disposizione del segretario del partito*. Rome: Nuova Europa.

Guerricchio, Rita. 1976. "Il modello di donna futurista." *Donne e politica* 4 (August–October): 35–37.

Hertz, Neil. 1985a. "Medusa's Head: Male Hysteria under Political Pressure." In *The End of the Line: Essays on Psychoanalysis and the Sublime*. Edited by Neil Hertz. New York: Columbia University Press.

———. 1985b. "In Reply." In *The End of the Line: Essays on Psychoanalysis and the Sublime*. Edited by Neil Hertz. New York: Columbia University Press.

Isidori Frasca, Rosella. 1983. *. . . e il duce le volle sportive*. Bologna: Pàtron.

———. 1988. "L'educazione fisica e sportiva, e la 'preparazione materna." In *La corporazione delle donne: Ricerche e studi sui modelli femminili nel ventennio fascista*. Edited by Marina Addis Saba. Florence: Vallecchi.

Kaplan, Alice Yaeger. 1986. *Reproduction of Banality: Fascism, Literature, and French Intellectual Life*. Minneapolis: University of Minnesota Press.

Labalme, Patricia H., ed. 1984. *Beyond Their Sex: Learned Women of the European Past*. New York: New York University Press.

Labriola, Teresa. 1918. *I problemi sociali della donna*. Bologna: Zanichelli.

———. 1924. "Il femminismo italiano nella rinascita dello spirito." *La donna italiana* 1 (January).

———. 1927a. "Nell'orbita del fascismo (Elogio della donna nuova)." *La donna italiana* 4 (September).

———. 1927b. "Nell'orbita del fascismo (Elogio della donna nuova)." *La donna italiana* 4 (October).

———. 1929. "Il nostro programma." *La donna italiana* 6 (December).

———. 1930a. "Problemi morali del femminismo." *La donna italiana* 7 (June).

———. 1930b. "Nell'orbita del femminismo: Valori reali e correnti fittizie nell'ora presente." *La donna italiana* 7 (October).

———. 1931. "Parlando con le lettrici." *La donna italiana* 8 (February).

———. 1932. "La donna nella cultura e nelle professioni (Conservazione e dispersione delle energie)." *La donna italiana* 9 (October).

———. 1933a. "L'assistenza quale dovere nazionale." *La donna italiana* 10 (February).

———. 1933b. "Per la riforma della cultura." *La donna italiana* 10 (July–August).

------. 1933c. "Sempre in tema di cultura." *La donna italiana* 10 (September).

------. 1934. "Spunto polemico." *La donna italiana* 11 (May).

------. 1935a. "Doveri di madri." *La donna italiana* 12 (January).

------. 1935b. "Suffragismo francese e sodalismo italiano." *La donna italiana* 12 (April).

------. 1936. "Madri e istitutrici." *La donna italiana* 13 (June–August).

------. 1938. "Il pericolo latente." *La donna italiana* 15 (January).

Laclau, Ernesto. 1977. "Fascism and Ideology." In *Politics and Ideology in Marxist Theory.* New York: Verso.

Lonzi, Carla. 1991. "Let's Spit on Hegel." In *Italian Feminist Thought.* Edited by Paola Bono and Sandra Kemp. Cambridge, Mass.: Basil Blackwell.

Macciocchi, Maria Antonietta. 1976. *La donna "nera": "Consenso" femminile e fascismo.* Milan: Feltrinelli.

Meldini, Piero, ed. 1975. *Sposa e madre esemplare: Ideologia e politica della donna e della famiglia durante il fascismo.* Florence: Guaraldi.

Milan Women's Bookstore Collective. 1990. *Sexual Difference: A Theory of Social-Symbolic Practice.* Translated by Patricia Cicogna and Teresa De Lauretis. Bloomington: Indiana University Press.

Mondello, Elisabetta. 1987. *La nuova italiana: La donna nella stampa e nella cultura del ventennio.* Rome: Riuniti.

Mosse, George. 1985. *Nationalism and Sexuality: Respectability and Abnormal Sexuality in Modern Europe.* New York: Howard Fertig.

Mussolini, Benito. 1961. "Macchina e donna." In *Opera omnia di Benito Mussolini.* Edited by Edoardo Susmel and Duilio Susmel. Florence: La Fenice. Originally published in *Il popolo d'Italia,* August 31, 1934.

Nozzoli, Anna. 1978. *Tabù e coscienza: La condizione femminile nella letteratura italiana del novecento.* Florence: La Nuova Italia.

Pieroni Bortolotti, Franca. 1963. *Alle origini del movimento femminile in Italia, 1848–1892.* Turin: Einaudi.

------. 1974. *Socialismo e questione femminile in Italia, 1892–1922.* Milan: Mazzotta.

------. 1978. *Femminismo e partiti politici in Italia 1919–1926.* Rome: Riuniti.

Re, Lucia. 1989. "Futurism and Feminism." *Annali d'italianistica* 7: 253–72.

Rich, Adrienne. 1980. "Compulsory Heterosexuality and Lesbian Existence." *Signs: Journal of Women in Culture and Society* 5, no. 4.

Rinaldi, Ivana. 1987. "Ines Donati: Realtà e mito di un' 'eroina' fascista." *Quaderni di resistenza Marche* 13 (January): 48–49.

Rivière, Joan, 1986. "Womanliness as Masquerade." In *Formations of Fantasy.* Edited by Victor Burgin, James Donald, and Cora Kaplan. New York: Routledge. Orginally published in *International Journal of Psychoanalysis* 10 (1929).

Robert, Enif. 1982. "Una parola serena." In Claudia Salaris, *Le futuriste: Donne e letteratura d'avanguardia in Italia (1909/1944).* Milan: Edizioni delle Donne. Originally published in *L'Italia futurista* 2 (October 7, 1917).

Saïd, Suzanne. 1983. "Féminin, femme, et femelle dans les grands traités biologiques d'Aristote." In *La femme dans les sociétés antiques: Actes des colloques de Strasbourg (mai 1980 et mars 1981).* Edited by Edmond Lévy. Strasbourg: AECR.

Santarelli, Enzo. 1976a. "Il fascismo e le ideologie antifemministe." *Problemi del socialismo* 4: 75–106.

------. 1976b. "Protagoniste femminili del primo novecento: Schede biobibliografiche." *Problemi del socialismo* 4: 248–49.

Saraceno, Chiara. 1991. "Redefining Maternity and Paternity: Gender, Pronatalism and Social Policies in Fascist Italy." In *Maternity and Gender Policies: Women and the Rise of the European Welfare States, 1880s–1950s*. Edited by Gisela Bock and Pat Thane. New York: Routledge.

Scaramuzza, Emma. 1983. "Professioni intellettuali e fascismo: L'ambivalenza dell'Alleanza muliebre culturale italiana." *Italia contemporanea* (September): 111–33.

Schiesari, Juliana. 1989. "In Praise of Virtuous Women? For a Genealogy of Gender Morals in Renaissance Italy." *Annali d'italianistica* 7: 66–87.

Scott, Joan W. 1990. "Deconstructing Equality-versus-Difference; or, The Uses of Poststructuralist Theory for Feminism." In *Conflicts in Feminism*. Edited by Marianne Hirsch and Evelyn Fox Keller. New York: Routledge.

Sighele, Scipio. 1910. *Eva moderna*. Milan: Treves.

Silverman, Kaja. 1980. "Masochism and Subjectivity." *Framework* 12: 2–9.

Sontag, Susan. 1980. "Fascinating Fascism." In *Under the Sign of Saturn*. New York: Farrar, Straus & Giroux. Originally published 1974.

Spackman, Barbara. 1990. "The Fascist Rhetoric of Virility." *Stanford Italian Review* 8, nos. 1–2: 81–101.

———. forthcoming-a. *Fascist Virilities: Rhetoric, Ideology, and Social Fantasy*. Minnneapolis: University of Minnesota Press.

———. forthcoming-b. "Mafarka and Son: Marinetti's Homo(phobic) Economics." *Modernism/Modernity*.

Sternhell, Zeev. 1986. *Neither Left nor Right: Fascist Ideology in France*. Translated by David Maisel. Berkeley: University of California Press.

Thomas, Yan. 1992. "The Division of the Sexes in Roman Law." In Georges Duby and Michelle Perrot, *A History of Women in the West: From Ancient Goddesses to Christian Saints*. Edited by Pauline Schmitt Pantel; translated by Arthur Goldhammer. Cambridge: Harvard University Press.

Zunino, Pier Giorgio. 1985. *L'ideologia del fascismo*. Bologna: Il Mulino.

6 / The Power of Style: Fashion and Self-Fashioning in Irene Brin's Journalistic Writing

Maurizia Boscagli

The Importance of Details

They say that in the period immediately following WWI, the photographic camera was the catalyst for many occasional encounters. "Miss, may I take your picture?" asked the soldiers who had survived the war, clad in extraordinarily short jackets and polished boots. And it seems that these requests had very positive consequences. But now it's frightening to think of the tons of film which, during these twenty years, have transmitted the memory of numberless faces, streets, beaches, wasted smiles with stretched lips, clouds lined with light, creased trousers, children, dogs, cats, old women, fishermen, groups of horrible bathers etc., etc. . . . all dross of a new vice.

IRENE BRIN, "Photography"[1]

Nothing could have better described Irene Brin's work in the eyes of official Fascist culture than her own words in this passage. Her journalistic production between 1920 and 1940—uniquely spanning the years of the Fascist *ventennio*—focused on the very elements that had been considered as bourgeois waste, and therefore made marginal, by Fascism: manners, fashion, international modernist art, women, and the middle class confronting modernity. That is, she privileged the trivial and apparently meaningless details that a culture chauvinistically interested in the monumental and anything national was trying to obscure.

In the midst of the stifling provinciality of Italian culture at the time, Brin invented a new type of journalistic writing that echoed the palimpsestic textuality of modernism: her page — characterized by a mixture of topics drawn from high and popular realms — reflects her wide-ranging gaze on the culture of modernity and, in particular, her interest in the effects that the new means of mechanical reproduction exercised on the everyday lives of people. In her brilliantly satirical style, Brin does not only describe modern manners and aspirations, but questions, probes, and interrogates the culture that produced them, so that her portrayal of modern mores is also an antisentimental and antimoralistic critique of Italian life under Fascism.

Brin's journalistic writing, collected in *Usi e costumi 1920–1940* for the first time by the Italian press Sellerio in 1981, originally appeared in the magazine *Omnibus,* one of the most anticonformist and unusual publications in Fascist Italy, eventually closed down by the Minculpop (Ministry of Popular Culture) and its censorship in the early 1940s. *Omnibus* published articles on contemporary art, literature, and music, and writings on that part of European and American culture that Fascism did not acknowledge, but branded as decadent. Together with pieces by such nonaligned critics as Alberto Savinio and Bruno Barilli appeared Irene Brin's *elzeviri* — short essays, or even vignettes of what today would be called cultural critique. These articles offered often humorous reflections on an array of topics (from hygiene to jazz, from unemployment to graphology and marriage) and prominent contemporary figures (including Gertrude Stein, Giorgio de Chirico, and Radclyffe Hall, as well as Barbette and Cordero, two famous transvestite actors of the time). This vertiginous variety implies, on Brin's part, a precise agenda concerning the female reader: through the multiplicity of her topics she addresses the New Italian Woman — culturally *à la page,* interested in more than the home and family life — and at the same time implicitly critiques the feminine identity being created by contemporary women's magazines, that of the *signorine* who read *Marie-Claire,* for instance.[2] Brin's production is an unusual example of women's writing during Italian Fascism. Neither on the side of official culture (as Margherita Sarfatti's writing was, for instance) nor on that of a very tolerated unofficial one (as exemplified by Liala and Delly's romances), her portrayal of modern women made available to her audience new images of femininity. In Brin's work the woman engineer, the *garçonne,* the lesbian, the actress, the poet, the traveler, and the artist were counterposed to the two most visible feminine stereotypes of the time, the robust rural housewife, who was awarded prizes by the regime for the number of children produced, and the pale, weak, and aristocratic heroine of romances, always looking for protection in the powerful body (often in uniform) of the male hero.

For the feminist critic of modern culture, Brin's writing matters for two reasons: it provides a critique of the stupefying and immobilizing representations of femininity that official and popular culture made available to women, and it stands as antagonist to Fascism. Here a brief parenthesis needs to be opened: although Brin held socialist views, her writing cannot be strictly defined as "resistant," particularly in light of the political meaning the term *resistance* possesses in Italian history. Indeed, the word *Fascism,* or even an allusion to the regime, never appears in her writing. And yet, the writings collected in *Usi e costumi* possess an oppositional quality, well disguised through their nonchalant, ironic tone, as well as through their apparently harmless, almost otiose and marginal choice of topics. In fact, Brin's writing is deeply antithetical to Fascism, both stylistically and thematically. Her fragmentary recording of modern "customs," her focus on the ephemeral, the trivial, the deeply inauthentic, stands in open opposition to the Fascist interest in totality and the epic. Brin's aim is to record and transmit historical memory: "This is neither intended to be nor can it be the history of two decades," she writes in the preface to *Usi e costumi,* "but only an aid to understanding a noisy, naive, and sad generation which existed under the illusion of living at an extraordinary pace" (Brin 1981, 11). Telescoping from epic continuity to the partiality of the everyday, Brin turns history into the story of a generation, that is, into a discontinuous narrative made out of apparently insignificant details. Her peculiar method of narrativizing history by breaking down its monumental continuity (what will be interpreted by the historian) into particles that are instead common experience for the individual also implies a redefinition of what counts as "culture." In Brin's writing culture does not encompass only the academic and military functions and the public spectacularity of the regime, but includes the minimal acts and the desires that arise in the everyday experiences of masses of people.

Brin's antiauthoritarian view of history corresponds to an understanding of culture equally adverse to totality. These qualities, together with her detached, ironic tone and the fragmentariness of her writing—a truly multivoiced encyclopedia of culture—qualifies her as a modernist writer. Insofar as she contributes to the project of demontage of the aura, she's certainly a modernist, but one who confronts, in T. S. Eliot's words, "the panorama of futility" constituting modernity without fear. Brin does not feel threatened by modern "futility"; in fact, she contributes to it herself. More modern than the high modernists themselves, she makes the trivial and the new the fulcrum of her social analysis. At the same time, she never celebrates these two categories blindly; rather, she astutely recognizes them as aleatory solutions to the problems posed by modernity. These are the very problems Walter Benjamin and Theodor Adorno, among other modern cultural critics, confront in their own work: the survival of the individual in the face of political totalitarianism and consumerism; the discourse of progress implied by capital's privileging of the new; the ephemerality and necessary fragmentation of subjectivity in the modern scene, and yet the imperative of maintaining a notion of active agency, of a subject endowed with critical capabilities, even though fetishistically reconstructed (an ersatz subject) out of its own ruins.

Although Brin's reflection does not take place in the same philosophical terms that characterize Benjamin's and Adorno's, her writing provides the discursive space where the same issues of individuality and totalitarianism can be once again articulated and debated. For Brin, fashion and the fashionable constitute the terrain where these questions take shape. At the time when the self is obliterated by Fascist rhetoric and cultural practices, fashion points to the possibility of a fleeting reconstruction of subjectivity, a self-fashioning whose ephemeral quality provokes reassurance and anxiety at the same time. What is reassembled through fashion and style is not the self, but a not-yet-complete, not-yet-finished and never real identity—the masquerade that for the feminist critic defines feminine identity and at the same time threatens the authenticity and the substantiality of the Phallus.[3] It is this threat Brin's discourse of fashion poses to the authentic and the natural that makes her writing antithetical to Fascism. With this essay I want to elucidate the terms of Brin's anti-Fascist style by looking at how fashion contributes to the critique of the Fascist liquidation of the self. The problem is twofold. On the one hand, fashion provides new strategies for producing subjectivity when individuality is deeply jeopardized by history. On the other—and here Brin's narrative seems to echo the terms of the poststructuralist feminist critique of phallogocentrism—fashion becomes the means for producing a never-concluded heterogeneity (what I will call the subjective) in the midst of historical homogeneity, that of a culture in uniform.

Staging the Self as Persona: Bricolage versus the Aura

After 1929, men's jackets became considerably longer, and so did hair. Charles Farrell and Johnny Weissmuller created big heads, which in Italy were called "a la Ghigo." ("Men's Wardrobe," in Brin 1981, 144)

At Santa Margherita, Amalia Guglielminetti used to wear striped, sleeveless dresses; Willa Cather, when she appeared on the beach, flaunted flowery cretonnes....Ninetta Moscatelli went to a ball in golden lamé. The city split into two parties: can a girl wear golden lamé or not? It was established that she could. ("Women's Wardrobe," in Brin 1981, 78–79)

There was a Crawford style...most of all there was a Crawford mouth, with the upper lip shaped like a liver sausage, the lower one like a slice of watermelon—critiqued at first, and then imitated everywhere. Her story seemed to complete the elegy of the spiteful face, of cheap clothes, and the self-made woman, whose story was repeated in the story of thousands of others, and then appeared dramatic and romantic. Typists swarmed out of offices in the evening, firmly convinced that they resembled her, and that, like her, they deserved a villa with swimming pool in California. ("Fashion and Cinema," in Brin 1981, 95)

To understand Brin's invisibly anti-Fascist writing through her use of fashion, we must keep in mind the nodal points of Fascist discourse: the production of the real through the epic, the gigantic, and the spectacular (what dwarfs the individual); its representation of history through the model of Hegelian teleology (a History with capital *h*, guarantor of eternity and universality for the Italian "race"); its dispersal of individuality into the oceanic (whose referent is the all-encompassing figure of the duce); its autarchic provincialism and its belief in nature; its contradictory relationship to modernity; and, last but not least, the representation of women as inferior to men. Although all these elements are in turn undermined and corroded in Brin's writing, it is nature and authenticity that she tacitly and frontally attacks through her interest in fashion. As a symbolic system in which desire, sexuality, style, and the social merge, fashion has been widely studied by past and contemporary critics—Leopardi, Balzac, Flaubert, Baudelaire, and Wilde in the nineteenth century, and Barthes, Baudrillard, Hebdige, Hollander, and Gaines, to name only a few, in the twentieth. But Benjamin's work is where the question of fashion is explored in the terms suggested by Brin's analysis, that is, vis-à-vis the cultural imperialism of Fascism and commodity fetishism. In the fragments of the unfinished *Passagenwerk,* his study of the Parisian arcades, Benjamin looks at fashion from a double point of view: as a form of perverted temporality (the mythic and phantasmagorical temporality of progress) and as the index of modern reification. In both cases fashion makes "modernity the time of Hell" (in Buck-Morss 1989, 96). Progress for Benjamin is an unending repetition of the new as always the same. Fashion signifies this mythic diachronicity, a continual transience without change. More significantly, for Benjamin fashion reifies the human capacity for change by displacing it onto things, so that by desiring, buying, and identifying with commodities, the subject will continually give up sovereignty and delegate it to the inorganic. For Benjamin, therefore, fashion signifies the subject's alienation ("Fashion prescribed the ritual through which the fetish commodity wished to be worshipped," as he wrote in the 1935 *Expose*; in Buck-Morss 1989, 97).

In her writing, Brin takes into account the question of temporality signified by fashion, but only secondarily. For her, the discourse of fashion implies another crucial category of Benjamin's theory, the aura, and thus poses two different questions: that of the opposition between artificiality (mediation) and authenticity (immediacy), and that of the possibility of reformulating individuality vis-à-vis the decline of the bourgeois ideology of the unique self on the one hand and the Fascist threat of oceanic homogeneity on the other.

The way Brin deals with fashion privileges not so much newness as artificiality—the unique style that in modernity comes to signify individuality and the self. The production of subjectivity through style (individuality as a personal aesthetic), achieved by juxtaposing and mixing already existing semiotic codes in fashion, as much as in literature and art, has been prominent in poststructuralist theory. I am thinking of

Roland Barthes in "The Death of the Author" (1977) as well as of contemporary feminist theory, as represented by Mary Ann Doane, Luce Irigaray, and Julia Emberley, for instance. The decentering of the phallogocentric subject through masquerade (and through fashion as a conspicuous embodiment of masquerade) has been taken as the representation of postmodern subjectivity par excellence, and as such has been saluted by different critics with exhilaration (Deleuze and Guattari 1983), with anxiety, if not despair (Jameson 1984) and, from another feminist critic, Rosi Braidotti (1989), with suspicion.[4] Yet, if in postmodernity the fashion apparatus works toward simulation and the disintegration of subjectivity, in the early twentieth century "modernist objects retained some capacity for symbolic investment, whether that of use value, prestige or the expression of identity" (Faurschou 1977, 81). Thus fashion could still provide a channel, no matter how unstable, for affirming individuality.

For Brin, reconstructing subjectivity through style (or perhaps it would be more accurate to talk of "the subjective") is a way of walking the slippery ground of a postbourgeois, post-nineteenth-century culture, where the individual has no safe space on which to establish her identity—unless she accepts identifying with the body of the nation and the body of the leader. It is not by chance that style (artificiality, affectation, cosmopolitanism) is ruled out and often demonized by Fascism. Fascist discourse associates style and fashion with the decadent bourgeoisie, the nationless Jew, the mundane life of the city, and the dishonest woman (the prostitute), against the life of the province, which is represented as simple, healthy, and most of all natural, because it is tied to the patriarchal and preindustrial land and to the cycles of nature. But nature, as Russell Berman (1986) makes clear, is appropriated by the Fascist imagination as a signifier of naturalization of elements that are per se highly "unnatural"—identity, gender, subjection, political activity:

> Perhaps more than any other motif, the desire—and as the alternative to the metropolis as the locus of individuality and democracy—marks the various literary fascist imaginations: the German literature of blood and soil, Pound's invocation of the natural order of ancient China, and above all, the culture of nature in Hamsun. Nature is the structure that precedes and predetermines individuality; subjectivity is merely a bourgeois illusion implicated in a liberal narrative of emancipation. (p. xvii)[5]

The way Fascism uses nature functions both to aestheticize politics and to reauraticize reality in the face of artificial and technological modernity. In fact, the Fascist notion of nature is accurately produced and staged exactly through those means of mechanical reproduction that Fascist imagination at least nominally disqualifies. For instance, the oceanic identity between the individual and the duce, always naturalized in Fascist discourse, is produced at the rally, thanks to the loudspeakers, or through the auratic presence of the leader staged by cinema or photography. In either case, the spectacle is supposed to produce in the viewer-listener a total feeling of "naturalness," so that the artificial functions as a channel for the authentic.

Fashion as well is "spectacular," but its staginess has a different quality and a different outcome from that of the totalitarian "show." The Fascist spectacle denies its fetishistic quality and demands from the spectator the same contemplation and passive absorption (a cessation of critical activity) that the aura of the bourgeois work of art studied by Benjamin demanded from its audience. The fashion apparatus, on the contrary, continually points to its own artificiality, to the work through which the body is clad, decorated, and fetishized, in a way that jeopardizes the notions of originality and authenticity that the aura implies. As a form of textuality — collage of different stylistic quotations — fashion declares, or at least makes visible, its status as a fetish. The spectacle of fashion is a work of montage whose shocking lack of authenticity (visible in the "apoplectic flower" Brin sees on the shoulder of a modern lady),[6] stands in place of what has never been there — nature.

The fashionable and its fragile ephemerality point to a figuration of the individual subject (built) in ruin(s) — the ersatz and fragmented version of individuality that follows the demise of bourgeois subjectivity under Fascism. Brin herself is a perfect representation of this ersatz self. She constitutes herself in absentia, through a series of personae, of which her noms de plume are the index (Maria Rossi, her real name, was displaced by "Oriane," "Mariu," "Maria del Corso," "Contessa Lara," and then Irene Brin, the name she used also outside her writing). Furthermore, her own individuality was totally mediated by her accurate staging of the self through fashion. Brin was an extremely elegant woman whose quirky cult of artifice made her quite famous at the time (at her dinner parties, her guests were presented with a dish of rice in the shape of a swan dyed with *blu di Mitilene*).

Her pleasure in surprising, in taking aback her interlocutor both with her writing and with her own person,[7] is also a form of play, a ludic attitude implicitly signaling that the discourse of plenitude advocated by bourgeois ideology and then refunctioned by Fascism is in ruin, gone bankrupt. Both with the staging of her own persona and with her writing, Brin is dancing on these ruins. At the same time, it must be added once again, her activity and her style cannot be read as a form of resistance to Fascism per se; rather, they inscribe resistance without voicing it explicitly. Both her staged presence and her writing were read by the Fascist institution fetishistically, as the Medusa's head that the regime needed to use apotropaically against its own castration anxiety. The fear of *absentia* and artificiality, of which Brin's fashion writing is a memento, is reabsorbed and exorcised by Fascist patriarchy (the totalitarian embodiment of Freud's little boy), by pushing this writing into the degraded and domestic(ated) sphere of feminine frivolity, and by labeling it as the mollified expression of the bourgeoisie. (Yet the apotropaic trick must have not been entirely effective; after all, *Omnibus* was ultimately censored by the Minculpop.) The image of a woman writing about trivial things is thus held apotropaically against the suspicion, if not the awareness, of a frightening absence (the absence of the subject, of the real itself), which Fascism manages to fill up with its own spectacularity and rhetoric. In this sense, we can define Fascism as a cultural and political agency truly, literally, running on empty.

The individuality one acquires through style and fashion is inauthentic, but cannot be renounced. What is renounced, instead, is the idea that identity, uniqueness, originality is an a priori, something innate in the individual, as bourgeois ideology had claimed. What confers individuality is no longer founded on the interiority of the subject, but rather on her exteriority (her attire, for instance), and on the operation of mixing codes to create a new hybrid. What is achieved — this is the lesson that Brin learns from modernity — is an unstable sense of identity, something that needs to be reestablished over and over again through the means one finds available (even though these are merely chiffon and Ermete watches, as Brin shows), but not relinquished. Brin's ironic, even stinging critique is often addressed to those who cannot live with this uncertainty, as well as to the passive consumers of modern culture, for whom style is not something to create, but rather something to imitate flatly, as for instance *le mitomani* do ("pale, long, sinewy women, almost always blond, often ill...child-ish and cruel," imitating Greta Garbo): "Soon young ladies who became bored by their reasonable husbands, and girls who were disappointed by their anonymous fiancés, imitated negligence, indifference, the art of sitting on a bus and feeling as if they were crossing...dangerous and unknown cities; the art of drinking cocktails as if about to com-mit suicide" ("Le mitomani," in Brin 1981, 30).

Brin wants the individual to be a producer of style, or at least a *bricoleur,* and an active—not passive—consumer of cultural myths. Hence her savage sarcasm toward one of the major sources of myth-making for women, *les magazines*: "Printed on shiny paper, with cig-arette ads which looked like paintings, paintings that looked like cig-arettes ads...French and more often American magazines announced important, often decisive news at the consulates in China and Ma-laysia, in Parisian metros, in Genoese villas in Belgrad ateliers: *Bon-wit-Teller fera de vous la femme de domain*" ("Les magazines," in Brin 1981, 27). This passage offers a metacommentary in reverse of her own work as a journalist: the *promesse de bonheur* voiced by the ad and the magazine's intent to bedazzle the reader are continually undermined by the "reality shocks" given by her text. Her writing presents itself as an unsutured surface whose fissures make visible the news that the glossy pages of ads and frivolous stories don't let in—war, unemployment, inflation, the homelessness of the refugees. These events and figures appear on Brin's page surreptitiously, in all their startling nudity. The shock experienced by the reader is empha-sized by her lack of commentary, her refusal to act as a mediator and an ideological and affective "cushion" for her audience: "The weekly dole for the German worker consisted of 9,60 mark in 1926. The cost of rent was generally 8 mark per week at that time (one only room, no matter how many members the family included). They had left, to live on, 0.23 cents per day" ("The Unemployed," in Brin 1981, 172). These data acquire a particularly bitter tone if read together with the other pieces included in the same section, titled "Some Prices" — where, for instance, she gives a detailed report, probably found in one of *les magazines,* about Mrs. Vanderbilt's expenses for her child Gloria, or the cost of one day at the resort of Mittersill: "One day at Mittersill cost 400 shillings. But the right to hunting was included" ("Daily Pensione a Mittersill," in Brin 1981, 174).

Although Gloria and Mrs. Vanderbilt, as well as such other socialites of the time as Wallis Simpson, Odette Pannetier, and Jane di San Faustino, appear in more than one sketch, the women Brin finds representative of her time are not primarily glamorous "celebs." As a resource of names and faces, the mundane chronicle is always displaced by Brin's own intellectual geography. Alongside the queen of Romania, Lady Mendl, and Coco Chanel, she inserts Marie Laurencin, painted with a feminist touch, "Don't tell us, please, that as a young woman she loved Apollinaire in vain, and consoled herself by drinking too much absynth" ("Female Protagonists," in Brin 1981, 65); Gertrude Stein and her "desire for baroque banality"; Catherine Mansfield, "almost certainly the major poet of our epoch"; and Mae West, resisting and winning over American puritanism: "Now she's almost fifty, and she's envied by the other Hollywood stars because she can eat all she likes, without dieting, and earns lots of money" ("Female Protagonists," in Brin 1981, 72).

Notwithstanding these excursus in the life of the rich and the famous, the real protagonist of Brin's analysis, and target of her critique, remains the middle class. Modernity, which Fascism approached through the futurist fascination with the machine, with the hardness and the geometric exactness of metal, is represented in Brin's page, through a careful analysis of the desires, awkwardness, and pettiness of different social classes. Brin is a particularly pointed critic of the petty bourgeoisie, whose tics, obsessions, fears, and illusions are scrutinized with the ironic and often blasé perspective of the class to which she belonged, the Italian and Mittel European haute bourgeoisie.

She shows a profound awareness that the object of her observation is a generation of consumers (of commodities, spectacles, fashions) who try to get rid of their provincialism by imitating foreign "costumes." The *tabarin* in Rome (the *Bal Tic-Tac*), the cocaine den in Bologna, the search for "a nice little place where we can wear our bathing suits all day long" ("Hygiene," in Brin 1981, 15) stood as the local embodiment of the great ideal of cosmopolitan modernity. Brin magnetically evokes the urban life of the metropolis as well as the opposite impulse to leave the metropolitan space for a return to wild, uncontaminated nature, "far away"—to which both Gauguin in the South Pacific islands and Erich Maria Remarque in Cannes succumbed, the latter described as "among duchesses seminaked like himself, greedily desiring simplicity and cosmic contacts" ("Hygiene," in Brin 1981, 16).

Some of the human fauna and locations Brin describes represent also the target of Adorno and Horkheimer's anxiously ferocious irony in *Dialectic of Enlightenment* (1969), in particular the theme of the return to nature, which the two German critics describe as a movement from the "blond beast" to the South Sea islanders of the "sarong film" (p. 233). But it is with the portrayal of the petty bourgeoisie—the image of the girl with the fashionable, made-up pale face, carrying two Upim bags on the bus—that Brin strikes a truly Adornian note. The aphoristic force of Adorno's prose, the same bitter and ironic tone of his mandarin materialist critique of culture, is echoed in Brin's lack of pity for the individual who lets herself be blindly interpellated by commodity culture—for the girls who, as Siegfried Kracauer (1974) put it, "cut their hair, go to the cinema and die" (quoted in Hake 1987, 425).

Brin shares with Adorno the same suspicion of the new and the same ambivalence toward the shipwreck of bourgeois values in the face of totalitarianism. The obliteration of the old in favor of the new shapes, for instance, the modern relationship between parents and children, which Brin registers in her writing. Before the absolute modernity of youth, the elders must step aside, in fact, must leave the scene as *bagages inutiles*. She tells us: "Parents, defined as '*Bagages Inutiles*'—invitation cards regularly brought the initials of the phrase *Sans Bagages Inutiles*, or *No Old People*—accepted, with masochistic complacence, their children's spite and boredom; they only desired to imitate them, to reach them, to be thin and dynamic, exhausted and amoral as they were" ("The Girls," in Brin 1981, 110). Adorno's (1987) reflection makes explicit Brin's perplexity and ambivalence in front of the modern foregrounding of the culture of youth, by pointing out the contiguity between this culture and its catastrophic outcome in the Fascist cult of youth:

> Our relationship to parents is beginning to undergo a sad, shadowy transformation. Through their economic impotence they have lost their awesomeness.... One of the Nazis' symbolic outrages is the killing of the very old. Such a climate fosters a late, lucid understanding with our parents.... The violence done to them makes us forget the violence they did.... Even the neurotic oddities and deformities of our elders stand for character, for

something humanly achieved, in comparison to pathic health, infantilism raised to the norm. (p. 22)

The iconoclastic value of the new, the young, is never taken at face value and uncritically celebrated by either critic; rather, it is cautiously examined. Adorno (1987) talks of newness, of the modern as the objective correlate of the "decay of experience": "The cult of the new and the idea of modernity is a rebellion against the fact that there is no longer anything new.... Itself unattainable, newness installs itself in the place of overthrown divinity amidst the first consciousness of the decay of experience" (p. 235). In subtle contrast, Brin associates the experience of modernity (the effects of listening to the radio, talking on the phone) with sadness:

> Once it became a mass medium, the radio soon meant the absolute abolition of silence, and, simultaneously, of absolute sociality.... As far as our generation was concerned, it seemed impossible to re-create silence, and we worked, ate, made love with the background music of spirituals, Bach, or, for indifference, habit, or fear of emptiness, of the Bulletin for the Sailor. Perhaps our rooms, which we wanted very empty, very white, very functional... amplified the volume of the complicitous voices of the *Comedien Harmonists,* and we were happy to feel so modern and so sad. ("Radiomania," in Brin 1981, 31)

For Brin, modernity is an experience of sadness and loss, but never of real mourning. The crisis of the nineteenth-century bourgeois world and the erosion of its hegemonic form of masculine subjectivity also brought with them the eclipse of a certain construction of femininity and the mandatory representation of women's activity as dilettantism, of which *"le signorine"* are the representatives:

> Young ladies were the perfect representatives of the complex and secret bourgeois world which, in the space of a decade, changed, came to a close, and actually ended. Their vocation to uselessness, to lies, led them into labyrinths of vain elegance, of superfluous precautions and—as real dilettantes—they badly learned some foreign languages, sewed for themselves badly—made clothes, and prepared inedible sandwiches—complicated, hyperdecorated—which made one think with anguish about the fact that their hands weren't always clean. ("The Girls," in Brin 1981, 111–12).

With the demise of feminine dilettantism (the role the bourgeois polity had reserved to women) the idea of masculine "professionalism" fell apart, too. At the end of the two decades examined by Brin, what is made visible is not only that *"le signorine" are* their clothes—their badly finished clothes—but that the emperor, too, the bourgeois himself, was naked, or at least was nothing more than a costume.

Adorno (1987) also acknowledges the reduction of the bourgeois masculine subject to nothing more than a vestige of himself:

> To think that the individual is being liquidated without traces is over-simplistic. The disaster does not take the form of a radical elimination of what existed previously; rather, the things that history had condemned are dragged along dead, neutralized and impotent as ignominious ballast. In the midst of standardized, organized human units, the individual persists.... But he is in reality no more than a mere function of his own uniqueness, an exhibition piece, like the foetuses that once drew the wonderment and laughter of children.... The individualities imported into America, and divested of individuality in the process, are called colorful personalities.... their "originality" even if it be only a peculiar odiousness, even their garbled language, turn human qualities into a clown's costume. (p. 135)

It is on the image of the clown's costume that the contiguity between Adorno's and Brin's texts breaks down. For Adorno, the notion of subjectivity that reason (*Vernunft*) had promised has been entirely perverted and dispersed by the logic of domination and abstraction of the Enlightenment. Thus the individual-as-costume is only a tattered, ersatz reproduction of a lost original (which should and could have been and never was, for Adorno). But for Brin, the costume is all that exists and matters; the clown costume thus testifies both to the impossibility of originality and of the authentic self and to the necessity of continually re-creating it anew through the commodified and spurious material provided by the modern age.

Furthermore, Brin experiences modernity as a key moment of cultural loss, but at the same time, she perceives it as a point of no return. There is no looking back, no nostalgia for *die Welt von Gestern* in her text. For her, the seat of the subject is—finally—empty (the king is dead, long live the clown) and ready to be filled by style. With her writing of fashion, Brin replicates the gaze of the modern cultural critic and of the fearless modernist, playfully focusing on the panorama of futility that constitutes the scene of modernity with a tinge of sadness but with no anxiety, and, above all, without the compulsive turn to order and totality characterizing both the aesthetic of high modernism and the discourse of Fascism. In doing so, she's positioning herself not as the artifex—the modernist Prosperolike author—but rather as the artifact, ready to negotiate her identity over and over again. Her sadness in the face of modernity is not mourning, but a warning to the generation whose story she records, "a generation," as she tells us, "which was terribly self-conscious, stubbornly searching for instincts and justifications, rights and rages, and unaware to have been called to subject itself to the most absolute constriction one can imagine; a generation so wrapped up in its conviction to be free from any moral, sentimental, and physical ties that it realized too late it had lost that freedom" (Brin 1981, 11). At the same time, Brin makes a call—useful for the modern as well as for the postmodern female subject—for more "fashioning," of herself and her world.

Notes

1. From Brin, *Usi e costumi 1920–1940* (1981). All the excerpts I quote from *Usi e costumi* in this chapter are my own translations.
2. The period Brin takes into examination, since the early 1920s, saw the birth of the first Italian modern women's magazines: "in 1919 *Novella,* by Rizzoli; in 1923 *Alba* (Alba Editions); in 1926 *Grazia* starts being published by Mondadori; and then *Rakam* in 1930; *Annabella,* by Rizzoli in 1934; *Eva* by Ottavia Vitagliano in 1934; in 1938 *Gioia,* Rusconi Paolozzi Editions, and then the aforementioned *Cordelia*" (Ghiazza 1991, 147).
3. I am thinking of the seminal work of the French psychoanalyst Joan Rivière (1929/ 1986) as well as of Mary Ann Doane (1982) and Michele Montrelay (1978), among others.
4. For Braidotti (1989), fashion in postmodernity has the dangerous effect of blurring sexual difference, so that neither the body (subjectivity), nor sexuality, nor gender is "taken seriously" by power: "The bodily surface, and the complex montage of organs that composes it, is thus reduced to pure surface, exteriority without depth, a movable theater of the self. One can find confirmation of the new economy of visual surfaces by looking at the images of the body conveyed by the dominant forms of fashion today: clothes, hairstyles, presentation of the self in everyday life. The emphasis placed on accessories... on 'design' or 'look'... as well as the powerful push towards androgynous, uni-sexed bodies, reveals the shift that has occurred in contemporary imagination. I'd sum them up by saying that not only is sexual difference systematically 'blurred,' but that with it, generational time is also arrested" (p. 172).
5. Alice Yaeger Kaplan also examines the Fascist interest in nature in chapter 1 of her book *Reproductions of Banality* (1986), this time by focusing on the psychoanalytic implication of the return to the semiotic/maternal that this interest implied.
6. "Season by season, women fell in love with their freedom, with their modesty.... A big string of Japanese pearls, an apoplectic flower on the shoulder, a chiffon scarf tied to the wrist, or a silk triangle knotted over the sporty blazer, were the only orna-

ments admitted by the women who swore they wanted to emancipate themselves from the hat — and so they substituted the stockings with socks, shoes with sandals." (from "Il guardaroba delle donne," in Brin 1981, 80).

7. Lietta Tornabuoni, in her foreword to *Usi e costumi*, tells how Brin's elegance struck even Diana Vreeland: "One afternoon in 1950 she wore a Fabiani suit and a Fath hat in Park Avenue, in New York. 'Where did she find it, who designed it?' she was asked by an aging woman-fetish with true American indiscretion, who stopped her on the street. But she was Diana Vreeland, the chief editor of *Harper's Bazaar,* and thus the fortune of Italian fashion in America began, as well as Brin's collaboration with the magazine that already had Truman Capote, Carson McCullers, Brassai, and Cartier Bresson among its contributors" (p. 232).

Works Cited

Adorno, Theodor. 1987. *Minima Moralia*. London: Verso.

Adorno, Theodor, and Max Horkheimer. 1969. *Dialectic of Enlightenment*. New York: Continuum.

Barthes, Roland. 1977. "The Death of the Author." In *Image-Music-Text*. New York: Hill & Wang.

Berman, Russell. 1986. "Foreword." In Alice Yaeger Kaplan, *Reproductions of Banality: Fascism, Literature, and French Intellectual Life*. Minneapolis: University of Minnesota Press.

Braidotti, Rosi. 1989. "Organs without Bodies." *differences* 1: 52–87.

Brin, Irene. 1981. *Usi e costumi* 1920–1940. Palermo: Sellerio.

Buck-Morss, Susan. 1989. *The Dialectics of Seeing: Walter Benjamin and the Arcades Project*. Cambridge: MIT Press.

Deleuze, Gilles, and Félix Guattari. 1983. *Antioedipus: Capitalism and Schizophrenia*. Minneapolis: University of Minnesota Press.

Doane, Mary Ann. 1982. "Film and Masquerade." *Screen* 23 (September–October): 30–57.

Faurschou, Gail. 1977. "Fashion and the Cultural Logic of Postmodernity." In *Body Invaders: Panic Sex in America*. Edited by Arthur Kroker and Marilouise Kroker. New York: St. Martin's.

Ghiazza, Silvana. 1991. "Così donna mi piaci." In *I best-sellers del ventennio: Il regime e il libro di massa*. Edited by Gigliola De Donato and Vanna Gazzola Stacchini. Rome: Riuniti.

Hake, Sabine. 1987. "Girls and Crisis: The Other Side of Diversion." *New German Critique* 42 (Fall): 420–36.

Jameson, Fredric. 1984. "Postmodernism and the Cultural Logic of Late Capitalism." *New Left Review* 146 (Fall): 216–62.

Kaplan, Alice Yaeger. 1986. *Reproductions of Banality: Fascism, Literature, and French Intellectual Life*. Minneapolis: University of Minnesota Press.

Kracauer, Siegfried. 1974. "Die kleine Ladenmädchen gehen in Kino." In *Das Ornament der Masse*. Edited by Karsten Witte. Frankfurt: Suhrkamp.

Montrelay, Michele. 1978. "Inquiry into Femininity." Translated by Parveen Adams. *m/f* 1: 330–46.

Rivière, Joan. 1986. "Womanliness as Masquerade." In *Formations of Fantasy*. Edited by Victor Burgin, James Donald, and Cora Kaplan. New York: Routledge. Originally published in *International Journal of Psychoanalysis* 10 (1929).

7 / Sibilla Aleramo: Writing a Personal Myth

Fiora A. Bassanese

In a journal entry dated December 5, 1940, an aging Sibilla Aleramo (1876–1960) pondered her extraordinary existence as an artist and woman, witnessing its mythic proportions with her characteristic self-reflection:

> Poetry incarnate, made life, life force. All that was life in me, all that, through time, was inscribed in my essence and made me a living symbol, a living poetic myth. All that I've barely expressed in words, quite possibly because I've gone on and on creating myself lyrically with that living material into a unique, almost demonic, work, every day, every instant. For, the person I am, I wanted to be, consciously availing myself of whatever mysterious fate gave me (oh, not only roses): fate I had no power to control, fate with its infinite obstacles and cruelties. I was proud to show it that nothing diminished me, even if it wounded me to the quick; indeed it all ineffably increased me, purified me, illuminated me. (1945, 31)[1]

Aleramo's self-appraisal points to several constants in the writer's life/works: the willed construction of an exceptional personal identity, the convergence of biography and art, and the tendency to self-exaltation and titanism. Sibilla Aleramo would spend thirty eventful years, which she called her third life, fashioning herself into a "living poetic myth" in both words and deeds, transcribing her life experience into textual self-representation. Curiously, her mythmaking coincides chronologically with the development of Benito Mussolini's own self-promotional image.[2] Intriguing parallels exist between the personas of the self-declared poet and the self-proclaimed duce, but Aleramo inherently challenges the gender norms of Fascist ideology in her pursuit of individual and literary fulfillment. In her view, literature is not merely self-referential, but "can profoundly influence individual and cultural self-understanding in the sphere of everyday life" (Felski 1989, 7). Following the model proposed by Leigh Gilmore in *Autobiographics* (1994), in this essay I will analyze how Aleramo uses "self-representation and its constitutive possibilities for agency and subjectivity to become no longer primarily subject to exchange but subjects who exchange the position of object for the subjectivity of self-representational agency" (p. 12).

Sibilla Aleramo's first life, as Rina Pierangeli Faccio, ended in 1902. The events of her youth are detailed in *Una donna* (A woman) (1906/ 1982), her most famous book. First published in 1906, this autobiographical novel traces the story of an unnamed woman from childhood to liberation. Today, it is generally acknowledged as Italy's seminal feminist novel, the progenitor of much contemporary women's fiction.

There exists a marked tendency on the part of readers and scholars alike to focus on this work among Aleramo's to the exclusion of others, and there is a continued temptation to identify Aleramo solely with the heroine of *Una donna,* an understandable lure given the modernity and unmistakable appeal of the character for a feminist audience. The protagonist emerges as a tormented but strong figure who gains personal and social awareness from her plight, gradually transforming herself from a suicidal victim into an advocate for women, the poor, and the oppressed. Moreover, such an identification is borne out by the author's early biography.

Devoted to the liberal social causes espoused in *Una donna,* Rina/ Sibilla fought the good fight for years. While still trapped in a patriarchal and abusive marriage, housebound Rina Pierangeli Faccio published articles and reviews in support of women's causes, such as sexual parity and universal suffrage.[3] After leaving her husband and embarking on her "second life," she volunteered in a clinic for the poor run by the Unione Femminile in Rome and joined Giovanni Cena, her then companion, in creating schools for day laborers and their children in the Roman countryside.[4] In 1908, Aleramo and Cena journeyed to Sicily and Calabria to assist earthquake victims. All the while, she remained active in feminist organizations and causes. Many years later, an elderly Aleramo would return to her youthful enthusiasms. Joining the Italian Communist Party after World War II, she dedicated herself to cultural activities: giving poetry readings in factories and assemblies or lecturing to her comrades, writing for the Communist daily *L'unità* and for the party's feminist journal *Noi donne,* even traveling to Eastern Europe as a party representative. It was a commited end to crown an idealistic youth. But what of Aleramo's middle years, her "third life," which corresponds to the rise and ascendancy of Fascism?

In 1910, Sibilla Aleramo set off on a romantic quest for ideal love, meaningful self-expression, and personal realization. She left behind Cena, a home, her social activism, the last vestiges of conventionality, and Rina Faccio. Aleramo's life became a series of peregrinations and liaisons as she moved from place to place, from man to man, all the while guarding her new individuality. As she herself recognized, the foundations for this existence were laid during her years with Giovanni Cena: "I became a free lover, I became a writer, I imposed my rebellion and my daring on society: and my name was changed to the one I now bear" (Aleramo 1945, 243).[5] The publication of *Una donna* made Aleramo a symbol of female emancipation; Sibilla's romantic attachments over several decades made her a celebrity, a literary femme fatale. After Cena came a succession of lovers: poets such as Vincenzo Cardarelli, Dino Campana, and Salvatore Quasimodo; artists such as Michele Cascella and Umberto Boccioni; and such intellectuals as Giovanni Papini and Giovanni Boine, to name only a famous few. With the lovers came a profusion of autobiographical writing — novels, novellas, plays, verse, letters, journals — that served to give voice to the emotions, thoughts, and meditations of the dis/enamored and narcissistic Sibilla.[6] However, whereas Rina Faccio had been a social critic and activist, the new Sibilla Aleramo was generally apolitical and self-absorbed, only vaguely conscious, for example, of the change in government after the March on Rome: "I began to interest myself in what was taking place, but without profound awareness" (Aleramo 1978a, 251; entry for November 6, 1949).[7]

Although Aleramo was relatively indifferent to the rise of Fascism, the tenor of her life and writing could hardly endear her to the early regime. As author of the polemical *Una donna,* she had challenged the patriarchal definition of womanhood, arguing for moral, intellectual, and sexual equality in marriage. More damning still, Aleramo had declared maternity unjust, concluding that it is immoral to sacrifice individuality to motherhood. Such positions clearly did not correspond to the Fascist categorization of women as mothers first, then wives or faithful widows, or to its reactionary antifeminism. Nevertheless, *Una donna,* polemical as it was, did find an appreciative audience in Fascist Italy: new editions appeared in 1919, 1921, 1930, and 1938. If Aleramo's early work had challenged the traditional position of women *within* social structures, her later works and chosen lifestyle altogether violated bourgeois and patriarchal gender definitions. Immodest free lover, agnostic, confessional writer, intellectual feminist, and unattached gypsy, Sibilla Aleramo post-1910 defied all definitions of approved Fascist femininity.

Having rejected conventional behavioral models for women, Aleramo viewed her irregular position as one of the sacrifices to be made to freedom and personal authenticity. Indeed, she interpreted her marginality as a sign of exceptionality rather than exclusion. Like Mussolini, she separated from the norm in order to construct an exemplary self-image for her public, but also for herself. The prime indicator of this singularity is Aleramo's chosen identity as "poet," not simply writer. Aleramo identified with this privileged role, derived from the orphic tradition of the artist as seer and magician, filtered through the romantics and French and Italian decadents. Her decision to assume the pseudonym Sibilla Aleramo as her identifier speaks to this association: she is a sibyl, the gifted prophet of a new femininity, the writer of books. But Aleramo suffered to give words to her inner truths, metaphors to her perceptions. This is especially true of her verse, the form of writing most clearly associated with the visionary artist. Although Aleramo occasionally composed with sudden bursts of inspiration, or illuminations, she often struggled with meter and cadence, as well as imagery and vocabulary. Yet she valued her poems as the outward sign of her lyric identity and artistic credentials; moreover, they illustrate key elements in the development of Sibilla's persona. In this essay I will focus on Aleramo's verse production, in part because it most literally and literarily defines her as "poet," but also because of the synthetic quality of verse, which expresses a great deal in a restricted space.

More than a profession, or even a vocation, "poetry" was Aleramo's mission, the locus where life and art fused.[8] Her quest was to create a style in which words and rhythms successfully rendered the movements of her experience and psyche, thus merging creativity and auto-biography and evoking several of her major influences: D'Annunzio's self-celebratory and sensual aestheticism; Nietzsche's dionysian spirit; Ibsen's somber morality; and the fragmentary, even lyrical, self-analysis favored by her friends, the restless young intellectuals surrounding the journal *La voce* (1908–16), whose autobiographical reflections tended to absolute candor. More often than not, living took precedence over writing:

> Woman to the utmost degree, I put into my life all the genius a man would have put into a masterpiece. I made my life the masterpiece I had dreamed of creating with poetry: I was, I still am, living poetry, oh, not perfect, indeed often confused, chaotic, but tremendous. (Aleramo 1945, 72; entry for April 29, 1941)[9]

Part of Sibilla Aleramo's self-portrait is the image of a writer in the making, a "living myth caught in the act of transforming life into writing," confusing the division between body and literary endeavor, which feminist critic Anna Nozzoli (1986) goes on to define as "the typology of the woman-poet" (p. 109). For Sibilla Aleramo, the issue of being a "woman" poet is essential to the understanding of her biography and her art. But, as Teresa De Lauretis (1982) has noted, in mythic structuration, the subject is gendered as male: "He is the active principle of culture, the establisher of distinction, the creator of difference" (p. 119).[10] As a female subject of a mythic self-representation, Aleramo is necessarily redefining gender categories and definitions.

Gender is at the core of Aleramo's mythology, just as it is essential to Mussolini's: both the woman poet and the leader of the nation postulate sexual difference, arguing for its necessity and desirability. From its inception, the ideology of Fascism excluded an active role for women, tacitly fostering a misogynistic attitude. As early as 1925, in a pronouncement on female suffrage, Mussolini declared, "Let's not digress into arguing if woman is superior or inferior; we contest that she is different" (quoted in Macciocchi 1976, 46).[11] Aleramo herself favored gender distinctions and constructed her lyric persona on her perception of the essentiality of biological difference. A believer in biologically based gender identity, Aleramo theoretically postulates sexual difference, arguing for its necessity and desirability, in two articles first published in *Il marzocco,* a major Florentine cultural journal, in 1911 and 1913, respectively: "Apologia dello spirito femminile" (Apologia of feminine spirit) and "La pensierosa" (The pensive woman) (see Aleramo 1920/1942).

Read together, the essays provide a poetics based on the gendered text, but they also implicitly propose a politically charged discourse on the cultural and ontological formation of women writers. The first piece, the "Apologia," begins as a response to two critiques of the current "excess production of feminine literature," deemed mediocre in both content and form by the male writer-reviewers. Giuseppe Antonio Borgese declares that women merely imitate male models with chronological delay (i.e., they possess no originality), and Luciano Zuccoli criticizes the weakness of female writing on the basis of women's limited existential experience (i.e., they have nothing to say). Both critiques serve up familiar platitudes, which Aleramo proceeds to deconstruct by altering Borgese's and Zuccoli's basic assumptions. Concurring that women are mediocre writers, she suggests that the cause of artistic failure must be attributed to the prevalence of imitative strategies and the inauthenticity of the subject. Women writers must learn to express their own psychological and biological difference: "Woman, who is different from man, copies him in art. She copies him rather than seeking her own vision of life and her own aesthetic laws within herself" (Aleramo 1920/1942, 61).[12] By believing in their separateness and gendered identities and reflecting them in their works, Aleramo continues, women could produce original art while remaining faithful to their artistic voice. To represent this ontologically sex-based difference, Aleramo models her conceptualization on Henri Bergson's *Évolution créatrice* (1907): intelligence is particularly male; intuition, particularly female.

In the "Apologia," Aleramo (1920/1942) goes on to declare that the "nonexistence of woman in art [inesistenza della donna in arte]" is the result of woman's lack of self-possession and her inability to give independent expression to "her own spiritual worth [il proprio valore spirituale]" (p. 62). Her conclusions are disheartening: "Instead of bringing her authentic soul to life and art, she has joined the action as a poor useless duplicate of man" (p. 63).[13] Aleramo's solutions reflect her personal belief in the indivisibility of art and life, where life is posited as a work of art, "a lengthy mysterious religious construction [una lunga misteriosa religiosa costruzione]" that leads to authentic self-expression. In short, women must acknowledge their inherent otherness in order to fulfill their artistic potential: "If we are convinced of a profound spiritual differentiation of men and women, we must convince ourselves that it implies a profound expressive difference" (p. 65).[14] For Aleramo, the female body is a figure of identity, a representation of the self that can (re)produce inherently gendered literary expression.

On the formal plane, gender difference translates into stylistic difference: "If woman will achieve the depiction of the feminine world of intuition, this more rapid contact between the human and universal spirits, it will certainly be with new movements, with impulses, tremors, pauses, transitions, vortexes unknown to masculine poetry" ("Apologia," in Aleramo 1920/1942, 66).[15] Two years later, in "La pensierosa," Aleramo (1920/1942) reinforces the points made in the "Apologia." Citing her own disciplined effort to reflect "the exigencies of virile brains [le esigenze dei cervelli virili]" (p. 126), she defines it a betrayal of her essential femaleness, lost to the demands of male intellectuality: "I reflect your representation of the world, a prioristically received, then understood by virtue of analysis; but I do not give you the image of things found deep within me, intuition, poetry, wonder, whether it is like your [image] or opposed to it" (p. 127).[16]

"La pensierosa" is a reflection on the difficulties encountered by women when confronting canonical authors and models or, to anticipate a bit, the Lacanian Law of the Father: "Oh, these words and these names, that you have taught me to use, these concepts that I have to present to you in the exact contours that you love, this clash between my inner rhythm and the rhythm of the forms you have found! How do I free myself?" (p. 128).[17] It is the communication of female essence that concerns Aleramo, the self-representation born of the "sensitivity of [her] maternal fibres [sensibilità delle mie fibre materne]," the awareness of female subjectivity emerging from Bergsonian intuition: "making my instinct my art [far del mio istinto la mia arte]" (pp. 131–32) — an art, here and elsewhere, defined in both existential and literary terms as the sign of her spirit and consciousness.[18] It is significant that Aleramo concludes a section of "La pensierosa" with a reversal of Descarte's idealist definition of man as reason with her own epistemological perception of female as intuition: "Amo, dunque sono [I love, therefore I am]" (p. 133). In philosophical terms:

"Celebrated 'pure thought' does not exist for women" (p. 135).[19] What does exist is the search for self and the quest for wholeness through love. In Aleramo's view, encoded gender does not divide the sexes or thwart their differing creative processes. Instead, she proposes a "human" identity of merged wholeness through the union of sexual opposites, recalling Jungian archetypal patterns for gender transcendence, in which each person incorporates both masculine and feminine aspects into the personality: the feminine "animus" and the masculine "anima" joining to achieve completeness.[20] Aleramo's essay does not reject the male in favor of the female, but calls for such union and fulfillment: "The Platonic myth can come true.... The [myth] of the human couple, of an intelligence and creative genius *a due* [in twos], can arise" (p. 140).[21]

Aleramo's views on sexual difference based on the traditional antithetical definition of male/female as intellect/intuition are markedly phallocentric and subject to criticism on philosophical and feminist grounds. As Leigh Gilmore (1994) has pointed out, "To construe the translation of anatomy and even experience into textual inevitability reduces the complex articulation of gender" (p. xii). Nevertheless, Aleramo's belief in the potential and desirability of original gendered writing provides a basis for self-expression that predates elements of Luce Irigaray's *différence* and Hélène Cixous's call for an *écriture féminine,* both of which incorporate bodily energies and the unconscious.[22] The Bergsonian model offered Aleramo a contemporary philosophical framework in which to situate her own awareness of literary alterity at ontological and epistemological levels. The theorizing of instinct and intuition as female categories allowed the poet to explore irrational and subconscious aspects of her self-consciousness and sexual identity. In her creative writing, Aleramo engages in self-representation as a female-gendered subject, particularly within the subjective realm of lyric poetry, which she so highly valued.

Passionate about her dream of "a greater femininity," Aleramo carried it well into old age "like a religion parallel, indeed grafted, to [the religion] of poetry." For Aleramo, the exploitation of female alterity promised "the salvation of [her] species," the coming of a new order in which a woman, "having acquired independence and personality, truly becomes a woman, truly [becomes] herself" (Aleramo 1945, 353–54; entry for December 2, 1944).[23] Immersed in embodying her own autonomous spirituality, the poet failed to grasp the threat that Fascist hegemony posed to the advancement of all women, including artists and intellectuals like herself. The sexual difference proposed by Mussolini and his theoreticians held no promise for feminine autonomy or spirituality: "I believe," the duce stated, "that woman does not have great synthetic power and that, therefore, she has no aptitude for great spiritual creations" (quoted in Macciocchi 1976, 46).

Sibilla Aleramo's indifference to the regime's antifeminist public policy and virulently patriarchal attitudes signals her ideological detachment throughout the 1920s and 1930s. Vaguely anti-Fascist, she was one of many intellectuals and artists to sign the Croce Manifesto in 1925, although she later blamed this action for closing establishment doors to her. Nevertheless, in times of great financial need, she felt no compunction about turning to the regime and the monarchy, eventually receiving small subsidies and a state pension.[24] Essentially apolitical at the time, Aleramo had a vast circle of friends, lovers, and acquaintances who included all shades of the ideological spectrum. She corresponded with well-known Fascist intellectuals such as the poet Arturo Onofri, who attempted to convert her to the cause; the philosopher-advocate Julius Evola, theorist of feminine inferiority; and Margherita Sarfatti, Mussolini's biographer, apologist, and lover. But Aleramo remained loyal to her idealistic and anti-Fascist friends, including Giovanni Amendola and Piero Gobetti, choosing her intimates from an odd assortment of intellectuals, critics, artists, and bohemians, as well as aristocrats, statesmen, and millionaires.[25] In 1925, Aleramo entered into a brief but ardent affair with political activist Tito Zaniboni, who soon afterward tried to assassinate Mussolini (November). A significant moment in Aleramo's life, the relationship led to her arrest and brief imprisonment. Ignorant of the crime, the poet was quickly released. She recorded the event lyrically in a famous poem, "Una notte in carcere" (A night in prison), a composition that exemplifies Aleramo's subjectivity, even on this inherently political occasion. The poem offers no historical references, no indignation, no mention of the poet's doomed lover.

After an atmospheric opening that stresses the tomblike physical environment of her cell — darkness, rain, peace, cold, silence, sleep — Aleramo's personal mythology dominates "Una notte in carcere":

Giaceva la mia libertà
quella notte come in una tomba,
il bel mito giaceva
per amor del quale ho vissuto ardendo.
Lungi le spiagge le rose le selve.
E creatura nessuna in pena per me,
nessuno nella notte ad attendermi lungi.
Nuda anima, quanta pace!...

Pure gli uomini e la lor giustizia
potevano, poveri uomini, ne l'errore persistere,
poteva l'alba non riportarmi libertà....
Sovra la notte di gran pioggia e sul mondo,
di là dalle sbarre di ferro,
l'errore forse infieriva....

Nella cella tutta ombra
una nuda certezza allora
in me sentii,
meravigliosamente
in me assolta sentii la vita intera,
folta di sogni, passionata ed aspra,
ogni giorno espiata,
vita d'opere e di lacrime,
e il cielo s'apriva ad archi sorridenti
di quando in quando, fuggitivi!

Meraviglia limpida, trasparente mistero,
nella notte di prigionia
trovarsi lieve, sì, alata come non mai,
nella cella simile ad una tomba. (Aleramo 1947/1980, 72–73)

My freedom lay prostrate
that night as in a tomb,
that beautiful myth for which
I lived aflame lay prostrate.
Shores and roses and woods a long way off.
And no creature grieved for me,
no one in the night to wait for me a long way off.
Naked soul, what peace!...

Yet men and their justice
might, poor men, persist in error,

dawn might not return my freedom...
On the rain-swept night and on the world
beyond these iron bars,
perhaps error flared...

In the cell's dark shadows
I then felt a naked certainty
arise in me,
marvelously
I felt all my life absolved,
dense with dreams, passionate and rough,
expiated every day,
a life of deeds and tears,
and the heavens opened now and again
to smiling arches, in flight.

Limpid marvel, transparent mystery,
to be light, yes, to have wings as
during this night of imprisonment
in the cell just like a tomb...[26]

The meditative serenity of Aleramo's somewhat prosaic blank verse underscores the theme of the inner self at peace with the world and the past. Alone, undefended, abandoned, and ill-used, the prisoner of injustice triumphs through the greatness of her being, which can encompass all of life, transforming captivity into the wings of lost freedom. Aleramo is manipulating some of the primary elements of her personal myth—the titanic struggle to affirm oneself and conquer adversity. Titanism in Aleramo is generally associated with her vital force, the ability to live to the fullest, to "live aflame." Sibilla's "beautiful myth" is transformational (smiling rainbows replace dreary rain), primordial ("the whole of life" and all of nature), regenerative (her "limpid marvel, transparent mystery"), and exclusive. It is not altogether surprising that she was drawn to similar mythic qualities found in the duce's public persona.

As the Fascist regime moved into its second decade, Aleramo's adherence was greater, if not ideologically motivated; put simply, she was charmed by its manifestations of energy and vitality. Rita Guerricchio (1974) explains Aleramo's "softening toward the regime" as an attraction to its exuberance, "inevitably exciting for an indiscriminate temperament like Sibilla's, who was predisposed toward it" (pp.

255–56).[27] Aleramo did not participate in the female delirium that greeted Mussolini during his public appearances, but his image held definite allure for the writer, who, when asked to describe the duce in 1931, responded, "Being a woman, I don't believe much in History, therefore I know little about it. But I do believe in human individualism and in mysterious power.... Mussolini is himself and that's that" (quoted in Passerini 1991, 119).[28] Nor was she the only female intellectual seduced by Fascist image building. In a study of feminine consensus and Fascism, *La donna "nera,"* Maria Antonietta Macciocchi (1976) points to a gradual sociological shift in women's involvement in the regime from the lower middle class to the upper classes and elite; party leadership began to pursue the support of important women, seeking out famous writers such as Grazia Deledda, Ada Negri, Matilde Serao, and, peripherally, Aleramo.

Mussolini's charisma, self-assurance, and egotism found echoes in Aleramo's own personality. Eschewing the "feminine" traits of submission, domesticity, renunciation, and silence, Sibilla forced herself on the world like a Nietzschean hero flexing her will to power. And, like the German philosopher's "superman," Aleramo thrived on her own singularity, her chosen role as an archetypal figure. As the new "woman poet," she could disdain normative expectations for women because she was alone of her kind, bringing to mind the Mussolini of contemporary propaganda. In a Nietzschean turn of phrase, Aleramo expressed her surrender to this titanic self:

> I had faith always and only in myself because I always knew that I was *the only reality* in a world of uncertain shapes.... But then, this self, with its instinct for love, for beauty, for harmony, is infinitely tyrranical and demands *for itself* the maddest of efforts, compensating them, it's true, with such rewards that, for a few instants, human substance is drawn near to the universal [substance]. *I am the slave of my instinct for greatness.* (quoted in Guerricchio 1974, 274)[29]

Yet, because of her gender, Aleramo's self-celebratory writing and narcissistic subjectivity were generally dismissed by the male critical establishment, which was unaccustomed to, and discomforted by, her fascination with the particulars of her unorthodox existence. Few were able to distinguish the artistic validity of her work and the novelty of her poetic voice from the irregularity of her behavior, a distinction made all the more difficult by Aleramo's repeated insistence that art and life are inseparable. Aleramo consciously nurtured her transgressive personality, inevitably encountering ostracism from friend and foe alike. Her ability to overcome and endure added to her agonistic self-image: loneliness and abuse are some of the sacrifices needed to sustain a life of freedom, essential to her mythic construction. The poem "Non ti curare" speaks to the pain of marginality and the will to conquer weakness; the final verse also points to Aleramo's belief in the transformational power of her exemplariness:

> Non ti curare della parola trista
> ch'uno a tuo danno intorno va spargendo,
> uno ch'ebbe da te soltanto bene.
> Non soffrirne, l'anima solleva,
> sii forte, donna, sola, invitto cuore.
> E scevra d'amarezza ancora sorridi:
> in te, beata, crede chi ti guarda. (Aleramo 1947/1980, 60)

[Don't heed the wicked word someone has spread about to injure you, someone who only received good from you. Don't suffer from it, your spirits raise; be strong, woman, alone, indomitable heart. Free of bitterness smile once again: who sees you, blessed one, believes in you.]

Given the historical moment, Aleramo's agonistic temperament suggests male, not female, prototypes. In addition to her much-admired Nietzsche, Aleramo found a secondary model in Gabriele D'Annunzio, whose works she began to read as an adolescent. Besides sharing a developed sense of their individual uniqueness, both writers attempted to translate this exceptionality creatively and existentially. D'Annunzio offered Aleramo an example of "inimitable life" (his term), life that is itself an artistic masterpiece. D'Annunzio's biography reads like pulp fiction, but he managed to transform such pulp into exquisitely refined literature that Aleramo drank in like an intoxicating ambrosia. Bewitched by D'Annunzio's verbal prowess and unrepressed personality, she called him "the white sorcerer."[30] Unfortunately for Aleramo, the surface similarities between their styles, psychological traits, and reputations led many reviewers and scholars to label Aleramo a mere imitator, a minor D'Annunzio in drag. Like others before him, Richard

Drake (1980) categorizes the fiction Aleramo produced between 1919 and the war as belonging "to that mysterious 'sibylline' realm of self-mythification, with close affinities to the worst qualities of D'Annunzian fiction: the decadent-romantic combination of the erotic with the spiritual, the deliberate mystification of the reader through the employment of peculiar syntax and enigmatic phrases, and the perversion of Nietzsche's celebration of the *Superuomo* [superman], modified by Aleramo to include the *Superdonna* [superwoman]" (p. xxx).[31] Throughout her long life, Aleramo continually rejected any such attempts to label her creative works as imitations or "literature," which she viewed as artifice and equivocation. Her lyrics, she declares in "Tempo, che irridi al numero!" (Time, you mock the number!), emerge as sensations and unexpected illuminations of life, itself a creation ("Poemi che non scrissi / ma vissi [Poems I did not write / but lived].") The moments of life, she declares, are destined to become art:

> s'inseriscono lievi,
> eran destino
> eran sangue,
> tornano ritmico vero,
> musicali baleni. (Aleramo 1947/1980, 36)

[They interject themselves lightly, they were fate, they were blood, they return rhythmic truth, musical flashes.]

Time and again, Aleramo declares that her writing is integral to her being, inseparable from her essence. It is, therefore, also inescapably female.

Aleramo's myth is constructed on the fact of gender and the devotion to absolute authenticity, her "personal law." Her confessional discourse affirms her status as a speaking subject, opening potential for expressing her "truth." If she equaled D'Annunzio in drive, vitality, agonistic spirit, even sensuality, she did not share his attraction to barbarism, violence, or perversity, or his elitism, grandiloquence, and artificiality. Moreover, D'Annunzian mythmaking extended beyond literature into the public arena, the male world of politics and war, closed to women. It is logical that such a living male legend would appeal to Mussolini and the Fascist hierarchy, who borrowed many of D'Annunzio's outward symbols and rhetoric as their own. Both the Fascists and D'Annunzio manipulated their respective images to influence public opinion and gain popularity, prestige, and position. D'Annunzio, the poet-hero, and Mussolini, the hero-leader, were emblems of mythic virility, appealing to the ingrained machismo of patriarchal Italy. On the other hand, though marginalized, Aleramo continued to manifest her sexually transgressive traits because they reflected her true self: it was not a question of self-promotion, but of morality. This uncompromising dedication to personal authenticity is at the heart of current scholarly reevaluations of Aleramo on a biographical, as well as literary, level. Viewed as brazen by many contemporaries, she appeals to current feminist scholarship, which is interpreting her obsessively autobiographical writing as an avant-garde, early example of female self-actualization and authenticity. Using descriptors often borrowed from Aleramo herself, scholars are exploring her "revealment," "consciousness," "savage modesty and savage nakedness," "lucid intuition," and "rage of self-creation," attempting to define the woman and her myth through her writing. To quote Olga Lombardi (1980): "The validity, indeed the nobility of this poetic experience, so tied to a specific era and so dated, . . . consists in the inner and authentic accord between the poet and her work: that is, in its intimate truth" (p. 752). In recent years, theoretician Rita Felski (1989) has indicated that the literary text is

> one important site for the struggle over meaning through the formulation of narratives which articulate women's changing concerns and self-perceptions. Writing should be grasped in this context as a social practice which creates meaning rather than merely communicating it; feminist literature does not reveal an already given female identity, but is itself involved in the construction of this self as a cultural reality. (p. 78)

In Aleramo's third life, the self was most often revealed through love. All her creative works from 1910 to 1940 focus on the amatory motif, as the events, emotions, sensations, and thoughts evolving from her personal experiences find their way onto paper. In many ways love, like freedom, forms a myth within the myth of Sibilla's self-construction. Like all aspects of her psyche, she persistently explored its roots and ramifications through written self-examination, seeking to account for her zealous pursuit of an ideal love through a series of less-than-ideal men:

> Something in me has remained eternally unsatisfied: the yearn-
> ing for a child of love, a being that was all together a masterpiece
> of my flesh, of my heart, of my spirit. And I loved, or thought to
> love, many men, waiting unawares. . . . My poetry was generated
> in this way. And the thousands of pages I've written to narrate
> myself, to explain myself. Even to this [page] today. A rage of
> self-creation, incessant. Moments, days, years. (Aleramo 1945,
> 33; entry for December 5, 1940)[32]

With incredible acuity, Aleramo exposes the egocentricity of her perceptions: frustrated physical maternity is transformed into sexual love,
then transfigured into words, only to return to the unfulfilled self. This
circularity is accentuated linguistically by Aleramo's lexical choices:
the *creatura* (child/being) is the masterpiece achieved in flesh, not
words; poetry is generated, like children; writing is equal to self-
creation, words made flesh. Significantly, the words *poet* and *poetry*
derive from the ancient Greek verb meaning "to create." Aleramo's
commingling of creativity and motherhood brings to mind Julia Kristeva's view of maternity as "a conceptual challenge to phallogocentrism: gestation and nurturance break down the oppositions between
self and other, subject and object, inside and outside" (in Jones 1985,
86). The motifs of maternity, love, and creativity merge here, as they
do throughout *Selva d'amore* (Woods of love).

Aleramo herself acknowledged that *Selva d'amore*, the 1947 edition of her verse in a single volume, contained an "absolute prevalence" of love poems, composed over thirty years. While considering
titles for the upcoming book, Aleramo mused on the possibilities *Pel-
legrina d'amore* (Pilgrim of love) and *Parabola d'amore e di poesia*
(Parable of love and poetry). Both are suggestive choices. The first
emphasizes the poetry's autobiographical genesis by identifying the
nature of the poet. Besides the obvious meaning of wanderer (from
man to man; city to city), "pilgrim" also connotes images of individual quests and religious devotion, undertaken in the service of a greater
good, love. Aleramo's alternative title stresses the positive exemplariness of her lyric experience; like all parables, the book offers an underlying moral to its audience. Whereas Aleramo perceived her poetry in spiritual terms, *Selva d'amore*, the title provided by her good
friend the literary critic Giacomo Debenedetti, aptly designates other
aspects of the volume. A *selva* is both a woods and a literary treasury,
referring to the book's function as a collection of love poems, but also

to the metaphorical woods of Dantesque tradition, a locus of fear, misgiving, and confusion: the labyrinth of love.

As a literary document, *Selva d'amore* is part of the long Italian tradition of the *canzoniere,* or songbook, of love. As a personal document, it is a fruit of Aleramo's "autonomous feminine spirituality," in which "love and poetry, eroticism and creative felicity tend to a single end, the tangible sign of feminine existence" (Luti 1986, 100). In keeping with the subjectivity inherent in all lyric poetry, love is perceived through a distinctly gendered perspective as a female experience, a sign of alterity. Aleramo clearly goes counter to the traditional construction of woman as the object, rather than subject, of desire, which has dominated art from the Greeks to Freud. But it is also an attempt at dialogue with the other, the male. As Mirella Serri (1988) notes: "Aleramo's entire lyric output unfolds like a single, uninterrupted conversation, developed along the lines of a love *canzoniere*" (p. 61). Serri signals love as the unifying motif of *Selva d'amore,* although the (unnamed) objects of such love vary. There is a well-defined metaphysical component to Aleramo's perception of love that can subsume any number of individual love objects. In his memoirs, Aleramo's good friend Primo Conti recalls days spent with her at the time of her amorous wanderings: "We spoke about poetry and her loves. Sibilla spoke willingly about her loves, but she never revealed their names. Even if her men changed, she only spoke of Love" (quoted in Conti and Morino 1981, 210).

The mystique of love that inspired Aleramo is concurrently physical and spiritual, affecting the total self. It is a mystical union where ecstasy and vision converge and difference is abolished. Through love, the poet aspires to the merger of male and female in a union meant to fulfill both, reconciling the separate gendered identities into a perfect whole that is greater than its imperfect parts. Akin to Platonic and neo-Platonic representations of the love experience, Aleramo's love proposes the exchange of identities and the loss of the self to the beloved at a metaphysical level. It is Aleramo's artistic attempt to attain that "creative genius *a due*" theorized in "La pensierosa." It is a far cry from the Fascist perception of women as sexless breeders or flawed sex objects and love as either patriarchal marriage or decadent encounters. Love is Aleramo's all-consuming "implacable god," in whose temple she worships. The poem "Fuoco" (Fire) captures the exalted tone of this personal credo:

> Avvampi da anni la vita mia,
> pur non posso toccarti,
> pur non posso spiegarti,
> fuoco sei e mistero,
>
> da anni si consuma la vita mia
> dinanzi alla tua fiamma bianca,
> solo a guardarti, solo a guardarti,
> mai di patire sono stanca. (Aleramo 1947/1980, 74)

[You've set my life ablaze for years, yet I cannot touch you, yet I cannot render you, fire are you and mystery, / for years my life has been consumed before your white flame, just looking at you, just looking at you, and never do I tire of pain.]

The "pain" of love in Aleramo's poetry is generally inflicted by the succession of unresponsive beloveds who rejected her vision, ending that particular dream if not the universal quest. Aleramo never wavered from her devotion to the "implacable god," but her love objects, more often than not, turned away. Insistently, the poet's voice demands, begs, pleads, cajoles, seduces, attempting to sway the recalcitrant male(s), who remains a relatively insignificant and generic figure when compared with the female persona. In scanning some two hundred compositions produced during a thirty-year span, it is difficult to distinguish one male interlocutor from another. Intrinsically, Aleramo's lyrics are instruments of self-expression and self-definition: to speak of love is to speak of self.

Writing in an official culture that denied female sexuality and viewed the female body as an instrument for propagation, Aleramo created an erotic identity charged with passion. Far from adhering to the duce's gendered worldview that "reduced the feminine to maternity and the masculine to power" that is, to "passivity" and "aggression" (Passerini 1991, 9), the poet proposes an assertive, venturesome, voluptuous femininity that can hold its own against the duce's well-publicized virility. If Mussolini used his vaunted sexuality to seduce the nation, Aleramo used hers to entice lovers and readers alike. Her representation of physical femininity functions as a myth of human agency. The poet repeatedly offers her body—her femaleness—to her audience as the mark of her uniqueness, in sharp contrast to the desexualized ideal proposed to Fascist womanhood:

Questa morbida mia forma di donna
fatta per la gioia,
or senza più carezze si vergogna
oscuramente e si tortura.
Castità,
stolto anticipo di vecchiezza e morte,
anche l'anima ormai ti respinge. ("Castità," in Aleramo
    1947/1980, 44)

[This soft womanly shape of mine, made for joy, left without ca-
resses, is darkly shamed and tortured. Chastity, foolish anticipa-
tion of old age and death, by now even my soul rejects you.]

Consequently, the body occupies a privileged space in Aleramo's lyrics
as an instrument for discovery and self-knowledge. As Adrienne Rich
(1986) has indicated, the "politics of location" for female self-representation begins in the body. *Selva d'amore* abounds in corporeal images of body parts, including such traditional feminine signifiers as
face, eyes, mouth, hair, hands, and breasts, found throughout lyric
poetry. To this canonical list, Aleramo adds her personal preferences:
arms, blood [including menstrual], veins, shoulders, palms. "The lyric
I shows itself through its parts. This metonymic process dominates the
poetry: the part refers to the whole. Parts of the body refer to the entire body" (Serri 1988, 61). Aleramo's lyric construction of the physical
self clearly produces a gendered self: a "female" poet, whose uniqueness is centered in biology. It is also a body that finds pleasure in itself, in the "little death" or orgasm, and the dissolution experienced
in pleasure; such themes recall Aleramo's theoretical emphasis on intuition and instinct as female qualities, bringing to mind Julia Kristeva's celebration of the rapture contained within the female body:
the theory of *jouissance*. Aleramo's lyrics re-create the sensations and
responses of her femaleness, reiterating Aleramo's belief in a gendered
text. The body itself is the receptacle of her chosen identity, her artistic destiny, as in the poem "Oh palme delle mani": "Oh palme delle
mani iscritte di segni, / triangoli, rami, croci, stelle, / tutta la mia vita
ch'è stata e sarà / ... / linee linee in catena in croce in danza, / oh
palme delle mie mani, scrittura d'astri! [Oh palms of my hands inscribed in signs, triangles, branches, crosses, stars, all my life that
was and will be ... lines lines chained crossed dancing, oh palms of
my own hands, written by the stars!]" (Aleramo 1947/1980, 70).

Facist propaganda also understood the centrality of the physical image to mythmaking. Whereas Aleramo extolled her womanly essence in writing, Mussolini's features and physique were "seen" as a sign of perfect manliness, from his singular physiognomy to his athletic prowess as horseman, swimmer, pilot, and so forth.[33] In either case, the body becomes a metaphor for the archetypal being proposed. If Mussolini was the incarnation of the "leader," savior of his nation, Aleramo embodied life force and generation. The conventional association of woman with nature and earth is a dominant theme throughout her poetry. Sometimes this motif takes on dionysian traits of sensual delight, when, like an Ovidian heroine, she undergoes metamorphosis, as in "Ciocche" (Locks), where her hair becomes a watery cascade in her lover's hands, or in "Come i flutti marini" (Like sea waves), in which she experiences "sulle mie membra / tacito scorrere di baci notturni / dolci come i flutti marini [a wordless flow of nocturnal kisses sweet as sea waves on my limbs]" (1947/1980, 54). Often the self is joined to floral images, the ideal natural metaphor for sensual femininity, for a body offering itself to be "plucked," as in the evocative "Pallore lucente":

> Pallore lucente, nell'aria e su me, e stupore.
> Son sola, tu lontano, denudo spalle e seno,
> una grande rosa bianca sono,
> ti parevo e sono, dolce di sole, che respira.
> Null'altro, e dunque comincia primavera.
> Vapora ogni ricordo che non sia d'amore. (Aleramo 1947/1980,
> 33–34)

[Shimmering pallor, in the air and on me, and astonishment. I am alone, you far away, revealing shoulders and breast, I am a large white rose, as I seemed to you and am, sweet with the sun and breathing. Nothing more, and so spring begins. Any memory that is not love evaporates.]

Suggestively, Aleramo's preferred flowers, roses, are symbols for both the goddess of love, Venus, and the perfect mother, Mary. These archetypal figures personify fertility and generation, as does the other mother, "earth" or nature, celebrated by Aleramo in her famous poem "Sì alla Terra" (Yes to the Earth) (translated in Allen et al. 1986, 46–47). The biological maternity glorified in Fascist propaganda is transformed into an ideal maternity by the poet, who offers her love as a fount of life, an instrument of rebirth. In a society that urged women to sacrifice themselves for their children and the nation, the poet surrenders her body and being to the beloved in a manner that is simultaneously selfless and selfish, hedonistic and spiritual, agonistic and plaintive. An erotic earth mother, she offers her being as sustenance to a son-lover, as in "Verde crescevi":

> Verde crescevi, o delicata pianta,
> e i giorni e gli anni e la linfa di mia vita
> erano per te pane e sole e vento,
> e se tanto io t'ho dato
> più nulla da me volendo se non di me nutrirti,
> dono m'è stato assai maggiore
> crescere vederti, giovinetta pianta. (Aleramo 1947/1980, 102–3)

[You grew green, O delicate plant, and the days and years and sap of my life were bread and sun and wind to you. If much was given, I wanted nothing in return if not to be your nourishment; my greatest gift has been to see you grow, young plant.]

In an odd coincidence, an article written by Fascism's major idealist philosopher, Giovanni Gentile, seems to echo Aleramo's views. While stating women's spiritual inferiority (an opinion repeatedly challenged by Aleramo), Gentile recognizes a strong connection between human love and the myth of *Terra generatrix,* the earth as generating mother. Through love, man is given the possibility of discovering himself in women, for the tie that binds men and women also binds us "through consciousness, to nature in which we exist, to our mother who gave birth to us in nature."[34] Lover and mother, Venus and Mary, converge in Aleramo's self-fashioning. As Giorgio Luti (1986) puts it: "Sibilla's eroticism appears as a new and diverse sign, an unrestrainable dispersion which gives birth to her being woman and artist, her only possibility for creation" (p. 93).

The child of Aleramo's erotic maternity is poetry, where matter becomes art. Love provides the impetus for transformation; it is a redemptive site for both lover and beloved. If the male is offered an opportunity to regenerate through the love of his mother-mistress, Aleramo as lover is no less altered: "L'amore! essere una e credersi il tutto! [Love! being one and believing oneself all!]."[35] Naturally, the male can reject the transfiguration proffered—the case of "Giunco non uomo": "in eterno / non mio né d'altre / né di sé mai, / negarsi all'ombra / e poi al sole, / giunco e non uomo [eternally neither mine nor another's, never his own, refusing the shadows, and then the sun, reed not man]" (Aleramo 1947/1980, 77). But for the poet herself, the experience, no matter how negative, is transcendental: love is recast as myth and poetry. "Sibilla's mystic impulse will always have a concrete start ... before revealing itself, essentially, as the love and creation of self" (Melandri 1988, 36).[36] Only art can afford Aleramo the permanence and mythic identity sought:

Miei versi,
mia nobiltà,
voi soli,
di tutto quanto,
somme immense,
alla vita donai,
voi soli restate,
piccoli in piccolo volume,
lucenti. ("Miei Versi," in Aleramo 1947/1980, 49–50)

[My verses, my nobility, only you, of all that, immense sums, I gave to life, you alone remain, slight in a slight volume, shining.]

Although Aleramo's "living poetic myth" of creative and sensual individuality, with its emphasis on gendered identity, received little approbation from the Fascist intellectual community, it did garner growing enthusiasm among female readers. In an informative essay on Aleramo's reception in the Italian women's magazines of the period, Elisabetta Mondello (1988) notes a definite shift in attitude from the 1920s to the 1930s. In the first decade of the Fascist regime, Aleramo was "branded in fiery terms" by the female press for her existential choices and "scandalous" contents, namely, her sexuality and sensual motifs, which were at odds with both tradition and the Fascist gospel. Incongruously, at the height of Mussolini's demographic campaign, when motherhood and marriage were publicly venerated, Aleramo was rehabilitated for the ladies, presented as the embodiment of whimsical female nonconformity and classified among the "great" women writers of the century (Mondello 1988, 261). Mondello quotes a 1931 article by journalist Dora Setti to emphasize her point:

She is presented as the ideal prototype of the modern feminine generation; the model of uniqueness; the woman whose cultural superiority has made her man's able collaborator. She is ahead of her time. Sibilla Aleramo, the first among women thinkers, seeks out the mysterious exigencies of the womanly spirit and works to validate them, to offer woman her autonomy, without, however, denaturalizing her. (p. 265)[37]

Setti's evaluation of Aleramo's singular position in the Italian world of letters is confirmed by her appeal for the new generation of women writers maturing under Fascism, including Fausta Cialente and Elsa Morante, who were attracted to her unfailing self-awareness. Having offered her "being" unconditionally as a sign of unique female subjectivity, Aleramo was finally discovering a receptive audience who understood its exemplary nature.

In life as in art, Sibilla Aleramo emerges as a countercultural figure, an outcast, a sociopolitical deviant. Yet, in her self-representation, she constructed a figure as exceptional in its way as the duce himself, a master of self-promotion. Just as Fascism constructed all-consuming myths in its aestheticization of politics, Aleramo built her own myth through aesthetics. Signed by difference and determined to give voice to "womanly genius," Aleramo wrote of herself for herself, but also about her sex for her sex. She wrote of her body, her desires, her loves, her thoughts, of the minute details of her existence, endlessly seeking to communicate her essence, giving birth to her life and her poetry. She wrote of her difference, as a woman and as a unique being. Asserting her right to speak, her subjectivity and her identity, she performed a highly politicized act of resistance to the objectification and silencing of women performed by Fascism. At the center of this incessant self-creation lay her belief in art and its power to grant her immortality, to project that mythic self into the future:

> Per tutta la vita volli de' miei giorni
> far cosa di luce, cosa d'amore,
> ed essi posi avanti ogni mia arte,
> e d'essi feci poesia perenne,
>
> oh giorni, trascoloranti riviere,
> giorni, miei duri diamanti! ("Lunare," in Aleramo 1947/1980, 86)

[All my life I wanted to make my days a thing of light, a thing of love, putting them before my art, and I made eternal poetry of them, / oh days, variegating rivers; days, my hard diamonds!]

Notes

All translations in this chapter are my own. Translation of the poetry does not conform to metrical rules.

1. Ma, poesia incarnata, fatta vita, forza vitale. Tutto ciò che è stato vita in me, e che, attraverso il tempo, s'è iscritto nella mia sostanza e m'ha reso un vivente simbolo, un vivente mito poetico. Tutto ciò ch'io non ho se non in minima parte espresso in parole, forse appunto perché sono andata via via creando me stessa liricamente con quel vivo materiale in una singolare, quasi demoniaca, opera, d'ogni giorno, d'ogni istante. Ché, quella che io sono, ho voluto io esserlo, valendomi coscientemente di quanto la misteriosa sorte mi dava, ah non rose soltanto, la sorte su cui io non avevo poteri, la sorte con le sue infinite difficoltà e crudeltà e verso la quale il mio orgoglio era appunto di mostrare che nulla mi diminuiva, s'anche nel più profondo mi feriva, e che anzi tutto ineffabilmente m'accresceva, m'affinava, m'illuminava.

The two published volumes of Aleramo's diary, kept between 1940 and her death in 1960, are rich sources for an understanding of her life, personality, and attitudes. *Dal mio diario* was reissued by Feltrinelli in 1979 with the new title *Un amore insolito*; it covers the war years 1940–44. The second volume is posthumous: *Diario di una donna: Inediti 1945–1960* (Aleramo 1978a).

2. Luisa Passerini has published an excellent study of the construction of Mussolini's public image. *Mussolini immaginario* (1991) traces the creation of the duce's mythology from his personal diaries and newspaper profiles to the stylized public propaganda of the 1930s.

3. Aleramo's early articles, reviews, and notes focusing on women's issues have been published in *La donna e il femminismo: Scritti 1897–1910.* (Aleramo 1978b). These writings include commentaries on sociological tracts, descriptions of feminist congresses, meditations on the psychological nature of Italian women, analyses of gender relations, even a discussion of feminism and pacifism. Even during her repressive marriage, Aleramo was active in the Unione Femminile, an organization that focused on the issue of universal suffrage and female emancipation. Although never politically allied in her youth, she leaned toward socialist ideals.

4. Rina Faccio first met Giovanni Cena in Milan while working briefly as an editor for a woman's magazine, *L'Italia femminile.* The two renewed their friendship in Rome in 1902, shortly after Rina abandoned her family. Cena was far more than a spouse; he became Rina's mentor, guiding her reading, editing her writing, introducing her to books and people. As a well-known poet and novelist and the editor of the prestigious *Nuova antologia,* Cena was frequently in the company of many of the significant intellectuals of the day. Although socially marginal as a separated wife, Rina Faccio lived with Cena in what she termed "something far more serious than a marriage [qualcosa di molto più grave di un matrimonio]" (1945, 234; entry for January 9, 1944). Besides her wifely duties, she also worked with him, reviewing books, editing his writing, embracing his humanitarian causes. Cena invented the pseudonym Sibilla Aleramo for the publication of *Una donna,* a work he helped mold. Although the new name was publicly recognized, for intimates she remained Rina, an identity she did not totally abandon for years. Cena had a great psychological and intellectual influence on Aleramo's development and personality.

5. Divenni libera amante, divenni scrittrice, imposi alla società la mia ribellione e la mia audacia: e il mio nome si mutò in quello che porto.

6. During her long life, Aleramo wrote more than four hundred articles for some of Italy's most prestigious journals and newspapers, four novels, a handful of dramas

and screenplays (some unpublished or unperformed), several volumes of verse, three prose anthologies, and her diaries, not to mention an extensive epistolary, some of which has been published. Aleramo was also a busy translator. However, she often considered herself unproductive because she tended to value her creative writing much more highly than her other works.

7. Incominciai a interessarmi a quanto avveniva, ma senza profonda coscienza.

The retrospective and regretful entry continues: "Today this void in my memory and, even more, this feeling of having been foreign, absent, all enclosed in my personal affairs for quite a long time, alarms me, almost horrifies me.... How was it possible? [Oggi questo vuoto della memoria e, piú ancora, questo senso d'esser stata cosí a lungo estranea, assente, tutta chiusa nelle mie vicende personali, mi sgomenta, mi fa quasi ribrezzo.... Come fu possibile?]."

8. Aleramo defined herself as "irremediably lyric" in personality and style; for her, "poetry" naturally included her entire creative production: dramas, novellas, fiction, as well as verse.

9. Donna alla massima potenza, ho messo nella vita tutto il genio che un uomo avrebbe messo in un capolavoro: ho fatto della mia vita il capolavoro che avevo sognato di creare con la poesia: sono stata, sono pur sempre, poesia vivente, oh, non perfetta, anzi spesso confusa, caotica, ma enorme.

10. De Lauretis goes on to define female as "what is not susceptible to transformation," effectively excluding women from the active role as either hero or poet.

11. Whereas Aleramo created a self-image through her own works, Mussolini used both personal writings, such as the early *Il mio diario* and *Diario di guerra,* and journalists and biographers to create and expand his self-image through books, profiles, and articles. It is interesting that Mussolini, like Aleramo, kept lifelong diaries, maintaining a constant dialogue with himself. See Passerini (1991) for more detail.

12. Sovra-produzione di letteratura femminile. La donna ch'è diversa dall'uomo, in arte lo copia. Lo copia anziché cercare in se stessa la propria visione della vite e le proprie leggi estetiche.

The two theoretical articles were reprinted in *Andando e stando,* a collection of Aleramo's essays. See pp. 59–69 and 126–41.

13. Invece di portare nella vita e nell'arte la sua autentica anima, è entrata nell'azione come un misero inutile duplicato dell'uomo.

14. Se siamo persuasi d'una profonda differenziazione spirituale fra l'uomo e la donna dobbiamo persuaderci che essa implica una profonda diversità espressiva.

15. Il mondo femmineo dell'intuizione, questo piú rapido contatto dello spirito umano con l'universale, se la donna perverrà a renderlo, sarà, certo, con movenze nuove, con scatti, con brividi, con pause, con trapassi, con vortici sconosciuti alla poesia maschile.

16. Rifletto la vostra rappresentazione del mondo, aprioristicamente ammessa, poi compresa per virtú d'analisi; ma non vi do l'immagine delle cose qual è nel mio profondo, intuizione, poesia, meraviglia tanto quando è simile alla vostra come quando è opposta.

17. Oh, queste parole e questi nomi, che voi m'avete insegnato ad adoperare, questi concetti che devo presentarvi nei contorni esatti che voi amate, questo cozzo fra il mio ritmo interno e il ritmo delle forme da voi trovate! Come liberarmi?

18. "Ch'io imprima alla mia volontà d'amore in tutte le sfere dell'essere il segno dello spirito, il fiero segno della coscienza" (p. 133).

19. Il famoso "pensiero puro" non esiste per la donna.

20. My thanks go to Professor Anna Meda of the University of Pretoria, South Africa, for suggesting the Jungian connection. Although Aleramo was an avid reader

in European and American literature and thought, I have been unable to discover any firsthand knowledge on her part of Jung's theories as early as 1913.

21. Il mito platonico vuol avverarsi.... Ecco innalzarsi [il mito] dell'individualità della coppia umana, quello d'un'intelligenza e di una genialità creativa a due.

22. For a succinct overview of these and other feminist theorists in the French tradition, consult Ann Rosalind Jones' essay "Inscribing Femininity: French Theories of the Feminine" (1985).

23. Come una religione parallela, anzi innestata, a quella della poesia.... Ho preferito sperare in una redenzione della mia specie, sperare in una epoca nella quale la donna, acquistata indipendenza e personalità, diventata veramente donna, veramente se stessa.

24. As early as 1928, Aleramo applied directly to Mussolini for economic assistance and patronage, noting her illustrious literary career that had brought glory to national letters. The duce received her within a month, impressing her with his "exceptionally strong individualism, but with a bull's strength, not a lion's [una individualità eccezionalmente forte, ma della forza più d'un toro che di un leone]." She left the interview impressed with the "omnipotent man," although she did not consider him a "great man" as did Gorky, Rodin, and D'Annunzio, all of whom she knew (Conti and Morino 1981, 237–38). In 1933 Aleramo received a monthly government subsidy. Queen Elena also helped Aleramo financially, offering her monetary gifts and paying for her hospitalization in 1935. As a token of her thanks, Aleramo wrote a handful of complimentary articles and poems.

25. Both Amendola and Gobetti used their journals to conduct social and cultural debates, including criticism of Fascism. Exiled to Paris, Gobetti died in 1926 as the result of a Fascist beating. That same year, Amendola's publication, *Il mondo,* was suppressed.

26. A lyric translation of "A Night in Prison" is available in Allen et al., (1986, 45–47). Most of Aleramo's lyric output is contained in the anthology *Selva d'amore,* originally published in 1947. All poetry quotations used in this essay are from this text. Unless otherwise indicated, all prose translations of the poetry are my own; I have made no attempt to capture the meter, alliterations, assonance, and so on of Aleramo's original blank verse. *Selva d'amore* contains three previously published collections of Aleramo's verse: *Momenti* (1912–20), *Poesie* (1921–27), and *Sì alla Terra* (1928–34). To these, Aleramo added a new, previously unpublished collection, *Imminente sera* (1936–42) and a section of fragmentary poems.

27. Di esuberanza prevedibilmente esaltante per un temperamento indiscriminatamente predispostovi come quello di Sibilla.

Guerricchio's monograph remains one of the most complete and careful studies of Aleramo's entire biography and literary output. Unlike most other authors, who tend to concentrate on *Una donna,* Guerricchio undertakes extensive literary and stylistic analysis. There has been a major revival of Aleramo studies in recent years, leading to a series of publications. The most important include Federzoni et al.'s *Sibilla Aleramo* (1980), Contorbia et al.'s *Sibilla Aleramo: Coscienza e scrittura* (1986), Melandri's highly personal *Come nasce il sogno d'amore* (1988), and Buttafuoco and Zancan's *Svelamento: Sibilla Aleramo: Una biografia intellettuale* (1988). Aside from a significant discussion in Guerricchio's volume, Aleramo's poetry has received relatively little attention from scholars, although it was generally well received by reviewers. For specific references to the verse, consult articles by Serri (1988), Solmi (1929/1980), and, in English, Bassanese (1992).

28. Donna, credo poco alla Storia, e quindi poco la conosco. Credo invece alla individualità umana, alla forza misteriosa.... Mussolini è se stesso e basta.

29. Ho avuto fede sempre soltanto in me perché mi son sentita sempre *la sola realtà* in un mondo di vaghe forme.... Ma ecco, questo io, col suo istinto d'amore, di bellezza, di armonia è infinitamente tirannico, ed esige *per sè* i più folli sforzi, compensandoli, è vero, con tali premi che avvicinano per attimi la sostanza umana alla universale. *Io sono la schiava del mio istinto di grandezza.*

The rewards mentioned probably refer to successful writing. Aleramo wrote this statement in the 1930s.

30. The relationship between Aleramo and D'Annunzio was both artistic and biographical. The two met on several occasions and corresponded. For a detailed yet synthetic account, see Costa (1986). Although both writers were considered living legends in their later years, their differing motivations and social acceptability resulted in contrasting socioeconomic rewards, as reflected in their final physical environments. D'Annunzio was surrounded by the memorabilia of his glory days (a gift of the thankful nation) in a luxurious villa aptly named Il Vittoriale (for victory!): a living icon inhabiting a personal shrine, far from the realities of daily life. Aleramo continued to inhabit a one-room attic in Rome, barely making ends meet, surrounded by trunks and armoires brimming with personal papers: the monuments to her life. See Conti (1986) for a discussion of Aleramo's paper legacy, left to the PCI (Italian Communist Party) at her death, now forming the Aleramo archive. Costa (1986) discusses Aleramo's literary debt to D'Annunzio, more visible in the lyrical cadences of her prose than in her more ascetic verse—a "closely woven network of tonal correspondences" (p. 124). Costa also lists the writers' similarities in motifs, metaphors, and images.

31. Although exhibiting some bias and presenting some minor inaccuracies, Drake's piece is the best available cultural and personal biography of Aleramo available in English; an English-language overview of Aleramo the writer is found in Jewell (1984). The best source in Italian, also harboring some inaccuracies, is Conti and Morino (1981). This unusual (auto)biography employs Aleramo's own writing as its basic source; the book quotes extensively from her diaries, correspondence, and fiction. It also cites articles, letters, memoirs, and reviews by her contemporaries. In 1992, French journalist René de Ceccatty published a fact-based but popularized biography of Aleramo, *Nuit en pays etranger,* translated into Italian as *Sibilla.*

32. Qualcosa in me è rimasto eternamente insoddisfatto, l'anelito ad un figlio dell'amore, a una creatura che fosse insieme un capolavoro della mia carne, del mio cuore, del mio spirito. E ho amato, o creduto d'amare, tanti uomini, in quell'inconsapevole attesa.... E la mia poesia è stata generata così. E le migliaia di pagine che ho scritto per narrarmi, per spiegarmi. Fino a questa d'oggi. Un furore di autocreazione, incessante. Istanti, giorni, anni.

Aleramo adored her son, Walter, born during her failed marriage. She left him with his father, hoping to regain custody legally; instead, she did not see him again for thirty years. She regretted the fact that she never again became pregnant, hoping for that total union with another being she had experienced with her son. Maternity, like romantic love, was a means to completion and total personal fulfillment.

33. See Passerini (1991) for an extensive discussion of Mussolini's personal and secondary myth building. It is a fascinating discussion of the gradual expansion of elements already inherent in the leader's early self-image, including an analysis of the growing importance of the duce's physical image, "as though he embodied and publicly exhibited something that was generally invisible, and the holiness surrounding it" (p. 70).

34. Gentile's article is titled "La donna nella coscienza moderna" (Woman in modern consciousness). It is discussed at length in Macciocchi (1976, 124–26).

35. This is from "Alla Psiche del Museo di Napoli," in Aleramo (1947/1980, 81).

36. Emphasizing the religious symbolism, Melandri states that Aleramo's dream of love is composed of "crosses and resurrections" utilized by the writer in creating "her narcissistic church."

37. Mondello attributes Setti's positive evaluation of the writer to her "uniqueness," the fact that she is not perceived as a "normal" woman (p. 266).

Works Cited

Aleramo, Sibilla. 1942. *Andando e stando,* 2d ed. Milan: Mondadori. Originally published 1920.

———. 1945. *Dal mio diario: 1940–1944.* Rome: Tumminelli.

———. 1978a. *Diario di una donna: Inediti 1945–1960.* Milan: Feltrinelli.

———. 1978b. *La donna e il femminismo: Scritti 1897–1910.* Edited by Bruna Conti. Rome: Riuniti.

———. 1979. *Un amore insolito: Diario 1940–1944,* 2d ed. Edited by Alba Morino. Milan: Feltrinelli.

———. 1980. *Selva d'amore.* Rome: Newton Compton. Originally published 1947.

———. 1982. *Una donna,* l5th ed. Milan: Feltrinelli. Originally published 1906.

Allen, Beverly, Muriel Kittel, and Keala Jane Jewell. 1986. *The Defiant Muse: Italian Feminist Poems from the Middle Ages to the Present.* New York: Feminist Press.

Bassanese, Fiora A. 1992. "Sibilla Aleramo: Rina Faccio" In *Dictionary of Literary Biography* (vol. 114) *Twentieth Century Italian Poets,* 1st series. Edited by Giovanna Wedel De Stasio, Glauco Cambon, and Antonio Illiano. Detroit/London: Bruccoli Clark Layman/Gale Research.

Buttafuoco, Annarita, and Marina Zancan, eds. 1988. *Svelamento: Sibilla Aleramo: Una biografia intellettuale.* Milan: Feltrinelli.

Ceccatty, René de. 1992. *Sibilla: Vita artistica e amorosa di Sibilla Aleramo.* Translated by Anna Maria Maccari. Milan: Mondadori. Originally published as *Nuit en pays etranger* (Paris: Julliard, 1992).

Conti, Bruna. 1986. "Due bauli: Le carte dell'Archivio." In *Sibilla Aleramo: Coscienza e scrittura.* Edited by Franco Contorbia, Lea Melandri, and Alba Morino. Milan: Feltrinelli.

Conti, Bruna, and Alba Morino, eds. 1981. *Sibilla Aleramo e il suo tempo: Vita raccontata e illustrata.* Milan: Feltrinelli.

Contorbia, Franco, Lea Melandri, and Alba Morino, eds. 1986. *Sibilla Aleramo: Coscienza e scrittura.* Milan: Feltrinelli.

Costa, Simona. 1986. "Sibilla e D'Annunzio." In *Sibilla Aleramo: Coscienza e scrittura.* Edited by Franco Contorbia, Lea Melandri, and Alba Morino. Milan: Feltrinelli.

De Lauretis, Teresa. 1982. *Alice Doesn't: Feminism, Semiotics, Cinema.* Bloomington: Indiana University Press.

Drake, Richard. 1980. "Introduction." In Sibilla Aleramo, *A Woman.* Berkeley: University of California Press.

Federzoni, Marina, Isabella Pezzini, and Maria Pia Pozzato. 1980. *Sibilla Aleramo.* Florence: La Nuova Italia.

Felski, Rita. 1989. *Beyond Feminist Aesthetics: Feminist Literature and Social Change.* Cambridge: Harvard University Press.

Gilmore, Leigh. 1994. *Autobiographics: A Feminist Theory of Women's Self-Representation.* Ithaca, N. Y.: Cornell University Press.

Guerricchio, Rita. 1974. *Storia di Sibilla.* Pisa: Nistri-Lischi.

Jewell, Keala Jane. 1984. "Un furore d'autocreazione: Women and Writing in Sibilla Aleramo." *Canadian Journal of Italian Studies* 7: 148–62.
Jones, Ann Rosalind. 1985. "Inscribing femininity: French theories of the feminine." In *Making a Difference: Feminist Literary Criticism*. Edited Gayle Greene and Coppelia Kahn. London: Methuen.
Lombardi, Olga. 1980. "Sibilla Aleramo." In *Letteratura italiana: Il Novecento* (vol. 1). Edited Gianni Grana. Milan: Marzorati.
Luti, Giorgio. 1986. "Sibilla Aleramo nell'esperienza letteraria del Novecento." In *Sibilla Aleramo: Coscienza e scrittura*. Edited by Franco Contorbia, Lea Melandri, and Alba Morino. Milan: Feltrinelli.
Macciocchi, Maria Antonietta. 1976. *La donna "nera": "Consenso" femminile e fascismo*. Milan: Feltrinelli.
Melandri, Lea. 1988. *Come nasce il sogno d'amore*. Milan: Rizzoli.
Mondello, Elisabetta. 1988. "L'immagine di Sibilla nella stampa femminile dei primi decenni del novecento." In *Svelamento: Sibilla Aleramo: Una biografia intellettuale*. Edited by Annarita Buttafuoco and Marina Zancan. Milan: Feltrinelli.
Nozzoli, Anna. 1986. "Il romanzo di sé: La narrativa di Sibilla Aleramo." In *Sibilla Aleramo: Coscienza e scrittura*. Edited by Franco Contorbia, Lea Melandri, and Alba Morino. Milan: Feltrinelli.
Passerini, Luisa. 1991. *Mussolini immaginario*. Rome: Laterza.
Rich, Adrienne. 1986. "Notes toward a Politics of Location." In *Blood, Bread, and Poetry*. New York: W. W. Norton.
Serri, Mirella. 1988. "La poesia: Specchio e autobiografia." In *Svelamento: Sibilla Aleramo: Una biografia intellettuale*. Edited by Annarita Buttafuoco and Marina Zancan. Milan: Feltrinelli.
Solmi, Sergio. "Eros e lirismo di Aleramo." In *Letteratura italiana: il novecento* (vol. 1). Edited by Gianni Grana. Milan: Marzorati. Originally published 1929.

8 / Antonietta Raphaël: Artist, Woman, Foreigner, Jew, Wife, Mother, Muse, and Anti-Fascist

Emily Braun

In the past fifteen years, feminist studies have led to critical revisions of art history, drawing attention to the cultural politics involved in the very writing of that history.[1] One of the most immediate repercussions was the (re)discovery of forgotten or altogether neglected women artists and the publication of numerous historical surveys with basic biographical information. Given the depth of scholarly research and sense of mission, it is surprising that, outside of Italy, the name of the painter and sculptor Antonietta Raphaël Mafai is repeatedly absent from the lot of gendered anthologies.[2] *Raphael* appears regularly in indexes, but it is that other one, without the umlaut — a sign for sexual difference if ever there was one.

Indeed, the prominence of certain names and life stories suggests that feminist art criticism is not without a bias of its own, especially favoring the French–American modernist mainstream. The formidable figure of Artemesia Gentileschi and the rich attention paid to the baroque period is followed by an enormous lacuna with regard to modern Italian artists. Aside from a lack of familiarity with the territory, the oversight is undoubtedly exacerbated by attitudes toward the Fascist period: preconceptions about both the repressed status of women and the cultural policies of the regime. In point of fact, women artists not only practiced under Fascism, they actually increased in number, as the state consolidated the professional gains achieved after the decline of the old academic system and the birth of independent exhibitions.

Within Italy, Antonietta Raphaël has commanded attention since her very first exhibition in 1929, where she was singled out by Roberto Longhi for her unusual expressionist style. Longhi (1929) also considered her to be the emblematic figure of a new group—the "school of via Cavour"—which included the painters Mario Mafai (her future husband) and Scipione. In the postwar years, this small bohemian coterie was elevated to mythical status as a kind of anti-Fascist resistance, as their art was considered a daring affront to the classical styles and nationalistic subjects favored by the regime.[3] Raphaël's status is such that she is the single woman artist to be included in Corrado Maltese's exemplary survey *Storia dell'arte in Italia 1785–1943* (1960, 386–89). (The only other woman discussed at length is the critic and cultural power broker Margherita Sarfatti [pp. 332–34], who was also, coincidentally, Jewish.)[4] Hence Raphaël's obscurity outside Italy is particularly ironic, given that she is arguably the only woman artist of the first half of the twentieth century to have sparked a new style or school.

It is not, however, the quality of her art per se but its eccentricity in the context of the Italian art scene of the late 1920s that accounts for her influence. Raphaël was the vehicle of a new style—the "school of Paris"—which was not only French, but specifically Jewish in origin, as Roberto Longhi (1929) was quick to observe when he dubbed her the "foster child of Chagall."[5] Moreover, in emphasizing her cultural difference (or indeed, being "without culture," in the sense of the classical or Christian tradition) critics inevitably elaborated a metaphor of her art's sexual difference as well. Her paintings and sculptures were described as "impetuous," "anarchic," or even "devilish," "imbued with a decorative grace," "fresh and happy colors," and a "primitive simplicity."

In the years following World War II, Raphaël built her second reputation as a sculptor. Here, too, critics considered her achievements all the more laudable for one of the weaker sex, given the physical effort of the work involved or, as one critic put it, the usual lack of a "plastic or constructive sense" in women. Unwittingly, Libero De Libero (1949) reinforced the prejudice when he claimed her "the only woman in the world who was a genuine sculptor" (in Mezio 1960, 24). Not surprisingly, Raphaël's sculpture was often described in masculine terms of strength, aggressiveness, and "virile fascination."[6]

Raphaël is both typical and atypical protagonist in the history of women artists of this century. The basic details of her biography confirm the obstacles of social expectations, lack of opportunities, and professional biases that confronted every woman taking up pen or brush. Yet added to these were extremes of familial crises, domestic hardships, and racial persecution that make her professional achievements all the more remarkable, or, alternatively, do much to explain the single-mindedness with which she pursued her art and her self-definition.

Raphaël's youth was marked by loss, economic difficulty, and a nomadic itinerary. She was born in 1895 in Kovno, Lithuania. Her father, De Simon Raphaël, a rabbi, died in 1903 when Raphaël was 8 years old.[7] In 1905, she emigrated to England with her mother and sisters; they settled in the predominantly Jewish East End of London. There Raphaël made a living as a music teacher after receiving a diploma in piano. After the death of her mother in 1919, and with so few roots to begin with, Raphaël's instinct was to move on. In 1924, she left England for good, traveling to Paris, through the south of France, and eventually arriving in Italy.

Once in Rome, Raphaël fell in with a group of art students at the Scuola Libero di Nudo, among them the 22-year-old Mario Mafai, with whom she began an affair. Mafai actually inspired her to take up painting, and her distinctive presence, in turn, proved an inspiration to his art.[8] Although Raphaël bore him three children (Miriam in 1926, Simone in 1928, and Giulia in 1930), the two did not marry until 1935. Between childbearing and child rearing, Raphaël continued to paint, and managed to exhibit in three shows in 1929, receiving considerable notice for a novice and an autodidact. From 1930 to 1933, she pursued her work in Paris and London, where she sought out the sculptor Jacob Epstein. She had brought the bulk of her paintings with her, and she left them behind in London in the hope of having an exhibition at the Redfern Gallery; all were subsequently lost or destroyed. Upon her return to Italy, she devoted her energies to sculpture, in an effort to avoid further competition and conflict with Mafai.

In 1938, with the passage of racial laws in Italy, Raphaël and the children removed themselves from Rome and lived under the protective eye of friends in Genoa. Mafai served in the army and then fought in the

Resistance. Despite the guarded existence, daily life continued apace. Moreover, with the children in school and Mafai away, Raphaël could give undivided attention to her work for the first time. Perhaps because of such freedoms, and Mafai's own formative wartime experiences, the two subsequently led separate lives, though they remained in constant contact until the latter's death in 1965. Compared with her youth and middle age, Raphaël worked more consistently and exhibited regularly for the first time in her career. Having developed as an artist with the handicap of being a woman, she now found herself in another underprivileged position: that of being a figurative and hence "retrograde" artist in a period when abstract art prevailed. Though convinced that she had not received her due, Raphaël nonetheless established a solid, if local, reputation in Rome in the 1950s and 1960s.[9]

One cannot begin to consider Raphaël's art, as she herself could not have begun to create it, without an awareness of her life circumstances and her sex. The question of her identity was constant and a constant subject of her art. It was a positive form made out of a series of negative presences, a self defined by what it was not: anything remotely connected to the dominant class, religious, and cultural conventions of modern Europe, specifically, the patriarchal, bourgeois, Catholic, and Latin faces of Fascist Italy.

Raphaël's involvement with her "self" is made evident by the degree to which she obscured or invented certain details of her life, from the basic facts of place and date of birth to the unverifiable stories of her professional contacts with the likes of Zadkine and Chagall.[10] Particularly indicative is the malleable and interchangeable series of names by which she called herself and signed her work: Antoinette or Antonietta Raphaël, Raphaël De Simon, Raffael, Raphaël Mafai (as noted by Mezio 1960, 12 n. 1). In an age of few role models, she constructed a narrative of self against a constantly shifting ground of nationality, language, and conjugal status. Raphaël does not belong to the category of victim or martyr, nor does she possess the tortured expression that has often seemed the precondition for "greatness" in the female pantheon. Ebullient and driven, she was endowed with an extraordinary sense of purpose that outweighed any potentially destructive self–doubt. Rather, her strength and self–assertion, so unconventional for a woman of her time, led her to doubt her essential femininity in other respects.

Despite a career marked by interruptions and detours, Raphaël's work demonstrates a fierce continuity of issues and themes. It addresses a series of dualities that relate, in turn, to her identity: lover and competitor, artist and mother, creator and procreator. Three particular subjects dominate: biblical scenes, images of women gazing into mirrors, and depictions of maternity (of both pregnancy and her growing children). Although Raphaël inevitably made reference to the history of art and styles, she also altered or subverted dominant traditions of image making to express novel points of view: those of the feminine and the matrilineal.

Raphaël's evolution as an artist was inseparable from her relationship with Mafai, from the affection and tensions of their sentimental lives to the support and competition between them professionally. In the early years, it was Raphaël who sustained Mafai's confidence, but neither the nurturing nor the sparring was ever one–sided. Though initially threatened by Raphaël — both by her talent and energy and by the changes she brought upon his life — Mafai went on to encourage her with advice and a large measure of freedom, sharing the burden of child care. Even with her strong will and independence (qualities Mafai chose not to resent but rather admired as part of her innate moral force), Raphaël could not have pursued her work so attentively without a tolerant partner and one equally disdainful of social convention.

Indeed, by working and living on the margins of bourgeois society, Raphaël and Mafai evaded the norms of familial life and of male/female stereotypes, which were accentuated during the Fascist period. Mafai, with his small stature and sweet demeanor — not to mention his "esthete" interests — possessed qualities traditionally associated with the feminine. Raphaël, by contrast, was physically hefty and an assertive personality who dared to enter into the male arena of "profession" rather than merely to dabble in a hobby or restrict her career to motherhood alone. As Mafai (1969a) recalled of their initial attraction: "She was full of life, exuberant, a little out of touch with reality and confident of the future with a rather ingenuous optimism. I liked her well-being and she my odd and romantic nature" (p. 18).

Perhaps most revealing of the lack of traditional gender identities (and ways of seeing) are Raphaël's early portraits of Mafai, painted while they were still in the throes of new romance. In *Mafai che beve*

(Mafai drinking; 1928), he raises a bottle to his lips, his head thrown back to expose the flesh of his neck down to his loosened tie; he drinks of the bottle as he would drink of a woman. The provocative placement of his hand on his hip and his thumb clasped over his belt furthers the sexual innuendo (Raphaël's naive, painterly style notwithstanding). The depiction of erotic interest on the part of a woman for a man is incomparable for its time. With the portrait of Kandinsky by Gabriele Munther, or of Lytton Strachey by Dora Carrington, for example, the aloof image of male intellect dominates and imparts a distance between artist and sitter, lover, and spouse.

When Raphaël did paint Mafai's creative persona in *Mafai che disegna* (Mafai drawing; 1928) (see Figure 8.1), it was in the act of reciprocal depiction: he is captured and captivated by her. The image also stands as a self-portrait: not only does Raphaël represent herself being drawn by Mafai, she also presents herself as the tiny nude with violin on the windowsill, and hence as both the object and inspiration of her companion's work. Though overemphasized and intense, Mafai's dark eyes bespeak infatuation rather than concentration. His dreamy look is complemented by Raphaël's heavily laid, unblended brush strokes, which seem to smother and possess the object of her gaze.

The intimacy of the early works, with their miniature proportions and insular mood, belie the trying relationship between the young Roman and the Lithuanian seven years his senior. Within months of their meeting in 1925, Raphaël left Rome for Montepulciano and then Florence, ostensibly to earn money teaching English, but also to avoid the growing conflict between them. Her letters to Mafai (written in English or in broken Italian) bemoan their separation, but also accuse him of selfishness in the face of her purported self–sacrifice and desire to shelter him. In December 1925, a few days before Christmas (which she spent alone in Florence), Raphaël wrote angrily to Mafai that he had done nothing for her "except share his room." She expressed irritation that he had never given her as much as a book or picture, though, as she claimed, "I have given you all that a woman could give to the man she loves," adding that she spent her last money with him. She continued: "What is love??! Does it mean forgiveness? Would I forgive another man if he were not you? No! Never!! Then it means being a slave, well I refuse to be a slave under any circumstances."[11]

Figure 8.1 *Mafai che disegna* (Mafai drawing), oil on canvas, 1928. (Courtesy Archivio della Scuola Romana. By permission.)

Raphaël's urge to build a nest with Mafai, in fact, stemmed from other reasons, as did her swift and decisive departure from Rome: she was pregnant. Whether or not she had informed Mafai of her circumstances, he was not present at the birth of their first child, Miriam, born on February 2, 1926: "The labor was difficult. I recall that the midwife stayed in my room listening to the baby breathing through some instrument placed on my belly. The whole night I was in terrible pain, a foreigner, alone and without family."[12]

Rather than returning to Rome, she sent Miriam to the country under the care of a wet nurse and continued to work in Florence. Her correspondence (in much-improved Italian) shows that matters continued to be difficult with Mafai. Still living under his mother's roof, the far more dependent Mafai was reticent about a life together with Raphaël and fearful of familial responsibilities.[13] Yet Raphaël never ceased to encourage him in his work. Clearly, she was aware that professional success for Mafai meant a successful resolution of their personal life as well: "I hope that you are working, especially drawing, and concentrating on the small things as well as the grand. If you work as you have promised me, I am sure that you will make wonderful progress and then we will be together with our little treasure."[14]

After some two years away, Raphaël returned to Rome to live with Mafai in November 1927. The reunion resulted in the fruitful, if brief, period of the "school of via Cavour," named for the street near the Colosseum where Mafai and Raphaël made their home and studio. Along with Scipione, Mafai and Raphaël worked intensely on evolving a new painting of eccentric subjects, torrid colors, and antimonumental forms that differed substantially from the dominant classicizing style of the time. Posterity has largely credited Raphaël with influencing Mafai and Scipione, and the evidence of the changes in their painting around the time of her return to Rome support this thesis.[15] But it was not merely her knowledge of foreign trends, specifically the lyrical expressionism of the school of Paris, but also her intense and spirited personality that proved the pivotal force behind their insouciant, bohemian way of life.

As a female and an exotic outsider, she played the "natural" role of muse. The colors of Mafai and Scipione's paintings betray the influence of Raphaël's warm and earthy palette, characteristically accented by rose, amber, and fiery reds. The color combinations also relate to the fabrics and stuffs of the caftans and Oriental tapestries in which Raphaël dressed herself and her home. In numerous paintings and ink studies of nudes, Mafai and Scipione paid homage to her general body type—the "blonde and pudgy" female (as Mafai once referred to her), in poses libertine and lyrical.[16] Scipione's appropri-

ately titled *Muse* (1928) depicts none other than Raphaël: the generous figure, full, wiry locks, incongruous hat (undoubtedly a nod to
her unconventional taste in fashion), and her ever-present guitar. A
bovine and a small drummer boy (personifications of Scipione and
Mafai, respectively) also appear, in wry acknowledgment of her inspiration.

The so-called brotherhood of via Cavour was rife with tension, as
Raphaël's return to Rome inevitably drove a wedge between the two
men. Between Raphaël and Scipione there was no love lost; they were
jealous of their respective relationships with Mafai and wary of each
other's influence.[17] In a letter to Renato Mazzacurati written in the
spring of 1929, Scipione disparagingly referred to Raphaël as just
another of a growing number of idiosyncratic painters, several women
among them.[18] The "ménage à trois" dissolved with Scipione's illness
and eventual death from tuberculosis in 1933. Raphaël, who was residing in Paris at the time, returned to Rome only after he passed
away; a year and a half later, she and Mafai finally married.

Raphaël and Mafai competed fiercely with each other in the early
years. They often painted the same sites, showed together in exhibitions, and even elicited reviews as a pair. The basis of constant comparison and Raphaël's sudden success at the end of the decade inevitably caused feelings of insecurity in Mafai. He also envied Raphaël's
ability to concentrate and her unrelenting discipline, which contrasted
with what he considered his lazy approach and distracted nature.[19]
While Raphaël was unintentionally ruthless in her frank assessments
of his work, he preferred the ironic turn of the knife when negating
hers (Mafai 1989). The writer Libero De Libero (1949) recalls visiting the studio on via Cavour, where Raphaël kept her paintings rolled
up in towels in a closet, "patiently putting up with the irritating laughter of Mafai" (p. 10). In later years, during the postwar reconstruction of the history of the period, Mafai downplayed Raphaël's role
and the significance of the school of via Cavour, emphasizing instead
his formative relationship with Scipione.[20]

Even when critical, Raphaël offered Mafai unfailing encouragement,
like a school mistress drilling her prize pupil or, conversely, like a
mother with blind praise for her child. She pushed him with the same
intensity that she demanded of herself, depleting valuable energies
and taking time away from her own work. "If you are near I don't
have the right to paint," she once lamented, and inevitably, Raphaël's

ambitions as a painter took second place to Mafai's.[21] By the early 1930s, she felt constrained to abandon the brush and take to sculpture in an effort to quell the competition between them. As she later confessed: "It was difficult for two artists to live together when they shared the same art of painting. I criticized him and he criticized me. And so I went to sculpture school at night."[22]

Yet Raphaël hardly faded into the background, sacrificing her art for his. True, she ceased to exhibit for many years after 1929, but privately she only increased her commitment to work. As late as 1960, Alfredo Mezio perpetuated the myth that for years Raphaël "was the brave girl who, putting her family above her art, withdrew modestly into the shadows and at a certain point disappeared right from the scene" (p. 17). Nothing was further from the truth: in 1930, only weeks after the birth of her third daughter, Giulia, she left with Mafai for Paris. She remained abroad, shuttling between the French capital and London for nearly four years, while Mafai joined her from Rome when possible and sent her money for livelihood in between. The children were left in the care of Mafai and their paternal grandmother, who, never fond of Raphaël in the first place, was indignant at her daughter-in-law's abdication of role.

During these years Mafai mothered the children, imparting to them an indelible memory of tenderness and care that differed sharply from the absent figure of Raphaël.[23] While allowing Raphaël the freedom to further her career, now in sculpture, and to broaden her contacts, the experience also proved a turning point in Mafai's sentimental life. As he confessed to Raphaël in the privacy of his diary: "Now I am enjoying certain joys unknown to me a few years ago and perhaps there are none greater outside one's own family. Nothing can equal even the slightest glance from the children, nor a word from you. I have little interest in the conversation of men" (Mafai 1984, 58; entry for January 2, 1932). The thought of Raphaël living alone, pushing herself and surviving on minimal means, filled Mafai with a new desire to comfort and nurture her. His imaginary conversations with her in his diary brim with tiny seductions and promises and pleas for her return. At the same time, Mafai's letters reveal a more difficult side of Raphaël's driven personality: her refusal to be pampered, to relax, or to accept the affection and protection she so desired. More than once, Mafai pleaded, "In God's name, why don't you let me do something for you?"[24]

Raphaël's determination to study in Paris betrayed the scope of her aspirations, as did the way she sought out the premier British sculptor, Jacob Epstein, when she decided to make sculpture her metier. The trip proved a rite of emancipation: Raphaël never again put her work in second place, regardless of connubial or maternal obligations. After her return to Italy in November 1933, the family moved into an apartment lodged within a hotel owned by Mafai's parents on the Piazza Indipendenza. A garage in the back garden served as her studio. Raphaël submitted herself to a rigorous schedule; up at the crack of dawn and into the studio, she "battled with her sculptures" until fatigue got the better of her. There was a staff to take care of everyday domestic chores, and the children took their meals in the hotel dining room. When the family moved to Genoa after the passage of the racial laws, she commanded the largest room in the house as her workplace. So far was her life from the standard routine of women that Mafai could prod her on with gentle sarcasm: "Now you are becoming a touch too lazy.... I wouldn't want you to turn into a good little housewife."[25]

The balance of affection shifted notably between Raphaël and Mafai during the second decade of their relationship: he became more attentive, and she turned her sense of purpose inward. As is evident in his diary and letters, Mafai readily sympathized with the responsibilities of motherhood and accepted Raphaël's ambition to continue her work regardless. Writing to her in London in 1931, he declared: "I'm sure of your success, you deserve it, and few artists have *suffered as you* have for art."[26] More confident of his own professional achievements (at this point his public reputation far exceeded hers), he also openly admitted his competitive instincts with humor and respect: "I paint everyday otherwise I feel badly and then...I don't want Antonietta to pass me by. So many times I have felt the superiority in some of your works, like certain ones of mine in the past, and I don't feel that I can do it like that again."[27] Correspondence from the war period indicates that Raphaël depended on Mafai for specific counsel on how to go about her work and to overcome creative impasse. Though the separation was painful for Mafai, he recognized that it allowed Raphaël to give undivided attention to her art, and he entreated her to use her time alone in the studio to the fullest. The war years marked a point of maturation for their partnership, which was perhaps best characterized by Mafai as a mutually enhancing battle of creative egos: "When you tell me that you cannot love anything more than your work, I could get jealous about it, but I understand it, and so another type of love evolves, full of the harmony of subtle yearnings and somewhat sublime."[28]

Details of the personal and professional lives of the Mafai family appear even more unconventional in the context of Fascist Italy. Raphaël's status as an unwed mother and her cohabitation with Mafai were in themselves not uncommon for the time: some one-fourth to one-third of all births were illegitimate.[29] More radical, instead, was the priority that Raphaël placed on her work and the domestic arrangements needed to accommodate it. After all, with the legislation of the Casti Connubi in December 1930 both church and state officially consigned women to the roles of wife and mother, with emphasis on the latter. Education and social services reinforced women's place as primary caretakers and domestic laborers, and the regime went so far as to reward the nation's most prolific women, putting them on parade like broodmares. Propaganda also infiltrated the realm of the fine arts, as images of demure expectant mothers, nursing peasant women, or even suckling animals populated the state exhibitions, complementing the state's campaign to increase the birthrate and stabilize women's place in the home. Although Raphaël's having borne three children conformed to official dictates, her complete lack of domestic inclination and her professional tenacity undermined established values (see De Grand 1976; De Grazia 1992).

In the Fascist era, devotion to the home was equated with devotion to the state. Raphaël was, of course, stateless, and worshiped no false patriotic idols or any form of governmental authority. As a foreigner and outsider to begin with, she perhaps found it easier than some women to resist societal and political pressures. The Mafai household inculcated individualistic and antiauthoritarian attitudes far removed from Fascist mass conformism. As Miriam Mafai (1992) recalls: "We lived an insulated life inside our proud little world: Jewish, artists, and opposed to the regime" (p. 135).

To be sure, Raphaël's metier as an artist allowed her greater freedoms than were found in other professions. The fine arts, along with literary pursuits, were acceptable "pastimes," because they functioned outside of the main economy and did not take jobs away from the male workforce. They could also be categorized as dilettante pursuits, within the realm of the aesthetic and hence the traditionally feminine. In addition, Italy had a long history of accomplished women artists, outnumbering other European nations during the Renaissance and until around 1700 (Krull 1989, 8–9). In the nineteenth century the figures dropped sharply, as women were excluded from the formal training of the academies. Only with the development of free exhibitions and the avant–garde in the early twentieth century did the number of women artists again begin to rise.[30] Under Fascism, state intervention in culture actually resulted in more exhibition opportunities for women on the regional and national levels. To take the newly created Rome Quadriennale, for example, the number of women artists in the state's most important public exhibition grew from 6.8 percent in 1931 to 11.8 percent in 1939—an increase in representation of 73 percent over a decade.[31] Furthermore, women's groups such as the Associazione Nazionale Donne Professioniste e Artiste (National Association of Professional Women and Artists) organized shows exclusively for women, continuing a tradition of independent exhibitions begun at the turn of the century.[32]

More revealing of the regime's attitude toward women in the visual arts, however, was the distribution of awards, purchases, and administrative positions. Women rarely entered into the echelons of power and success and remained a marginal group within the official cultural arena. Countess Mimi Pecci Blunt and Margherita Caetani may have wielded considerable reputations as private patrons of the arts, but Margherita Sarfatti was the only woman ever to preside on any of the national organizing committees of the Biennale, Triennale, or Quadriennale, and no woman ever participated on either the appointed or elected selection juries.[33] (Nor did Sarfatti, a self–proclaimed feminist, go out of her way to promote women in the arts: no women were invited to either of the exhibitions of the "Novecento italiano" [Italian Twentieth Century], which she organized in 1926 and 1929.)

Furthermore, the number of purchases of works by women artists from the Quadriennale and Biennale did not increase in proportion to the number of female exhibitors.[34] Accordingly, personal exhibitions at the Quadriennale or Biennale remained exclusive to men. Most indicative is the absence of women from the mural movement of the 1930s, which provided the most significant means of employment and public recognition.[35] Because of either lack of training or lack of opportunity, no women worked on a large public scale or joined in the critical debates on art for the state.

Raphaël had little interest in catering to official propaganda, and as a woman, foreigner, and autodidact she was not in a position to compete for public commissions. Mafai, however, executed a large fresco, the *Triumph of Caesar,* for the Palazzo del Littorio in 1935.[36] Raphaël inevitably participated in the culture of the regime by exhibiting in the regional syndicate exhibitions, for which she ostensibly needed a party card. She made her debut as a painter in the Prima Mostra del Sindacato Fascista (First Fascist Syndicate Exhibition) in 1929, and returned to the public eye as a sculptor in the Lazio syndicate exhibitions of 1936, 1937, and 1938.

When Raphaël appeared on the Roman scene in 1929 she was as much identified as a "woman artist" as she was as a cohort of Scipione and Mafai. Though critics singled out her expressionist edge, several of her peers had earlier cultivated modern postimpressionist or fauve styles, among them Deiva de Angelis (1885–1925), Pasquarosa Bertoletti (1896–1973), Edita Broglio (1886–1977), and Leonetta Pieraccini Cecchi (1882–1977). All had affiliations with the Roman avantgarde before Raphaël's arrival, having participated in the exhibitions of the Roman Secession during the war. And typically, they were all linked with successful male artists or writers.

Raphaël carved a more singular profile in the 1930s as a "woman sculptor" — a rare occupation during the Fascist period. The medium itself was also more resistant to stylistic innovation and was predisposed toward a public, ceremonial role. The few women who exhibited sculpture in state exhibitions, such as Lidia Franchetti, Antonietta Paoli Pogliani, Maria Chiaromonte, and Federica Aloisi, worked in conservative academic or art deco styles and with themes congenial to the regime. Yet barely had Raphaël emerged as a sculptor in the syndicate exhibitions of the mid-1930s than she was forced to retreat from public view because of the passage of anti-Semitic legislation.

Ironically, her isolation and displacement from the already marginal position of woman artist proved beneficial to her career. During the war years, as other women were forced to abandon their interests to the home front and submit to greater restrictions on their daily lives, Raphaël was able to concentrate on her work undisturbed. And at a time of increasing challenge to creative freedom, Raphaël proceeded uninhibited by official prescriptions concerning style and subject.

While Raphaël was shunted from the mainstream, Mafai's reputation only grew. He was represented in all four Quadriennale, including a personal show of twenty-nine works in 1935. He also continued to exhibit within the system after the passage of the racial laws, largely out of necessity, to support his family with his earnings. Raphaël's position outside official culture — by choice, circumstance, and later racial persecution — may have protected her artistic integrity, but it also limited her commercial viability. Her economic dependence on Mafai was an unavoidable consequence, which she nonetheless considered an affront to her personal dignity (see Mafai 1989).

Undoubtedly, the number and choice of biblical images painted by Raphaël throughout her career resulted from her awareness of her position as a woman within an oppressive, patriarchal society. Drawn to the stories of irrepressible women, she rendered several versions of the archetypal female heroine Judith, slayer of Holofernes, and of the lesser-known story of Tamar (*Er and Tamar*, 1967), who had the foresight and cunning to ensure her familial line.[37] In addition, she chose female protagonists for the general biblical theme of flight, as in the grand *Fuga* of 1936 and in *La fuga* (The flight; 1958), a sculpture of a mother carrying her three children in protection and haste (see Figure 8.2). The biblical scenes, virtually all taken from the Old Testament, also underline her Jewish identity, which she asserted in other paintings of her family and of the rite of blessing the candles on Shabbat. Yet above and beyond Raphaël's religious affinities, the images of Judith and Tamar show an identification with women who triumphed over adversity through daring and independence of mind.

It is perhaps less remarkable that Raphaël pursued an artistic career under the regime than that she did so despite being the mother of three children. Few of the most successful women artists of the twentieth century had children to raise as well as their careers: Gwen John, Marianne von Werefkind, Gabriele Munther, Natalie Goncharova, Emily Carr, Georgia O'Keeffe, Leonor Fini, Meret Oppenheim, Frida Kahlo, Kay Sage, to name but a few, were all childless. Suzanne Valadon, Sonia Delaunay, and Louise Nevelson each had one offspring.

Figure 8.2 *La fuga* (The flight), bronze, 1958. (Courtesy Archivio della Scuola Romana. By permission.)

Vanessa Bell and Alice Neel each had three children, and Barbara Hepworth had four, including a set of triplets. Yet only two other artists explored the actual theme of motherhood in such depth: Käthe Kollwitz and Paula Modersohn-Becker. Not surprisingly, Raphaël also integrated her two identities, choosing pregnancy and her children as the central subjects of her art: "All my life I sculpted motherhood," she confirmed in 1961 (quoted in Berenice 1961). In addition to numerous portrait busts of her young daughters, she devoted a series to the pregnant female figure and another to the themes of maternal protection and bonding between mother and child. At her death, the last work upon her easel was an unfinished canvas of a woman giving birth.

Ironically, only by placing her work above her children could Raphaël so devote herself to the art of maternity. She began to cultivate the subject after a long period of absence from her infant daughters, during which time she reached maturity in her own career. Upon her return from Paris and London at the end of 1933, she modeled portrait busts of Miriam and Simone, combining their barely defined features with her own tentative expressions in a new art form. They provided a subject with which she was intimately familiar, and they were readily available, submissive models. Though infused with tenderness and affection, the sculptures actually evolved from a rigorous relationship between mother and child, artist and model. The young girls were instructed to remain absolutely still and quiet, or to strike exacting poses. "You must sleep," she commanded the 7-year-old Miriam when modeling her in closed-eyed slumber, oblivious to whether the child wanted to or could oblige. By contrast, on the rare occasions when Mafai sketched his daughters, he allowed them to relax, talk, or read a book.

As a mother, Raphaël demanded the same of her daughters as she did of herself. She expected discipline and devotion to work, and she pushed them to excel at music, gymnastics, and schoolwork, submitting them to endless drills and practice. Miriam Mafai remembers that her mother would emerge from her studio only to ask, "How goes the homework?" or to announce, "Now it's time to play the piano." Only their "sweet, lazy and distracted" father provided refuge from Raphaël's authoritarian zeal. From an early age the three girls learned that a career, rather than marriage, was the essential goal, and that no matter what the task, one was to do it well. Books were the standard gifts on birthdays and holidays; intellectual life held the highest value for the Mafai family, and little attention was paid to fashion, home economics, coquetry, or other standard feminine concerns. Though birth and child imagery dominated her work, maternity was the central theme of Raphaël's art, not her life, as was made painfully clear to her daughters: "I'm not sure if I ever asked her: what meant more to her — we or her statues. I knew that she wouldn't have given me a satisfactory answer, because she would have said: the statues" (Mafai 1992, 139).[38]

The demeanor of *Le tre sorelle* (The three sisters; 1936) (Figure 8.3) says much about the qualities Raphaël wished to impart to her daughters, while also reflecting her own self-worth. Massed together in a

Figure 8.3 *Le tre sorelle* (The three sisters), cement, 1936. (Courtesy Archivio della Scuola Romana. By permission.)

united front, the sisters bear their sturdy bodies with a noble carriage, as yet unaffected by the self-consciousness of adolescence. The bust of Miriam at the front forms the apex of the compositional triangle and a metaphoric bulwark against the world. With her arms crossed and held close to her chest, she appears both defiant and self-con-

tained. The motif of the crossed arms was likely borrowed from Jacob Epstein, who began to use it around 1930, replacing the typical
passivity or coquetry of female portrait busts with a new assertive
pose. Raphaël depicted herself in similar fashion in her *Autoritratto*
(Self-portrait) (Figure 8.4) several years later. Despite their firm and
stalwart presence, the three sisters glance downward with a pensive,
introspective air. The disposition of Miriam's head resting heavily in
her hand also alludes to Rodin's *Thinker,* the pose of melancholy, and
to a long tradition of depicting creative introspection, traditionally associated with the male.

Equally as daring, *La fuga* depicts a child springing forth from the
head of its mother, refashioning the myth of the birth of Athena from
Zeus (see Figure 8.2). The allusion to the goddess of wisdom confirms
Raphaël's supreme valuation of knowledge and the power it brings.
Though the child is of necessity positioned above the shoulders (to
make room for the two others borne on the back of the mother) the
metaphor is unmistakable; it is visually reinforced by the overpower-
ing presence of the child's head and the barely perceptible delineation
of her arms clutched under the mother's chin. Raphaël repeated the
motif in the more explicitly titled *Maternità* (Maternity) in 1961. The
patriarchal figure of Zeus is replaced by a matriarch, but this does
not diminish the significance of a birth from the head rather than
from the belly and the opposition implied therein: mind versus body,
culture versus nature, spirit versus flesh.

Raphaël explored the emotive force of maternal bonding and duress
in the very forms and modeling of her sculpture. In the *Niobe* series
(1938–53; see Figure 8.5) a mother shields her child from danger
in the protective embrace of her own body. In the final, and least
naturalistic, version they are merged together, as the body of the child
pushes inward, literally reentering the maternal womb. The mother
propels herself forward on one foot, accentuating the sense of urgency
and the weight of responsibility she bears. (Another version of the
clasped figures, sculpted in 1960, is titled, appropriately, *Angoscia*
[Anxiety].) By disregarding anatomical correctness and breaking
open the sculptural mass, Raphaël creates a dynamic relationship
between solid and void, interior and exterior, that doubles back on
the thematic concern of shelter and vulnerability, origin and offspring.

Figure 8.4 *Autoritratto* (Self-portrait), terra-cotta, 1952. (Courtesy Archivio della Scuola Romana. By permission.)

Paradoxically, Raphaël used the fragment or part to stress physical and emotional connection, as in the assemblage of heads, torsos, and limbs that form *La fuga* (Figure 8.2). She also made new sculptures from partial casts of earlier works: the standing child at the base of *La fuga*, for example, was also turned into a sculpture in its own right, a part from a whole, extending the reproductive cycle in fact and metaphor. Her distended belly is now slit open where it was once connected to the mother, baring the deep hollow of the interior form. Raphaël juxtaposes this gaping absence to the commensurable presence of two legs on the back of the figure (a modified cast of the second child in the original *La fuga*) that seem to rise upward through the sheer force of delivery. Though an independent form severed from

Figure 8.5 *Niobe,* bronze, 1948. (Courtesy Archivio della Scuola Romana. By permission.)

its origins, the fragment remains bound to the supporting figure, like a child to the parent.

Raphaël exploited the concepts of the partial or the broken and adapted figure to evolve a formal language consonant with the experience of the female body, and hence at odds with the idealism of the classical tradition. *Genesi I* (Genesis I; 1947) (Figure 8.6), her first version of the pregnant form, is headless, emphasizing the sheer weight and sinking posture of the figure. The swollen breasts and limbs address the actual biological functions of pregnancy while asserting a proud mass of flesh. She sculpted maternity from the inside out—from an awareness of her own bodily experience—and in do-

Figure 8.6 *Genesi I* (Genesis I), bronze, 1947. (Courtesy Archivio della Scuola Romana. By permission.)

ing so, broke with age–old conventions of chaste madonnas and earthy matriarchs.

Though her focus on motherhood appears on the surface to conform to patriarchal interests, nothing could be further from the norm of representation, or more confrontive of fear, shame, or disgust, than the nakedness of her pregnant bellies in the *Genesis* series. In *La grande genesi, n. 4* (The large genesis, no. 4; 1962–68) (Figure 8.7), the seated nude is playing with her hair, boldly asserting, rather than denying, the sexuality of the expectant woman.

Motherhood also inspired many works by Jacob Epstein. Raphaël undoubtedly knew his enormous *Genesis* of 1929–31, completed shortly before she arrived in London. The *Genesis* figure proved an important point in Epstein's career and in the history of the sculpted

Figure 8.7 *La grande genesi, n. 4* (The large genesis, no. 4), bronze, 1962–68.
(Courtesy Archivio della Scuola Romana. By permission.)

female figure, for he wanted to capture, as he put it, "the profoundly elemental in motherhood, the deep down instinctive female, without the trappings and charm of what is known as feminine." According to Epstein (1955), the brute directness of the work, its lack of eroticism and conventional charm, induced the ire of the public. He claimed that it was a particular affront to women, who saw in it "an attempt to undermine their attractiveness, their desire to please and seduce" (pp. 139–40).[39] Despite his pretense to the contrary, Epstein's vision was blinded by stereotype, in this case of woman as earth mother and primal creature, fated to nature and not to the intellect.

Not only does Raphaël's conception of genesis lack the patent archaism of Epstein's work, it is made by a woman and hence by one of the only sex able to produce both sculpture and babies. For Raphaël maternity was more than a contemporary realistic subject—she was, after all, a mother—it was also a concrete metaphor for her creative work. As she mothered children, so she gave birth to art, in a double process of gestation and labor. Late into her life she continued to use the metaphor to express creative process: "What I am truly looking for I don't know how to explain, but I know that something has to merge, be born, born. But when? This I do not know."[40]

The pairing of procreativity and creativity has a long and venerable literary history, traditionally among men, who, as the dominant force in cultural production, have used the birthing metaphor to express both the anxieties and the fulfillment of their work.[41] Unable to reproduce in fact, men reproduce in fiction, begetting immortality through art and usurping the procreative role for the furthering of humanity in an intellectual sense. Conversely, the metaphor underlines the traditional divisions of labor in society—men create, women procreate. Whereas the former are freed from the burdens of childbearing to pursue other interests, the latter are constrained from producing otherwise. Until the twentieth century, when women used the poetic metaphor of birthing it often underlined the incompatibility rather than the harmony between roles.

Sculpture is a privileged site for the birthing metaphor; the original myth of creation, after all, holds God as a sculptor who fashioned man out of clay. No one more enjoyed the parallels between the making of sculpture and the making of babies than did Raphaël's contemporary Arturo Martini, who spoke of drawing forth from the "poetic sack" and likened the modeling of form to a "pushing from within." "Form is nothing but chaos," he wrote, "that composes itself little by little, as if in a maternal womb." Martini went so far as to lament, "Why was I not born a woman? At least I could have satisfied myself making children" (Martini 1982, 59, 62, 95).

Yet Martini actually sculpted few versions of motherhood, his most important incarnation of the theme being the carved wood *Maternity* of 1927. Though Martini's subject of three children clinging to their mother in defense may well have influenced Raphaël's *La fuga* of 1958, his treatment of the figures pales in comparison with Raphaël's bold rearrangements of the human anatomy. For Raphaël, the language of sculpture was inseparable from the language of female form, analogous in fact and concept to the swollen masses and rotund volumes of her own body, or to the fragmented composition of her sexual identity. She bridged the division between maternity and creativity that habitually confronted women in arts and letters; in the history of early modern sculpture, her contribution is unique.

Given Raphaël's emancipated position within a private and public context, it is surprising to note the number of images she rendered of women as objects of erotic delight. Some dozen sculptures and paintings, from the 1920s until her death, represent women primping and preparing themselves for view. They fall primarily into two types: women gazing into mirrors and women combing their hair (see Figure 8.8). There are also several versions of female dancers or seated nudes in which the women display themselves provocatively while playing with their abundant tresses. Painted in luxuriant colors of violet and red with golden flesh tones, the canvases exude a vibrant sensuality, an impression furthered by the richly textured impasto. Similarly, the broken surfaces of the sculptures impart a warm physicality and emphasize the pleasure of the touch.

The self-adulating figures, viewed in the privacy of their toilette, allude to the societal pressures brought to bear on women to be beautiful and seductive. The dressing table and the ritual of the bath symbolize the intimate landscape, in short, the sexuality of the female, as depicted over centuries of art by male artists. As John Berger (1977, 45–65) has noted, the tradition of the nude gazing into the mirror doubly implicates the female sex: she is there for the delight of the male viewer while simultaneously condemned as an embodiment of vanitas. Recent psychoanalytic studies have also argued that the crux of female identity is constituted in dialogue with the outside gaze — either by a woman's own reflection in the mirror or the appraising view of the male.[42]

On the one hand, Raphaël's nudes betray her ambition to paint one of the most ubiquitous and prestigious subjects in the history of Western art. On the other, they present a blatant twist on that same venerable tradition: a woman exploring the image of female sexuality developed in response to male desire.[43] These are, after all, images of women looking at themselves painted by a woman, not by a man,

Figure 8.8 *La pettinatrice* (Combing the hair), oil on canvas, 1957. (Courtesy Archivio della Scuola Romana. By permission.)

implicating the female viewer, as well as the male, in the position of voyeur. Yet there is also an identification between viewing subject and painted object, because the female viewer inevitably reflects upon herself in a reciprocal position. The additional presence of another woman in the picture—the one who is combing the hair—reinforces the sense of complicity. The image of the woman is not that of the "other," but of kind; clearly Raphaël was evaluating the schisms among her sense of self, her sexuality, and the socially constructed feminine archetype.

On the most general level, Raphaël's fixation on the mirror derived from her need to determine her own identity. The first picture in the series, *Giudetta e lo specchio* (Judith and the mirror; c. 1928), is clearly an essay on the search for self rather than a vanitas or erotic theme, given that the woman is fully clothed. Nor does the subject have anything to do with the biblical story line: Judith serves as a stand-in for Raphaël and an acknowledgment of her Semitic origins—one of Raphaël's few solid points of identification. As a youthful work, painted early in her career and in her relationship with Mafai, it represents a literal moment of reflection, a pause between a personal history of displacement and a life still to be formed. Rendered as a shard, the mirror refers to the fragmentary nature of the self, a whole constructed piecemeal from exterior impressions. In another painting from the same period, *Mafai che disegna* (Figure 8.1), even the act of painting becomes a kind of mirroring: Raphaël sees herself in him and as he would see her.

The notion of specularity also dovetails with that of narcissism or the completion of the self through the image of another, be it a mirror reflection, a lover, or a child. Perhaps because of her lack of rooted identity, Raphaël was constantly in search of a unified, seamless whole, finding herself in every aspect of external reality. Hence Alberto Moravia (1974) characterizes her as a consummate narcissist: "Every painting by Raphaël is in reality a mirror over which she bends to see the reflection of—her own image." Her features—the slanted almond eyes, wavy hair, and rounded face—permeate every portrait, in addition to those of her children, who naturally embody an extension of herself. Objects recognizably her own—Oriental fabrics, Judaica, playing cards, and instruments—invade every setting (see Figure 8.9). And in this self-reflecting world, Moravia argues, all the men are in love with Raphaël, whether they are actually present in the picture (as in the portraits of Mafai) or their gazes merely implied. In 1940, she explicitly acknowledged her fascination with the theme in her own sculpture of *Narcissus,* which depicts the beautiful young man frozen on all fours, enraptured with his own image.

Figure 8.9 *Natura morta con chitarra* (Still life with guitar), oil on canvas, 1928.
(Courtesy Archivio della Scuola Romana. By permission.)

As unconventional as her life may have been, Raphaël was very much preoccupied by perceptions of conventional femininity. She lied about her date of birth out of vanity and competition, denying the seven years that separated her from the younger Mafai. With broad Slavic features, she was not a beautiful woman according to prevailing canons, and age accentuated the lack of delicacy so favored in Western cultures. Raphaël's self-consciousness about her appearance revealed itself in passing references to her nose. "You want to know if my nose is still so ugly?" she coyly asked Mafai in a letter of 1925. "It seems to me to have become even uglier." Yet it was clearly a point of insecurity, as evident in an angry letter the next month: "I loved you devotedly sincerely... but devotion is a thing of little importance for you, for you could easily change me for any other woman regardless of her thoughts or her ideals as long as she would be the happy possessor of a beautiful nose."[44] Stout and plump, her figure complied handsomely with the needs of childbearing, but not with the ideal of the modern female body promoted in the mass media.

She dressed in large, flowing caftans that covered her body while drawing attention to her ethnicity.

Miriam Mafai recalls that while she was growing up, her mother avoided discussions of sex and sexual education, neglecting even to inform her of the facts of menstruation. Describing her mother as slightly fearful of sex, Mafai believes that Raphaël viewed physical passion as a weakness (despite her clearly emotionally passionate relationship with her husband), as a threat, no doubt, to the stringent creative life that Raphaël so ardently pursued. Her daughters wore their hair cropped like boys, and she dressed them in ungainly, unfashionable clothes that prompted the ridicule of their peers in elementary school (Mafai 1992, 135–36).

Emancipation clearly made Raphaël aware of the dichotomy between her "masculine" drive and priorities and the sociocultural expectations of feminine seduction and acquiescence. In the images of Judith and Salome the traits are merged, as these particular heroines used their wily ways to achieve their goals. Significantly, the number of her self–attentive female nudes increased in the postwar years, along with Raphaël's age and decreasing possibilities as a lover. Well over 50 years old, she no longer lived with Mafai, who pursued sexual relationships with other women. In this period of greater professional security, and with her battles behind her, Raphaël had the luxury of considering those aspects of the stereotypical feminine she had long ago dismissed or denied.

Whether wanting or questioning, the late "boudoir" pictures and sculptures express full awareness of a divided or multiple self, as explicitly articulated in one of her late paintings, *Io e i miei fantasmi* (My phantoms and I; 1961). Here Raphaël places herself at left, fully clothed and brush in hand, standing before a seated nude. The pictorial structure reinforces the notion of division and confrontation: two figures on either side, one clothed and one naked, one aggressively looking, the other averting her gaze. The phantoms are none other than the female nudes, ghosts of the grand tradition in Western art and of the traditionally feminine that continued to both elude and inspire Raphaël. Significantly, it is the only self-portrait in which she depicts herself at work, and she uses the occasion to revert to the usual gender relationship between male artist and female model, between surveyor and surveyed. Through the compositional dichotomy of *Io e i miei fantasmi,* Raphaël acknowledges the leap of faith still necessary to identify herself as both woman and artist, even after four decades of a creative life.

Notes

   I thank Miriam Mafai for her countless conversations, as well as Netta Vespignani of the Archivio della Scuola Romana, who generously provided the unpublished letters and diaries of both Antonietta Raphaël and Mario Mafai. I am also grateful to Francesca Morelli, curator of the archive, for her research assistance. All translations are my own.

   1. Thalia Gouma–Peterson and Patricia Mathews (1987) provide a summary of the state of the research in feminist art–historical scholarship, with a qualitative emphasis on the methods expounded by Rozsika Parker and Griselda Pollock in their book *Old Mistresses: Women, Art, and Ideology* (1981). Their review is challenged by Norma Broude and Mary D. Garrard (1989).

   2. Antonietta Raphaël does not appear in any of some dozen standard surveys of women artists. Exceptionally, she is listed in Penny Dunford's *A Biographical Dictionary of Women Artists in Europe and America since 1950* (1989, 243). Raphaël does appear in the important Italian exhibition devoted to women artists of the first half of the twentieth century organized by Lea Vergine, *L'altra metà dell'avanguardia 1910–1940* (1980, 57–58).

   3. For a revisionist view of the postwar interpretation of Roman painting in the 1920s and 1930s, see Braun (1988).

   4. Jesse Boswell is mentioned only in passing, as one of the members of the "6 di Torino" (Maltese 1960, 365).

   5. Similarly, Virgilio Guzzi (1955; in Mezio 1960, 30–31) called her work a "feminine distillation of Soutine and Chagall." Raphaël herself was aware of the critics' tendency in the postwar years to view her as an oddity, reinforcing a kind of "ghetto" distinction between her art and that of the mainstream. As her daughter Miriam Mafai (1989) has acknowledged, "Some critics began to bring to light her role in the Scuola Romana, but she felt that she was being assigned a rather marginal and eccentric position, as the one who had introduced to Rome certain dark and burning colors, or the sort of drunken mark of Chagall."

   6. "The sculptor Raphaël breaks the rules: usually women do not have much of a plastic or constructive sense" (Borghese 1947; in Mezio 1960, 23). Fortunato Bellonzi (1955), preferring her painting to her sculpture, nonetheless admitted that "her aggressive and barbaric modeling achieves felicitous moments, without affectation, in sculpted portraits or in the lively small bronzes" (in Mezio 1960, 31–32). See also the review by Antonio del Guercio (1955): "This humane and poetic continuity, which excludes any reference to the archaic...confers a virile fascination on Raphaël's collection of works" (in Mezio 1960, 33).

   7. Raphaël's exact surname remains unknown: her father is referred to as both Simone (Simon) and Simone De Raphaël. The surname Raphael (without the umlaut) appears on her British passport dated 1924. Miriam Mafai believes it may be an invented name, either chosen by the family when they began a new life in England or the personal choice of the artist herself (personal communication, May 20, 1992).

8. After visiting Mafai's studio for the first time, in 1925, Raphaël told him she did not like his paintings, that she found them "too sad." A month later, on his birthday, he brought her a bunch of violets and a challenge: " 'Make me a present: paint these.' He returned two hours later and said, 'It's fantastic, you must continue,' and thus I began" (Antonietta Raphaël, unpublished diary; in D'Amico 1991, 50).

9. For a complete bibliography of catalogs, exhibitions, and reviews in the postwar period, see D'Amico (1991, 121–27).

10. Although Raphaël often gave her birth date as 1899 or 1900, on her marriage certificate her date of birth reads 1895; see the biographical summary by D'Amico (1991, 49). She claims to have had a friendship with Zadkine during her early years in London, but, as D'Amico argues, it could not have been significant, given that the sculptor moved to Paris from London in 1909 (p. 50). Her relationship with Chagall, both in 1924 when she passed through Paris and again in the early 1930s, is unsubstantiated. She clearly worked with Epstein while in London in the early 1930s, but writings by the British sculptor, including his autobiography, make no mention of Antonietta Raphaël (see Epstein 1955).

11. Antonietta Raphaël, Florence, December 23, 1925, to Mario Mafai, Rome.

12. Antonietta Raphaël, unpublished diary, entry for February 2, 1966.

13. In a letter to Raphaël of July 1929, written from nearby Trevi, Mafai admitted: "I would have wanted you near, especially in this life without obligations and without a home, eating fruit and running with joy and without a care.... But it's terrible to think of such things for they raise the curtain on our life of struggle and sacrifice and, even worse, it reflects my own weakness, which turns into a cowardice I am ashamed to confront."

14. Antonietta Raphaël, Florence, March 13(?), 1926, to Mario Mafai, Rome. See also the letter from Raphaël to Mafai, Florence, June 28, 1927.

15. See Maltese (1960, 386–88), Purificato (1965, 11), and Guttuso (1952, in Mezio 1960, 26).

16. Mario Mafai, Rome, August 17, 1941, to Antonietta Raphaël, Genoa.

17. As Libero De Libero (1981) commented of Raphaël: "She was truly the mythic python in between the two painters. But this is a story still to be written" (p. 22). Miriam Mafai (1989) attests that Raphaël "was jealous of Scipione, frightened by his illness and by his happy licentious bent, which she feared would influence my father."

18. "One could call it the show of freaks, freaks that are becoming commonplace given that the numbers grow ever larger: Ceracchini, Pieraccini Leonetta Cecchi, Pieraccini, Pasquarosa [Pasquarosa Bertoletti Marcelli], Vanda Biagini, Antonietta Raphaël, Ciucci, etc." (in D'Amico 1991, 52).

19. "Their relationship was never easy. She was jealous.... My father was jealous of Antonietta, of her sunny character, her inexhaustible energy, fantasy and ability to work" (Mafai 1989). In a letter to Raphaël in Genoa, written from Rome, March 14, 1942, Mafai observed: "Your love and energies strive towards more definition and creation. I also aim for this, but it happens that I love too many things and so I get distracted; I'm interested in different issues, I read a variety of books and it isn't always easy for me to decide on my goals."

20. Curiously, Mafai never acknowledged any specific debt to Raphaël, and credited his and Scipione's awareness of contemporary French painting to other sources (see Mafai 1969a, 15–20). He gave little import to the school of via Cavour, noting that it lasted only a short while. In a more specific article on the period titled "La pittura del 1929," he summarized Raphaël's influence in a line: "Often Scipione accompanied me on my return home to via Cavour, and there we would find Raphaël com-

ing to grips with her painting, which raised curiosity and admiration in us because of its strange bounty of impasto and unexpected solutions" (Mafai 1969b, 43).

21. Letter from Antonietta Raphaël, London, August 27, 1931, to Mario Mafai, Rome (in Fagiolo dell'Arco and Coen 1978). In her recollections of her parents' relationship, Miriam Mafai (1992) acknowledges that "she greatly helped Mafai to become that which he was. It was she who pushed him continually" (p. 138).

22. Antonietta Raphaël, unpublished diary, in D'Amico (1991, 54–55).

23. As the eldest of the three daughters, Miriam Mafai saw the least of her mother: she was tended by a nurse from shortly after her birth, and was reared for the most part by her grandmother. Her proximity to Raphaël was the closest in 1939–44, during the war years, in Genoa. During Raphaël's absence in the early 1930s, Miriam Mafai (1992, 133) recalls, she was put to bed by her father, who made her write to her mother and then often fell asleep in the children's room.

24. For instance, see Mafai (1984, 50, 53, 56–58; entries for November and November–December 1931 and for January 2, 1932).

25. Letter from Mario Mafai, Rome, March 7, 1942, to Antonietta Raphaël, Genoa.

26. The only date on this letter is 1931.

27. Letter from Mario Mafai, Rome, July 17, 1941, to Antonietta Raphaël, Genoa.

28. Letter from Mario Mafai, Rome, March 14, 1942, to Antonietta Raphaël, Genoa.

29. These statistics are taken from Victoria De Grazia's *How Fascism Ruled Women* (1992, 61–62). For the regime's policies toward women, see especially De Grazia's chapter on motherhood (pp. 41–76).

30. The Ca' Pesaro exhibitions, to take but one example, show a dramatic increase, from a paltry three or four women per show in the years before the war to eleven exhibitors in 1919. The list of participants can be found in *Venezia: Gli anni di Ca' Pesaro 1908–1920* (1987, 274–76).

31. These figures are approximate. They are based on an accounting of names from the catalogs of the Quadriennale d'Arte Nazionale, Rome: in 1931, 26 out of 384 exhibitors were women (6.8 percent), followed by 56 out of 677 in 1935 (8.3 percent), and 69 out of 586 in 1939 (11.8 percent).

32. Enrico Crispolti, in a letter to Lea Vergine dated February 18, 1979, states that annual exhibitions devoted to women artists were begun in Rome in 1902 (in Vergine 1980, 15).

33. On Margherita Sarfatti, see Cannistraro and Sullivan (1993).

34. See the statistics compiled by Maria Cecilia Mazzi (1980), which include the purchases by various government agencies from the Quadriennale of 1935, 1939, and 1943 and the Biennale throughout the 1930s.

35. Since the end of World War I, Italian artists had theorized about the return to a monumental public art of murals, mosaics, and other traditional forms. With Mussolini's building program in the 1930s, the regime regularly commissioned painters and sculptors to work on Fascist headquarters and other new government buildings. A percentage of the budget for new buildings was set aside specifically for decorative programs, a practice that became official in 1942 with the passage of the "2 Percent for Art Law." Aside from providing employment in economically difficult times, the mural movement catered to those artists who wanted a special role in the shaping of a new Fascist society and believed they could fulfill such a role through the style and content of public art. See, for example, the "Manifesto della pittura murale," signed by Mario Sironi, Carlo Carrà, Massimo Campigli, and Achille Funi, originally published in *La colonna,* December 1933.

36. Details about the commission remain vague, and it is not listed in the standard biographies on Mafai. It has been recalled by Ziveri (see D'Amico 1991, 55), who shared the project with Mafai, with the assistance of Raphaël and Mazzacurati.

37. I discuss Raphaël's Jewish themes and her Jewish identity in Braun (1989, 172–74, 179–80, 183).

38. The preceding discussion of Raphaël's work habits and her rapport with her daughters is drawn from the recollections of Miriam Mafai (1989, 1992) and an unpublished letter to Alda Guidi (courtesy of Miriam Mafai).

39. Valentino Martinelli (1960, 23) notes that Raphaël's sculptures of the genesis theme were completely opposed to the stylized primitivism of Epstein's version.

40. Antonietta Raphaël, unpublished diary, entry for September 3, 1968.

41. This discussion of the birth metaphor, its history and applications, is informed by Susan Stanford Friedman's "Creativity and the Childbirth Metaphor" (1989).

42. The prevailing attitudes toward the female nude in Western art are discussed by Parker and Pollock (1981; see especially the chapter "Painted Ladies," 114–33). For a summary of Lacanian theories and their pertinence to depictions of women in art, see Kate Linker (1984).

43. Whitney Chadwick (1990, 266–72) notes how the female nudes by Suzanne Valadon and Paula Modersohn–Becker also "challenge and collide" with the visual tradition established by male artists.

44. Antonietta Raphaël, Florence, November 2, 1925, and December 23, 1925, to Mario Mafai, Rome.

Works Cited

Bellonzi, Fortunato. 1955. "Raphaël Mafai." *Fiera letteraria* (Rome), May 29, 1955.

Berenice [Iolena Baldini]. 1961. "Recensioni." *Paese Sera*, May 25–26.

Berger, John. 1977. *Ways of Seeing*. London: British Broadcasting Corporation/Penguin.

Borghese, Leonardo. 1947. "Mostre d'arte." *Corriere della sera*, May 29.

Braun, Emily. 1988. "Scuola Romana: Fact or Fiction?" *Art in America* 76 (March): 128–36.

———. 1989. "From the Risorgimento to the Resistance: One Hundred Years of Jewish Artists in Italy." In *Gardens and Ghettos: The Art of Jewish Life in Italy* (exhibition catalog, Jewish Museum, New York). Edited by Vivian Mann. Berkeley: University of California Press.

Broude, Norma, and Mary D. Garrard. 1989. "Discussion: An Exchange on the Feminist Critique." *Art Bulletin* 71: 124–27.

Cannistraro, Philip V., and Brian R. Sullivan. 1993. *Il Duce's Other Woman*. New York: William Morrow.

Chadwick, Whitney. 1990. *Women, Art, and Society*. New York: Thames & Hudson.

D'Amico, Fabrizio, ed. 1991. *Antonietta Raphaël* (exhibition catalog, Galleria Civica, Modena). Bologna: Nuova Alfa Editoriale.

De Grand, Alexander. 1976. "Women under Italian Fascism." *Historical Journal* 19: 947–68.

De Grazia, Victoria. 1992. *How Fascism Ruled Women: Italy, 1922–1945*. Berkeley: University of California Press.

del Guercio, Antonio. 1955. "Antonietta Raphaël Mafai." *Rinascita*, May.

De Libero, Libero. 1949. *Mafai*. Rome: De Luca Editore.

———. 1981. *Roma 1935*. Rome: Edizioni della Cometa.

Dunford, Penny. 1989. *A Biographical Dictionary of Women Artists in Europe and America since 1950.* Philadelphia: University of Pennsylvania Press.

Epstein, Jacob. 1955. *An Autobiography,* 2d ed. London: Hulton.

Fagiolo dell'Arco, Maurizio, and Ester Coen. 1978. *Raphaël: Scultura lingua viva* (exhibition catalog). Rome: Galleria Incontro d'Arte.

Friedman, Susan Stanford. 1989. "Creativity and the Childbirth Metaphor: Gender Difference in Literary Discourse." In *Speaking of Gender.* Edited by Elaine Showalter. New York: Routledge.

Gouma-Peterson, Thalia, and Patricia Mathews. 1987. "The Feminist Critique of Art History." *Art Bulletin* 69: 326–57.

Guttoso, Renato. 1952. "Antonietta Raphaël Mafai." *Rinascita,* March.

Guzzi, Virgilio. 1955. "A. R. Mafai." *Il tempo,* May 21.

Krull, Edith. 1989. *Women in Art.* London: Studio Vista.

Linker, Kate. 1984. "Representation and Sexuality." In *Art after Modernism: Rethinking Representation.* Edited by Brian Wallis. New York/Boston: New Museum of Contemporary Art/D. R. Godine.

Longhi, Roberto. 1929. "La mostra romana degli artisti sindicati — II: Clima e opere degli irrealisti." *L'Italia letteraria,* April 14.

Mafai, Mario. 1969a. "Autobiografia." In Valentino Martinelli, Jacopo Recupero, and Livia Velani, *Mafai* (exhibition catalog, Palazzo Barberini, Rome). Rome: De Luca Editore.

———. 1969b. "La pittura del 1929." In Valentino Martinelli, Jacopo Recupero, and Livia Velani, *Mafai* (exhibition catalog, Palazzo Barberini, Rome). Rome: De Luca Editore.

———. 1984. *Diario 1926–1965.* Rome: Edizioni della Cometa.

Mafai, Miriam. 1989. "Mia madre, la Raphaël." *La repubblica,* June 24.

———. 1992. "Miriam Mafai." In *Nel segno della madre.* Edited by Anna Maria Mori. Como: Frassinelli.

Maltese, Corrado. 1960. *Storia dell'arte in Italia 1785–1943.* Turin: Einaudi.

Martinelli, Valentino. 1960. *Antonietta Raphaël Mafai.* Rome: De Luca Editore.

Martini, Arturo. 1982. *La scultura lingua morta.* Edited by Mario De Micheli. Milan: Jaca Book.

Mazzi, Maria Cecilia. 1980. " 'Modernità e tradizione': Temi della politica artistica del regime fascista." *Ricerche di storia dell'arte* 12: 27–32.

Mezio, Alfredo. 1960. *Antonietta Raphaël e la pittura romana del 1930* (exhibition catalog). Ivrea: Centro Culturale Olivetti.

Moravia, Alberto. 1974. "Il narcisismo della Raphaël." In *Antonietta Raphaël: Dipinti, sculture, disegni, incisioni* (exhibition catalog). Rome: Galleria Cassiopea Due.

Parker, Rozsika, and Griselda Pollock. 1981. *Old Mistresses: Women, Art, and Ideology.* New York: Pantheon.

Purificato, Domenico. 1965. *I colori di Roma.* Bari: Adriatica.

Venezia: Gli anni di Ca' Pesaro 1908–1920 (exhibition catalog, Ala Napoleonica e Museo Correr, Venice). 1987. Milan: Mazzotta.

Vergine, Lea, ed. 1980. *L'altra metà dell'avanguardia 1910–1940* (exhibition catalog, Ripartizione Cultura, Comune di Milano). Milan: Mazzotta.

9 / Alba De Céspedes's *There's No Turning Back*: Challenging the New Woman's Future

Carole C. Gallucci

Woman must obey.... My idea of her role in the State is in opposition to all feminism. Naturally she shouldn't be a slave, but if I conceded her the vote, I'd be laughed at. In our State, she must not count.
BENITO MUSSOLINI, in Emil Ludwig, *Talks with Mussolini* (1933)

You can't go home again.... those who stayed behind will never forgive us for having seen new things, new faces, for having had the key to our own room, for having been able to come and go as we wanted.
ALBA DE CÉSPEDES, *Nessuno torna indietro* (1938)[1]

In 1938, Alba De Céspedes (1911-) made her explosive debut on the Italian literary scene with the novel *Nessuno torna indietro* (There's no turning back). Soon thereafter, the critic Silvio Benco (1938) proclaimed his admiration for De Céspedes's ability to combine "the material of eight different novels into a single text." Likewise, in 1939 Maria Borgese called the novel "unforgettable," underlining its relation to contemporary film. The story about eight young women living in a boardinghouse in Rome went through nineteen editions by December 1940. That same year, Fascist censors banned the book, claiming that it did not reflect the "Fascist ethic."[2] Indeed, the way

De Céspedes fashions her female characters as they study, work, and live independently stands in sharp contrast to the Fascist cultural model of the "New Woman" as "exemplary wife and mother" (*sposa e madre esemplare*; Meldini 1975). By means of propaganda, repression, and censorship, Fascist discourses exalted and perpetuated this traditional female image in an effort to confine real women to socially accepted roles and behaviors. But De Céspedes defended her novel before a Fascist investigative committee, arguing that she had only depicted society as it really was. She insisted that the text presented many different ways of looking at the world. Despite the ban, *Nessuno torna indietro* sold more than 150,000 copies by 1943 and was translated into thirty languages (see Giocondi 1978, 16–23).[3]

Given the constant attention *Nessuno torna indietro* attracted among the literary elite, general readers, and Fascist detractors alike, it is surprising that this novel has not received extensive study in recent scholarship on Italian women during Fascism.[4] To be sure, De Céspedes's polemical novel, which specifically interrogates issues of gender and class, invites us to reassess the forms of self-articulation women elaborated during the regime and the ways they may have contested the dominant image of woman in culture and society, a major project in historiographic and literary studies on Italian Fascism.[5] Precisely how models of "Woman" are constructed in Fascist thought is admittedly outside the scope of this brief analysis. By focusing on the interrelations between history and story in *Nessuno torna indietro*, I will argue that as De Céspedes maneuvers amid dominant discourses, she creates a gendered female space that counters prevailing constructions of gender, sex, class, and religion. By reading De Céspedes's representations of women's social life in the regime against the ideals and myths promoted by Fascist ideologues, I intend to show how she strategically challenges, for instance, the models of the "New Woman" and the "crisis woman," and the (un)holy alliance between church and state, as part of an overall critique of sociopolitical conditions under Fascism. I am also particularly interested in the narrative practices devised by De Céspedes to invent female roles for social transformation.[6]

Freedom at the Pensione Grimaldi

In the sequence of narratives that constitutes *Nessuno torna indietro*, De Céspedes evokes the complexity of each character's attempts to shape her identity as she negotiates social boundaries. De Céspedes does this by employing a narrative strategy that involves several overlapping levels of interpretation. The novel is written in the third person. We learn about each female character first through her own thoughts (the novel liberally employs the device of the interior monologue); second, through other characters' perceptions; and finally, through the narrator herself, who mediates between the two other viewpoints. These forms of interpellation and self-reflection illustrate the poles of the characters' positionalities as well as the spaces they refashion during their identity formation. All of the eight characters display changing awareness of self; each must live out the consequences of her "choices," and thereby construct her identity.[7]

The institutional restraints that the young female students must negotiate in their quest for self-knowledge are evoked by the setting, which has far-reaching historical and social implications. The action takes place between November 1934 and the summer of 1936, and is set at the Pensione Grimaldi, a convent, which serves as a boarding-house for women students in downtown Rome. The young women view the Grimaldi as a "bridge" between one phase of life and the next, a place that traditionally guides females through the passage from adolescence to marriage and motherhood. From the opening lines, the narrator transforms space into symbols of women's literal and figurative confinement: "The front door of the huge, gray house opened up like a dark throat; a glass door separating the hall halted the last rays of twilight. Beyond this nebulous black forms occasionally passed. Outside, people walked slowly across the piazza" (p. 9). These lines clearly draw on conventional gothic imagery. Binary oppositions, such as inside/outside, imprisonment/freedom, and darkness/light, are established from the outset and pervade the text. Not surprisingly, given the conventional formula of the gothic and the historical context of Fascism, the public/private spaces are gendered: the author depicts the outside world as masculine space, whereas the inside appears strictly feminine.[8]

From the very beginning of the novel, the author represents the Grimaldi using the imagery of a jail. Life outside is more inviting. As the young women glimpse the Villa Borghese from the Grimaldi's barred windows, or comment on the Roman streets filled with passersby, they feel like "prisoners" trying to escape. Although the women have chosen to reside at the convent while pursuing their university studies, convent life is structured by rules and forms of policing that regulate the students' movements between these private and public spheres. They are permitted to go out during the day, primarily to attend classes at the university, but there is, of course, a curfew. Thus, the Grimaldi offers only the illusion of freedom and independence. Victoria De Grazia (1992) underscores the significance of the Grimaldi as a metaphor for women's oppression in the regime: "Under fascism, women's freedom to go out could be compared to the freedom reigning at the Pensione Grimaldi, a halfway house with fixed hours, closely watched group routines, and the strictures of newly internalized conventions" (p. 233).[9] However, De Céspedes dramatizes the tactics used to subvert the rules. For example, sometimes the young women pretend they are going out to attend university lectures, and then sneak away to stroll along the streets alone, deep in thought, or to meet a male friend. She thus attends to the strategies of resistance that, at the symbolic level, infringe upon the patriarchal law, while asserting female desires.

The images De Céspedes employs in her depiction of the Grimaldi also articulate the interrelatedness of story and history in her narrative, a quality that some critics have minimized, through a purely literary approach. For instance, Maria Assunta Parsani and Neria De Giovanni (1984) argue that De Céspedes uses historical events as a framing device in order to increase our understanding of a particular character:

> The historical event is placed in a crucial moment of our national life and with much probability even in the lives of our women writers. And yet little importance is given to external, historical events; they are only mentioned in a few passing lines and are strictly dependent on the facts of the characters' private lives. So a historical event, a chronological framing, is given only if knowing it increases our understanding of the private life of the characters. (p. 8)[10]

Certainly, the passage of narrative time is not marked in the fashion of conventional history. The author provides only one chronological date: December 2, 1934. The passing of time is marked by changes from night to day and the changes in the seasons. Historical events of international importance are noted, such as the outbreak of the Spanish Civil War and the war in Libya. Moreover, De Céspedes attends to the way Fascism structures the forms of everyday living in contemporary Italian society. She describes, for instance, the presence of the Casa del Fascio (the Fascist meeting hall), the obligatory Roman salute, and the beginning of food rationing in Italy. Likewise, her representation of the convent, its rules, and the nuns resonates with images of Fascism and hints at historical forms of institutional and ideological collusion.

An (Un)holy Alliance

A brief outline of the relations between Fascist and Catholic thought on womanhood would be useful here. In his *Prison Notebooks,* Antonio Gramsci analyzes the nature of politics in the modern age, including the (inter)relationship between church and state in Italy (see Gramsci 1966, 87).[11] He reminds us that one of the key issues in Italy, as opposed to those in Germany, was whether Fascist policies and images differed significantly from Catholic thought on womanhood. It is perhaps an irony of history that Mussolini's dictatorial regime was the first Italian government in modern Italian history to be recognized officially by the Vatican (Mack Smith 1982, 161).[12] The policies advanced by the regime and by the church with regard to gender, social policy, and education show striking correspondence. Catholic thought on the family and sexuality — exalting the figure of the paterfamilias, promoting the sanctity of marriage, and defining women primarily in a familial role — constituted a familiar discourse that underwrote Fascist policies relating to the subordination of women in virtually all aspects of public life. Pius XI's encyclical *Casti connubi* (On Christian marriage), issued on December 31, 1930, displays the ideological similarities between the Roman Catholic Church and Fascism. The text reiterated the traditional teachings of the church, defining woman as wife and mother, arguing against the emancipation of women (see Fremantle 1956, 235–43). The emphasis on women as wives and mothers in Fascist discourse of the 1930s is no doubt connected both to the Italian state's reconciliation with the Catholic Church orchestrated by Mussolini in 1929 and to economic factors brought about by the Great Depression (Noether 1982, 75).[13] A good case in point regards the distribution of contraceptives, which, under Fascism, became a crime against the state. In addition, the regime increasingly criminalized abortion and deferred any talk of divorce to unsympathetic church authorities.[14]

As we will see, De Céspedes dares to speak about abortion and contraception, taboo subjects for both the church and Fascist ideologues. Her portrayal of religious ceremonies and religious figures underscores this (un)holy alliance. Obligatory religious ceremonies are presented as empty rituals. The young women, for example, say the rosary "without praying," while in the chapel their thoughts are always elsewhere (p. 143). After Milly dies from a "weak heart," the narrator describes the nuns not as pious, self-abnegating women, but rather as "demonic" beings who populate the morbid comedy (p. 134). The important critic Maria Borgese (1939, 232) even called them "hard-hearted Fascists." Although she did not provide further explanation, we may assume that she drew her assessment from De Céspedes's representation of the nuns as authoritarian.

In fact, the uncharitable Suor Lorenza does not "seem like a nun at all"; she stands "guard" to prevent the young women from escaping (pp. 54–55). The narrator compares her to both Mother Superior and Suor Prudenzina in order to underline her "different" nature. Unlike the other nuns, Suor Lorenza is jealous of the young women's freedom of movement, however restricted it actually is. Suor Lorenza even goes so far as to convey her belief that prayer is futile. Indeed, De Céspedes presents none of the nuns in terms of an exemplary life to imitate in the tradition of *vita esemplare*. It is thus fitting that Suor Lorenza is forced to replace the Mother Superior, "an old fixture," becoming "imprisoned in the role she herself has created," which almost led to her insanity (pp. 209ff.). Like the young women she has tried to sequester, in the end even Suor Lorenza "can't go back," which is to say, life will never be the same as it was before Fascism.

Rewriting Motherhood

Thus, at the intersections between what we might call micro- and macrohistory, De Céspedes represents women's social life in the regime. She interweaves the historical realities of Italian Fascism with women's daily lives, and thus makes explicit a different perspective on Fascism as historical movement and ideology through the women's stories. She achieves this, in part, by recontextualizing and contesting the codes that structure such female models as the exemplary wife and mother, the intellectual woman and the rural woman, representations that the regime desired to promote or discourage.

The realities of maternal experience are best illustrated by De Céspedes's portrayal of Emanuela Andori, the most complex character in the novel. This character, a beautiful, wealthy Florentine woman who seems to "know nothing" (p. 10), reconfigures motherhood while allowing De Céspedes to give serious attention to the social problems besetting single mothers. Through a series of flashbacks, we learn of her love affair with an aviator, Stefano Mirovich, who was killed in a plane crash before learning of Emanuela's pregnancy. Emanuela attained sexual awareness in spite of social strictures, and now must visit her daughter Stefania, who resides in a nearby school for girls, only secretly. Emanuela's thoughts on being a mother and her relationship with her daughter present motherhood as a choice, not a destiny — a learned behavior, not the natural fulfillment of female biological and psychological needs.

In fact, when Emanuela suspects she may be pregnant, she fears that the "terrible thing" could be true, that the "horrible creature" is growing inside her. She fantasizes throwing herself into the Arno river, an act that she believes will eject the fetus from her body: "She would have let that weight fall into the river," allowing her to swim to the surface "free" (pp. 114–15). Thus, in one of the most transgressive elements of the novel, the image of Emanuela's potential suicide may reasonably be read as a metaphor for a rebirth of self through abortion. It would be a mistake to attribute Emanuela's fantasy only to fear of the social ostracism that an "illegitimate" child would bring upon her. During one of their meetings in Rome, after Emanuela gives Stefania a doll, Stefania decides to name it after her mother: "But what's your name, mom?" the child asks, puzzled (p. 44). Then, in a crucial flashback to Emanuela's childhood, the narrator recounts Emanuela's feeble attempts to play with a doll. Although her young girlfriend, speaking in a "strange voice," tries to teach her how to play "Mother," Emanuela does not understand: "You're not a real mother; it's just a game" (p. 77). Maternal love is understood not as inborn self-sacrifice, but rather as social conditioning; Emanuela insists that a woman must learn to love "that little bundle of flesh" (p. 83).

Although the material demands of motherhood are located in Stefania's school, where Emanuela reluctantly assumes the role of mother, the psychic costs relentlessly take their toll. Refusing to assume the culturally constructed identity of mother, Emanuela must work through an existential crisis triggered by the birth of her daughter. She is everyone and no one, as evidenced in one of several allusions to Pirandellian themes: "At home, in the Grimaldi and with Stefania, everywhere she had a different life, and a different face for everyone. But who was she really?" (p. 50). The mother attributes her alienation from self to her child, perceived as a source of oppression; she is "a sort of tumor, a malign tumor" (p. 265). At one point, for example, Emanuela fantasizes that Stefania, sick with scarlet fever, willingly seeks death in order to liberate her mother. The open-ended story line De Céspedes creates for these two characters reveals the complexity of the mother-daughter relationship. At the end of the novel, Emanuela's "secret" is revealed, and she is forced to leave the Grimaldi. She does not attempt to fabricate another life, given the current conditions in Italy. Instead she embarks, with her daughter, on a long ocean voyage aboard—significantly—a ship named the *Amazon*.[15] She thus leaves her past behind as she goes in search of other possibilities for herself and her daughter.

The different concerns and aspirations De Céspedes articulates with her female characters call into question conventional representations (constructed in the 1930s, as today) of marriage as institution and the ideal of all young Italian women. She breaks down the hierarchies of gender and class with the "love story" between Emanuela and Andrea; here the woman is older, richer, and socially superior to the man. Afraid of being doomed to a nightmarish existence as a housewife, Emanuela even consciously rejects the petit bourgeois Andrea.

The Intellectual Woman

Silvia and Augusta—representative versions of the intellectual woman—critique normative codifications of male-female relations and female desire. In the portrayal of Silvia, a woman from Calabria who represents the "successful intellectual,"[16] the author contrasts her perception of her own intellectual initiations with those of others.

For instance, Silvia is variously described as "unfeminine," "ugly," "not a woman" at all (e.g., pp. 102, 139, 141, 183–85, 413, 452).[17] Her intelligence makes her "like men," thus others perceive her characteristics as "manlike." Such cultural stereotypes of sexual difference and deviant femininity that blurs gender boundaries draws upon nineteenth-century essentialist notions of woman from positivist anthropology, which Fascist thinkers elevated to the status of scientific theory. We clearly see these contrasting attitudes when Silvia proudly tells the other women of her new job as a "collaborator" with her admired professor of literature, Belluzzi. Vinca then argues that Silvia's work is a sublimation of heterosexual love: "Work for you is like a surrogate for love between a man and a woman. You give yourself to it as if to a man. . . . Your femininity disappears in your brain" (p. 122). It is highly significant that Silvia's femininity is thought to disappear in her brain, a familiar stereotype that connects the development of intelligence in women to heterosexual desire.

Likewise, in a crucial dialogue between Silvia and the esteemed professor, De Céspedes highlights both the reductive definition of woman and how Silvia transgresses it. Professor Belluzzi argues that his wife Dora is a "donna proprio . . . proprio donna [woman really . . . a real woman]" (p. 183). Silvia, firmly on the side of reason, thus participates (albeit marginally) in a man's world. Belluzzi explains: "Those of us who think, who are always studying, need beside us a person who does not think at all. Because if they did we would suffocate" (p. 183). Dora is, therefore, "a real woman" because of her "incredible ignorance of things" (p. 183). In another important comparison, Silvia asks her pregnant sister Immacolata what she thinks about while she busies herself with "feminine tasks": "and she replied, smiling, 'I never think'" (p. 404).

One could argue that Silvia eventually rejects the male ideal of romantic love in order to pursue her own independence. In a recurring fantasy finally resolved near the end of the novel, Silvia rejects the imaginary bandit who has come to take her away on an adventure: "No, I won't light your campfire, bandit, I will go away alone to the mountains in search of a grotto of my own" (p. 362). Here De Céspedes alludes to Virginia Woolf: Silvia can be the master of her own destiny only if given the material conditions, a space of her own, to do so. This grotto may also be a classical allusion in which Silvia contests the notion of woman as empty vessel.[18] Thanks to Belluzzi's contacts, Silvia eventually ends up with a teaching position in a secondary school in Littoria, a Fascist "new city" with no past (pp. 430–31).[19]

The politics of writing is best illustrated by Augusta. In contrast to Silvia, Augusta is the "failed intellectual," also perceived as unwomanly by the others. She is the oldest, "the old maid," a label Emanuela later applies to her writing (pp. 329, 410–11). Augusta comes from Sardinia, birthplace of Nobel Prize-winning novelist Grazia Deledda, a catalyst to Augusta's own writing (p. 160). Augusta may well represent one of the "scribblers" decried by male critics of the 1920s and 1930s (see Ruinas 1930). She is a prolific writer of short stories, "all love stories," but her work has been rejected by publishers. So she has begun "a great novel." This "great novel" shows the workings of ideology and its relation to objective, material structures of oppression. It will be, she tells us:

> A great novel of universal appeal. A novel against men. I maintain that we can certainly do at least as much as they do. I show that if we put up with them it's only in order to create for ourselves a social role and not for any sexual attraction. I talk about the instinctive disgust that a woman feels for that beast, about the absurdity of women's social position in marriage. A revolutionary book. (p. 259)

Augusta devotes her entire life to this "feminist utopian book,"[20] where women create a "woman's-only" space, a space that recalls Christine de Pisan's "City of Women." Such a space would allow women to reevaluate such concepts as female aging and death. Even Emanuela becomes drawn into this vision, imagining Augusta as a "prophetess" calling women to arms (p. 329).[21]

Augusta's character challenges the heterosexual contract, and provides configurations of lesbian desire. In a pivotal scene, Vinca, Silvia, and Augusta share their intimate thoughts on love. Vinca says:

> "As children, we loved everything equally, whether it was an object, our female schoolteacher, or a female classmate. Love exists within us in a potential state from the moment we are born. With the point of a pin I wrote the name of a friend, Bellita, on the skin of my arm. I never told her. Naturally, if I think about it now, I laugh." "We all did things like that," Augusta admitted. (p. 122)

Vinca accepts the possibility of love for a girlfriend only during childhood, adding that it is something "naturally" left behind. Augusta,
however, accepts without qualification the possibility of lesbian desire.[22] Indeed, her ideas on marriage and her behavior with Valentina
may be read as a form of desire that dared not speak its name in the
Fascist regime. In fact, the Codice Rocco, the 1930 penal code, strictly
prohibited homosexuality. Furthermore, since the late 1800s, sociological and scientific discourses had shown concern over the so-called
fiamme—relationships between adolescent Italian girls in boarding-
schools (see De Giorgio 1992, 118–25).

The final images of Augusta at the Grimaldi, still writing, show a
striking resemblance to visual representations of the "crisis woman,"
given to excessive drinking and smoking (see De Grazia 1992, 216).
Nonetheless, she refuses to renounce her dream or to return home to
Sardinia, a place polarized by rigid gender roles and patriarchal social customs. Furthermore, De Céspedes represents, through Augusta
and Silvia, the value of knowledge and books as tools for social and
political transformation; neither character is contained within the
heterosexual economy.

Vinca Ortiz, a powerful symbol of female rebellion and ethnic difference, historicizes the novel by focusing on events in Spain and the
outbreak of the Spanish Civil War (1936–39). De Céspedes herself
later underscored the importance of Vinca's function within the narrative economy, criticizing the director Franco Giraldi for eliminat-
ing the character from the 1987 television movie version of the book
(Serri 1987). Unlike the other students, Vinca shows outward disre-
spect for the nuns. More important, she is a "foreigner" who speaks
Spanish, "hiding securely behind her strange idiom" (p. 10). However, through her, the reader participates in the small Spanish Nationalist community surrounding Donna Inez. Through this group and
through Luis's subsequent letters from Spain, we learn of the horrors
of war and the destruction of Vinca's homeland (pp. 171–77, 236,
268–74).[23]

Vinca is a constant reminder of contemporary historical events beyond the convent and Italian territory, perhaps symbolizing a collective sense of disenfranchisement from community and nation. Indeed,
as much as Emanuela would like to forget the war in Spain, Silvia reminds the women that they are all alienated from contemporary so-

ciety, all "foreigners, even if we are living in the fatherland [*sic*]" (p. 82). Although economically independent, Vinca is homeless at the end of the novel; she cannot go back to Spain because of a conflict with her father's new young wife, nor can she remain at the Grimaldi. Before leaving, Emanuela observes that Vinca's apartment reflects "the disorder of the rooms of women who live alone" (p. 439).

The Rural Woman

Here it is useful to recall the dominant representation of the Rural Woman circulated as part of the rural campaign. In visual as well as ideological representations, she is robust, healthy-looking, and prolific. This image is no doubt connected to the demographic campaign and the regime's attempt at autarchy. Within this context, De Céspedes examines modern conflicts between urban and rural life, and between generations, as exemplified by Xenia and Anna. Both characters challenge the idyllic vision of life in the countryside, a favorite myth of the regime. Though both of these characters have been raised in rural areas of Southern Italy, they have drastically different ideas, beliefs, and hopes as they attempt to fashion lives for themselves, positions that are also the result of class differences between the two families. The material conditions in which Xenia grew up show us the grittier side of rural life. She is able to study in Rome only because her parents mortgaged the family farm and lived on a diet of potatoes for a year. In a vivid description of Xenia's birthplace and town life, De Céspedes highlights women's restricted mobility and scarce job opportunities.

Thus, when Xenia fails her exams, she refuses to return to what she sees as a monotonous, unfulfilling way of life. Instead, she seeks "success" in Milan, where she tries to find a job. In a not-so-subtle critique of policies and laws instituted by the Fascists to manage the labor market and stem internal immigration, De Céspedes gives literary voice to the plight of unemployed single women, even investigating prostitution, another taboo subject under the regime.[24] Although enrolled in the GUF (Fascist University Groups), Xenia has neither a Fascist identification card nor references, and is virtually locked out of legal employment. She wryly notes that the system prevents women from being economically independent while it favors young women living at home who are simply consumers before marrying. Xenia thus calls attention to class struggle and the plight of women workers (pp. 70–72, 149, 333). She argues against capitalist inequities on both economic and moral grounds, proclaiming: "There do not exist honest and dishonest people in the world. Only poor and rich exist.... There's only one force in the world...money. And with that you can even buy honesty" (p. 332). A metaphor of prostitution is clearly at play here. Thus, we see that oppressive political practices instituted to manage the forms of society are the reason she ends up servicing the male sexual needs of her boss and later of his business rival. More important, the author's sympathetic treatment of Xenia's moral quandary over her life, over the fact that she "can't go back," prevents us from morally judging her.

In sharp contrast to Xenia, Anna desperately hangs on to the conservative values of her upbringing and struggles against the cultural and economic changes of modernity, which have transformed her middle-aged parents' attitudes and the place she called home. Her inner conflicts between traditionalism and modernity are amply apparent when she visits her parents at their newly urbanized house:

> Everything was gone now: the walls were bare, the light cold. Even mom and dad were no longer the same people within those walls; the familial intimacy which she always thought about with nostalgia at the boardinghouse was missing. It was as if something new and different was about to take over. (p. 218)

With a sense of profound loss, and a longing for things to be as they were, Anna must reconcile herself to the bourgeois customs and values taking root even in the south.[25] Her parents want to climb the social ladder. Her mother insists that "it's time to follow progress," which Anna believes is a betrayal of the past (pp. 218ff.). Anna finds security in the land, whereas her parents desire new possessions to fill the house. Anna is directly contrasted to her mother not only in terms of her vision of life, but also regarding her taste in music: Anna prefers "popular music" based on oral traditions; her mother enjoys the radio (pp. 225–26, 235). What does this rejection of the past on the part of her parents signify? It signals one of the more glaring contradictions in Fascist thought: that of reconciling modernity and traditionalism. That is, although the Fascists glorified a cult of youth and the "new," they also propagated a cult of rural life and "tradition."

Interestingly, Anna shares more beliefs with her matriarchal grandmother than with her mother. Yet the aging woman must live out this tragic conflict between old and new: she remains sequestered in her room, yelling out the window, "I am still the boss!" She refuses to appear as anything other than "an old peasant woman" (p. 215).[26] Anna sides with her grandmother, who is respected by the neighboring peasants, in contrast to her father, and fearfully suspects the new changes. Although we might expect Anna to entertain conventional ideas on matrimony — she is in fact the only main character to espouse the tenets of Catholic dogma — she participates in the pervasive female discourse that represents women's lack of economic opportunities as the chief reason women marry men (pp. 120, 261–62, 397, 401). Anna, the only young woman in the group who marries, describes the pressure to do so, claiming: "All women are . . . starved. They marry whoever shows up and then yelp under his blows. The essential thing is to be able to say to your friends: 'I'm getting married.' To see them die of anger" (p. 231). Anna's decision to marry a neighbor, Mario Aponte, is, in fact, presented as a pragmatic strategy to keep the farm in her family. Critic Bruce Merry (1990) interprets this character as little more than a "husband-hunt opportunist," but the narrator suggests that prevailing social custom would not have allowed her to inherit and retain ownership of the land.

In the range of attitudes on marriage that De Céspedes represents, only Valentina displays an obsession with finding a husband, yet this is also apparently because of economic concerns. She comes from the same small town as Anna, yet belongs to a lower socioeconomic stratum. After her father dies, she and her mother become little more than domestic servants to her paternal uncles. Valentina thinks of nothing else but getting married, which for her signifies "victory": "I'm poor and will have the responsibility to take care of my mother. I can't leave her, so who will want me under those conditions?" (p. 230). De Céspedes again reminds us that class and regional biases condition marriage, which is presented not as a realistic possibility for all women, but as limited to a select few.

While focusing on Valentina's profound wish to marry, De Céspedes also gives literary representation to female sexuality and autoeroticism.

214 / Carole C. Gallucci

The narrator vividly describes Valentina's erotic nocturnal fantasies of a young Indian prince, in which the boundaries between reality and fantasy are conflated (p. 296). One night, Valentina's affectionate tendencies quickly become masochistic and suicidal. At this point, the narration changes from the first person to the third, with the entrance of the phantom prince, once again described in great detail. Yet this time Valentina does not welcome him:

> She backed up against the wall; she drew back. Tonight the prince frightened her. She felt he was not a real man; he would have disappeared, drowned in her sleep, faded like a shadow. In the morning she would not have found him next to her. A nonexistent being, her man: made of nothing, of shadows, of desire. She could not free herself from him; he was in her; she herself gave him life. . . . she could never be with anyone else except her phantom. (pp. 402–3)

Indeed, the prince has been with Valentina since childhood, and will disappear only if an actual man comes along. She is powerless to do anything but cry: "At the sound of her tears, he disappeared" (p. 404). This passage is especially significant for the way De Céspedes situates woman as the subject of her own desire, the creator of a prince who satisfies her different desires. The Indian prince, dressed in silk, complete with velvet slippers and dangling gold bracelets, caringly attends to her. He stands in stark contrast to the images of "male virility" promoted by the regime.[27] Significantly, Valentina does not meet the man of her dreams; she remains at the Grimaldi with Augusta, making no further mention of the Indian prince.

Overall, De Céspedes creates a dismal picture of male-female sexual relationships as brief and unfulfilling. Vinca refuses to have sex with Luis and then later offers herself with one word, "Vuoi? [Do you want to?]," but he refuses because of the impending war (pp. 190–91). Dino wastes few words, saying to Xenia, "I think by now that it's time we went to bed together, no?" after which he joyfully tells Horsch, "A virgin, I had a virgin!" (pp. 151, 207). Given these situations, it is difficult to find any evidence to support Silvio Benco's (1938) interpretation that the men in the text "represent passion." On the contrary, they apparently lack the ability to arouse or meet the forms of female desire as De Céspedes portrays them.

Writing and Resistance

De Céspedes's own political activities in the Resistance underscore a strong commitment to the engagement between life and art. In 1943, during the Nazi occupation of Northern Italy, she crossed the German lines in order to reach the Allies in the south. She then worked for Radio Free Bari, using the pseudonym Clorinda. After the liberation of Rome, she founded and edited the important journal *Mercurio,* which, in 1948, provided the forum for an insightful debate between Natalia Ginzburg and De Céspedes on the "fate" of women. Using provocative imagery, Ginzburg likened women's fate to the condition of "always falling into a well," because of both "women's temperament" and "a long tradition of subordination and slavery." Such a fate befalls even women "who feel strong and intelligent and beautiful," which renders them powerless. De Céspedes then commented on Ginzburg's article with humor, maintaining that the well has a didactic function to show women "all the most painful and sublime truths of love." Thus, the well becomes a locus of self-discovery for women, where "we embrace all of human suffering, which is made up almost entirely of women's suffering" (1948, 111).

By focusing on young women's suffering during Fascism, *Nessuno torna indietro* attempts to force the reader to see the material conditions within which and against which women—such as De Céspedes— struggled to invent roles for social and political transformation. In *Nessuno torna indietro* De Céspedes creates a space within which the main objective is to counter prevailing constructions of gender, sex, class, and religion. She accomplishes this task in four ways. First, her text explicitly opposes (and in many cases completely rejects) ideals promoted by the regime, including the image of the "New Woman" as mother. Her explorations of contraception, abortion, and female prostitution, taboo subjects in the regime, are clear statements of opposition to repressive sexual politics and restrictive social policies. Second, De Céspedes portrays women, albeit ambiguously, as "successful intellectuals," capable of pursuing and obtaining economic independence. Third, she emphasizes the collusion between church and state in their attempts to confine women to repressive patriarchal institutions and organizations. Finally, she demystifies the cultural constructions of the bourgeois family, romantic love, and femininity.

De Céspedes's critical rewriting of these cultural constructions of femininity, romantic love, marriage, and motherhood is vital to our understanding of women as inventors of culture during Fascism. The novel's huge international success is evidence that her work appealed to a mass audience at the same time it attracted the serious attention of eminent critics of her time. In her literature, De Céspedes shows the importance of female self-representation to a mass female public. Moreover, De Céspedes's narrative talents and her insightful treatment of feminist issues have assured both her rightful place in the literary canon and our continued reading interest and pleasure.

Notes

I would like to thank the following people for their insightful comments on the development of this essay: Professor Robert Dombroski, Professor Robin Pickering-Iazzi, Mary Gallucci, Meg Gallucci, Jerry Phillips, and Menina Combs. I also want to thank the helpful staff of the Interlibrary Loan Office of the Homer Babbidge Library at the University of Connecticut, especially Lynn and Bob.

1. This and all subsequent translations are mine. All citations of *Nessuno torna indietro* refer to the 1938 edition published by Mondadori.

2. De Céspedes's own comments on the censorship and repression she suffered are particularly insightful (see Petrignani 1984, 37–45). A similar fate would befall also the short stories collected in *Fuga* (De Céspedes 1940). See De Céspedes's interview in Paris on the television movie made from *Nessuno torna indietro* in Serri (1987).

3. Alessandro Blasetti adapted the novel to film in 1943, and in 1987 it was adapted into a movie for television. See also Jacqueline Reich's forthcoming dissertation, "Women on the Verge of a Discourse: The Supporting Actress and Italian Cinema, 1936–1943."

4. Among the recent literature are Robin Pickering-Iazzi's, "Unseduced Mothers" (1990–91) and *Unspeakable Women* (1993), Victoria De Grazia's *How Fascism Ruled Women* (1992), Gigliola De Donato and Vanna Gazzola Stacchini's *I best-seller del ventennio* (1991), Marina Addis Saba's, *La corporazione delle donne* (1988), Elisabetta Mondello's, *La nuova italiana* (1987), and David Forgacs's *Rethinking Italian Fascism* (1986).

5. See in particular Ellen Nerenberg (1991), as well as Maria Assunta Parsani and Neria De Giovanni (1984) and Bruce Merry (1990). An article by Maria Rosaria Vitti-Alexander (1991) was brought to my attention too late to be incorporated into this essay.

6. In her literature, De Céspedes devoted attention to women's issues, often analyzing the oppressive dynamics of male-female relations. Her subsequent work includes *Fuga* (1940), *Dalla parte di lei* (1949), *Quaderno proibito* (1952), *Quaderno proibito: Commedia in due tempi* (1962), *Invito a pranzo* (1955a), *Prima e dopo* (1955b), *Il rimorso* (1963), *La bambolona* (1967), *Le ragazze di maggio* (1968), and *Il buio della notte* (1973).

7. Nerenberg (1991) focuses on three of the eight main characters because their positions toward love, work, maternity, and matrimony are most easily identifiable. I

have chosen instead to examine a fuller range of the characters, as they represent differing positions on Fascist ideology and politics. This essay is part of a book in progress, in which I explore women's fiction in relation to the images of women propagated by Fascist ideology.

8. Many of the themes and symbols of the gothic thriller are tied to women's bodies: images of the prison and sexual anxiety. In the novel we (over)hear female adolescents voicing fears about motherhood and sexuality, as well as protesting against the constructed cultural ideal of femininity and gendered power relations. The young women are not passive objects, as might be expected in the convention of the gothic thriller, but rather active subjects. On the symbolic meanings of space, see Michel de Certeau (1984).

9. In an opening scene, Milly reassures Emanuela that she will get used to living "in fear, in subordination" (p. 24).

10. Merry (1990, 56) also argues for this distinction.

11. Although it was during Fascism that most social policies on women were initiated, earlier "protective" legislation concerning women and children was passed in 1902 and later amended.

12. Mack Smith (1982) notes that in February 1929 Mussolini reached an agreement with the Catholic Church formally known as the Lateran Pacts.

13. Victoria De Grazia (1992, 89ff.) in particular highlights how Fascist family policy reiterated Catholic dogma. The similarities between Catholic and Fascist images of "Woman" explain in part the "success" of the regime in implementing policies directly relating to the subordination of women.

14. The only systematic attempt to reconcile state and family within both Fascist and Catholic contexts was proposed by the Catholic Fascist ideologue Ferdinando Loffredo in his *Politica della famiglia* (1938).

15. The use of the name *Amazon,* a literary image of warrior women throughout history, further underscores the significance of women's history.

16. This phrase is used by Parsani and De Giovanni (1984, 19–20), who argue that Silvia is the novel's protagonist.

17. Nerenberg (1991) argues that Silvia is distinguished by "her work ethic and her homeliness" (p. 268).

18. I would like to thank Robin Pickering-Iazzi for bringing this possibility to my attention.

19. I agree with Nerenberg (1991) that Silvia should not be interpreted within the rather narrow categories of "success" and "failure" that Parsani and De Giovanni (1984) construct. It is interesting to note, however, that De Céspedes changed the final portrait of Silvia after the 1938 edition.

20. Nerenberg (1991, 271) uses this term to describe Augusta's "great novel."

21. Nerenberg (1991, 273) interprets Augusta's slapping of Emanuela after learning of her deceit as exiling her from the community.

22. Nerenberg (1991, 270–73) also comments on this exchange. See also Adrienne Rich (1983). Lillian Faderman (1981) argues that the boardingschool was a site of female romantic friendships.

23. On Italian intervention during the Spanish Civil War, see John F. Coverdale (1975).

24. It is important to recall that as early as 1923 prostitutes suffered severe penalties under the Public Security Laws (see De Grazia 1992, 44–45). On the history of the regulation of prostitution in nineteenth- and early-twentieth-century Italy, see Mary Gibson (1986).

25. The countryside is described as surreal, suggesting that Anna is living out a fable (p. 226; see also pp. 221–22, 224, 227).

26. Later she envisions the peasants rising up in revolt, shouting, "We want the old proprietress!" (p. 234). Both Merry (1990, 63) and Parsani and De Giovanni (1984, 32) discuss the figure of the grandmother in De Céspedes's fiction.

27. See Barbara Spackman's (1990) remarks on the Fascist "rhetoric of virility."

Works Cited

Addis Saba, Marina, ed. 1988. *La corporazione delle donne: Ricerche e studi sui modelli femminili del ventennio fascista.* Florence: Vallecchi.

Benco, Silvio. 1938. "Una romanziera." *Il piccolo della sera,* December 15, 3.

Borgese, Maria. 1939. "Letteratura femminile." *Nuova Antologia,* July 16, 232–35.

Coverdale, John F. 1975. *Italian Intervention in the Spanish Civil War.* Princeton, N. J.: Princeton University Press.

de Certeau, Michel. 1984. *The Practice of Everyday Life.* Translated by Steven F. Rendall. Berkeley: University of California Press.

De Céspedes, Alba. 1938. *Nessuno torna indietro.* Milan: Mondadori.

———. 1940. *Fuga.* Milan: Mondadori.

———. 1948. "Lettera a Natalia Ginzburg." *Mercurio* 36–39: 110–12.

———. 1949. *Dalla parte di lei.* Milan: Mondadori.

———. 1952. *Quaderno proibito.* Milan: Mondadori.

———. 1955a. *Invito a pranzo.* Milan: Mondadori.

———. 1955b. *Prima e dopo.* Milan: Mondadori.

———. 1962. *Quaderno proibito: Commedia in due tempi.* Milan: Mondadori.

———. 1963. *Il rimorso.* Milan: Mondadori.

———. 1967. *La bambolona.* Milan: Mondadori.

———. 1968. *Le ragazze di maggio.* Milan: Mondadori.

———. 1973. *Il buio della notte.* Paris: de Seuil.

De Donato, Gigliola, and Vanna Gazzola Stacchini, eds. 1991. *I best-sellers del ventennio: Il regime e il libro di massa.* Rome: Riuniti.

De Giorgio, Michela. 1992. *Le italiane dall'unità a oggi: Modelli culturali e comportamenti sociali.* Rome-Bari: Laterza.

De Grazia, Victoria. 1992. *How Fascism Ruled Women: Italy, 1922–1945.* Berkeley: University of California Press.

Faderman, Lillian. 1981. *Surpassing the Love of Men: Romantic Friendship between Women from the Renaissance to the Present.* New York: William Morrow.

Forgacs, David, ed. 1986. *Rethinking Italian Fascism: Capitalism, Populism and Culture.* London: Lawrence & Wishart.

Fremantle, Anne, ed. 1956. *The Papal Encyclicals in Their Historical Context.* New York: Mentor.

Gibson, Mary. 1986. *Prostitution and the State in Italy, 1860–1915.* New Brunswick, N. J.: Rutgers University Press.

Ginzburg, Natalia. 1948. "Discorso sulle donne." *Mercurio* 36–39: 105–10.

Giocondi, Michele. 1978. *Lettori in camicia nera: Narrativa di successo nell'Italia fascista.* Messina-Florence: G. D'Anna Editrici.

Gramsci, Antonio. 1966. *Note sul Machiavelli, sulla politica e sullo stato.* Turin: Einaudi.

Loffredo, Ferdinando. 1938. *Politica della famiglia.* Milan: Bompiani.

Ludwig, Emil. 1933. *Talks with Mussolini.* Translated by Eden Paul and Cedar Paul. Boston: Little, Brown.

Mack Smith, Denis. 1982. *Mussolini: A Biography.* New York: Vintage.

Meldini, Piero, ed. 1975. *Sposa e madre esemplare: Ideologia e politica della donna e della famiglia durante il fascismo.* Florence: Guaraldi.

Merry, Bruce. 1990. *Women in Modern Italian Literature: Four Studies Based on the Work of Grazia Deledda, Alba De Céspedes, Natalia Ginzburg and Dacia Maraini.* Townsville, Australia: James Cook University of North Queensland, Department of Modern Languages.

Mondello, Elisabetta. 1987. *La nuova italiana: La donna nella stampa e nella cultura del ventennio.* Rome: Riuniti.

Nerenberg, Ellen. 1991. " 'Donna proprio . . . proprio donna': The Social Construction of Femininity in *Nessuno torna indietro.*" *Romance Languages Annual* 3: 267–73.

Noether, Emiliana P. 1982. "Italian Women under Fascism: A Reevaluation." *Italian Quarterly* 32 (Fall): 69–80.

Parsani, Maria Assunta, and Neria De Giovanni. 1984. *Femminile a confronto: Tre realtà della narrativa contemporanea: Alba De Céspedes, Fausta Cialente, Gianna Manzini.* Rome: Lacaita Editore.

Petrignani, Sandra. 1984. *Le signore della scrittura: Interviste.* Milan: Tartaruga.

Pickering-Iazzi, Robin. 1990–91. "Unseduced Mothers: The Resisting Female Subject in Italian Culture of the Twenties and Thirties." Working Paper No. 1, fall–winter, University of Wisconsin-Milwaukee Center for Twentieth Century Studies.

———, ed. 1993. *Unspeakable Women: Selected Short Stories Written by Italian Women during Fascism.* New York: Feminist Press.

Reich, Jacqueline. Forthcoming. "*Women on the Verge of a Discourse: The Supporting Actress and Italian Cinema, 1936–1943.*" Doctoral dissertation, University of California, Berkeley.

Rich, Adrienne. 1983. "Compulsory Heterosexuality and Lesbian Existence." In *The Signs Reader: Women, Gender, and Scholarship.* Edited by Elizabeth Abel and Emily Abel. Chicago: University of Chicago Press.

Ruinas, Stanis. 1930. *Scrittrici e scribacchine d'oggi.* Rome: Accademia.

Serri, Mirella. 1987. "Alba De Céspedes [*sic*] accusa: Il mio libro in tv stravolta dall'erotismo." *Tuttolibri,* March 21, 5.

Spackman, Barbara. 1990. "The Fascist Rhetoric of Virility." *Stanford Italian Review* 8, nos. 1–2: 81–101.

Vitti-Alexander, Maria Rosaria. 1991. "Il passaggio al ponte: L'evoluzione del personaggio femminile in Alba De Céspedes." *Campi immaginabili: Rivista quadrimestrale di cultura* 3: 103–12.

10 / Reading, Writing, and Rebellion: Collectivity, Specularity, and Sexuality in the Italian Schoolgirl Comedy, 1934–43

Jacqueline Reich

Introductory Lesson

From the Fascist regime's earliest days, educational reform was a major preoccupation of the newly established government. It was seen as essential to preserving the original youthful spirit of the Fascist revolution and to providing a proper "breeding ground" for new zealous party members and future political leaders. In fact, the schools became the subject of the first serious test of Fascist policy.[1] Beginning in February 1923, barely four months after the March on Rome and two years before the "official" inauguration of Fascist dictatorship, Giovanni Gentile, the regime's initial minister of education, proposed and instituted a series of sweeping changes in the primary and secondary school system, as well as in the universities. This focus on education continued throughout the *ventennio,* culminating in Giuseppe Bottai's much touted, but more or less ineffective, 1939 School Charter.

In Italian cinema, an analogous emphasis on schooling occurs. In the films produced in the nine-year period from 1934 to 1943, no fewer than eighteen take place in a scholastic setting.[2] The locales vary in scope, ranging from a ski school to the more traditional boarding schools, to an orphanage, and even to a reform school. Some of these films are melodramas, but the cinematic form of choice was the comedy, reinforced by such amusing titles as *Maddalena, zero in condotta* (Maddalena, zero in behavior) (Vittorio De Sica 1941) and *Il diavolo va in collegio* (The devil goes to boarding school) (Jean Boyer 1943).

Given the importance of education to the Fascist regime, it is somewhat surprising that almost all of these films have little or no overt connection with the greater historical climate of Fascist educational reform. Never is the spectator's attention drawn to the obligatory picture of Mussolini hanging on the classroom wall (if it appears there at all), nor does he or she notice the students reading the new required Fascist textbooks. In fact, these films exist in a vacuum. Unlike propagandistic films produced during the era, they are lacking political orientation and historical anchoring to a site of intense Fascist ideological indoctrination. Moreover, they have as their principal characters female students, despite the regime's discriminatory policies with respect to "feminine" education.[3]

There are several plausible explanations for this want of correspondence between cinematic realization and extracinematic reality. First, these films seek to emulate an established and successful cinematic formula: many of the Italian films are direct remakes of Hungarian texts (films, plays, and novels) or generic imitations of the American screwball comedy. In addition, as Francesco Savio (1975) has noted, the Italian film industry used these films in a concerted attempt to cash in on the ever-increasing popularity of up-and-coming young female stars, many of whom debuted in this genre.[4] Finally, one of the primary objectives of Italian cinema during the Fascist period was not just to highlight the regime's policies and values but also to divert attention away from pressing social problems and grim political situations. Their chief function was to entertain audiences rather than to instruct them (Brunetta 1975, 42).

These films, although escapist in both plot lines and cinematic style, raise some very interesting issues with respect to proper feminine conduct. In the schoolgirl comedy, the young women's primary iconological function is to be the object of the spectator's gaze. Their bodies, clothing, and makeup are designed, packaged, and sold to the filmgoing audience.[5] But this commodification of the female body, corollary to the notion of woman as spectacle, is thwarted on the narrative level. Such untraditional and, moreover, un-Fascist behavior as female rebellion, ingenuity, resourcefulness, and intelligence is both privileged and rewarded. In many instances these uncontrollable women are "tamed" or "converted" (usually by particular men and the institution of marriage), but often they are not. The result of this contrast between iconologic presentation and the film's diegesis is a heightened tension between collectivity, so essential to the Fascist state, and individuality, precisely what the regime was trying to eradicate with its programs of "political socialization" (Koon 1985, 20). However, contradiction is endemic to this ideological position in itself. By emphasizing the collective, the schoolgirl comedy increases the subversive potential for mass insurrection; by deemphasizing the individual, it discourages heroic initiative and spirit — an integral part of Fascist dogma. This is a problem that is not easily or necessarily resolved at the films' conclusions, creating a text in which meaning is far from absolute.

In this essay I wish to explore these issues of women as spectacle, the collective versus the individual, and their implications for the portrayal of female subjectivity in Italian cinema during the Fascist years. My work uses previous research on this subject by film scholars such as Gian Piero Brunetta (1975, 1979) and Marcia Landy (1986) as a point of departure.[6] Although these scholars' insightful analyses of the films' narratives within the context of extracinematic considerations are indispensable, it is my aim to expand upon their observations by formally defining the Italian schoolgirl comedy as a specific film genre. These films have more in common than the perfunctory setting of the scholastic institution. They share many additional compositional elements, including characterization, plot structure, and themes. By isolating the films' common characteristics and examining how they function both with and against one another, I will show how meaning is produced and female subject positions are constructed therein. However, the messages contained within these constructions are often conflicting and contradictory, particularly in how they address the female spectators of the era. It is my opinion that this lack of ideological coherence reflects the very nature of Italian Fascism and its policies toward women, which were themselves riddled with conflict and contradictions. My examination will focus on the schoolgirl comedies that best epitomize the genre and illustrate this phenomenon: Mario Mattoli's Ore 9, lezione di chimica (Nine o'clock, time for chemistry class; 1941), De Sica's Teresa Venerdì (Theresa Friday; 1941), and Raffaello Matarazzo's Il birichino di papà (Daddy's little devil; 1943).

Rules and Regulations: Fascism and Education

Educational policy before the Fascist era had three principal objectives: to increase the literacy rate, to decrease the dropout rate by raising the years of required school attendance, and to preserve the interests of the ruling class by reserving the preparatory schools (the *ginnasio* and the *liceo classico*) for the socially privileged and academically gifted. Giovanni Gentile, the Fascist "philosopher-in-residence," continued the scope of many of these programs in his attempt to standardize Italian education during the regime's early years. Instruction was divided along class (and gender) lines with the creation of technical and vocational schools, teacher training institutes, and the *liceo femminile* (a form of girls' finishing school). In 1929, five years after Gentile's departure, a new period of school reforms began, one characterized by an increased "Fascistization" (Koon 1985, 63). Teacher training and indoctrination became more intense; all elementary and secondary school teachers were required to take an oath of loyalty to the regime; and classes on Fascist culture were introduced, as were state-produced, ideologically correct textbooks. Giuseppe Bottai, the regime's last and perhaps most powerful minister of education (1936–43), attempted to combine schooling with practical applications, stressing vocational training, manual labor, physical fitness, and Fascist indoctrination. For the most part, these initiatives were never implemented, as criticism and reluctance were high.

From their inception, many of these educational reforms reinforced the sexual division of societal roles endemic to the regime's overall ideological position. Gentile's *liceo femminile* offered a separate but "unequal" alternative to the *liceo classico,* in which the traditional study of the humanities took second place to subjects more appropriate for young girls: singing, sewing, and other "feminine tasks." Bottai's school charter later established two postprimary institutes for the preparation and training of women, the Women's Training College (three years) and the Women's Teachers' Training College (two years), which would "impart a moral preparation for household tasks as well as teaching in the kindergarten schools" (Bottai 1939, 15, 19). Female students were discouraged from advancing in their studies, even more so than their male counterparts. For example, 20 percent more boys than girls continued past fifth grade.[7] As an additional deterrent, university tuition doubled for female students in 1928 (Saracinelli and Totti 1983, 120). The regime also attempted to rid the teaching profession of what it believed to be an overabundant and detrimental female presence. In 1926, women were excluded from teaching such subjects as Latin, Greek, history, and philosophy in the *liceo* and the *ginnasio* and were later barred from major positions of authority in both middle and technical schools (De Grand 1976, 949).

Ironically, the results of the government's various policies often thwarted their original intentions. This expanded focus on education became a tool for female empowerment and advancement. The literacy rate for women actually increased substantially, as did female enrollment in all levels of schooling. The regime's various "feminine" schools were an overall failure (the *liceo femminile* disappeared as early as 1928) (De Grazia 1992, 154; Koon 1985, 56). Active participation in government and church-sponsored extracurricular activities, while preaching order, collectivity, and subordination, still combined with these other forces in cultivating a growing sense of autonomy, independence, and individuality among young Italian women (De Grazia 1992, 146–48, 196–97, 160–61).

Theories and Formulas: The Italian Schoolgirl Comedy as Genre

These internal contradictions within Fascist ideology find expression in the Italian schoolgirl comedies in question. But in order to examine this sociohistorical phenomenon and its cinematic correspondences (or lack thereof), it is necessary to clarify the relevant terminology, beginning with what exactly defines a film genre.[8] A particular genre consists of a set of structures or a framework based on shared characteristics within a subset of films. It establishes conventions, plays on expectations, and achieves closure and coherence in the end. Moreover, genre, like cinema itself, is a signifying practice in constant movement and fluctuation, involving many operations on cinema's different levels of interpretation: the formal or iconological level; the iconographic or syntactic level; and the level of signification, in which the previous two levels unite to form the text's meaning.[9] Yet these discursive levels are not separated from one another by strict boundaries. On the contrary, they are characterized by an inherent permeability: they can collaborate with or work in opposition against one another in order to produce a particular message, be it in accordance with or contrary to the dominant ideological discourse.

Any film genre must have a referent in the cinematic tradition upon which it bases its structure and from which it distinguishes itself by means of its own characteristics.[10] In the case of the Italian school-girl comedy, these models are two: contemporary Hungarian cinema and theater, and the American screwball comedy.[11] Hungarian popular culture, with its ability to entertain and captivate an audience, its guiding principle of evasion, and its pristine sexual attitudes, conformed to much of the Fascist government's agenda and would thus cause few problems with the censors (Laura 1991). Between 1931 and 1943, the *commedia all'ungherese* (comedy, Hungarian style) formed the basis for approximately twenty-six films that were grounded in Hungarian materials (films, plays, novels), revolved around Hungarian characters, or were produced in Hungary, usually in bilingual versions, and then released in Italy.

The influence of the American screwball comedy surfaces in a more general way, as Hollywood, and American culture as a whole, held such a powerful fascination for both the Italian film industry and the filmgoing public.[12] The American model of the comedy, much like its Italian imitations, concerned itself with creating the illusion of social harmony in a time of crisis (see Schatz 1981, 158). Many popular films centered on the antagonistic couple, whose witty repartee and opposing points of view provided both the obligatory narrative conflicts and much of the humor. This sexual antagonism was often the result of contradictions between the more liberated female characters who dominated both the Hungarian and American comedies of the era and the more traditional attitudes of their male counterparts. Although tamed or domesticated in the end through marriage, the modern woman nevertheless presented a new model for female behavior, designed to arouse the audience's curiosity, laughter, and perhaps even envy.[13]

Before diving into an in-depth exploration of the individual films, it is first essential to establish the singular characteristics of the Italian schoolgirl comedy. In most genres, the films' raw material, that is, their formal and basic compositional elements, are subordinate to and contained by the dominating iconographic elements, or rather any genre's three building blocks: setting, characterization, and plot structure. Settings, here the girls' school, provide an Aristotelian unity of place as well as play on culturally conditioned expectations. The characters subscribe to set formulae. First and foremost among them in the schoolgirl comedy is the independent, rebellious, and resourceful young female student (the protagonist), who, although not talented scholastically (she inevitably receives poor to failing grades), is intelligent and wise beyond her years. She pursues a love interest, almost always an older man in a position of authority within the school. The rest of the dramatis personae include her nemesis, always female and usually another member of the school community; a sympathetic and comic male character who comes to the protagonist's aid even if his actions violate the school's codes of conduct; the collective, formed by the other female students; the teachers, who provide comic relief with their deadpan severity and incompetence; and the harsh yet compassionate headmistress, who is able to both punish and forgive. Finally, the use of the term *plot structure* is deliberate in its rigidity, because a genre film's narrative is constructed around a specific conflict and its necessary resolution. It is based on the principles of dispersal and regulation, disequilibrium and the indispensable restoration of the status quo, involving a disturbance and then refiguration of subject positions within a given social order (Neale 1980, 21–28).[14] The schoolgirl plot centers more on the courtship and inevitable union of the male-female couple than on the female students; its main function is to bring the man and woman (or girl) together, thereby taming (or attempting to tame) individual female rebellious behavior and restoring proper social order. The love story is also the focal point of the films' major themes: love conquers all; a girl's dreams can come true; and honesty, benevolence, and self-sacrifice will always win in the end.

The schoolgirl comedy's fundamental conflict and resolution, however, do not simply concern ensuring the male and female protagonists' amorous destiny and instilling proper ideological values in the process. This kind of interpretation is limited to the secondary level of cinematic meaning, what Erwin Panofsky (1967) calls the "conventional subject matter," in which the artistic text's motifs and images are connected to themes and concepts. Panofsky goes on to isolate a third level of meaning, which he describes as "intrinsic" or "symbolic," and "is apprehended by ascertaining those underlying principles which reveal the basic attitude of a nation, a period, a class, a religious or philosophical persuasion" (p. 7).[15] It is on this last plane of interpretation, what I prefer to call the level of signification, that the idea of genre loses its rigidity as a category of analysis. Whereas form and content consolidate to produce conventional meaning, on the level of signification they have the potential to work against each other in order to reveal the gaps and contradictions that are part of the dominant discourse (Neale 1980, 13). Thus the conflict is not merely one of good versus evil or uniting a couple destined to be together. It addresses larger issues, such as law and order, social hierarchies, and gender relations.

Any analysis of film genre, then, should focus not only on the structural rules by whose principles the cinematic text is organized, but also, if not predominantly, on the various contradictions that emerge from those very constructions. The scholastic setting, as Brunetta (1979) rightly concludes, provides "a place where clashes can occur between a society founded on authoritarian, educational principles and a different morality of the young, particularly young women, who were aware of their own powers of attraction, of the power of their bodies, and used them as weapons in fighting and attempting to dismantle the educational system's forms of repression" (p. 484). I would like to expand this cogent but somewhat limited interpretation of the restrictive school system as metaphor for Fascist Italy with a few additional observations. First, these girls are not only rebelling against a repressive "educational system." The revolt is also directed against Fascist politics as a whole. Second, the female characters in these films do not use their physical presence and "powers of attraction" solely as a means of attaining their goals. If anything, their bodies, commodified by the genre's iconology, weaken their status as autonomous and independent characters. Certainly an awareness of their own sexual powers plays an important role in the female protagonists' ability to manipulate situations for their own gain, but this use is contained predominantly in the narrative's amorous plot. Instead, their intellectual powers of resourcefulness, initiative, and creativity, although unable to flourish in the repressive classroom atmosphere, are their primary tools for success. Their ingenuity, cunning, and independence not only help them get the man but also right what has been wronged, teach moral lessons, and ultimately preserve that very autonomy.

In the schoolgirl comedy, both the female protagonist's spirit of rebellion against (Fascist) tradition and her gifts of acumen and perspicacity highlight the principal tension released in these films at the level of signification: collectivity versus individuality. These frictional elements are metaphorically represented in the ubiquitous symbol of Fascism: the *fascio* itself. Roland Sarti (1974), in stressing the non-monolithic character of Fascist ideology, has noted:

> The internal diversity [of Italian Fascism] was appropriately reflected in the fasces, the bundle of sticks with an ax blade protruding that became the political emblem of the movement, and historians ever since have wondered whether to attach greater significance to the diversity of the components or to the bond that held them together. (p. 2)

Similarly, this political imagery reflects the conflictual potential between the individual and the collective in Fascist dogma, for both components are essential in its representation: the "diversity" of the single branches as well as the "bond" of the collective experience. This ambiguity is also reflected in life under Fascism for girls and young women. As noted above, increasing female enrollment at all levels of schooling, coupled with the required (and voluntary) array of extracurricular activities, had the effect of exposing girls and young women to new experiences and ideas to which they never would have had access had they remained within the confines of the more traditional and limiting familial structure. Most of these organizations involved group activities and focused on instilling a sense of Fascist community spirit as well as the values of female domesticity and subordination. Nevertheless, the very nature of the collective experience introduced their participants to different social and cultural subject positions through contact with other group members. It also encouraged acts of heroism that both corresponded to other Fascist ideals and served to set the individual apart from the group.

In the films under discussion, individual instances of rebelliousness abound and are usually enacted by the female protagonist. They run contrary to prescribed Fascist codes of female behavior, which are evident in the period's numerous films and in various other Fascist discourses, such as speeches, policies, and propagandistic publications.[16] Nonetheless, cases of subversion on the part of a single character are tolerated in the interests of the narrative. Most of these acts of rebellion are performed with the aim of uniting the male and female protagonists in the bond of love and thus ensuring the obligatory happy conclusion, because conflict and closure form the obligatory principles according to which a genre film is structured. Thus, episodes of female rebelliousness by the protagonist are both praised and rewarded, and accordingly, individuality in this instance is the victor over the homogeneous collective. It is interesting to note that as the genre progresses in the early 1940s (and Fascist rule begins to topple), this individual rebellion becomes the principal focus of the plot; the coupling, if it exists at all, plays a secondary role, hastily developed and resolved.

More intriguing, however, are the scenes of group disobedience that surface in these films. The schoolgirl comedies showcase the adventures and misadventures of the female student body. These scenarios range in scope from spying on other students to playing mischievous pranks on their teachers and undermining school authority in general. Usually employed for comic purposes, these scenes of disrupture, although severely punished by the authorities they threaten, nevertheless stress the power of the collective force. These episodes, however, are necessarily located on the text's margins with respect to the central narrative conflict (i.e., the love story). As Stephen Heath (1981) suggests, the narrative is the organizing principle and process of the filmic space, and, similarly, space in frame is constructed as narrative space: "Film makes space, takes place as narrative, and the subject, too, set—sutured—in the conversion of the one to the other" (p. 62). Narrative displacement is necessary in order to create a safe space for a concept more frightening and potentially more subversive than individual acts of rebellion: female solidarity.

Another significant characteristic of the Italian schoolgirl comedy, which also plays on the idea of the individual and his or her relationship to the collective, is the scenes of performance or spectacle that abound in these films. These spectacular moments can be as brief as a gym class in which the girls perform calisthenics in form-fitting outfits or as elaborate as staged theatrical numbers. Patricia Mellencamp (1991) defines the spectacle as an "enclosed unit" within the narrative that momentarily halts the diegetic flow by bracketing the sequence through musical score (i.e. a complete song) and identical opening and closing shots. It is characterized by Laura Mulvey's (1989, 14–26) concept of "to-be-looked-at-ness" for three primary reasons:

(1) all "looks" are directed at the performer, (2) there exists an eroti-
cally charged pleasure of looking at the performer as sexual object of
unbound exhibitionism, and (3) the spectacle is characterized by "excessive style" that is designed to capture the film viewer's attention
(see also Feuer 1982, 34–36). According to Richard Dyer (1985), the
American musical comedy's main purpose is "escape" and "wish-ful-
fillment," and this quest for utopianism corresponds to five emotions
or "sensibilities" it aims to portray: energy, abundance, intensity, trans-
parency, and community. Although Dyer states that the notion of community, which in the musical manifests itself in the camaraderie among
the showgirls, is of little importance to capitalist imperatives, it is instead of primary significance for the sequences of performance in the
Italian schoolgirl comedy. In these films, gymnastic routines, musical
numbers, and other instances of performance and spectacle, rather
than privileging the individual in framing and camera angles, as can
the Hollywood musical, necessarily showcase the female collective.
In their roles as objects of the gaze, their "potentially disruptive sexuality, a threat to the sanctity of marriage and the family," is contained
(Mellencamp 1991, 5).[17] However, in the guise of featuring the actresses' musical talents and/or physical attributes, these self-contained
units also have the potential to subvert the films' key themes. It is this
idea of collectivity, or more precisely homogenization and socialization, that is the primary target of ridicule and scorn in these films;
submission and subordination to authority are undermined as the rebellious protagonist disrupts, appropriates, or even destroys the show.
These acts of sabotage and sedition are allowed because, like all scenes
of performance, they are set apart from the diegesis. Here the concept of marginality and cinematic space returns, but this time the frame
of reference is the narrative as a whole.

The significance of the conflicts raised in the schoolgirl comedies
produced during Fascism should not be minimized, because, as I have
stated above, the beginning and end are established and immutable
conditions.[18] These conflicts serve to ruffle the status quo in order to
either restore it or reorder it in accordance with societal norms.[19] However, as Stephen Neale (1980, 20) points out, this unity is an impossibility, because the cracks in the film's discourse, as manifested in the
conflict in question, can never be fully repaired. They are only "sutured" over, stitched up hastily in order to achieve a final coherence
and unity.[20] In many schoolgirl comedies, this resolution is in fact

hurried and hassled: not all questions and points of contention are answered and sealed with a kiss. While the pairing off of the female protagonist is a given, her autonomy and individuality remain intact. Thus, the operation of suture, which attempts to effect ideological coercion by persuading the viewer to accept cinematic images as an accurate reflection of his or her subjectivity, is incomplete.[21] Instead, the gaps in the sutures create a narrative situation that can be processed and perceived by the spectator as he or she wishes. However, this is not an open text in accordance with Umberto Eco's widely accepted definition of the term. Rather, it is an example of what Eco (1979) refers to as a potential "open reading" of a "closed text" (pp. 8–9). The task of the "open reader" is to fill in the gaps that are an integral and inevitable part of any closed text, be it literary, theatrical, or cinematic (Carlson 1990). Transposed to the arena of film theory, an opportunity is created for the "open spectator" to negotiate interpretation and meaning. In the case of the Italian schoolgirl comedy, the holes in the films' discourse on female individuality and collectivity allow for a reading in which the former is preserved and even rewarded and the latter is utilized subversively to disrupt prescribed codes and modes of feminine, Fascist behavior.

Rebels with a Cause: The Italian Schoolgirl Comedy as Text

Although Goffredo Alessandrini's 1934 film *Seconda B* (Tenth grade, class B), the first Italian schoolgirl comedy, differs in many ways from what later was to develop into the full-fledged genre, it nonetheless becomes the point of reference for subsequent films.[22] The setting, a school for daughters of wealthy families, soon became standard.[23] The characters (the wimpy male professor, the spinster teacher, the unruly student leader, the comically compassionate male character, the female collective) all survived in future manifestations of the genre. A gymnastics class constitutes the scene of performance and is here used as a site of confrontation between authority and rebellion. The emphasis here, however, is not the rebellious female student but rather the male teacher who learns to choose the "correct" object of his affections. The teacher is the female protagonist and the student is her nemesis, a formula that would subsequently be reversed. The female students, as Marcia Landy (1986, 48–49) notes, are depicted unsympathetically. Closure is more or less complete: authority and discipline are maintained, insubordination is curtailed, and class divisions are preserved.

The first full-fledged return to the *Seconda B* model came five years later with Massimiliano Neufeld's *Assenza ingiustificata* (Unexcused absence; 1939). This jump in time can be explained in several contexts. Genre represents an intersection between culture and cinema: films of a particular type flourish in specific historical, social, political, and economic conditions. In the early to mid-1930s, the film industry was just getting back on its feet after many years of neglect by both the private and public sectors. It was not until 1934, when Luigi Freddi took charge and founded a government-run film agency (the Direzione Generale per la Cinematografia), that a definitive program for renovation was entered upon. During this period, American films flooded the market. Among them were the films of Deanna Durbin, an actress perceived as an older Shirley Temple who enjoyed immense success in both the United States and Italy. In 1938, with the introduction of the Alfieri laws, which prohibited the importation of American films from the four major studios (MGM, Warner Brothers, Paramount, and Twentieth Century Fox), a large gap had to be filled. Capitalizing on both Durbin's popularity and fresh young female talent coming out of the Centro Sperimentale di Cinematografia, the recently created film school in Rome, the schoolgirl comedy was reborn.[24] The first full-scale success was Vittorio De Sica's immensely popular *Maddalena, zero in condotta.* It was quickly followed by that of another schoolgirl comedy with a similarly ridiculous title, Mario Mattoli's *Ore 9, lezione di chimica,* the first film I will now examine in detail.

Despite the film's advertising slogan describing itself as "Fresh, gentle, and serene, like the dreams of adolescence," *Ore 9* packs a rather subversive punch in its condemnation of abusive power and intrusive rule.[25] The story takes place at the Collegio di Valfiorita, an opulent and elite girls' boarding school formerly reserved for nobility, but now open to members of the upper bourgeoisie. The students have little interest in their studies. Most of their attention is focused instead on their handsome chemistry teacher, Professor Marini (Andrea Checchi). The main culprit is Anna Campolmi (Alida Valli), the daughter of an extremely wealthy industrialist and the leader of the school's power-wielding clique. Conflict erupts when the headmistress's overly zealous assistants confiscate the students' diaries. Although the head-mistress disagrees with their methods, she nevertheless seizes the op-portunity to pry into her underlings' minds. Noticing that there are two missing diaries, those of Anna and her nemesis, the "model stu-dent" Maria (Irasema Dilian), she summons Anna and Maria to her office. Once confronted, Anna openly protests this initiative. For this action she is punished, whereas Maria, who had destroyed her diary, is not. In order to avenge this injustice, that evening Anna and her friends go in search of Maria, only to find her bed empty; they subse-quently discover her embracing a man in the school's garden. At first Anna and the others, in an act of solidarity, do not inform on Maria even when confronted by the headmistress. But Anna later changes her mind when she jealously spies Maria talking to Professor Marini, her beloved, and suspects him to be Maria's mystery man. Conse-quently, Maria is confined to her room. During a torrential thunder-storm she escapes, only to injure herself seriously by falling into a ditch. A repentant Anna valiantly offers to give Maria a desperately needed blood transfusion in order to save her life. Later it is revealed that the mystery man was in fact Maria's father, who, on the run from the law after being unjustly convicted of a crime, has finally turned himself in with proof of his innocence. The stage is now set for the happy ending: Maria survives, is accepted socially into the collective, and Anna and Marini run off to be married.

The film's narrative and iconological emphasis rests on the school-girls as a unified entity.[26] Iconologically, conformity is reinforced be-cause the Valfiorita students are required to wear uniforms for activ-ities both inside and outside the classroom (not always the case in the schoolgirl comedy). Visual emphasis thus rests on similarity and not difference. In their various activities, solidarity is the motivating drive, with Anna continually expounding inspirational mottoes, such as "All for one and one for all" and "We must stick together when confronted by the headmistress." The greatest crime among these girls is to rat on the others, regardless of social dynamics, and Anna vio-lates this sacred trust when she selfishly betrays Maria. To atone for her transgression, Anna performs the ultimate act of solidarity: the sharing of blood.

Anna's various acts of rebellion are considered positive when their in-tent benefits the greater good of the collective. The proper target of these seditious exploits is the overly restrictive and repressive *collegio*.

Whereas in earlier films discipline was confined to the classroom, at the Collegio di Valfiorita the areas of jurisdiction include the girls' rooms and even their personal thoughts and feelings; the sequestering of their diaries, which constitutes an invasion of both private and emotional property, is a perfect example. Anna, aware of these frequent intrusive raids, explains to the headmistress when asked why she doesn't keep a diary:

> ANNA: In a diary, you either write down things that other people should not read, and then it's better not to write them, or you write things that other people can read, and then it's pointless to write them down.
>
> HEADMISTRESS: That's right.
>
> ANNA: In fact, ma'am, allow me to protest this abuse.
>
> HEADMISTRESS: Protest? Abuse? What do you think you're talking about?
>
> ANNA: Yes, ma'am, because you can expect discipline, obedience, and study from us, but you do not have the right to pry into our thoughts.
>
> HEADMISTRESS: It is not a question of rights, it's about duty.

A potential explanation for this extraordinarily active interest in the girls' personal lives could stem from the fact that the *collegio* is a boarding school, not a day school. However, the headmistress's emphasis is on obligation (to whom is never quite clarified) over individual liberties. The overtones to her discourse are clearly sinister and covertly Fascist. Thus, couched within this pleasing and amusing story of attractive schoolgirls is a metaphorical critique of authoritarian excess, which should be interpreted within the context of Italian Fascism and its policies of frequent intrusion into the private lives of its citizens.

Mattoli's film is also a perfect example of how narrative signification and visual representation work against one another in order to reveal contradictions in a film's various discourses. The mutinous collective intent on undermining this excessive authority and the strong-willed and self-righteous protagonist who stands up for her rights against that authority are all elements that somehow had to be presented in a nonthreatening form in order to avoid trouble with the censors. Because the perpetrators of these various seditious acts are female, a possible way to counter their effects is through classical, iconological commodification of the female body. The camera lingers on the girls, using the traditional cinematic devices of soft focus and close-ups of their perfectly made-up faces as well as other body parts. The many group activities in which they engage, such as horseback riding, swimming, and gymnastics, provide an opportunity not only to showcase their attractive and lithe bodies in (often sexually suggestive) action but also for numerous costume changes, including equestrian outfits, see-through nightgowns, bathing suits, and gym uniforms featuring tight bodices and short skirts. In many ways, *Ore 9* is a fashion show, a scene of performance; the girls' attire is certainly not chosen for its practicality.[27]

However, the fact that all the girls are obliged to wear the same clothes (except in evening wear) is not without significance. Fashion is power, whether employed as a means of personal expression or, if imposed from without, as a way of curbing dangerous and threatening individuality and sexuality. Anna laments this very predicament:

> Me? A little girl? Because I am required to wear this ridiculous uniform? If only I could dress like this: hair up, a slightly bared shoulder, a soft wrap around me, advancing slowly at a languid pace, with a slightly disdainful look in my eyes.

The school's multiple uniforms serve two primary functions: they deprive the female collective of their individual freedom, attempting to contain their rebellion and blossoming sexual awareness (as evident in their not so innocent lust for Marini). At the same time, however, they visually unify the collective and hence strengthen their position as group.[28] By relegating the young women to iconological object of the gaze, their iconographic subject positions as agents of action and change are undermined. However, because this particular process of commodification involves the privileging of the group over the individual, the menacing potential of mass subversion is iconologically fortified. Thus, the conflictual knot involving the tension between the individual and the collective is never fully untangled.

Although not technically a schoolgirl comedy, as the action takes place in an orphanage and there are no classroom scenes, Vittorio De Sica's *Teresa Venerdì* nonetheless contains many elements common to the genre but with an added twist, particularly in its portrayal of female subjectivity. The film focuses on the exploits of Dr. Pietro Vignali, played by De Sica himself, an incompetent but well-meaning pediatrician with a nonexistent practice and a mountain of debt. Given an ultimatum by his wealthy father, Vignali takes a position as a health inspector at the Orfanotrofio Santa Chiara, an orphanage for young girls. There he meets Teresa Venerdì (Adriana Benetti, in her film debut), one of the older orphans, who assists him in his medical duties. She is immediately taken with the dashing doctor. However, her contact with him is threatened when she is punished for what the school authorities call an "immodest act," which consisted of clandestinely performing a love scene from *Romeo and Juliet*. The doctor convinces the headmistress to pardon the young woman, but her nemesis, the obedient but malevolent Alice, pens a love letter to Pietro in Teresa's name, which the teachers conveniently discover. When Teresa realizes she is about to be punished for something she did not do (and is told by an antagonistic teacher that as a result she will be sent to be a butcher's maid), she runs away to the doctor's home, where she learns of his financial and personal troubles (he has since acquired a vacuous but wealthy fiancée). Assuming various identities, she resolves the doctor's many predicaments. Pretending to be his sister, Teresa tells his showgirl mistress Loletta Prima (Anna Magnani) that the family is broke and Pietro must marry Lillì Passalacqua, the wealthy fiancée. Confessing that she is not Pietro's sister, she then begs Lillì to marry the doctor in order to save him from financial ruin. Believing Teresa is Vignali's mistress, Lillì's father later comes to bribe her in order to save his family's reputation, and with that sum she is able to absolve the doctor's debts. Pietro ultimately realizes the extent of Teresa's generosity and kindness, and, in a scene that would fulfill anyone's romantic fantasy, leads her away from the orphanage to become his wife.

Despite the film's title, the plot is structured more around Pietro and his misadventures than around Teresa, although she does play a fundamental role in the various narrative conflicts. This film, like many others of the period, sets up a situation in which the male protagonist must choose his proper mate. In the standard Hollywood formula, the relationships between the male and female characters are often constructed triangularly, with one (usually the male) torn between Miss Right and Miss Wrong. Here, however, there are three women from whom Pietro must pick: Loletta, the self-proclaimed "artist"; Lillì, the flighty ingenue with bourgeois pretensions of being a poet because of her uncanny rhyming ability; and Teresa, ever humble and kind. It is through Teresa's ingenuity, love for the doctor, and goodwill that not only are the narrative's conflicts resolved in a satisfactory manner but is she also able to receive her just reward—liberation from the orphanage and a life with the man of her romantic dreams.

Teresa Venerdì is an example of a classical Hollywood text, involving archetypal characters, the standard screwball comedy situation, and emotional investment.[29] The film's lighthearted musical score as well as strategic cinematography, especially of the charming and endearing girls who constitute the collective (close-ups and group shots of smiling, adorable waifs abound), reinforce its comedic and sentimental characteristics. Female sexuality, although not as explicitly treated as in the German *Mädchen in Uniform,* is nevertheless an undercurrent in the film's various discourses on the feminine romantic imagination. Secret diaries, love letters, and clandestine performances of amorous scenes (these girls prefer *Romeo and Juliet* to historical tragedies) all attest to the fact that, contrary to the doctor's opinion, these girls think a great deal about love. Sexual fantasy is a force that must be and subsequently is successfully contained in the film's happy ending. Closure itself is fairly complete, leaving little room for negotiation of meaning. Unlike Anna, Teresa has never been the rebellious one who openly defies authority: when punished, she accepts responsibility for her actions as well as her fate.

The key to the film's signification, however, lies in its conceptualization of performance. There are three principal performers in the film, all of whom are women: Loletta, the vaudeville star of "The Queen of Jazz"; Lillì, reciting her ridiculous poetry; and of course Teresa, who enacts both romantic and historical tragedies (a play titled *Grief That Kills* and the famous balcony scene in *Romeo and Juliet*). As Marcia Landy (1986) observes, Pietro must choose "the best performer, one whose role-playing corresponds with socially desirable attitudes. Teresa's role, like Juliet's, is chaste, devoted, and self-sacrificing, whereas the other two women are portrayed as self-indulgent and self-aggrandizing" (p. 54). However, what Landy fails to note is that Teresa's performances take several forms and are not necessarily placed within a theatrical context. In order to rectify Pietro's complicated circumstances, she masquerades, both voluntarily and involuntarily, as various personae. As his sister, she even quotes word for word the dramatic monologue she performed in *Grief That Kills*. This sequence's theatricality is reinforced through shot composition: Teresa is framed in a pensive medium close-up as well as positioned in front of the window draperies, a clear substitute for the stage curtain. The result of Teresa's fairly aggressive acquisition of new subject positions is that traditional notions of female performance are reversed. Teresa is not merely the passive object of the gaze, as is the woman's function in the classical Hollywood narrative. Instead, she is the primary active agent, one who takes control of a situation by using her performative capabilities. In *Teresa Venerdì,* performance is not mere spectacle or art, as it is for Loletta or Lillì: as Teresa herself says, "Theater is a serious matter." It functions as an arena of action and reaction; performance is a means of achieving one's goals.

These very acts, moreover, have profound implications for both gender and Fascism. Judith Butler (1990) has theorized:

> Gender ought not to be construed as a stable identity or locus of agency from which various acts follow; rather, gender is an identity tenuously constituted in time, instituted in an exterior space through *a stylized repetition of acts.* . . . Significantly, if gender is instituted through acts which are internally discontinuous, then the *appearance of substance* is precisely that, a constructed identity, a performative accomplishment which the mundane social audience, including the actors themselves, come to believe and to perform in the mode of belief. (pp. 140–41)

Gender constructions are in turn parodied through such sexual "plays" as cross-dressing and drag: "The performance [of drag] suggests a dissonance not only between sex and performance, but sex and gender, and gender and performance" (Butler 1990, 136–37).[30] Taking Butler one step further, this concept of gender toying with reference to performance can also be applied within the contextual framework of female sexual and gender roles. Conscious assumptions of different configurations of gender roles or new "sexual personae" metaphorically comment on both the general constructed nature of gender and sexuality and their prescribed codes within the given "social temporality" (Butler's term). Thus, with what can be called scenes of "metaperformance," Teresa's various subject posturings constitute a critique of both femaleness and femininity in the given social and historical context, here Italian Fascism. They subvert traditional notions of female performance, female passivity, and socially prescribed gender roles and codes of behavior, stressing and rewarding instead action, initiative, and ingenuity.

Raffaello Matarazzo's *Il birichino di papà* immediately sets itself apart from other schoolgirl comedies with its strikingly fiercer critique of Fascist ideology. Nicoletta (Chiaretta Gelli, an Italian carbon copy of Deanna Durbin) is both a tomboy and a true rebel; she has little regard for traditional rules of conduct. When her sister Livia (Anna Vivaldi) marries Roberto (Franco Sandurra), the son of the wealthy Marchesa Della Bella (Dina Galli), Nicoletta is constrained by her family to enter a boarding school run by none other than the marchesa herself. The attempt to tame her wild disposition fails completely, for at the *collegio* Nicoletta is even more disobedient and rebellious. When she learns of her sister's unhappiness with her new husband, she escapes, determined to rescue Livia. Upon entering the Della Bella home, Nicoletta spies Roberto embracing his former fiancée and convinces Livia to leave. Seeking the help of an inept but benevolent attorney, Nicoletta, in Livia's name, threatens divorce proceedings unless certain conditions are met. In the end, the couple is reconciled when Roberto, finally breaking free of his family's hold on him, confesses his true love for Livia. Nicoletta, because she has saved the day, is permitted to leave the *collegio,* return to her family, and, most important, lead her life as she chooses.

Reeking with militaristic and Fascist connotations, this film's *collegio* lacks the gaiety, vivacity, and charm of those found in other films. The various characters depart from the previously established norm: there is no student antagonist, no love interest, no compassionate character, no benevolence on the part of the headmistress. The marchesa's institution is depicted as prisonlike from the opening shot sequence, where the schoolgirls are shown marching in unison formation to lugubrious music in a series of six swipes from various angles: front, back, side. Visual imagery reinforces this theme of incarceration. The school's interior walls are patterned with shadows resembling the bars of prison cells; the sound of clicking heels echoes through the long, vacant corridors; and the students' behavior therein is strictly monitored by guards and escorts. The marchesa's motto is "Discipline above all else"; as a result, Nicoletta spends much time in solitary confinement (the *cella di rigore*).

Strong willed, independent, and self-righteous, Nicoletta is even further from the traditional "feminine" ideal than Anna and Teresa.[31]

She wears pants, assumes "masculine" body poses, and addresses her father by his first name. Among her various crimes, she engages the marchesa's chauffeur in a wild-goose chase around the living room and later deliberately sends a rolled-up carpet careening into none other than the marchesa herself. These "defects" in Nicoletta's character are blamed, in the eyes of the Della Bellas, on two primary influences: the savagery of country life (they refer to her as "a little beast") and the fact that her father has raised her in a more masculine than feminine fashion. He calls her Nicola (the Italian form of Nicholas) and refers to her as the son he always desired and never had. It is the marchesa's belief that enrolling Nicoletta in her school will set the girl on the moral and behavioral path toward gender and social correctness. However, in the end, Nicoletta refuses to conform to either the "feminine" or the "socially appropriate," resulting in the utter failure of the marchesa's mission. Thus, not only are Nicoletta's individuality and rebelliousness preserved, but implicit in this acceptance is a condemnation of both bourgeois privileging of city over country life, which Nicoletta personifies, and rigid codes of expected gender conduct, which Nicoletta rejects. The film's bucolic conclusion brings the spectator full circle, back to the beginning, reinforced in both iconology and narrative: the final scene exactly parallels the first, complete with a frenetic carriage ride and an exuberant Nicoletta vibrantly singing the same song.

In *Ore 9*, the scenes of performance, although minimal, serve the purpose of countering the dangerous implications of the narrative's discourse on female solidarity and sexuality through iconological commodification. In *Il birichino*, performance, primarily in the guise of song, has a dual function: it counters both iconology and ideology. These scenes condemn Fascist educational and youth policies, authoritarianism, and restrictions on individual rights and liberties. There are three possible explanations for how such subversive discourses managed to squeak by the censors. First, it should not be forgotten that the film was released in 1943, a year of confusion and growing dissent in Italy. With most of its attention focused on the war effort, the regime's control over its various public and private institutions was beginning to dissipate, leaving room for the creation of more overtly oppositional discourses; cinema, controlled by the Ministry of Popular Culture, was no exception. Second, Nicoletta's vivacity and rambunctiousness have connections to extrafilmic considerations. This

film was designed to launch Chiaretta Gelli as a major young star à la
Deanna Durbin, whose American characters personified those very attributes. In this aim it was quite successful, owing in part to the popularity of the schoolgirl comedy as well as the perfect match of actress and character.[32] Finally, these scenes of performance are isolated
moments in the narrative, constituting breaks in the action. Their narrative status as separate and distinct, moreover, allows them greater
freedom in their disruptive potential. Their diegetic position and significance may be marginal, but their implications on the level of signification are central.

The school's repression of adolescent longings and desires is the
subject of the first of Nicoletta's songs while *in collegio*. Reminiscent
of a scene in *Ore 9*, the girls gather around the piano in a rare free
moment while their protagonist leads them in a song lamenting their
plight: "For youth, one needs happiness / Without freedom, there is
only sadness." Nicoletta goes on to bemoan her predicament in a
solo: "And yet I am here languishing / No one hears my sighs."
The song concludes with their collective desire for liberation: "We
only dream of air, light, and freedom." The scene's choreography ac-
cents the contrast between the regimental drudgery of their everyday existence and their yearning for emancipation. The girls dance
among themselves or sway in time to the music. Never are they still,
and rarely are they synchronized with one another, as opposed to
their strictly prescribed, uniform actions while under *collegio* super-
vision.

The second scene of performance, a rhythmic gymnastics exhibition for visiting day at the school, shifts the emphasis from the characters to the educational institution itself. The sequence begins with
an establishing long shot of the *collegio*'s elegant exterior as the girls
come marching proudly down the stairs, holding their hoops up high,
to the enthusiastic applause of their proud parents. With deliberate and
precise movements, they create formations designed to highlight their
athletic prowess as they sing:

> We are clever, we are good,
> In behavior we get tens.
> Either we study our lessons
> Or we don't pass our exams.
> A little bit here, a little bit there
> We learn to breathe well.

Suddenly, a lone singing voice is heard. The camera slowly pans up to the building's right-hand corner window, where Nicoletta, in solitary confinement, disrupts the performance with her musical improvisations and subversive words:

A little bit here, a little bit there,
This prison is killing me with boredom.
A little bit up, a little bit down
I can't stand your muzzles anymore!

Audience reactions to this disturbance vary: the parents are scandalized, the headmistress and her cohorts look embarrassed and uncomfortable, and Nicoletta's father Leopoldo and her aunt beam with pride. Nicoletta in turn is hurried away to the infirmary, a room on the other side of the building, where she can no longer cause trouble while the show continues.

The severity of Nicoletta's actions would be enough in and of itself to draw the conclusion that this scene is a critique of Fascist educational policy. However, given the nature of this performance and its historical context, further inferences can be drawn. Another important arena of Fascist concern was the health of Italian citizens, for the glory of the Italian empire, the order and efficiency of the regime, and the prosperity of the nation were all tied up in the image of happy, robust, and fit Italian men and women. Athletic contests as well as noncompetitive sporting events were organized, and physical education became a requirement in the schools as well as the focus of many extracurricular group activities. Although fitness messages were aimed primarily at boys and men, women were also encouraged to participate in such sports as tennis, skiing, roller-skating, and, of course, rhythmic gymnastics (a particular Fascist favorite), which would create lithe and supple bodies as well as instill grace. In the regime's later years, these talents were showcased in the *sabato fascista* (Fascist Saturday), in which Italians of all ages, in the splendor of their Fascist uniforms, would participate in a variety of activities intended to impart military, political, and athletic values through homogenization.[33]

Il birichino's gymnastics exhibition is a direct parody of Fascist rhetoric on physical fitness, education, recreation, and programs of socialization. The girls' movements are supervised by a robust blond drill sergeant barking militaryesque orders. The song even cites the appropriate Fascist motto, word for word:

> In order to follow our saying,
> "Mens sana in corpore sano"
> We combine gymnastics and
> The hoop with our studies.

The girls move slowly, deliberately, and rigidly, as is typical of Fascist displays of physical prowess. In other films of this genre, their movements on such gymnastics apparatus as the parallel bars, vaults, and balance beam are sexually suggestive, featuring their outstretched and parted legs. Short gym skirts have all but disappeared here; in this film the girls instead wear their everyday Fascist uniforms of longer jumpers, white blouses, white sneakers, and socks. Fetishistic commodification is impeded by two important iconological factors: the lighting is natural and full of shadows, and the shots are predominantly from long and medium-long range, rendering scopophilic gazing next to impossible. The end result is a deeroticization of the female body.

Nicoletta's disruption, the disturbance that ensues as a result, and the harsh words she uses to describe the school and its abuses of power coupled with this deliberate use of Fascist imagery constitute one of the most severe critiques of Fascist ideology in the entire cinematic production of the *ventennio*. This visual deemphasis of female sexuality is a radical departure from previous schoolgirl comedies and has a specific function. The intended target of parody and commentary is not female rebellion or sexual repression as concepts in and of themselves. Rather, the object of focus is the very institutions that attempt to crush the former and construct the latter. With *Il birichino*, criticism has passed from the inherent tension and contradictions in Fascist education and other policies to those very policies and ideological discourses in and of themselves and the apparatuses that propagate and maintain them.

Lessons Learned

Read on the superficial levels of character, setting, and narrative, the Italian schoolgirl comedy appears to be little more than fluff entertainment for the masses, designed to play off the audience's fascination with and the popularity of young female starlets. With their quaint story lines, angelic images of adorable faces, and perfunctory happy endings, these films have the added function of diverting attention from an often troubling and trying contemporary reality. However, when these films are analyzed on the level of signification, a different picture emerges, for it is there that the various levels of the cinematic discourse (iconological, iconographic, and symbolic) work not synthetically but dialectically to reveal the multiple ideological subtexts at work therein. For example, in *Ore 9*, iconology and iconography function against one another in order that the menacing potential of individual rebellion, group solidarity, and active female sexuality endemic to the film's narrative discourse are countered and checked through the commodification of the female body. Nevertheless, the deliberate use of school uniforms, while possessing the iconological function of deemphasizing the individual, simultaneously reinforces the power of the collective. In *Teresa Venerdì*, with its emphasis on the concept of performance in and of itself and as metaphor for the individual's role in society, the protagonist's active assumption of subject positions both reverses the traditional status of women's "to-be-looked-at-ness" characteristic of cinematic spectacles and questions the concept of female passivity in general.

In this process of negotiation between cinema's discursive elements and practices, the gaps and contradictions within the filmic text highlight the gaps and contradictions within the dominant ideology's own discourses and its often muddled attempts to both implement and maintain them. Taken within the context of the given historical, cultural, and political framework, the primary object of criticism is a school system concerned more with discipline than with education. In *Il birichino*, the target includes specific Fascist discourses on nationalism and socialization. Yet the school is a metaphor for Fascist institutions in general, and as the genre progresses (and Fascist control dwindles), reproach deepens. The *collegio*/school/orphanage becomes more and more repressive, culminating in *Il birichino*'s militaristic prison camp. As intimidation and abuse intensifies, subversion becomes all the more powerful and critical.

One final notion needs to be addressed: the genre's relation to its audience. There are several explanations for a particular genre's appeal, all of which can be applied to the schoolgirl comedy. On a psychological level, its popularity can be attributed to the spectator's desire to repeat an initial pleasurable experience. The point of reference here is not only *Seconda B*, the first of the genre, but also the corresponding Hungarian and American models and subsequent Italian films of the same type. Second, according to Schatz (1981, 30–31, 35), a genre's popularity to a large extent is based on "the essentially unresolvable, irreconcilable nature" of the conflicts in question. Rather than reestablishing the status quo, in these films the problems are resolved for the time being, only to resurface in the next film pertaining to this genre. The many ideological conflicts that arise on the schoolgirl comedy's level of signification (collectivity versus individuality, rebellion versus submission, and group harmony versus selfish interest) are far from conclusively aligned with the dominant ideology at the film's end. Although Anna and Teresa are to be married, there is either only a slight or brief allusion, iconographic or narrative, to any relinquishing of their active independence; *Il birichino*'s conclusion involves Nicoletta's total liberation from social expectations. The opportunity for an "open" and potentially dissident reading arises, in which confrontation of authority and steadfastness in one's beliefs, even if they do not conform with those of the dominant ideology, are prized. This effect is rendered possible by two nonnarrative cinematic devices: (1) the dominant point of view throughout the films is that of the female protagonist, and the spectator is encouraged to identify with her; and (2) the extracinematic discourse further concentrated on, promoted, and sold the product, in this case the insubordinate teenager whose rebelliousness, resoluteness, and individuality are privileged and preserved.

Finally, there exists a potential cathartic relationship between audience and film character. The spectator is encouraged to work out unacceptable social behavior through subject identification with one or more of the film's players (hence another function of the deliberate point-of-view constructions in the film's formal composition). Subversive conduct is intended to be contained within the parameters of the cinematic text (Sobchack 1986, 111). However, because the locus of that containment is the proper resolution to a given problem in the film's happy ending, and because that resolution is in fact nothing more than a cultural and cinematic illusion, those boundaries that circumscribe the rebellious catharsis are themselves ephemeral and subject to rupture. Thus, the counterideology at the heart of these films' discourse has the capacity to cross the traditional cinematic boundaries of text, screen, and theater and accompany the spectator into the "real" world. It is in this notion of narrative and ideological transgression that the real subversive potential of the schoolgirl comedy lies. Couched within a seemingly harmless and innocent facade, these films provided alternative models of modes of behavior and rules of conduct to a generation of viewers who, having grown up during the Fascist era, were ready for something new.

Notes

I would like to thank the following people for their invaluable help on this project: Gianna Landucci and the staff of the Mediateca Regionale Toscana in Florence, Roberto Benati and Gianluca Farinelli of the Cineteca Comunale di Bologna, the librarians at the Biblioteca Nazionale in Florence and the Biblioteca del Museo Nazionale del Cinema in Turin, and my colleagues and professors Gavriel Moses, Gian Paolo Biasin, Carol J. Clover, Piero Garofalo, Robin Pickering-Iazzi, John Alcorn, and Carole Gallucci. Unless otherwise noted, all translations in this chapter are my own.

1. For the theoretical and political justifications of Fascist educational policies as well as a description of the individual programs and initiatives, see Tracy Koon's comprehensive work, *Believe, Obey, Fight: The Political Socialization of Youth in Fascist Italy, 1922–1943* (1985).

2. These films include Gennaro Righelli's *Amazzoni bianche* (White amazons; 1936), Max Neufeld's *Assenza ingiustificata* (Unexcused absence; 1939), Nunzio Malasomma's *Dopo divorzieremo* (We'll divorce later; 1940), C. L. Bragaglia's *Violette nei capelli* (Violets in their hair; 1941), Vittorio De Sica's *Un garibaldino al convento* (A Garibaldian in a convent; 1942), Giorgio Bianchi's *La maestrina* (The little teacher; 1942), Mario Mattoli's *Stasera niente di nuovo* (Nothing new tonight; 1942), Luigi Zampa's *Signorinette* (Little ladies; 1942), Akos Rathany's *Una volta alla settimana* (Once a week; 1942), and Alessandro Blasetti's *Nessuno torna indietro* (No one goes back; 1943). For complete descriptions of all these films, see Francesco Savio (1975) and Gianfranco Casadio (1991).

3. To my knowledge, there are only three films that have as their settings boys' schools or whose plots center on the male student body: Flavio Calzavara's *Piccoli naufraghi* (Little castaways; 1939), Domenico Paolella's *Gli ultimi della strada* (The lowest ones on the streets; 1940), and Ferdinando Maria Poggioli's *Addio giovinezza* (Farewell youth; 1940).

4. Savio (1975, xxi) was among the first to notice this trend of using the *film di collegio* (boarding school films) as promotional vehicles for aspiring young actors and actresses. Foremost among those who gained fame with the schoolgirl comedy are Alida Valli, Carla Del Poggio, Irasema Dilian, and Chiaretta Gelli.

5. My theoretical position on gender, cinema, and spectatorship has been influenced by several seminal texts in the field of feminist film theory. These include Jeanne Allen's "The Film Viewer as Consumer" (1980), Teresa De Lauretis's *Alice Doesn't: Feminism, Semiotics, Cinema* (1984), Mary Ann Doane's *The Desire to Desire: The Woman's Film of the 1940s* (1987), Annette Kuhn's *The Power of the Image: Essays on Representation and Sexuality* (1985), Laura Mulvey's *Visual and Other Pleasures* (1989), and D. N. Rodowick's *The Difficulty of Difference: Psychoanalysis, Sexual Difference, and Film Theory* (1991).

6. Gian Piero Brunetta (1979, 484) interprets the school environment as a place where conservative norms and transgressive desires (especially those pertaining to women) could clash. Marcia Landy (1986, 46–57) provides the most exhaustive study to date with her detailed analysis of five of these texts (*Seconda B, Addio giovinezza,*

Maddalena zero in condotta, Teresa Venerdì, and *Il birichino di papà*). She continues along much the same lines as Brunetta, noting the implicit (and/or explicit) critique of authoritarian discipline as well as generational, gender, and class conflicts.

7. Victoria De Grazia (1992, 151–55) provides a cogent analysis of Fascist educational reform with respect to women.

8. My working definition of *genre* owes to several important works in the field of film genre theory: Stephen Neale's *Genre* (1980), Thomas Schatz's *Hollywood Genres: Formulas, Filmmaking and the Studio System* (1981), Andrew Tudor's "Genre" (1986), Rick Altman's "A Semantic/Syntactic Approach to Film Genre" (1986), Thomas Schatz's "The Structural Influence: New Directions in Film Genre Study" (1986), and Thomas Sobchack's "Genre Film: A Classical Experience" (1986).

9. My definitions of *iconology* and *iconography* may differ from standard usage. Using Erwin Panofsky's (1967, 3–17) theories as my point of departure, I take *iconology* to mean the formal characteristics of the cinematic image. These include framing, lighting, costume, proxemic patterns between objects on screen, and proxemic patterns between the camera and the objects on screen. The *iconographic*, on the other hand, denotes film's narrative, characters, and themes: in other words, the syntactical combination of words and images.

10. New genres are born when "either a relatively stable set of semantic givens is developed through syntactic experimentation into a coherent and durable syntax, or an already existing syntax adopts a new set of semantic elements" (Altman 1986, 34–35).

11. Francesco Savio, in his introduction to *Ma l'amore no* (1975), erroneously attributes the dominant cultural influence to German popular cinema. He supports his argument by citing one film, *La segretaria privata,* which in actuality was adapted from a Hungarian novel (see Bolzoni 1988, 12).

12. For an insightful discussion of American cinema's influence in Italy, see James Hay (1987, 37–63).

13. For more on the depiction of female characters in Hungarian cinema, see Bolzoni (1988, 21–22) and Laura (1991, 47–48); on Hollywood comedies, consult Molly Haskell (1974, 90–152).

14. Thomas Schatz (1981, 30) also outlines the four elements or stages into which the story is organized: (1) the establishment of the setting and the conflict in question, (2) animation of the conflicts through actions and attitudes of characters, (3) intensification of the conflict "by means of conventional situations and dramatic confrontations until the conflict reaches crisis proportions," and (4) resolution of the crisis "in a fashion which eliminates the physical and/or ideological threat and thereby celebrates the (temporarily) well-ordered community."

15. Although Panofsky's point of reference is the visual arts, and the Renaissance humanist tradition in particular, he nonetheless provides extremely useful categories of analysis for film studies. See Panofsky (1967, 3–17).

16. De Grazia's *How Fascism Ruled Women* (1992) is an invaluable resource for Fascist constructions of the "feminine," as are De Grand's "Italian Women under Fascism" (1976), Piero Meldini's *Sposa e madre esemplare: Ideologia e politica della donna e della famiglia durante il fascismo* (1975), and Emiliana Noether's "Italian Women under Fascism: A Reevaluation" (1982).

17. "In this respect patriarchy does not so much institute the woman as sexual object in the cinema as offer the female body as an accepted and acceptable image on to which to deflect the erotic component in the scopophilic drive" (Neale 1980, 57).

18. "The filmmakers who created the quality comedies knew that what is appeal-

ing in their films is not the naive promise of romantic love or of some utopian dream, but rather, the conflict itself" (Schatz 1981, 172).

19. The social or situation comedy, according to Neale (1980), "tends to specify its disorder as the disturbance of socially institutionalised discursive hierarchies.... The order is disturbed in order for its hierarchy to be rearranged" (24–25).

20. For a more detailed historical and theoretical overview of the concept of suture, see Silverman (1983, 194–236) and Heath (1981, 76–112).

21. This particular effect is based on Althusser's concept of ideology and interpellation: "Ideology 'acts' or 'functions' in such a way that it 'recruits' subjects among the individuals (it recruits them all), or 'transforms' the individuals into subjects" (Althusser 1971, 174). On the relationship between ideology and suture, see Silverman (1983, 215–22) and Heath (1981, 101–7).

22. *Seconda B* was heavily influenced by the immensely popular and now classic 1931 German film *Mädchen in Uniform* (Girls in uniform), directed by Leontine Sagan. *Mädchen in Uniform* is in itself a fascinating text, treating such themes as excess authority, human compassion, and highly charged female eroticism. Siegfried Kracauer (1947, 226–29) provides an excellent summary of the film's plot as well as an incisive analysis.

23. The notable exception here is De Sica's *Teresa Venerdì*.

24. For more on the history of the Italian film industry, see Luigi Freddi's *Il cinema* (1949), Jean Gili's *Stato fascista e cinematografia: Repressione e promozione* (1981), and Massimo Mida and Lorenzo Quaglietti's *Dai telefoni bianchi al neorealismo* (1980). Savio's (1979, 2:487) interview with Vittorio De Sica expands upon the relationship between Durbin and the Italian schoolgirl comedy.

25. The film's advertising campaign is cited in Savio's *Ma l'amore no* (1975, 245).

26. A review in the October 6, 1947, edition of *Variety* observed that the "film's chief asset is Valli and a comprehensive assortment of young, attractive femininity." See also the *New York Herald Tribune* (October 18, 1947). For the Italian perspective, consult Sandro De Feo's review in *Il Messaggero* (September 7, 1941) and Giuseppe Isani's in *Cinema* (November 10, 1941). Isani also gave the film three out of a possible four stars.

27. Roland Barthes (1983) has observed, " 'Real' clothing is burdened with practical considerations (protection, modesty, adornment); these finalities disappear from 'represented' clothing, which no longer serves to protect, to cover, or to adorn, but at most to signify protection, modesty, or adornment" (8). For more on the idea of fashion and film, see Herzog (1990).

28. Jane Gaines (1990) sees costume as employed primarily as a means of giving iconological expression to a character's essence and/or advancing the narrative; however, here the opposite is at work.

29. The main players and plot can all be traced back to what Stephen Harvey (n. d.) calls "Hollywood prototypes." The cinematic model, however, was the Hungarian film *Penték Rézi*, directed by Laszlo Vadja and based on the novel of the same name by Rezsö Török. When Vittorio De Sica saw the Hungarian version at the 1938 Venice Film Biennale, he is reported to have commented, "After seeing it, I thought I could do better" (quoted in Laura 1991, 42).

30. Similarly, "gender, or the feminine in this case, is itself performative in nature, and this 'act' of identity construction, while 'performed' by the subject, is constituted not by the acts themselves but rather by their expression" (Butler 1990, 24–25).

31. Landy (1986, 55–57) focuses on gender in her cogent analysis of the film.

32. Gelli's main appeal, according to both Savio and Gelli herself, rested in the spontaneity and uninhibitedness that she projected in her on-screen characters. See Savio's interview with Gelli in *Cinecittà anni trenta* (1979, 2:569–78).

33. For more on Fascism and physical fitness, see Saracinelli and Totti (1983, 105–16), De Grazia (1992, 218–21), Fabrizio (1976), and Isidori Frasca (1983).

Works Cited

Allen, Jeanne. 1980. "The Film Viewer as Consumer." *Quarterly Review of Film Studies* 5: 481–99.

Althusser, Louis. 1971. "Ideology and Ideological State Apparatuses (Notes towards an Investigation)." In *Lenin and Philosophy and Other Essays*. New York: Monthly Review Press.

Altman, Rick. 1986. "A Semantic/Syntactic Approach to Film Genre." In *Film Genre Reader*. Edited by Barry Keith Grand. Austin: University of Texas Press.

Barthes, Roland. 1983. *The Fashion System*. Translated by Matthew Ward and Richard Howard. New York: Hill & Wang.

Bolzoni, Francesco. 1988. "La commedia all'ungherese nel cinema italiano." *Bianco e nero* 49, no. 3: 7–41.

Bottai, Giuseppe. 1939. *The School Charter in Fascist Italy*. Rome: Laboreremus.

Brunetta, Gian Piero. 1975. *Cinema italiano tra le due guerre. Fascismo e politica cinematografica*. Milan: Mursia.

———. 1979. *Storia del cinema italiano, 1895–1945*. Rome: Riuniti.

Butler, Judith. 1990. *Gender Trouble: Feminism and the Subversion of Identity*. New York: Routledge.

Carlson, Marvin. 1990. "The Theatre Audiences and the Reading of Performance." In *Theatre Semiotics: Signs of Life*. Bloomington: Indiana University Press.

Casadio, Gianfranco, et al. 1991. *Telefoni bianchi: Realtà e finzione nella società e nel cinema degli anni quaranta*. Ravenna: Longo Editore.

De Grand, Alexander. 1976. "Women under Italian Fascism." *Historical Journal* 19: 947–68.

De Grazia, Victoria. 1992. *How Fascism Ruled Women: Italy, 1922–1945*. Berkeley: University of California Press.

De Lauretis, Teresa. 1984. *Alice Doesn't: Feminism, Semiotics, Cinema*. Bloomington: Indiana University Press.

Doane, Mary Ann. 1987. *The Desire to Desire: The Woman's Film of the 1940's*. Bloomington: Indiana University Press.

Dyer, Richard. 1985. "Entertainment and Utopia." In *Movies and Methods* (vol. 2). Edited by Bill Nichols. Berkeley: University of California Press.

Eco, Umberto. 1979. *The Role of the Reader*. Bloomington: Indiana University Press.

Fabrizio, Felice. 1976. *Sport e fascismo*. Florence: Guaraldi.

Feuer, Jane. 1982. *The Hollywood Musical*. Bloomington: Indiana University Press.

Freddi, Luigi. 1949. *Il cinema* (2 vols.). Rome: L'Arnia.

Gaines, Jane. 1990. "Costume and Narrative: How the Dress Tells the Woman's Story." In *Fabrications: Costume and the Female Body*. Edited by Jane Gaines and Charlotte Herzog. New York: Routledge.

Gili, Jean A. 1981. *Stato fascista e cinematografia: Repressione e promozione*. Rome: Bulzoni.

Harvey, Stephen. n. d. *"Teresa Venerdì."* *Circulating Film Notes 13* (Museum of Modern Art, New York).

Haskell, Molly. 1974. *From Reverence to Rape: The Treatment of Women in the Movies.* Chicago: University of Chicago Press.

Hay, James. 1987. *Popular Film Culture in Fascist Italy: The Passing of the Rex.* Bloomington: Indiana University Press.

Heath, Stephen. 1981. *Questions of Cinema.* Bloomington: Indiana University Press.

Herzog, Charlotte. 1990. " 'Powder-Puff' Promotion: The Fashion Show-in-the-Film." In *Fabrications: Costume and the Female Body.* Edited by Jane Gaines and Charlotte Herzog. New York: Routledge.

Isidori Frasca, Rosella. 1983. *. . . e il duce le volle sportive.* Bologna: Pàtron.

Koon, Tracy. 1985. *Believe, Obey, Fight: The Political Socialization of Youth in Fascist Italy, 1922–1943.* Chapel Hill: University of North Carolina Press.

Kracauer, Siegfried. 1947. *From Caligari to Hitler: A Psychological History of the German Film.* Princeton, N.J.: Princeton University Press.

Kuhn, Annette. 1985. *The Power of the Image: Essays in Representation and Sexuality.* London: Routledge & Kegan Paul.

Landy, Marcia. 1986. *Fascism in Film: The Italian Commercial Cinema, 1930–1943.* Princeton, N.J: Princeton University Press.

Laura, Ernesto G. 1991. "Il mito di Budapest e i modelli ungheresi." In Gianfranco Casadio et al., *Telefoni bianchi: Realtà e finzione nella società e nel cinema degli anni quaranta.* Ravenna: Longo Editore.

Meldini, Piero, ed. 1975. *Sposa e madre esemplare: Ideologia e politica della donna e della famiglia durante il fascismo.* Florence: Guaraldi.

Mellencamp, Patricia. 1991. "Spectacle and Spectator: Looking through the American Musical Comedy." In *Explorations in Film Theory: Selected Essays from Ciné-tracts.* Edited by Ron Burnett. Bloomington: Indiana University Press.

Mida, Massimo, and Lorenzo Quaglietti. 1980. *Dai telefoni bianchi al neorealismo.* Bari: Laterza.

Mulvey, Laura. 1989. *Visual and Other Pleasures.* Bloomington: Indiana University Press.

Neale, Stephen. 1980. *Genre.* London: British Film Institute.

Noether, Emiliana. 1982. "Italian Women under Fascism: A Reevaluation." *Italian Quarterly* 32 (Fall): 69–80.

Panofsky, Erwin. 1967. *Studies in Iconology: Humanistic Themes in the Art of the Renaissance.* New York: Harper.

Rodowick, D. N. 1991. *The Difficulty of Difference: Psychoanalysis, Sexual Difference, and Film Theory.* New York: Routledge.

Saracinelli, M., and N. Totti. 1983. *L'Italia del duce: L'informazione, la scuola, il costume.* Rimini: Panozzo.

Sarti, Roland, ed. 1974. *The Ax Within: Italian Fascism in Action.* New York: New Viewpoints.

Savio, Francesco. 1975. *Ma l'amore no: Realismo, formalismo, propaganda e telefoni bianchi nel cinema italiano di regime (1930–1943).* Milan: Sonzogno.

———. 1979 *Cinecittà anni trenta. Parlano 116 protagonisti del secondo cinema italiano (1930–1943)* (3 vols.). Rome: Bulzoni.

Schatz, Thomas. 1981. *Hollywood Genres: Formulas, Filmmaking and the Studio System.* New York: Random House.

———. 1986. "The Structural Influence: New Directions in Film Genre Study." In *Film Genre Reader.* Edited by Barry Keith Grand. Austin: University of Texas Press.

Silverman, Kaja. 1983. *The Subject of Semiotics*. New York: Oxford University Press.
Sobchack, Thomas. 1986. "Genre Film: A Classical Experience." In *Film Genre Reader*. Edited by Barry Keith Grand. Austin: University of Texas Press.
Tudor, Andrew. 1986. "Genre." In *Film Genre Reader*. Edited by Barry Keith Grand. Austin: University of Texas Press.

Appendix / Selected Chronology of Italian Fascism and Women in History and Selected Criticism

1918   Publication of Teresa Labriola's *Problemi sociali della donna* (The social problems of women).

1919   Founding of the first *fascio di combattimento,* in Milan.

Sacchi Law excludes women from high-ranking positions in the military and public office.

Publication of Futurluce's "Le donne e il futurismo" (Women and futurism).

New edition of Sibilla Aleramo's feminist work *Una donna* (A woman; 1906), followed by editions published in 1921, 1930, 1938.

1920   First women's *fascio,* formed at Monza.

The Federazione Italiana fra Laureate e Diplomate Degli Istituti Superiori, an association for women high school and university graduates, is founded (dissolved by government request in 1935).

Irene Brin begins prolific period of journalistic writing, contributing articles to *Omnibus* and women's publications.

Publication of Sibilla Aleramo's *Andando e stando* (Going and staying).

1921   Formation of the Communist Party of Italy.

Formation of the National Fascist Party.

1922   March on Rome by Fascist squads.

Mussolini becomes prime minister of Italy.

1923   Passage of the Acerbo electoral law, guaranteeing two-thirds of the seats in Parliament to the party with the majority of votes.

As part of Gentile school reform implemented to restrict overall university admissions, female students must pay higher instructional fees.

1924   Giacomo Matteotti, deputy of the Social-Democrat Party, kidnapped and murdered after denouncing Fascists for election fraud.

Italian women and men stage demonstrations.

"Aventine secession": members of parties opposing Fascist government refuse to participate in Parliament.

Publication of Teresa Labriola's essay "Il femminismo italiano nella rinascita dello spirito" (Italian feminism in the spiritual rebirth).

Publication of Benedetta Cappa Marinetti's *Le forze umane: Romanzo astratto con sintesi grafiche* (Human strengths: Abstract novel with graphic syntheses).

1925   Passage of law extending voting rights in administrative elections to specific groups of women, among them, female heads of household and war widows.

Passage of law establishing Opera Nazionale Maternità ed Infanzia (National Agency for Maternity and Childhood) to oversee agencies for mothers and children.

Anna Kuliscioff dies in Milan.

1926   Passage of law abolishing local elections.

Introduction of incentive and punitive pronatalist legislation.

Grazia Deledda is awarded the Nobel Prize for Literature.

Passage of law forbidding women to occupy chairs in Greek, history, Latin, letters, and philosophy at classical and scientific institutions of higher learning.

Antonio Gramsci arrested and incarcerated.

1927   Women rice workers strike for better working conditions.

1928   Law passed prohibiting women from being appointed middle-school directors.

1929   Lateran Accords finalized between Mussolini and the Vatican, normalizing church-state relations.

Antonietta Raphaël makes her debut as painter in Rome in the *Prima mostra del sindacato fascista* (The first Fascist syndicate exhibition).

1930   Luigia Pirovano founds national support organization for working-class women, Alleanza Muliebre Italiana (Italian Female Cultural Alliance).

Publication of Mario Gastaldi's book on Italian women writers, *Donne, luce d'Italia* (Women, the light of Italy).

1931   Publication of Benedetta Cappa Marinetti's *Il viaggio di Gararà: Romanzo cosmico per teatro* (Gararà's journey: Cosmic novel for theater).

1933   Regina Terruzzi organizes the Massaie Rurali, an organization conceived by the Fascist state for rural housewives.

1935   Italy invades Abyssinia.

Mussolini begins campaign for women to donate their wedding rings for the war effort.

1936   Mussolini and Hitler form political alliance with the Rome-Berlin Axis.

The Italian Women's Union (Unione Donne Italiane) organized in France.

Antonietta Raphaël exhibits sculpture, with exhibitions to follow in 1937 and 1938.

1938   Passage of law limiting female workers to 10 percent of the total employees in state and private offices (rescinded in 1940).

Passage of the anti-Semitic racial laws.

Publication of Alba De Céspedes's international best-seller *Nessuno torna indietro* (English translation, *There's No Turning Back,* published in 1941).

1939   *Carta della scuola* (school charter) reforms the Gentile education system and provides for future creation of institutions for female instruction.

Pact of Steel: Italy and Germany form a military alliance.

Paola Masino completes *Nascita e morte della massaia* (Birth and death of the housewife).

1940   Italy enters World War II as an ally of Germany.

1941   Publication of Maria Bandini Buti's *Poetesse e scrittrici* (Women poets and writers); second volume published in 1942.

1943   Women demonstrate for "bread and peace."

Mussolini receives a vote of no confidence in the Fascist Grand Council and is imprisoned.

Badoglio government formed and Italy declares armistice; Nazi troops occupy Central and Northern Italy.

Formation of the Committees of National Liberation and the Partisan movement to liberate Italy from Italian Fascists and German Nazis.

Mussolini rescued by Germans; forms the Republic of Salò in northern Italy.

Women's Resistance organization, Gruppi di Difesa della Donna e per l'Assistenza ai Combattenti per la Libertà (Groups for the Defense of Women and for the Aid of the Freedom Fighters) formed in Turin.

De Céspedes crosses lines of Nazi-occupied Northern Italy and reaches Allies in the south. Works for Radio Free Bari, using the name Clorinda.

1944   The Italian Women's Union journal *Noi donne* published in Italy for the first time.

Rita Rosani, one among thousands of women contributing to the Resistance, is killed by the Nazis and posthumously receives the Italian Gold Medal.

1945   Partisans execute Mussolini and Clara Petacci.

Women receive the right to vote.

———

1975   Piero Meldini, ed., *Sposa e madre esemplare: Ideologia e politica della donna e della famiglia durante il fascismo.*

1976   Alexander De Grand, "Women under Italian Fascism."

Maria Antonietta Macciocchi, *La donna "nera": "Consenso" femminile e fascismo.*

1978   Franca Pieroni Bortolotti, *Femminismo e partiti politici in Italia 1919–1926.*

Ilva Vaccari, *La donna nel ventennio fascista (1919–1943).*

1982   Stefania Bartolini, "La donna sotto il fascismo."

Claudia Salaris, *Le futuriste: Donne e letteratura d'avanguardia in Italia (1909/1944).*

1983   Rosella Isidori Frasca, ... *e il duce le volle sportive.*

Emma Scaramuzza, "Professioni intellettuali e fascismo: L'ambivalenza dell'Alleanza muliebre culturale italiana."

1984   Luisa Passerini, *Torino operaia e fascismo.*

1985   Nuto Revelli, *L'anello forte.*

1986   Lesley Caldwell, "Reproducers of the Nation: Women and the Family in Fascist Policy."

David Dollenmayer, "Alfred Döblin, Futurism, and Women: A Relationship Reexamined."

Maria Fraddosio, "Le donne e il fascismo: Ricerche e problemi di interpretazione."

Enzo Santarelli, "Il fascismo e le ideologie antifemministe."

1987   Elisabetta Mondello, *La nuova italiana: La donna nella stampa e nella cultura del ventennio.*

Luisa Passerini, *Fascism in Popular Memory: The Cultural Experience of the Turin Working Class.*

1988   Marina Addis Saba, ed., *La corporazione delle donne: Ricerche e studi sui modelli femminili nel ventennio fascista.*

Emily Braun, "Scuola Romana: Fact or Fiction?"

1989   Lucia Re, "Futurism and Feminism."

1990   Robin Pickering-Iazzi, "Unseduced Mothers: The Resisting Female Subject in Italian Culture of the Twenties and Thirties."

1991   Anna Bravo, "Simboli del materno."

Annarita Buttafuoco, "Motherhood as a Political Strategy: The Role of the Italian Women's Movement in the Creation of the *Cassa Nazionale di Maternità.*"

Victoria De Grazia, "La nazionalizzazione delle donne: Modelli di regime e cultura commerciale nell'Italia fascista."

Ellen Nerenberg, " 'Donna proprio ... proprio donna': The Social Construction of Femininity in *Nessuno torna indietro.*"

Chiara Saraceno, "Redefining Maternity and Paternity: Gender, Pronatalism and Social Policies in Fascist Italy."

1992   Victoria De Grazia, *How Fascism Ruled Women: Italy, 1922–1945.*

1993   Giuliana Bruno, *Streetwalking on a Ruined Map: Cultural Theory and the City Films of Elvira Notari.*

Philip V. Cannistraro and Brian R. Sullivan, *Il Duce's Other Woman.*

Robin Pickering-Iazzi, ed., *Unspeakable Women: Selected Short Stories Written by Italian Women during Fascism.*

1994   Conservative Silvio Berlusconi, head of the Forza Italia movement, becomes prime minister of Italy, with a coalition government including Gianfranco Fini—leader of the neo-Fascist Italian Social Movement, now called the National Alliance—and the right-wing Umberto Bossi, head of the separatist Northern League, as well as Pierferdinando Casini, leader of the CCD, the Catholic Christian Democratic Party.

Selected Bibliography

Addis Saba, Marina, ed. *La corporazione delle donne: Ricerche e studi sui modelli femminili nel ventennio fascista*. Florence: Vallecchi, 1988.

L'audacia insolente: La cooperazione femminile 1886–1986. Venice: Marsilio, 1986.

Bartolini, Stefania. "La donna sotto il fascismo." *Memoria* 10 (1982): 124–32.

Blum, Cinzia. "Rhetorical Strategies and Gender in Marinetti's Futurist Manifesto." *Italica* (Summer 1990): 196–211.

Braun, Emily. "Scuola Romana: Fact or Fiction?" *Art in America* 76 (March 1988): 128–36.

———. "From the Risorgimento to the Resistance: One Hundred Years of Jewish Artists in Italy." *Gardens and Ghettos: The Art of Jewish Life in Italy* (exhibition catalog, Jewish Museum, New York). Edited by Vivian Mann. Berkeley: University of California Press, 1989.

Bravo, Anna. "Simboli del materno." In *Donne e uomini nelle guerre mondiali*. Edited by Anna Bravo. Rome-Bari: Laterza, 1991.

Brin, Irene. *Usi e costumi 1920–1940*. Palermo: Sellerio, 1981.

Brunetta, Gian Piero. *Storia del cinema italiano, 1895–1945*. Rome: Riuniti, 1979.

Bruno, Giuliana. *Streetwalking on a Ruined Map: Cultural Theory and the City Films of Elvira Notari*. Princeton, N.J.: Princeton University Press, 1993.

Buttafuoco, Annarita. "Motherhood as a Political Strategy: The Role of the Italian Women's Movement in the Creation of the *Cassa Nazionale di Maternità*." In *Maternity and Gender Policies: Women and the Rise of the European Welfare States, 1880s-1950s*. Edited by Gisela Bock and Pat Thane. New York: Routledge, 1991.

Caldwell, Lesley. "Reproducers of the Nation: Women and the Family in Fascist Policy." In *Rethinking Italian Fascism: Capitalism, Populism and Culture*. Edited by David Forgacs. London: Lawrence & Wishart, 1986.

Cannistraro, Philip V., and Brian R. Sullivan. *Il Duce's Other Woman*. New York: William Morrow, 1993.

Casadio, Gianfranco, et al. *Telefoni bianchi: Realtà e finzione nella società e nel cinema degli anni quaranta*. Ravenna: Longo Editore, 1991.

Casalini, Maria. *La signora del socialismo italiano*. Rome: Riuniti, 1987.

Chang, Heesok. "Fascism and Critical Theory." *Stanford Italian Review* 8, nos. 1–2 (1990): 13–33.

Coverdale, John F. *Italian Intervention in the Spanish Civil War*. Princeton, N.J.: Princeton University Press, 1975.

Davies, Judy. "The Futures Market: Marinetti and the Fascists in Milan." In *Visions and Blueprints: Avantgarde Culture and Radical Politics in Early Twentieth-Century Europe*. Edited by Edward Timms and Peter Collier. Manchester: Manchester University Press, 1988.

De Donato, Gigliola, and Vanna Gazzola Stacchini, eds. *I best-seller del ventennio: Il regime e il libro di massa*. Rome: Riuniti, 1991.

De Felice, Renzo. *Intervista sul fascismo*. Bari: Laterza, 1976.

————, comp. *Bibliografia orientativa del fascismo*. Rome: Bonacci, 1991.

De Giorgio, Michela. *Le italiane dall'unità a oggi: Modelli culturali e comportamenti sociali*. Rome-Bari: Laterza, 1992.

De Grand, Alexander. "Women under Italian Fascism." *Historical Journal* 19 (1976): 947–68.

De Grazia, Victoria. "La nazionalizzazione delle donne: Modelli di regime e cultura commerciale nell'Italia fascista." *Memoria* 33, no. 3 (1991): 95–111.

————. *How Fascism Ruled Women: Italy, 1922–1945*. Berkeley: University of California Press, 1992.

Dollenmayer, David. "Alfred Döblin, Futurism, and Women: A Relationship Reexamined." *Germanic Review* (Fall 1986): 138–45.

"Fascism and Culture." *Stanford Italian Review* 8, nos. 1–2 (1990).

"Fascist Aesthetics." *South Central Review* 6 (Summer 1989).

Fraddosio, Maria. "Le donne e il fascismo: Ricerche e problemi di interpretazione." *Storia contemporanea* 1 (1986): 95–135.

Gagliani, Dianella, et al. "Culture popolari negli anni del fascismo." *Italia contemporanea* 157 (1984): 63–90.

Giocondi, Michele. *Lettori in camicia nera: Narrativa di successo nell'Italia fascista*. Messina-Florence: G. D'Anna Editrici, 1978.

Golsan, Richard J., ed. *Fascism, Aesthetics, and Culture*. Hanover: University Press of New England, 1992.

Hay, James. *Popular Film Culture in Fascist Italy: The Passing of the Rex*. Bloomington: Indiana University Press, 1987.

Hewitt, Andrew. *Fascist Modernism: Aesthetics, Politics, and the Avant-Garde*. Stanford: Stanford University Press, 1993.

Isidori Frasca, Rosella. *. . . e il duce le volle sportive*. Bologna: Pàtron, 1983.

Kaplan, Alice Yaeger. *Reproductions of Banality: Fascism, Literature, and French Intellectual Life*. Minneapolis: University of Minnesota Press, 1986.

Koon, Tracy. *Believe, Obey, Fight: The Political Socialization of Youth in Fascist Italy, 1922–1943*. Chapel Hill: University of North Carolina Press, 1985.

Laclau, Ernesto. "Fascism and Ideology." In *Politics and Ideology in Marxist Theory*. New York: Verso, 1977.

Landy, Marcia. *Fascism in Film: The Italian Commercial Cinema, 1930–1943*. Princeton, N.J.: Princeton University Press, 1986.

Macciocchi, Maria Antonietta. *La donna "nera": "Consenso" femminile e fascismo*. Milan: Feltrinelli, 1976.

Meldini, Piero, ed. *Sposa e madre esemplare: Ideologia e politica della donna e della famiglia durante il fascismo*. Florence: Guaraldi, 1975.

Mondello, Elisabetta. *La nuova italiana: La donna nella stampa e nella cultura del ventennio*. Rome: Riuniti, 1987.

————. "L'immagine di Sibilla nella stampa femminile dei primi decenni del novecento." In *Svelamento: Sibilla Aleramo: Una biografia intellettuale*. Edited by Annarita Buttafuoco and Marina Zancan. Milan: Feltrinelli, 1988.

Mosse, George. *Nationalism and Sexuality: Respectability and Abnormal Sexuality in Modern Europe*. New York: Howard Fertig, 1985.

Nerenberg, Ellen. " 'Donna proprio . . . proprio donna': The Social Construction of Femininity in *Nessuno torna indietro*." *Romance Languages Annual* 3 (1991): 267–73.

Passerini, Luisa. *Torino operaia e fascismo*. Bari: Laterza, 1984.

———. *Fascism in Popular Memory: The Cultural Experience of the Turin Working Class.* Translated by Robert Lumley and Jude Bloomfield. Cambridge: Cambridge University Press, 1987.

———. "Immaginare l'immaginario: Rassegna di termini e di libri." *Linea d'ombra* 42 (1989): 19–23.

———. *Mussolini immaginario.* Rome: Laterza, 1991.

Pickering-Iazzi, Robin, ed. *Unspeakable Women: Selected Short Stories Written by Italian Women during Fascism.* New York: Feminist Press, 1993.

Pieroni Bortolotti, Franca. *Alle origini del movimento femminile in Italia, 1848–1892.* Turin: Einaudi, 1963.

———. *Socialismo e questione femminile in Italia, 1892–1922.* Milan: Mazzotta, 1974.

———. *Femminismo e partiti politici in Italia 1919–1926.* Rome: Riuniti, 1978.

Re, Lucia. "Futurism and Feminism." *Annali d'italianistica* 7 (1989): 253–72.

Runcini, Romolo. "La parola e il gesto tra futurismo e fascismo." *Problemi: Periodico quadrimestrale di cultura* (September/December 1981): 262–74.

Salaris, Claudia. *Le futuriste: Donne e letteratura d'avanguardia in Italia (1909/1944).* Milan: Edizioni delle Donne, 1982.

Salvatorelli, Luigi. *Nazionalfascismo.* Turin: Einaudi, 1977.

Santarelli, Enzo. "Il fascismo e le ideologie antifemministe." *Problemi del socialismo* 4 (1976): 75–106.

Saraceno, Chiara. *La famiglia operaia sotto il fascismo.* Milan: Fondazione Gian Giacomo Feltrinelli, 1979–80.

———. "Redefining Maternity and Paternity: Gender, Pronatalism and Social Policies in Fascist Italy." In *Maternity and Gender Policies: Women and the Rise of the European Welfare States, 1880s-1950s.* Edited by Gisela Bock and Pat Thane. New York: Routledge, 1991.

Saracinelli, M., and N. Totti. *L'Italia del duce: L'informazione, la scuola, il costume.* Rimini: Panozzo, 1983.

Savio, Francesco. *Cinecittà anni trenta. Parlano 116 protagonisti del secondo cinema italiano (1930–1943)* (3 vols.). Rome: Bulzoni, 1979.

Scaramuzza, Emma. "Professioni intellettuali e fascismo: L'ambivalenza dell'Alleanza muliebre culturale italiana." *Italia contemporanea* (September 1983): 111–33.

Schnapp, Jeffrey. "Forwarding Address." *Stanford Italian Review* 8, nos. 1–2 (1990): 53–80.

Schnapp, Jeffrey, and Barbara Spackman. "Selections from the Great Debate on Fascism and Culture." *Stanford Italian Review* 8, nos. 1–2 (1990): 235–72.

Sontag, Susan. "Fascinating Fascism." In *Under the Sign of Saturn.* New York: Farrar, Straus & Giroux, 1980. Originally published 1974.

Spackman, Barbara. "The Fascist Rhetoric of Virility." *Stanford Italian Review* 8, nos. 1–2 (1990): 81–101.

Sternhell, Zeev. *Neither Left nor Right: Fascist Ideology in France.* Translated by David Maisel. Berkeley: University of California Press, 1986.

Vaccari, Ilva. *La donna nel ventennio fascista (1919–1943).* Milan: Vangelista, 1978.

Viazzi, Glauco, ed. *I poeti del futurismo 1909–1944.* Milan: Longanesi, 1978.

Zunino, Pier Giorgio. *L'ideologia del fascismo.* Bologna: Il Mulino, 1985.

Contributors

Rosalia Colombo Ascari is a professor at Sweet Briar College in Virginia. She has taught at Bocconi University in Milan, Italy, and in several American colleges and universities. She has published articles on social and feminist issues in contemporary Italy and on Italian and French modern cinema. She is coauthor of *L'analyse du texte* (1994) and is working on a critical anthology of Italian literature. She is also doing research for a book dealing with the biographies of anti-Fascist women, including Anna Kuliscioff.

Fiora A. Bassanese is associate professor of Italian at the University of Massachusetts, Boston, and has long been active in the area of women's studies and Italian culture. She is the author of *Gaspara Stampa* (1982) and numerous articles on both Renaissance and twentieth-century women writers, such as Veronica Franco, Sibilla Aleramo, and Armanda Guiducci.

Maurizia Boscagli is assistant professor of English at the University of California, Santa Barbara, where she teaches classes in gender studies and critical theory. She has written articles on feminist theory, film, and the cultural politics of modernism, and is currently completing a manuscript on the male body as spectacle in early-twentieth-century European consumer culture.

Emily Braun is assistant professor at Hunter College, City University of New York, where she teaches classes in twentieth-century art and theory. She specializes in Italian culture between the world wars, and has authored numerous articles and exhibition catalogs on artists and cultural politics under Fascism. She is editor of *Italian Art in the Twentieth Century* (1989) and coauthor of the catalog *Gardens and Ghettos: The Art of Jewish Life in Italy* (1989).

Carole C. Gallucci received her Ph.D. in Italian from the University of Connecticut in 1994; her dissertation addresses the relationship between Italian Fascist ideology and women's fiction. She was awarded a Fulbright grant to conduct research in Italy in 1994–95. She has published translations of Italian works, such as *Sex and Gender in Historical Perspective: Selections from Quaderni Storici* (1990), as well as numerous book reviews.

Mariolina Graziosi is professor of sociology at the University of Milan. She has a Ph.D. from the University of Wisconsin-Madison, and is currently a training candidate at the C. G. Jung Institute in Zurich. Her publications include articles on various areas of sociology. She has just completed a book on the social text of patriarchy in Italy during the Liberal and Fascist eras and is currently working on a research project, financed by the National Research Council, on the symbolic use of women's images in the process of building national identities.

Clara Orban is assistant professor of Italian and French at DePaul University. Her publications include articles on several aspects of Italian and French literary studies, as well as language pedagogy. She has completed a textbook for advanced commercial French and has also written on the Columbian quincentennial and on the phenomenon of *préciosité*. Her main areas of research are word and image studies in the early-twentieth-century avant-garde, which she has examined in her articles on Boccioni, Marinetti and Cendrars, and medicine. She is nearing completion on a book on words and images in futurism and surrealism.

Robin Pickering-Iazzi is associate professor of Italian at the University of Wisconsin-Milwaukee. She has published articles on nineteenth- and twentieth-century Italian writers and culture, and, most recently, edited *Unspeakable Women: Selected Short Stories Written by Italian Women during Fascism*. She is finishing up a book on cultural theory and the discourses Italian women authors produced in high and mass literature during Fascism.

Lucia Re is associate professor of Italian and comparative literature at the University of California, Los Angeles. Her publications include

Calvino and the Age of Neorealism: Fables of Estrangement (1990) and articles on D'Annunzio, futurism and feminism, and contemporary Italian women poets and philosophers.

Jacqueline Reich is currently the graduate fellow in Italian at Trinity College in Hartford, Connecticut, where she teaches Italian language, literature, and cinema. She recently completed her Ph.D. at the University of California, Berkeley, with a dissertation on constructions of female subjectivity in Italian cinema during the Fascist period. Her articles and reviews have appeared in *Italica, VIA: Voices in Italian Americana,* and *Differentia.*

Barbara Spackman is associate professor of Italian at New York University. She is the author of *Decadent Genealogies: The Rhetoric of Sickness from Baudelaire to D'Annunzio* (1989) and of essays on Folengo, Machiavelli, Marinetti, D'Annunzio, and others. She is currently working on a study of the rhetoric of Italian Fascism.

Index

267